ALCOHOL, TOBACCO, AND ILLICIT DRUGS

ISSN 1938-8896

ALCOHOL, TOBACCO, AND ILLICIT DRUGS

Sandra M. Alters

INFORMATION PLUS® REFERENCE SERIES
Formerly Published by Information Plus, Wylie, Texas

GALE
CENGAGE Learning™

Detroit • New York • San Francisco • New Haven, Conn • Waterville, Maine • London

Alcohol, Tobacco, and Illicit Drugs

Sandra M. Alters

Paula Kepos, Series Editor

Project Editors: Kathleen J. Edgar, Elizabeth Manar

Rights Acquisition and Management: Tracie Richardson, Kelly Quin, Robyn Young

Composition: Evi Abou-El-Seoud, Mary Beth Trimper

Manufacturing: Cynde Lentz

Gale
27500 Drake Rd.
Farmington Hills, MI 48331-3535

ISBN-13: 978-0-7876-5103-9 (set)
ISBN-13: 978-1-4144-3370-7

ISBN-10: 0-7876-5103-6 (set)
ISBN-10: 1-4144-3370-0

ISSN 1938-8896

This title is also available as an e-book.
ISBN-13: 978-1-4144-5765-9 (set)
ISBN-10: 1-4144-5765-0 (set)
Contact your Gale sales representative for ordering information.

Printed in the United States of America
1 2 3 4 5 6 7 13 12 11 10 09

TABLE OF CONTENTS

PREFACE

Alcohol, Tobacco, and Illicit Drugs is part of the *Information Plus Reference Series*. The purpose of each volume of the series is to present the latest facts on a topic of pressing concern in modern American life. These topics include the most controversial and studied social issues in the twenty-first century: abortion, capital punishment, care of senior citizens, crime, the environment, health care, immigration, minorities, national security, social welfare, women, youth, and many more. Even though this series is written especially for high school and undergraduate students, it is an excellent resource for anyone in need of factual information on current affairs.

By presenting the facts, it is the intention of Gale, Cengage Learning to provide its readers with everything they need to reach an informed opinion on current issues. To that end, there is a particular emphasis in this series on the presentation of scientific studies, surveys, and statistics. These data are generally presented in the form of tables, charts, and other graphics placed within the text of each book. Every graphic is directly referred to and carefully explained in the text. The source of each graphic is presented within the graphic itself. The data used in these graphics are drawn from the most reputable and reliable sources, such as from the various branches of the U.S. government and from major independent polling organizations. Every effort has been made to secure the most recent information available. Readers should bear in mind that many major studies take years to conduct and that additional years often pass before the data from these studies are made available to the public. Therefore, in many cases the most recent information available in 2009 is dated from 2006 or 2007. Older statistics are sometimes presented as well if they are of particular interest and no more-recent information exists.

Even though statistics are a major focus of the *Information Plus Reference Series*, they are by no means its only content. Each book also presents the widely held positions and important ideas that shape how the book's subject is discussed in the United States. These positions are explained in detail and, where possible, in the words of their proponents. Some of the other material to be found in these books includes historical background, descriptions of major events related to the subject, relevant laws and court cases, and examples of how these issues play out in American life. Some books also feature primary documents or have pro and con debate sections that provide the words and opinions of prominent Americans on both sides of a controversial topic. All material is presented in an even-handed and unbiased manner; readers will never be encouraged to accept one view of an issue over another.

HOW TO USE THIS BOOK

Both legal and illicit drugs—substances that can affect a person's mood or physiology—are used by people from all segments of American society. Legal drugs include prescription medications as well as popular and widely available substances such as alcohol, tobacco, and caffeine. Illegal drugs are those with no currently accepted medical use in the United States, such as heroin, lysergic acid diethylamide, ecstasy, and inhalants. This book provides an overview of legal and illicit drugs, including their health impact, addictive nature, and potential for abuse. Also discussed are the political and economic ramifications of such substances; their use among youth; possible treatments; drug trafficking; antidrug efforts and campaigns; and criticisms of the war on drugs.

Alcohol, Tobacco, and Illicit Drugs consists of nine chapters and three appendixes. Each chapter is devoted to a particular aspect of alcohol, tobacco, and illicit drugs in the United States. For a summary of the information covered in each chapter, please see the synopses provided in the Table of Contents at the front of the book. Chapters generally begin with an overview of the basic facts and background information on the chapter's topic, then proceed to examine subtopics of particular interest. For example, Chapter 7, How Alcohol, Tobacco, and Drug Use Affect Economics and Government begins with a discussion of alcohol sales and consumption in the United States. It details how much Americans drink and spend on beer, wine, and distilled spirits. Next, tobacco production and consumption are examined. Topics covered include farming trends, manufacturing, exporting, and the world tobacco markets. Then the chapter looks at alcohol and tobacco advertising and taxation, specifically by noting how much these industries spend on advertising, how youth are affected by it, and the amount of taxes that are collected from the sale of these products. The chapter then outlines the government regulation of alcohol and tobacco, such as the direct shipments of alcohol, the selling of alcohol and tobacco over the Internet, and the regulation of tobacco by the U.S. Food and Drug Administration. Also discussed are the economic costs of alcohol, tobacco, and other drug use; the tobacco companies' responsibility for the costs of tobacco use; and the ending of the tobacco quota system. Readers can find their way through a chapter by looking for the section and subsection headings, which are clearly set off from the text. They can also refer to the book's extensive Index if they already know what they are looking for.

Statistical Information

The tables and figures featured throughout *Alcohol, Tobacco, and Illicit Drugs* will be of particular use to readers in learning about this issue. These tables and figures represent an extensive collection of the most recent and valuable statistics on alcohol, tobacco, illicit drugs, and related issues—for example, graphics cover the amount of alcoholic beverages consumed per capita by American citizens over the past several decades; alcohol's involvement in fatal automobile crashes; the diseases associated with tobacco use; the number of youth who use illicit drugs; and the prevalence rates of hallucinogen use among students. Gale, Cengage Learning believes that making this information available to readers is the most important way to fulfill the goal of this book: to help readers to understand the issues and controversies surrounding alcohol, tobacco, and illicit drugs in the United States and to reach their own conclusions.

Each table or figure has a unique identifier appearing above it for ease of identification and reference. Titles for the tables and figures explain their purpose. At the end of each table or figure, the original source of the data is provided.

To help readers understand these often complicated statistics, all tables and figures are explained in the text. References in the text direct readers to the relevant statistics. Furthermore, the contents of all tables and figures

are fully indexed. Please see the opening section of the Index at the back of this volume for a description of how to find tables and figures within it.

Appendixes

Besides the main body text and images, *Alcohol, Tobacco, and Illicit Drugs* has three appendixes. The first is the Important Names and Addresses directory. Here, readers will find contact information for a number of government and private organizations that can provide further information on alcohol, tobacco, and/or illicit drugs. The second appendix is the Resources section, which can also assist readers in conducting their own research. In this section the author and editors of *Alcohol, Tobacco, and Illicit Drugs* describe some of the sources that were most useful during the compilation of this book. The final appendix is the Index.

ADVISORY BOARD CONTRIBUTIONS

The staff of Information Plus would like to extend its heartfelt appreciation to the Information Plus Advisory Board. This dedicated group of media professionals provides feedback on the series on an ongoing basis. Their comments allow the editorial staff who work on the project to make the series better and more user-friendly. The staff's top priority is to produce the highest-quality and most useful books possible, and the Advisory Board's contributions to this process are invaluable.

The members of the Information Plus Advisory Board are:

- Kathleen R. Bonn, Librarian, Newbury Park High School, Newbury Park, California

- Madelyn Garner, Librarian, San Jacinto College, North Campus, Houston, Texas

- Anne Oxenrider, Media Specialist, Dundee High School, Dundee, Michigan

- Charles R. Rodgers, Director of Libraries, Pasco-Hernando Community College, Dade City, Florida

- James N. Zitzelsberger, Library Media Department Chairman, Oshkosh West High School, Oshkosh, Wisconsin

COMMENTS AND SUGGESTIONS

The editors of the *Information Plus Reference Series* welcome your feedback on *Alcohol, Tobacco, and Illicit Drugs*. Please direct all correspondence to:

Editors
Information Plus Reference Series
27500 Drake Rd.
Farmington Hills, MI 48331-3535

CHAPTER 1
DRUGS: A DEFINITION

Drugs are nonfood chemicals that alter the way a person thinks, feels, functions, or behaves. This includes everything from prescription medications to illegal chemicals such as heroin to popular and widely available substances such as alcohol, tobacco, and caffeine. A wide variety of laws, regulations, and government agencies exist to control the possession, sale, and use of drugs. Different drugs are held to different standards based on their perceived dangers and usefulness, a fact that sometimes leads to disagreement and controversy.

Illegal drugs are those with no currently accepted medical use in the United States, such as heroin, lysergic acid diethylamide (LSD), and marijuana. It is illegal to buy, sell, possess, and use these drugs except for research purposes. They are supplied only to registered, qualified researchers. (Some states and local jurisdictions have decriminalized certain uses of certain amounts of marijuana, but federal laws supersede these state and local marijuana decriminalization laws. See Chapter 9.)

Legal drugs, by contrast, are drugs whose sale, possession, and use as intended are not forbidden by law. Their use may be restricted, however. For example, the U.S. Drug Enforcement Administration (DEA) controls the use of legal psychoactive (mood- or mind-altering) drugs that have the potential for abuse. These drugs, which include narcotics, depressants, and stimulants, are available only with a prescription and are called controlled substances. The term *illicit drugs* is used by the Substance Abuse and Mental Health Services Administration to describe both controlled substances that are used in violation of the law and drugs that are completely illegal.

The goal of the DEA is to ensure that controlled substances are readily available for medical use or research purposes while preventing their illegal sale and abuse. The agency works toward accomplishing this goal by requiring people and businesses that manufacture, distribute, prescribe, and dispense controlled substances to register with

the DEA. Registrants must abide by a series of requirements relating to drug security, records accountability, and adherence to standards. The DEA also enforces the controlled substances laws and regulations of the United States by investigating and prosecuting those who violate these laws.

The U.S. Food and Drug Administration (FDA) also plays a role in drug control. This agency regulates the manufacture and marketing of prescription and nonprescription drugs. It also requires that the active ingredients in a product be safe and effective before allowing the drug to be sold.

Alcohol and tobacco are monitored and specially taxed by the Alcohol and Tobacco Tax and Trade Bureau (TTB). The TTB was formed in January 2003 as a provision of the Homeland Security Act of 2002, which split the Bureau of Alcohol, Tobacco, and Firearms (ATF) into two new agencies. One of these agencies, the TTB, took over the taxation duties for alcohol, tobacco, and firearms and remained a part of the U.S. Department of the Treasury. The TTB also ensures that alcohol and tobacco products are legally labeled, advertised, and marketed; regulates the qualification and operations of distilleries, wineries, and breweries; tests alcoholic beverages to ensure that their regulated ingredients are within legal limits; and screens applicants who wish to manufacture, import, or export tobacco products.

The other agency split from the former ATF is the reformed ATF: the Bureau of Alcohol, Tobacco, Firearms and Explosives. The ATF has become a principal law enforcement agency within the U.S. Department of Justice enforcing federal criminal laws and regulating the firearms and explosives industries. It also investigates illegal trafficking of alcohol and tobacco products.

On April 2, 2009, the U.S. House of Representatives approved legislation that would give the FDA authority over the sale and advertising of tobacco, but the U.S. Senate had yet to vote on the bill. The legislation would grant the FDA various liberties, including regulating the levels of nicotine and other ingredients in cigarettes, banning tobacco manufacturers from selling candy-flavored or menthol cigarettes, forcing larger warning signs on tobacco packaging, and preventing the sale of alleged "mild" or "lite" cigarettes. After the vote of approval in the House of Representatives, the administration of President Barack Obama (1961–) spoke out in favor of the bill.

FIVE CATEGORIES OF SUBSTANCES

Drugs may be classified into five categories:

- Depressants, including alcohol and tranquilizers—these substances slow down the activity of the nervous system. They produce sedative (calming) and hypnotic (trance-like) effects as well as drowsiness. If taken in large doses, depressants can cause intoxication (drunkenness).

- Hallucinogens, including marijuana, phencyclidine, and LSD—hallucinogens produce abnormal and unreal sensations such as seeing distorted and vividly colored images. Hallucinogens can also produce frightening psychological responses such as anxiety, depression, and the feeling of losing control of one's mind.

- Narcotics, including heroin and opium, from which morphine and codeine are derived—narcotics are drugs that alter the perception of pain and induce sleep and euphoria (an intense feeling of well-being; a "high").

- Stimulants, including caffeine, nicotine, cocaine, amphetamine, and methamphetamine—these substances speed up the processing rate of the central nervous system. They can reduce fatigue, elevate mood, increase energy, and help people stay awake. In large doses stimulants can cause irritability, anxiety, sleeplessness, and even psychotic behavior. Caffeine is the most commonly used stimulant in the world.

- Other compounds, including anabolic steroids and inhalants—anabolic steroids are a group of synthetic substances that are chemically related to testosterone and are promoted for their muscle-building properties. Inhalants are solvents and aerosol products that produce vapors that have psychoactive effects. These substances dull pain and can produce euphoria.

Table 1.1 provides an overview of alcohol, nicotine, and other selected psychoactive substances. It includes the DEA schedule for each drug listed. Developed as part of the Controlled Substances Act (CSA) of 1970, the DEA drug schedules are categories into which controlled substances are placed depending on characteristics such as medical use, potential for abuse, safety, and danger of dependence. The types of drugs categorized in each of the five schedules, with examples, are shown in Table 1.2.

DRUGS DISCUSSED IN THIS BOOK

This book focuses on substances widely used throughout the world: alcohol, tobacco, and illicit drugs. Not only are alcohol and tobacco legal, relatively affordable, and more or less socially acceptable (depending on time, place, and circumstance), but also they are important economic commodities. Industries exist to produce, distribute, and sell these products, creating jobs and income and contributing to economic well-being. Thus, whenever discussions of possible government regulation of alcohol and tobacco arise, the topic brings with it significant economic and political issues.

Illicit drugs are those that are unlawful to possess or distribute under the CSA. Some controlled substances can be taken under the supervision of health care professionals licensed by the DEA. The CSA provides penalties for the unlawful manufacture, distribution, and dispensing of controlled substances, based on the schedule of the drug or substance and enforced by the DEA. Nonetheless, illicit drugs have fostered huge illicit drug marketing and drug trafficking (buying and selling) networks (see Chapter 8). Tobacco, beer, wine, and spirits are exempt from the CSA and the DEA drug schedules.

Figure 1.1, Figure 1.2, and Figure 1.3 show trends in cigarette, illicit drug, and alcohol use in the 20th century and into the beginning of the 21st century. They also provide an overview of the ebb and flow of the use and abuse of these substances in the United States. This chapter will take a historical look at the use and abuse of each substance, and the chapters that follow will present more up-to-date information.

WHAT ARE ABUSE AND ADDICTION?

Many drugs, both legal and illicit, have the potential for abuse and addiction. Research and treatment experts identify three general levels of interaction with drugs: use, abuse, and dependence (or addiction). In general, abuse involves a compulsive use of a substance and impaired social or occupational functioning. Dependence (addiction) includes these traits, plus evidence of physical tolerance (a need to take increasingly higher doses to achieve the same effect) or withdrawal symptoms when use of the drug is stopped.

The progression from use to dependence is complex, as are the abused substances themselves. Researchers find no standard boundaries between using a substance, abusing a substance, and being addicted to a substance. They believe these lines vary widely from substance to substance and from individual to individual.

In addition, scientists have been working to answer the question of why some people who use addictive substances become addicted and others do not or can more easily break the addiction. The results of many studies of identical and fraternal (nonidentical) twins and families with histories of substance abuse and addiction indicate there is a genetic component to addiction. In "Are There Genetic Influences on Addiction: Evidence from Family, Adoption, and Twin Studies" (*Addiction*, vol. 103, no. 7, July 2008), Arpana Agrawal and Michael T. Lynskey of the Washington University School of Medicine in St. Louis, Missouri, review studies that examined the genetic basis for addition. The researchers determine that evidence shows inheritance

TABLE 1.1

Commonly abused drugs

Substance: category and name	Examples of *commercial* and street names	DEA Schedule[a]/how administered[b]	Intoxication effects/potential health consequences
Depressants			
Alcohol	Beer, wine, hard liquor	Not scheduled/swallowed	Reduced anxiety; feeling of well-being; lowered inhibitions; slowed pulse and breathing; lowered blood pressure; poor concentration/fatigue; confusion; impaired coordination, memory, judgment; addiction; respiratory depression and arrest, death
Barbiturates	*Amytal, Nembutal, Seconal, Phenobarbital;* barbs, reds, red birds, phennies, tooies, yellows, yellow jackets	II, III, V/injected, swallowed	Also, for barbiturates—sedation, drowsiness/depression, unusual excitement, fever, irritability, poor judgment, slurred speech, dizziness, life-threatening withdrawal.
Benzodiazepines (other than flunitrazepam)	*Ativan, Halcion, Librium, Valium, Xanax;* candy, downers, sleeping pills, tranks	IV/swallowed, injected	For benzodiazepines—sedation, drowsiness/dizziness
Flunitrazepam[c]	*Rohypnol;* forget-me pill, Mexican Valium, R2, Roche, roofies, roofinol, rope, rophies	IV/swallowed, snorted	For flunitrazepam—visual and gastrointestinal disturbances, urinary retention, memory loss for the time under the drug's effects
GHB[c]	*gamma-hydroxybutyrate;* G, Georgia home boy, grievous bodily harm, liquid ecstasy	I/swallowed	For GHB—drowsiness, nausea/vomiting, headache, loss of consciousness, loss of reflexes, seizures, coma, death
Methaqualone	*Quaalude, Sopor, Parest;* ludes, mandex, quad, quay	I/injected, swallowed	For methaqualone—euphoria/depression, poor reflexes, slurred speech, coma
Cannabinoids (hallucinogens)			
Hashish	Boom, chronic, gangster, hash, hash oil, hemp	I/swallowed, smoked	Euphoria, slowed thinking and reaction time, confusion, impaired balance and coordination/cough, frequent respiratory infections; impaired memory and learning; increased heart rate, anxiety; panic attacks; tolerance, addiction
Marijuana	Blunt, dope, ganja, grass, herb, joints, Mary Jane, pot, reefer, sinsemilla, skunk, weed	I/swallowed, smoked	
Dissociative anesthetics (hallucinogens)			
Ketamine	*Ketalar SV;* cat Valiums, K, Special K, vitamin K	III/injected, snorted, smoked	Increased heart rate and blood pressure, impaired motor function/memory loss; numbness; nausea/vomiting
			Also, for ketamine—at high doses, delirium, depression, respiratory depression and arrest
PCP and analogs	*phencyclidine;* angel dust, boat, hog, love boat, peace pill	I, II/injected, swallowed, smoked	For PCP and analogs—possible decrease in blood pressure and heart rate, panic, aggression, violence/loss of appetite, depression
Hallucinogens			Altered states of perception and feeling; nausea; persisting perception disorder (flashbacks)
LSD	*Lysergic acid diethylamide;* acid, blotter, boomers, cubes, microdot, yellow	I/swallowed, absorbed through mouth tissues	Also, for LSD and mescaline—increased body temperature, heart rate, blood pressure; loss of appetite, sleeplessness, numbness, weakness, tremors
Mescaline	Buttons, cactus, mesc, peyote	I/swallowed, smoked	For LSD—persistent mental disorders
Psilocybin	Magic mushroom, purple passion, shrooms	I/swallowed	For psilocybin—nervousness, paranoia
Opioids and morphine derivatives (narcotics)			
Codeine	*Empirin with Codeine, Fiorinal with Codeine, Robitussin A-C, Tylenol with Codeine;* Captain Cody, Cody, schoolboy; (with glutethimide) doors & fours, loads, pancakes and syrup	II, III, IV/injected, swallowed	Pain relief, euphoria, drowsiness/nausea, constipation, confusion, sedation, respiratory depression and arrest, tolerance, addiction, unconsciousness, coma, death
Fentanyl and fentanyl analogs	*Actiq, Duragesic, Sublimaze;* Apache, China girl, China white, dance fever, friend, goodfella, jackpot, murder 8, TNT, Tango and Cash	I, II/injected smoked, snorted	Also, for codeine—less analgesia, sedation, and respiratory depression than morphine
Heroin	*Diacetylmorphine;* brown sugar, dope, H, horse, junk, skag, skunk, smack, white horse	I/injected smoked, snorted	For heroin—staggering gait
Morphine	*Roxanol, Duramorph;* M, Miss Emma, monkey, white stuff	II, III/injected, swallowed, smoked	
Opium	*Laudanum, paregoric;* big O, black stuff, block, gum, hop	II, III, V/swallowed, smoked	
Oxycodone HCL	*Oxycontin;* Oxy, O.C., killer	II/swallowed, snorted, injected	
Hydrocodone bitartrate, acetaminophen	*Vicodin;* vike, Watson-387	II/swallowed	

accounting for a wide range of influence on addiction—from 30% to 70%. Other factors, such as gender, age, social influences, and cultural characteristics, interact with one's genetics, resulting in an individual's susceptibility to addictive behavior.

Physiological, Psychological, and Sociocultural Factor

Some researchers maintain that the principal causes o substance use are external social influences, such as pee pressure, whereas the principal causes of substance abus and/or dependence are psychological and physiologica

TABLE 1.1

Commonly abused drugs [CONTINUED]

Substance: category and name	Examples of *commercial* and street names	DEA Schedule[a]/how administered[b]	Intoxication effects/potential health consequences
Stimulants			*Increased heart rate, blood pressure, metabolism; feelings of exhilaration, energy, increased mental alertness/rapid or irregular heart beat; reduced appetite, weight loss, heart failure, nervousness, insomnia*
Amphetamine	*Biphetamine, Dexedrine;* bennies, black beauties, crosses, hearts, LA turnaround, speed, truck drivers, uppers	II/injected, swallowed, smoked, snorted	*Also, for amphetamine—rapid breathing/tremor, loss of coordination; irritability, anxiousness, restlessness, delirium, panic, paranoia, impulsive behavior, aggressiveness, tolerance, addiction, psychosis*
Cocaine	*Cocaine hydrochloride;* blow, bump, C, candy Charlie, coke, crack, flake, rock, snow, toot	II/injected, smoked, snorted	*For cocaine—increased temperature/chest pain, respiratory failure, nausea, abdominal pain, strokes, seizures, headaches, malnutrition, panic attacks*
MDMA (methylenedioxy-methamphetamine)	Adam, clarity, ecstasy, Eve, lover's speed, peace, STP, X, XTC	I/swallowed	*For MDMA—mild hallucinogenic effects, increased tactile sensitivity, empathic feelings/impaired memory and learning, hyperthermia, cardiac toxicity, renal failure, liver toxicity*
Methamphetamine	*Desoxyn;* chalk, crank, crystal, fire, glass, go fast, ice, meth, speed	II/injected, swallowed, smoked, snorted	*For methamphetamine—aggression, violence, psychotic behavior/memory loss, cardiac and neurological damage; impaired memory and learning, tolerance, addiction*
Methylphenidate (safe and effective for treatment of ADHD)	*Ritalin;* JIF, MPH, R-ball, Skippy, the smart drug, vitamin R	II/injected, swallowed, snorted	
Nicotine	Cigarettes, cigars, smokeless tobacco, snuff, spit tobacco, bidis, chew	Not scheduled/smoked, snorted, taken in snuff and spit	*For nicotine—additional effects attributable to tobacco exposure, adverse pregnancy outcomes, chronic lung disease, cardiovascular disease, stroke, cancer, tolerance, addiction*
Other compounds			
Anabolic steroids	*Anadrol, Oxandrin, Durabolin, Depo-Testosterone, Equipoise;* roids, juice	III/injected, swallowed, applied to skin	*No intoxication effects/hypertension, blood clotting and cholesterol changes, liver cysts and cancer, kidney cancer, hostility and aggression, acne; in adolescents, premature stoppage of growth; in males, prostate cancer, reduced sperm production, shrunken testicles, breast enlargement; in females, menstrual irregularities, development of beard and other masculine characteristics*
Dextromethorphan (DXM)	*Found in some cough and cold medications; Robotripping, Robo, Triple C*	Not scheduled/swallowed	*Dissociative effects, distortive visual perceptions to complete dissociative effects*
Inhalants	*Solvents (paint thinners, gasoline, glues), gases (butane, propane, aerosol propellants, nitrous oxide), nitrites (isoamyl, isobutyl, cyclohexyl);* laughing gas, poppers, snappers, whippets	Not scheduled/inhaled through nose or mouth	*Stimulation, loss of inhibition; headache; nausea or vomiting; slurred speech, loss of motor coordination; wheezing/unconsciousness, cramps, weight loss, muscle weakness, depression, memory impairment, damage to cardiovascular and nervous systems, sudden death*

Schedule I and II drugs have a high potential for abuse. They require greater storage security and have a quota on manufacturing, among other restrictions. Schedule I drugs are available for research only and have no approved medical use; schedule II drugs are available only by prescription (unrefillable) and require a form for ordering. Schedule III and IV drugs are available by prescription, may have five refills in 6 months, and may be ordered orally. Some schedule V drugs are available over the counter

Taking drugs by injection can increase the risk of infection through needle contamination with staphylococci, HIV, hepatitis, and other organisms.

Associated with sexual assaults.

SOURCE: Adapted from "Commonly Abused Drugs," National Institutes of Health, National Institute on Drug Abuse, 2008, http://www.nida.nih.gov/DrugPages/DrugsofAbuse.html#ASSOCIATED (accessed December 8, 2008)

needs and pressures, including inherited tendencies. Additionally, psychoactive drug use at an early age may be a risk factor (a characteristic that increases likelihood) for subsequent dependence.

Physically, mood-altering substances affect brain processes. Most drugs that are abused stimulate the reward or pleasure centers of the brain by causing the release of dopamine, which is a neurotransmitter—a chemical in the brain that relays messages from one nerve cell to another.

Psychologically, a person may become dependent on a substance because it relieves pain, offers escape from real or perceived problems, or makes the user feel more relaxed or confident in certain social settings. A successful first use of a substance may reduce the user's fear of the drug and thus lead to continued use and even dependence.

Socially, substance use may be widespread in some groups or environments. The desire to belong to a special group is a strong human characteristic, and those who use one or more substances may become part of a subculture that encourages and promotes use. An individual may be influenced by one of these groups to start using a substance, or he or she may be drawn to such a group after starting use somewhere else. In addition, a person—especially a young person—may not have access to alternative rewarding or pleasurable groups or activities that do not include substance use.

TABLE 1.2

Drug schedules established by the Controlled Substances Act (CSA), 1970

Schedule I

- The drug or other substance has a high potential for abuse.
- The drug or other substance has no currently accepted medical use in treatment in the United States.
- There is a lack of accepted safety for use of the drug or other substance under medical supervision.
- Examples of Schedule I substances include heroin, lysergic acid diethylamide (LSD), marijuana, and methaqualone.

Schedule II

- The drug or other substance has a high potential for abuse.
- The drug or other substance has a currently accepted medical use in treatment in the United States or a currently accepted medical use with severe restrictions.
- Abuse of the drug or other substance may lead to severe psychological or physical dependence.
- Examples of Schedule II substances include morphine, phencyclidine (PCP), cocaine, methadone, and methamphetamine.

Schedule III

- The drug or other substance has less potential for abuse than the drugs or other substances in Schedules I and II.
- The drug or other substance has a currently accepted medical use in treatment in the United States.
- Abuse of the drug or other substance may lead to moderate or low physical dependence or high psychological dependence.
- Anabolic steroids, codeine and hydrocodone with aspirin or Tylenol, and some barbiturates are examples of Schedule III substances.

Schedule IV

- The drug or other substance has a low potential for abuse relative to the drugs or other substances in Schedule III.
- The drug or other substance has a currently accepted medical use in treatment in the United States.
- Abuse of the drug or other substance may lead to limited physical dependence or psychological dependence relative to the drugs or other substances in Schedule III.
- Examples of drugs included in Schedule IV are Darvon, Talwin, Equanil, Valium and Xanax.

Schedule V

- The drug or other substance has a low potential for abuse relative to the drugs or other substances in Schedule IV.
- The drug or other substance has a currently accepted medical use in treatment in the United States.
- Abuse of the drug or other substances may lead to limited physical dependence or psychological dependence relative to the drugs or other substances in Schedule IV.
- Cough medicines with codeine are examples of Schedule V drugs.

SOURCE: Adapted from *Drugs of Abuse, 2005 Edition*, U.S. Department of Justice, Drug Enforcement Administration, 2005, ttp://www.usdoj.gov/dea/pubs/abuse/doa-p.pdf (accessed December 8, 2008)

FIGURE 1.1

Trends in cigarette use, 1900–2004

Annual per capita consumption 18 years and over

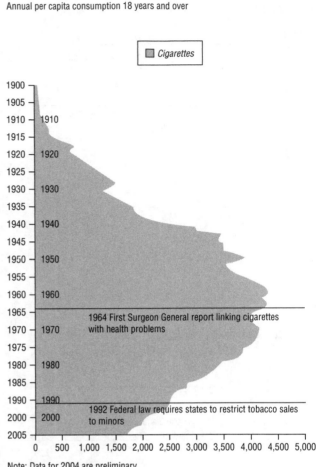

Note: Data for 2004 are preliminary.

SOURCE: "Trends in Cigarette Use, 1900–2004," in *Current State of Drug Policy: Successes and Challenges*, Executive Office of the President of the United States, Office of National Drug Control Policy, March 2008, http://www.whitehousedrugpolicy.gov/publications/successes_challenges/successes_challenges.pdf (accessed August 18, 2008). Data from Miller, R. U.S. cigarette consumption 1900 to date. In Harr W. ed. Tobacco Yearbook. Bowling Green KY. Cockrel Corporation 1981.

Figure 1.4 illustrates some relationships between physiological, psychological, and cultural factors that influence drinking and drinking patterns. Constraints (inhibitory factors) and motivations influence drinking patterns. In turn, drinking patterns influence the relationship between routine activities related to drinking and acute (immediate) consequences of drinking.

Definitions of Abuse and Dependence

Two texts provide the most commonly used medical definitions of substance abuse and dependence. The *Diagnostic and Statistical Manual of Mental Disorders* (*DSM*) is published by the American Psychiatric Association. The *International Classification of Diseases* (*ICD*) is published by the World Health Organization (WHO). Even though the definitions of dependence in these two manuals are almost identical, the definitions of abuse are not.

THE *DSM* DEFINITION OF ABUSE. The text revision of the fourth edition of the *DSM*, *Diagnostic and Statistical Manual of Mental Disorders-IV Text Revision* (*DSM-IV-TR*) was published in 2000 and was the most recent revision available in 2009. (The publication of the *DSM-V* in its final form is expected in 2012.) The *DSM-IV-TR* defines abuse as an abnormal pattern of recurring use that leads to "significant impairment or distress," marked by one or more of the following in a 12-month period:

- Failure to fulfill major obligations at home, school, or work (e.g., repeated absences, poor performance, or neglect)

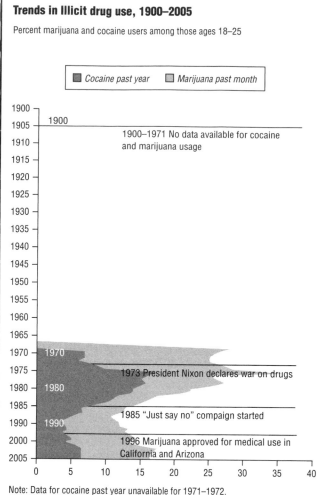

FIGURE 1.2

Trends in Illicit drug use, 1900–2005

Percent marijuana and cocaine users among those ages 18–25

◼ Cocaine past year   ◼ Marijuana past month

1900–1971 No data available for cocaine and marijuana usage

1973 President Nixon declares war on drugs

1985 "Just say no" compaign started

1996 Marijuana approved for medical use in California and Arizona

Note: Data for cocaine past year unavailable for 1971–1972.

SOURCE: "Trends in Illicit Drug Use, 1900–2005," in *Current State of Drug Policy: Successes and Challenges*, Executive Office of the President, Office of National Drug Control Policy, March 2008, http://www.whitehousedrugpolicy.gov/publications/successes_challenges/successes_challenges.pdf (accessed August 18, 2008)

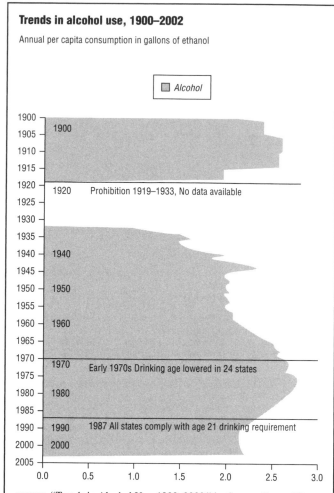

FIGURE 1.3

Trends in alcohol use, 1900–2002

Annual per capita consumption in gallons of ethanol

◼ Alcohol

1920 Prohibition 1919–1933, No data available

Early 1970s Drinking age lowered in 24 states

1987 All states comply with age 21 drinking requirement

SOURCE: "Trends in Alcohol Use, 1900–2002," in *Current State of Drug Policy: Successes and Challenges*, Executive Office of the President of the United States, Office of National Drug Control Policy, March 2008, http://www.whitehousedrugpolicy.gov/publications/successes_challenges/successes_challenges.pdf (accessed August 18, 2008)

- Use in hazardous or potentially hazardous situations, such as driving a car or operating a machine while impaired

- Legal problems, such as arrest for disorderly conduct while under the influence of the substance

- Continued use in spite of social or interpersonal problems caused by the use of the substance, such as fights or family arguments

THE *ICD* DEFINITION OF HARMFUL USE. The 10th and most recent revision (as of 2009) of the *ICD* (*ICD-10*), which was endorsed by the 43rd World Health Assembly in May 1990 and has been used in WHO Member States since 1994, uses the term *harmful use* rather than *abuse*. (The publication of the *ICD-11* in its final form is expected in 2015.) It defines harmful use as "a pattern of psychoactive substance use that is causing damage to health," either physical or mental.

Because the *ICD* manual is targeted toward international use, its definition must be broader than the *DSM* definition, which is intended for use in the United States. Cultural customs of substance use vary widely, sometimes even within the same country.

DEFINITIONS OF DEPENDENCE. In general, the *DSM-IV-TR* and the *ICD-10* manuals agree that dependence is present if three or more of the following occur in a 12-month period:

- Increasing need for more of the substance to achieve the same effect (occurs as the user builds up a tolerance to the substance), or a reduction in effect when using the same amount as used previously

- Withdrawal symptoms if use of the substance is stopped or reduced

- Progressive neglect of other pleasures and duties

- A strong desire to take the substance or a persistent but unsuccessful desire to control or reduce the use of the substance

FIGURE 1.4

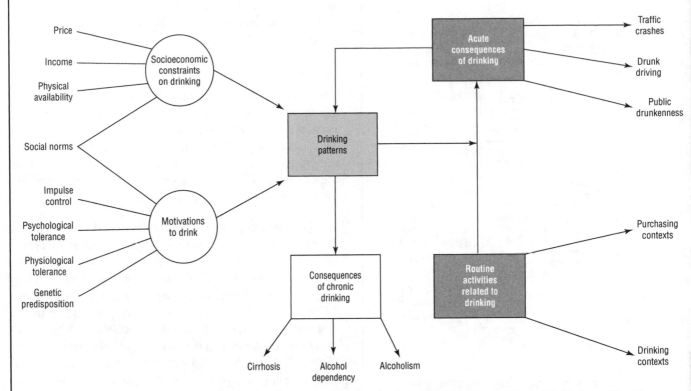

An ecological model of drinking behavior

SOURCE: Paul J. Gruenewald and Alex B. Millar, "An Ecological Model of Drinking Behavior," in "Alcohol Availability and the Ecology of Drinking Behavior," *Alcohol Health & Research World*, vol. 17, no. 1, 1993 (updated October 2000), http://www.niaaa.nih.gov/Resources/GraphicsGallery/TreatmentPrevention/gruen.htm (accessed August 5, 2008)

- Continued use in spite of physical or mental health problems caused by the substance

- Use of the substance in larger amounts or over longer periods of time than originally intended, or difficulties in controlling the amount of the substance used or when to stop taking it

- Considerable time spent in obtaining the substance, using it, or recovering from its effects

Progression from Use to Dependence

The rate at which individuals progress from drug use to drug abuse to drug dependence (or addiction) depends on many of the aforementioned factors. In general, each level is more dangerous, more invasive in the user's life, and more likely to cause social interventions, such as family pressure to enter treatment programs or prison sentences for drug offenses, than the previous level.

Figure 1.5 is a diagram of the progression to addiction. Notice that the intensification of use leads to abuse and that abuse leads to dependence. The right side of the diagram shows social interventions that are appropriate at various stages of drug use, abuse, and dependence. The dotted lines to the left show that relapse after recovery may lead to renewed drug use, abuse, or dependence.

THE HISTORY OF ALCOHOL USE

Ethyl alcohol (ethanol), the active ingredient in beer, wine, and other liquors, is the oldest known psychoactive drug. It is also the only type of alcohol used as a beverage. Other alcohols, such as methanol and isopropyl alcohol, when ingested even in small amounts, can produce severe negative health effects and often death.

The basic characteristics of alcoholic beverages have remained unchanged from early times. Beer and wine are created through the natural chemical process called fermentation. Fermentation can produce beverages with an alcohol content of up to only 14%. More potent drinks such as rum or vodka—known as spirits or liquors—can be produced through distillation. This is a process that involves using heat to separate and concentrate the alcohol found in fermented beverages and can result in drinks that have an alcoholic content of 50% or more.

Early Uses and Abuses of Alcohol

Beer and wine have been used since ancient times in religious rituals, celebrations of councils, coronations, war, peacemaking, festivals, hospitality, and the rites of birth, initiation, marriage, and death. In ancient times, just as in the 21st century, the use of beer and wine sometimes led to

FIGURE 1.5

Drug use, abuse, and dependence

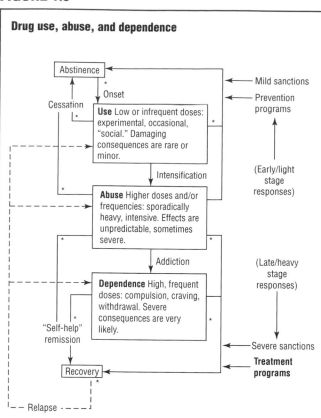

*Indicates the influence of biological, physiological, and social factors that condition changes in behavior.

SOURCE: "Figure 2.1. Drug Use, Abuse, and Dependence," in *Technologies for Understanding and Preventing Substance Abuse and Addiction*, U.S. Congress, Office of Technology Assessment, September 1994, www.fas.org/ota/reports/9435.pdf (accessed August 11, 2008). Data from the National Academy of Sciences, Institute of Medicine.

drunkenness. One of the earliest written works on temperance (controlling one's drinking or not drinking at all) was written in Egypt nearly 3,000 years ago. These writings can be thought of as similar to present-day pamphlets espousing moderation in alcohol consumption. Similar recommendations have been found in early Greek, Roman, Indian, Japanese, and Chinese writings, as well as in the Bible.

Drinking in Colonial America

In colonial America people drank much more alcohol than they do in the 21st century, with estimates ranging from three to seven times more alcohol per person per year. Liquor was used to ease the pain and discomfort of many illnesses and injuries such as the common cold, fever, broken limbs, toothaches, frostbite, and the like. Parents often gave liquor to children to relieve their minor aches and pains or to help them sleep. Until 1842, when modern surgical anesthesia began with the use of ether, only heavy doses of alcohol were consistently effective to ease pain during operations.

As early as 1619 drunkenness was illegal in the Virginia Colony. It was punished in various ways: whipping, place-

ment in the stocks, fines, and even wearing a red D (for "drunkard"). By the 18th century all classes of people were getting drunk with greater frequency, even though it was well known that alcohol affected the senses and motor skills and that drunkenness led to increased crime, violence, accidents, and death.

Temperance

In 1784 Benjamin Rush (1746–1813), a physician and signer of the Declaration of Independence, published the booklet *An Inquiry into the Effects of Ardent Spirits on the Mind and Body*. The pamphlet became popular among the growing number of people who were concerned about the excessive drinking of many Americans. Such concern gave rise to the temperance movement.

The temperance movement in the United States began in the early 1800s and lasted until roughly 1890. Initially, the goal of the movement was to promote moderation in the consumption of alcohol. By the 1850s large numbers of people were completely giving up alcohol, and by the 1870s the goal of the temperance movement was to promote abstinence from alcohol. Reformers were concerned about the effects of alcohol on the family, the labor force, and the nation, all of which needed sober participants if they were to remain healthy and productive. Temperance supporters also saw alcoholism as a problem of personal immorality.

Prohibition

In 1919 reform efforts led to the passage of the 18th Amendment of the U.S. Constitution, which prohibited the "manufacture, sale, or transportation of intoxicating liquors" and their importation and exportation. The Volstead Act of 1919, which passed over President Woodrow Wilson's (1856–1924) veto, was the Prohibition law that enforced the 18th Amendment.

Outlawing alcohol did not stop most people from drinking; instead, alcohol was manufactured and sold illegally by gangsters, who organized themselves efficiently and gained considerable political influence from the money they earned. In addition, many individuals illegally brewed alcoholic beverages at home or smuggled alcohol from Canada and Mexico. Ultimately, the 18th Amendment was repealed in 1933 with the passage of the 21st Amendment.

Understanding the Dangers of Alcohol

As the decades passed, recognition of the dangers of alcohol increased. In 1956 the American Medical Association endorsed classifying and treating alcoholism as a disease. In 1970 Congress created the National Institute on Alcohol Abuse and Alcoholism, establishing a public commitment to alcohol-related research. During the 1970s, however, many states lowered their drinking age to 18 when the legal voting age was lowered to this age.

Traffic fatalities rose after these laws took effect, and many such accidents involved people between the ages of 18 and 21 who had been drinking and driving. Organizations such as Mothers against Drunk Driving and Students against Drunk Driving sought to educate the public about the great harm drunk drivers had done to others. As a result, and because of pressure from the federal government, by 1988 all states raised their minimum drinking age to 21. In *Traffic Safety Facts, 2007 Data—Young Drivers* (2008, http://www-nrd.nhtsa.dot.gov/Pubs/811001.PDF), the National Highway Traffic Safety Administration estimates that laws making 21 the minimum drinking age have saved an estimated 26,333 lives since 1975. By 1989 warning labels noting the deleterious effects of alcohol on health were required on all retail containers of alcoholic beverages. Nonetheless, the misuse and abuse of alcohol remain major health and social problems in the first decade of the 21st century.

THE HISTORY OF TOBACCO USE

Tobacco is a commercially grown plant that contains nicotine, an addictive drug. Tobacco is native to North America, where since ancient times it has played an important part in Native American social and religious customs. Additionally, Native Americans believed that tobacco had medicinal properties, so it was used to treat pain, epilepsy, colds, and headaches.

From Pipes to Cigarettes

As European explorers and settlers came to North America in the 15th and 16th centuries, Native Americans introduced them to tobacco. Its use soon spread among the settlers, and throughout Europe and Asia, although some rulers and nations opposed it and sought to outlaw it. At this time tobacco was smoked in pipes, chewed, or taken as snuff. Snuff is finely powdered tobacco that can be chewed, rubbed on the gums, or inhaled through the nose.

Cigar smoking was introduced to the United States in about 1762. Cigars are tobacco leaves rolled and prepared for smoking. The U.S. consumption of cigars exceeded 4 billion in 1898, according to various tobacco-related Web sites. Cigarettes (cut tobacco rolled in a paper tube) would soon become the choice of most smokers, however, thanks to the 1881 invention of a cigarette-making machine that allowed them to be mass-produced and sold cheaply.

Early Antismoking Efforts in the United States

The first antismoking movement in the United States was organized in the 1830s (just as the temperance movement was growing in the country). Reformers characterized tobacco as an unhealthy and even fatal habit. Tobacco use was linked to increased alcohol use and lack of cleanliness. Antismoking reformers also suggested that tobacco exhausted the soil, wasted money, and promoted laziness, promiscuity, and profanity. Their efforts to limit or outlaw smoking met with only small, temporary, successes until well into the 20th century.

A Boom in Smoking in the United States

The National Center for Chronic Disease Prevention and Health Promotion reports in "Consumption Data" (2006, http://www.cdc.gov/tobacco/data_statistics/tables/economics/consump1.htm) that cigarette usage increased dramatically in the early 1900s, with the total consumption increasing from 2.5 billion cigarettes in 1901 to 13.2 billion cigarettes in 1912. In 1913 the R. J. Reynolds Company introduced Camel cigarettes, an event that is often called the birth of the modern cigarette. During World War I (1914–1918) cigarettes were shipped to U.S. troops fighting overseas (this also occurred during World War II, 1939–1945). They were included in soldiers' rations and were dispensed by groups such as the American Red Cross and the Young Men's Christian Association. Women began openly smoking in larger numbers as well, something tobacco companies noticed; in 1919 the first advertisement featuring a woman smoking cigarettes appeared.

Cigarette smoking was very common and an accepted part of society, but doubts about its safety were growing. On July 12, 1957, following a joint report by the National Cancer Institute, the National Heart Institute, the American Cancer Society, and the American Heart Association, the U.S. surgeon general Leroy E. Burney (1906–1998), a smoker himself, delivered the official statement "Lung Cancer and Excessive Cigarette Smoking" (http://caonline.amcancersoc.org/cgi/reprint/8/2/44.pdf), in which he declared that "the weight of the evidence is increasingly pointing in one direction: that excessive smoking is one of the causative factors in lung cancer." Nevertheless, cigarette ads of the 1950s touted cigarette smoking as pleasurable, sexy, relaxing, flavorful, and fun. (See Figure 1.6.)

Health Risks Lead to Diminished Smoking

In 1964 the U.S. surgeon general Luther L. Terry (1911–1985) released *Smoking and Health: Report of the Advisory Committee to the Surgeon General of the Public Health Service* (http://profiles.nlm.nih.gov/NN/B/B/M/Q/_/nnbbm.pdf). This landmark document was the United States' first widely publicized official recognition that cigarette smoking is a cause of lung cancer and laryngeal cancer in men, probable cause of lung cancer in women, and the most important cause of chronic bronchitis.

Increased attention was paid to the potential health risks of smoking throughout the rest of the 1960s and 1970s. The first health warnings appeared on cigarette packages in 1966. In 1970 the WHO took a public stand against smoking. On January 2, 1971, the Public Health Cigarette Smoking Act of 1969 went into effect, removing cigarette advertising from radio and television in the United States. A growing number of individuals, cities, and states filed lawsuits against U.S. tobacco companies. Some individuals claimed they had been deceived about the potential harm of smoking. A few states filed lawsuits to recoup money spent on smokers' Medicaid

FIGURE 1.6

A cigarette advertisement from the 1950s. © *Robert Landau/Corbis.*

ills. In 1998, 46 states, 5 territories, and the District of Columbia signed the Master Settlement Agreement (http://g.ca.gov/tobacco/msa.php) with the major tobacco companies to settle all state lawsuits for $206 billion. Excluded from the settlement were Florida, Minnesota, Mississippi, and Texas, which had already concluded previous settlements with the tobacco industry. Chapter 8 includes more recent information on the Master Settlement Agreement and its long-term effects.

THE EARLY HISTORY OF NARCOTIC, STIMULANT, AND HALLUCINOGEN USE

Humans have experimented with narcotic and hallucinogenic plants since before recorded history, discovering their properties as they tested plants for edibility or were attracted by the odors of some leaves when the leaves were burned. Ancient cultures used narcotic plants to relieve pain or to heighten pleasure and hallucinogenic plants to induce trancelike states during religious ceremonies. Natural substances, used directly or in refined extracts, have also served simply to increase or dull alertness, to invigorate the body, or to change the mood.

Narcotic Use through the 19th Century

As mentioned earlier, narcotics, including heroin and opium, are drugs that alter the perception of pain and induce sleep and euphoria. Opium is a dried powdered extract derived from the opium poppy plant *Papaver somniferum.* Morphine and heroin are made from opium, and all three of these addicting narcotics are called opiates.

Opium itself has been used as a pain reliever in Europe and Asia for thousands of years. In 1803 Friedrich Wilhelm Sertürner (1783–1841), a German pharmacist, discovered how to isolate the highly potent morphine from opium. In 1832 the French chemist Pierre-Jean Robiquet (1780–1840) isolated codeine from opium, which is milder than morphine. It came to be used in cough remedies. The development of the hypodermic needle in the early 1850s made it easier to use morphine. It became a common medicine for treating severe pain, such as battlefield injuries. During the U.S. Civil War (1861–1865), so many soldiers became addicted to morphine that the addiction was later called soldier's disease.

The most potent narcotic derived from opium is heroin, which was first synthesized in 1874 by C. R. Alder Wright (1844–1894) at St. Mary's Hospital in London. The Bayer Company in Eberfeld, Germany, began to market the drug as a cough remedy and painkiller under the brand name Heroin; the word was derived from the German word for "heroic," which was intended to convey the drug's power and potency. The drug was an instant success and was soon exported.

Stimulant Use through the 19th Century

The use of stimulants dates back to about 3000 BC with South American societies. Even then, the people of this region knew that cocaine, which was extracted from the leaves of the coca tree *Erythroxylon coca*, was capable of producing euphoria, hyperactivity, and hallucinations. This small coca tree is native to tropical mountain regions in Peru and Bolivia.

After the Spanish conquest of the Incas in the early 1500s and the ensuing Spanish immigration into South America, coca was grown on plantations and used as wages to pay workers. The drug seemed to negate the effects of exhaustion and malnutrition, especially at high altitudes. Many South Americans still chew coca leaves to alleviate the effects of high altitudes.

The spread of the use of coca is attributed to Paolo Mantegazza (1831–1910), an Italian physician who came to value the restorative powers of coca while living in Lima, Peru, in the 1850s. He praised the drug, which led to interest in coca in the United States and Europe. In 1863 the French chemist Angelo Mariani (1838–1914) extracted cocaine from coca leaves and used it as the main ingredient in his coca wine, called Vin Mariani. Shortly thereafter, cough syrups and tonics holding drops of cocaine in solution became popular. Eventually, extracts from coca leaves not only appeared in wine but also in chewing gum, tea, and throat lozenges.

The temperance movement in the United States from 1800 to 1890 helped fuel the public's fondness for nonalcoholic products containing coca. In the mid-1880s Atlanta, Georgia, became one of the first major U.S. cities to forbid the sale of alcohol. It was there that the inventor John Stith Pemberton (1831–1888) first marketed Coca-Cola, a syrup that then contained extracts of both coca and the kola nut, as a "temperance drink."

Hallucinogen Use through the 19th Century

Naturally occurring hallucinogens, which are derived from plants, have been used by various cultures for magical, religious, recreational, and health-related purposes for thousands of years. For more than 2,000 years Native American societies often used hallucinogens, such as the psilocybin mushroom (*Psilocybe mexicana*) of Mexico and the peyote cactus (*Lophophora williamsii*) of the U.S. Southwest, in religious ceremonies. Even though scientists were slow to discover the medicinal possibilities of hallucinogens, by 1919 they had isolated mescaline from the peyote cactus and recognized its resemblance to the adrenal hormone epinephrine (adrenaline).

Cannabis, also a hallucinogen, is the term generally applied to the Himalayan hemp plant *Cannabis sativa* from which marijuana, bhang, and ganja (hashish) are derived. Bhang is equivalent to the U.S.-style marijuana, consisting of the leaves, fruits, and stems of the plant. Ganja, which is prepared by crushing the flowering tips of cannabis and collecting a resinous paste, is more potent than marijuana and bhang.

Cannabis dates back more than 5,000 years to Central Asia and China; from there it spread to India and the Near East. Cannabis was highly regarded as a medicinal plant used in folk medicines. It was long valued as an analgesic (painkiller), topical anesthetic, antispasmodic, antidepressant, appetite stimulant, antiasthmatic, and antibiotic.

NARCOTIC, STIMULANT, AND HALLUCINOGEN USE AT THE TURN OF THE 19TH CENTURY AND BEYOND

In late 19th-century America it was possible to buy, in a store or by mail order, many medicines (or alleged medicines) containing morphine, cocaine, and even heroin. Until 1903 the soft drink Coca-Cola contained cocaine. The cocaine was later removed and more caffeine (already present in the drink from the kola nut) was added. Pharmacies sold cocaine in pure form, as well as many drugs made from opium, such as morphine and heroin.

Beginning in 1898 heroin became widely available when the Bayer Company marketed it as a powerful cough suppressant. According to the Office of Technology Assessment in *Technologies for Understanding and Preventing Substance Abuse and Addiction* (September 1994, http://www.princeton .edu/~ota/disk1/1994/9435/9435.PDF), physician prescriptions of these drugs increased from 1% of all prescriptions in 1874 to between 20% and 25% in 1902. These drugs were not only available but also widely used, with little concern for negative health consequences.

Soon, however, cocaine, heroin, and other drugs were taken off the market for a number of reasons. A growing awareness of the dangers of drug use and food contamination led to the passage of laws such as the Pure Food and Drug Act of 1906. Among other things, the act required the removal of false claims from patent medicines. Medical labels also had to state the amount of any narcotic ingredient the medicine contained and whether that medicine was habit-forming. A growing temperance movement, the development of safe, alternative painkillers (such as aspirin), and more alternative medical treatments contributed to the passage of laws limiting drug use, although these laws did not completely outlaw the drugs.

Besides health-related worries, by the mid- to late 1800s drug use had come to be associated with "undesirables." When drug users were thought to live only in the slums, drug use was considered solely a criminal problem; but when it was finally recognized in middle-class neighborhoods, it came to be seen as a mental health problem. By the turn of the 19th century the use of narcotics was considered an international problem. In 1909 the International Opium Commission met to discuss worldwide drug use. This meeting led to the signing of a treaty two years later in the Netherlands requiring all signatories to pass laws limiting the use of narcotics for medicinal purposes. After nearly three years of debate, Congress passed the Harrison Narcotic Act of 1914, which called for the strict control of opium and coca (although coca is a stimulant and not a narcotic).

Regulating Narcotics, Stimulants, and Hallucinogens

During the 1920s the federal government regulated drugs through the U.S. Department of the Treasury. In 1930 President Herbert Hoover (1874–1964) created the Federal Bureau of Narcotics and selected Harry J. Anslinger (1892–1975) to head it. Believing that all drug users were deviant criminals, Anslinger vigorously enforced the law for the next 32 years. Marijuana, for example, was presented as a "killer weed" that threatened the very fabric of American society.

Marijuana is thought to have been introduced to the United States by Mexican immigrants. Thus, according to the Office of Technology Assessment, in *Technologies for Understanding and Preventing Substance Abuse and Addiction*, it was widely believed that anti-Mexican attitudes, as well as Anslinger's considerable influence, prompted the passage of the Marijuana Tax Act of 1937. The act made the use or sale of marijuana without a tax stamp a federal offense. Because by this time the sale of marijuana was illegal in most states, buying a federal tax stamp would alert the authorities in a particular state to who was selling drugs. Naturally, no marijuana dealer wanted to buy a stamp and expose his or her identity to the authorities.

From the 1940s through the 1960s the FDA, based on the authority granted by the Food, Drug, and Cosmetic Act

of 1938, began to police the sale of certain drugs. The act had required the FDA to stipulate if specific drugs, such as amphetamines, barbiturates, and sulfa drugs, were safe for self-medication.

After studying most amphetamines (stimulants) and barbiturates (depressants), the agency concluded that it simply could not declare them safe for self-medication. (See Table 1.1 for listings of stimulants and depressants.) Therefore, it ruled that these drugs could only be used under medical supervision—that is, with a physician's prescription. For all pharmaceutical products other than narcotics, this marked the beginning of the distinction between prescription and over-the-counter (without a prescription) drugs.

For 25 years, undercover FDA inspectors identified pharmacists who sold amphetamines and barbiturates without a prescription and doctors who wrote illegal prescriptions. In the 1950s, with the growing sale of amphetamines, barbiturates, and, eventually, LSD and other hallucinogens at cafés, truck stops, flophouses, and weight-reduction salons and by street-corner pushers, FDA authorities went after these other illegal dealers. In 1968 the drug-enforcement responsibilities of the FDA were transferred to the Department of Justice.

War on Drugs

From the mid-1960s to the late 1970s the demographic profile of drug users changed. Previously, drug use had generally been associated with minorities, lower classes, or young "hippies" and "beatniks." During this period drug use among middle-class whites became widespread and more generally accepted. Cocaine, an expensive drug, began to be used by middle- and upper-class whites, many of whom looked on it as a nonaddictive recreational drug and status symbol. In addition, drugs had become much more prevalent in the military because they were cheap and plentiful in Vietnam.

Whereas some circles viewed drug use with wider acceptance, other public sectors came to see drugs as a threat to their communities—much as, 40 years earlier, alcohol had acquired a negative image, leading to Prohibition. Drugs not only symbolized poverty but also were associated with protest movements against the Vietnam War (1955–1975) and the so-called Establishment. Many parents began to perceive the widespread availability of drugs as a threat to their children. By the end of the 1960s such views began to acquire a political expression.

When he ran for president in 1968, Richard M. Nixon (1913–1994) included a strong antidrug plank in his law-and-order platform, calling for a war on drugs. After he was elected president, Nixon created the President's National Commission on Marihuana and Drug Abuse, which published its findings in *Marihuana: A Signal of Misunderstanding* (March 1972, http://www.druglibrary.org/Schaffer/Library/studies/nc/ncmenu.htm). Nixon ignored the commission's findings, which called for the legalization of marijuana. Since that time the U.S. government has been waging the war on drugs. In 1973 Congress authorized the formation of the Drug Enforcement Administration (DEA) to reduce the supply of drugs. A year later the National Institute on Drug Abuse (NIDA) was created to lead the effort to reduce the demand for drugs and to direct research, federal prevention, and treatment services.

Under the Nixon, Ford, and Carter administrations federal spending tended to emphasize the treatment of drug abusers. Meanwhile, a growing number of parents, fearing that their children were being exposed to drugs, began to pressure elected officials and government agencies to do more about the growing use of drugs. In response, the NIDA began widely publicizing the dangers of marijuana and other drugs once thought not to be particularly harmful.

President Ronald Reagan (1911–2004) favored a strict approach to drug use, popularized the phrase "war on drugs," and increased enforcement efforts. In *Technologies for Understanding and Preventing Substance Abuse and Addiction*, the Office of Technology Assessment states that the budget to fight drugs rose from $1.5 billion in 1981 to $4.2 billion in 1989. By the end of the Reagan administration, two-thirds of all drug control funding went for law enforcement and one-third went for treatment and prevention. First Lady Nancy Reagan (1921–) vigorously campaigned against drug use, urging children to "just say no!" The Crime Control Act of 1984 dramatically increased the penalties for drug use and drug trafficking.

INTRODUCTION OF CRACK COCAINE. Cocaine use increased dramatically in the 1960s and 1970s, but the drug's high cost restricted its use to the more affluent. In the early 1980s cocaine dealers discovered a way to prepare the cocaine so that it could be smoked in small and inexpensive but powerful and highly addictive amounts. The creation of this so-called crack cocaine meant that poor people could now afford to use the drug, and a whole new market opened. In addition, the acquired immune deficiency syndrome (AIDS) epidemic caused some intravenous drug users to switch to smoking crack to avoid exposure to the human immunodeficiency virus (HIV), which can be contracted by sharing needles with an infected user.

Battles for control of the distribution and sale of the drug led to a violent black market. The easy availability of sophisticated firearms and the huge amounts of money to be made selling crack and other drugs transformed many areas of the nation—but particularly the inner cities—into dangerous places.

The widespread fear of crack cocaine led to increasingly harsh laws and penalties. Authorities warned that crack was instantly addictive and spreading rapidly, and they predicted a subsequent generation of "crack babies"—that is, babies born addicted to crack because their mothers were using it during pregnancy.

HEROIN GETS CHEAPER AND PURER. The dangers associated with crack cocaine caused changes in the use of heroin in the 1990s. Many reported deaths from heroin overdosing had lessened the drug's attraction in the 1980s. In addition, heroin had to be injected by syringe, and concerns regarding HIV infection contributed to the dangers of using the drug. In the 1990s an oversupply of heroin, innovations that produced a smokable variety of the drug, and the appearance of purer forms of the drug restored its attractiveness to the relatively small number of people addicted to "hard" drugs. It was no longer necessary to take the drug intravenously—it could be sniffed like cocaine—although many users continued to use needles.

The War Continues: The Office of National Drug Control Policy

The Anti-drug Abuse Act of 1988 created the Office of National Drug Control Policy (ONDCP), to be headed by a director—popularly referred to as the drug czar—who would coordinate the nation's drug policy. The Office of Technology Assessment reports in *Technologies for Understanding and Preventing Substance Abuse and Addiction* that spending for drug control rose from $4.2 billion in 1989 under President Reagan to $12.7 billion in 1993 under President George H. W. Bush (1924–). As was the case during the Reagan administration, the monetary split was roughly two-thirds for law enforcement and one-third for treatment and prevention. By 1990 every state that had once decriminalized the use of marijuana had repealed those laws.

The Office of Technology Assessment indicates that when President Bill Clinton (1946–) took office in 1993 he cut the ONDCP staff from 146 to 25, while at the same time raising the director of the ONDCP to cabinet status. Clinton called for 100,000 more police officers on the streets and advocated drug treatment on demand. According to the ONDCP, in *The National Drug Control Strategy, FY 2004 Budget Summary* (February 2003, http://www.whitehouse.drugpolicy.gov/publications/policy/04budget/fy04budgetsum.pdf), drug control funding totaled $8.2 billion in 1998, with the split 52% for law enforcement and 48% for treatment and prevention. (It is important to note that in the mid-1990s changes were made in the list of expenditures included in this tally, and in 2003 the national drug control budget was restructured, thus making it difficult to analyze historical drug control spending trends before and after 1995. The FY 2004 budget summary provides a recalculation of historical tables from 1995 to 2004.)

Taking office in 2001, President George W. Bush (1946–) promised to continue national efforts to eradicate illicit drugs in the United States and abroad. On May 10 2001, he appointed John Walters (1952–) as the new drug czar. Together, they pledged to continue to reduce illicit drug use in the United States. Their proposed goals included increased spending on treatment, intensified work with foreign nations, and an adamant opposition to the legalization of any currently illicit drugs. The Bush administration also wove its antidrug message into its arguments for invading Afghanistan. Even though Bush's case was built primarily on the notion that Afghanistan's Taliban leaders had harbored the terrorist Osama bin Laden (1957–), he regularly referred to Afghanistan's role as the world's biggest producer of opium poppies.

The ONDCP indicates that at the start of the Bush administration federal spending on drug control started at $10.4 billion in 2001 (as shown in the FY 2004 budget summary). By 2009 the ONDCP notes in *National Drug Control Strategy: FY 2009 Budget Summary* (February 2008, http://www.whitehousedrugpolicy.gov/publications/policy/09budget/fy09budget.pdf) that drug control grew to a requested $14.1 billion in 2009, with treatment accounting for 34.8% of the total in the requested 2009 budget.

Questioning the War on Drugs

By 2007 there was considerable controversy surrounding the necessity and effectiveness of the war on drugs. Decades of effort had led to large numbers of people serving prison sentences for manufacturing, selling, or using drugs. Yet, the illicit drug trade continued to thrive. Many critics argued that a different approach was necessary and questioned whether illicit drugs were an enemy worth waging war against, especially such a costly war during a time of rapidly rising federal budget deficits.

The American public also appeared to view the war on drugs as a low priority. In *Economy Runaway Winner as Most Important Problem* (November 21, 2008, http://www.gallup.com/poll/112093/Economy-Runaway-Winner-Most-Important-Problem.aspx), Jeffrey M. Jones of the Gallup Organization notes that in 2008, 58% of adult Americans rated the economy as the top problem in the United States; drugs were not listed among the top 13 most important problems. Other problems seen as having a higher priority than drugs were the war in Iraq, unemployment, dissatisfaction with government leaders, national security, education, and terrorism.

In the fall of 2008 two reports were published that also documented inadequacies with the war on drugs. In October 2008 the U.S. Government Accountability Office (GAO) released *Plan Colombia: Drug Reduction Goals Were Not Fully Met, but Security Has Improved; U.S. Agencies Need More Detailed Plans for Reducing Assistance* (http://www.gao.gov/new.items/d0971.pdf). The GAO examines progress made toward the Colombian government's strategy "Plan Colombia," the goals of which included reducing the production of illicit drugs by half in six years (with a focus on cocaine) and improving security in areas of Colombia that were held by illegal armed groups. The United States sup-

ported this plan and provided nearly $6 billion for its implementation. The GAO found that security had been increased and that opium poppy cultivation and heroin production had decreased by about half. Coca cultivation and cocaine production, however, had increased.

In November 2008 the Partnership for the Americas Commission of the Brookings Institution released *Rethinking U.S.-Latin American Relations: A Hemispheric Partnership for a Turbulent World* (http://www.brookings.edu/reports/2008/~/media/Files/rc/reports/2008/1124_latin_america_partnership/1124_latin_america_partnership.pdf). The report notes that "current U.S. counternarcotics policies are failing by most objective measures" and that "the only long-run solution to the problem of illegal narcotics is to reduce the demand for drugs in the major consuming countries, including the United States." The report suggests that the United States work to reduce the flow of guns to Mexico, which would help curb the flow of drugs to the United States; expand drug prevention programs in schools, especially those that emphasize drugs' disfiguring attributes to young people; and promote drug courts, which merge treatment with incarceration.

In the months following the inauguration of President Barack Obama (1961–), his administration already showed signs of rethinking existing drug policy in the United States. Carrie Johnson and Amy Goldstein reported in the *Washington Post* (March 12, 2009, http://www.washingtonpost.com/wp-dyn/content/article/2009/03/11/AR2009031103567.html) that the White House, in announcing its nominee for the administration's so-called drug czar, said that "it will push for treatment, rather than incarceration, of people arrested for drug-related crimes." Johnson and Goldstein went on to say that the administration's "choice of drug czar and the emphasis on alternative drug courts . . . signal a sharp departure from Bush administration policies, gravitating away from cutting the supply of illicit drugs from foreign countries and toward curbing drug use in communities across the United States."

Drug-related violence in Mexico surged in 2008, with an estimated 65,000 deaths blamed on Mexican drug cartels that year ("Obama to Beef Up Mexico Border Policy, March 25, 2009, http://www.cnn.com/2009/POLITICS/03/24/obama.mexico.policy). By early 2009 the violence was spilling over into U.S cities, and on March 24 the White House announced an initiative to ease violence and drug trafficking at the Mexican border ("Administration Officials Announce U.S.-Mexico Border Security Policy: A Comprehensive Response and Commitment," http://www.whitehouse.gov/the_press_office/Administration-Officials-Announce-US-Mexico-Border-Security-Policy-A-Comprehensive-Response-and-Commitment). According to the official statement, the White House is "investing $700 million this year to work in collaboration with Mexico on law enforcement and judicial capacity"; the Department of Justice, the Department of Homeland Security, and the Department of Treasury "are all ramping up personnel and efforts directed at the Southwest border" and "we are renewing our commitment to reduce the demand for illegal drugs here at home." The following day, U.S. Secretary of State Hillary Rodham Clinton (1947–) was in Mexico endorsing the policy and admitting that the United States shares the blame for the violence. Mark Landler in the *New York Times* ("Clinton Says U.S. Feeds Mexico Drug Trade," March 25, 2009, http://www.nytimes.com/2009/03/26/world/americas/26mexico.html) quoted Clinton as saying, "Our insatiable demand for illegal drugs fuels the drug trade."

CHAPTER 2
ALCOHOL

Contrary to popular belief, ethanol (the alcohol in alcoholic beverages) is not a stimulant, but a depressant. Even though many of those who drink alcoholic beverages feel relaxation, pleasure, and stimulation, these feelings are caused by the depressant effects of alcohol on the brain.

WHAT CONSTITUTES A DRINK?

In the United States a standard drink contains about 0.5 ounces (12.5 mL) of pure alcohol. The following beverages contain nearly equal amounts of alcohol and are approximately standard drink equivalents:

- One shot (1.5 ounces, or 44.4 mL) of spirits (80-proof whiskey, vodka, gin, etc.)

- One 2.5-ounce (73.9-mL) glass of a cordial, liqueur, or aperitif

- One 5-ounce (147.9-mL) glass of table wine

- One 3- to 4-ounce (88.7- to 118.3-mL) glass of fortified wine, such as sherry or port

- One 12-ounce (354.9-mL) bottle or can of beer

- One 8- to 9-ounce (236.6- to 266.2-mL) bottle or can of malt liquor

ALCOHOL CONSUMPTION IN THE UNITED STATES

After caffeine, alcohol is the most commonly used drug in the United States. Even though researchers frequently count how many people are drinking and how often, the statistics do not necessarily reflect the true picture of alcohol consumption in the United States. People tend to under-report their drinking. Furthermore, survey interviewees are typically people living in households; therefore, the results of survey research may not include the homeless, a portion of the U.S. population traditionally at risk for alcoholism (alcohol dependence).

Per Capita Consumption of Alcohol

The yearly per capita (per person) consumption of alcoholic beverages peaked at 28.8 gallons (109 L) in 1981. (See Table 2.1.) Per capita consumption declined to 24.7 gallons (93.5 L) in 1997 and 1998 and has climbed only slightly since then. In 2006 the per capita consumption of alcoholic beverages was 25.3 gallons (95.8 L).

Beer remained the most popular alcoholic beverage in 2006, being consumed at a rate of 21.6 gallons (81.8 L) per person. Beer consumption peaked in 1981 at 24.6 gallons (93.1 L) per person, but its consumption declined steadily to its present relatively stable level by 1995. The per capita consumption of wine and spirits in the United States is much lower than that of beer. The 2006 per capita consumption of wine was 2.3 gallons (8.7 L) and of distilled spirits (liquor), 1.4 gallons (5.3 L).

A complex set of factors contributes to variations in alcohol use over people's life spans. Part of the decline in alcohol consumption is a result of population trends. In the 1980s and 1990s the number of people in their early 20s—the leading consumers of alcohol—declined fairly steadily. The United States is also seeing a growing number of residents in their 50s and 60s. This is a group that is, in general, unlikely to consume as much alcohol as younger people.

Individual Consumption of Alcohol

The data for alcohol consumption mentioned in the previous section are per capita figures, which are determined by taking the total consumption of alcohol per year and dividing by the total resident population, including children. This figure is useful to see how consumption changes from year to year because it takes into account changes in the size of the resident population. Nonetheless, babies and small children generally do not consume alcohol, so it is also useful to look at consumption figures based on U.S. residents aged 12 and older.

TABLE 2.1

Per capita consumption of beer, wine, and distilled spirits, 1966–2006

Year	Total resident population			
	Beer	Wine[a]	Distilled spirits	Total[b]
Gallons				
1966	16.5	1.0	1.6	19.0
1967	16.8	1.0	1.6	19.4
1968	17.3	1.1	1.7	20.1
1969	17.8	1.2	1.8	20.8
1970	18.5	1.3	1.8	21.6
1971	18.9	1.5	1.8	22.3
1972	19.3	1.6	1.9	22.8
1973	20.1	1.6	1.9	23.6
1974	20.9	1.6	2.0	24.5
1975	21.3	1.7	2.0	25.0
1976	21.5	1.7	2.0	25.2
1977	22.4	1.8	2.0	26.1
1978	23.0	2.0	2.0	26.9
1979	23.8	2.0	2.0	27.8
1980	24.3	2.1	2.0	28.3
1981	24.6	2.2	2.0	28.8
1982	24.4	2.2	1.9	28.5
1983	24.2	2.3	1.8	28.3
1984	24.0	2.4	1.8	28.1
1985	23.8	2.4	1.8	28.0
1986	24.1	2.4	1.6	28.2
1987	24.0	2.4	1.6	28.0
1988	23.8	2.3	1.5	27.6
1989	23.6	2.1	1.5	27.2
1990	23.9	2.0	1.5	27.5
1991	23.1	1.8	1.4	26.3
1992	22.7	1.9	1.4	25.9
1993	22.4	1.7	1.3	25.5
1994	22.3	1.7	1.3	25.3
1995	21.8	1.8	1.2	24.8
1996	21.7	1.8	1.2	24.8
1997	21.6	1.9	1.2	24.7
1998	21.7	1.9	1.2	24.7
1999	21.8	1.9	1.2	24.9
2000	21.7	1.9	1.3	24.9
2001	21.8	1.9	1.3	24.9
2002	21.8	2.0	1.3	25.1
2003	21.6	2.1	1.3	25.1
2004	21.7	2.2	1.4	25.2
2005	21.5	2.2	1.4	25.1
2006	21.6	2.3	1.4	25.3

Notes: Alcoholic beverage per capita figures are calculated by the Economic Research Service (ERS) using industry data. Uses U.S. resident population, July.
[a]Beginning in 1983, includes wine coolers.
[b]Computed from unrounded data.
Data last updated March 15, 2008.

SOURCE: "Alcoholic Beverages: Per Capita Availability," U.S. Department of Agriculture, Economic Research Service, March 15, 2008, http://www.ers.usda.gov/data/foodconsumption/spreadsheets/beverage.xls#PccLiq!a1 (accessed August 11, 2008)

Table 2.2 shows the percentage of respondents aged 12 and older who reported consuming alcohol in the past month in 2006 and 2007 when questioned for the annual National Survey on Drug Use and Health, which is conducted by the Substance Abuse and Mental Health Services Administration. In 2007, 51.1% of this total population had consumed alcohol in the month before the survey, as opposed to 50.9% of the total population in 2006. A higher percentage of males consumed alcoholic beverages in the past month than did females in both years. Table 2.2 also shows that alcohol consumption varies by race. A higher percentage of whites had used alcohol within the month before the survey than had African-Americans or Hispanics.

Prevalence of Problem Drinking

Table 2.2 also shows the percentages of Americans aged 12 and older who engaged in binge drinking or heavy alcohol use in the month before the survey. Binge drinking means a person had five or more drinks on the same occasion, that is, within a few hours of each other. Heavy alcohol use means a person had five or more drinks on the same occasion on each of five or more days in the past 30 days. All heavy alcohol users are binge drinkers, but not all binge drinkers are heavy alcohol users.

In both 2006 and 2007 people aged 18 to 25 were more likely than people in other age groups to be binge drinkers and heavy alcohol users. Much higher percentages of males binge drank and used alcohol heavily than females in the month before each of these surveys. In addition, Native Americans and Alaskan natives were the most likely to have engaged in binge drinking in 2006 and 2007. However, Native Hawaiians and other Pacific Islanders were more likely than all other groups to have engaged in heavy alcohol use in 2006. Data were unavailable for this group for 2007. The percentage of Native Americans and Alaskan natives who engaged in heavy alcohol use rose from 2006 to 2007, giving them the highest percentage of heavy alcohol use among all groups shown.

DEFINING ALCOHOLISM

Most people consider an alcoholic to be someone who drinks too much and cannot control his or her drinking. Alcoholism, however, does not merely refer to heavy drinking or getting drunk a certain number of times. The diagnosis of alcoholism applies only to those who show specific symptoms of addiction, which the Institute of Medicine defines in *Dispelling the Myths about Addiction: Strategies to Increase Understanding and Strengthen Research* (1997) as a brain disease "manifested by a complex set of behaviors that are the result of genetic, biological, psychological, and environmental interactions."

In "The Definition of Alcoholism" (*Journal of the American Medical Association*, vol. 268, no. 8, August 26, 1992), Robert M. Morse and Daniel K. Flavin define alcoholism as "a primary, chronic disease with genetic, psychosocial, and environmental factors influencing its development and manifestations. The disease is often progressive and fatal. It is characterized by impaired control over drinking, preoccupation with the drug alcohol, use of alcohol despite adverse consequences, and distortions in thinking, most notably denial. Each of these symptoms may be continuous or periodic."

"Primary" refers to alcoholism as a disease independent from any other psychological disease (e.g., schizophrenia), rather than as a symptom of some other underlying

TABLE 2.2

Percentage of past-month alcohol use, binge alcohol use, and heavy alcohol use among drinkers aged 12 and older, by demographic characteristics, 2006 and 2007

Demographic characteristic	Type of alcohol use					
	Alcohol use		Binge alcohol use		Heavy alcohol use	
	2006	2007	2006	2007	2006	2007
Total	50.9	51.1	23.0	23.3	6.9	6.9
Age						
12–17	16.6	15.9	10.3	9.7	2.4	2.3
18–25	61.9	61.2	42.2	41.8	15.6	14.7
26 or older	53.7	54.1	21.4	21.9	6.0	6.1
Gender						
Male	57.0	56.6	31.2	31.7	10.7	10.6
Female	45.2	46.0	15.2	15.4	3.3	3.3
Hispanic origin and race						
Not Hispanic or Latino	52.4	52.6	22.9	23.3	7.1	7.1
White	55.8	56.1	24.1	24.6	7.8	7.8
Black or African American	40.0	39.3	19.1	19.1	4.6	4.1
American Indian or Alaska Native	37.2	44.7	31.0	28.2	9.0	11.6
Native Hawaiian or other Pacific Islander	36.7	*	24.1	*	11.0	
Asian	35.4	35.2	11.8	12.6	2.4	2.6
Two or more races	47.1	47.5	22.8	23.2	6.3	7.3
Hispanic or Latino	41.8	42.1	23.9	23.4	5.7	5.5

*Low precision; no estimate reported.
Notes: Binge alcohol use is defined as drinking five or more drinks on the same occasion (i.e., at the same time or within a couple of hours of each other) on at least 1 day in the past 30 days. Heavy alcohol use is defined as drinking five or more drinks on the same occasion on each of 5 or more days in the past 30 days; all heavy alcohol users are also binge alcohol users. Difference between estimate and 2007 estimate is statistically significant at the 0.05 level. Difference between estimate and 2007 estimate is statistically significant at the 0.01 level.

SOURCE: "Table 2.42B. Alcohol Use, Binge Alcohol Use, and Heavy Alcohol Use in the Past Month among Persons Aged 12 or Older, by Demographic Characteristics: Percentages, 2006 and 2007," in *2007 National Survey on Drug Use and Health: Detailed Tables*, U.S. Department of Health and Human Services, Substance Abuse and Mental Health Services Administration, Office of Applied Studies, September 2008, http://oas.samhsa.gov/NSDUH/2k7NSDUH/tabs/Sect2peTabs1to42.htm#Tab2.42B (accessed December 8, 2008)

disease. "Adverse consequences" for an alcoholic can include physical illness (such as liver disease or withdrawal symptoms), psychological problems, interpersonal difficulties (such as marital problems or domestic violence), and problems at work. "Denial" includes a number of psychological maneuvers by the drinker to avoid the fact that alcohol is the cause of his or her problems. Family and friends may reinforce an alcoholic's denial by covering up his or her drinking (e.g., calling an employer to say the alcoholic has the flu rather than a hangover). Such behavior is also known as enabling. In other words, the friends and family make excuses for the drinker and enable him or her to continue drinking as opposed to having to face the repercussions of his or her alcohol abuse. Denial is a major obstacle in recovery from alcoholism.

ALCOHOLISM AND ALCOHOL ABUSE

The American Psychiatric Association (APA), which publishes the *Diagnostic and Statistical Manual of Mental Disorders* (*DSM*), first defined alcoholism in 1952. *DSM-III*, the third edition of the APA's publication, renamed alcoholism as alcohol dependence and introduced the term *alcohol abuse*. According to *DSM-III*'s definitions of alcohol abuse, the condition involves a compulsive use of alcohol and impaired social or occupational functioning, whereas alcohol

dependence includes physical tolerance and withdrawal symptoms when the drug is stopped. *DSM-IV-TR*, the most recent edition as of 2009, refines these definitions further, but the basic definitions remain the same.

The World Health Organization publishes the *International Classification of Diseases* (*ICD*), which is designed to standardize health data collection throughout the world. The 10th edition (*ICD-10*) generally defines abuse and tolerance similarly to the *DSM-IV-TR*.

The National Institute on Alcohol Abuse and Alcoholism (NIAAA), in *Five Year Strategic Plan FY09–14* (2008, http://pubs.niaaa.nih.gov/publications/StrategicPlan/StrategicPlan.doc), states that "*alcohol dependence*, typically considered to be synonymous with *alcoholism* (alcohol addiction), is a complex disease characterized by persistent and intense alcohol-seeking, which results in a loss of control over drinking, a preoccupation with drinking, compulsion to drink or inability to stop, and the development of tolerance and dependence." This definition of alcohol dependence includes the following four symptoms: craving, loss of control, physical dependence, and tolerance. These symptoms are described in Table 2.3 and are a result of changes in the functioning of the brain and underlying changes in gene expression as its cells adapt to the chronic heavy use and abuse of alcohol.

TABLE 2.3

Four symptoms of alcoholism

Alcoholism, also known as "alcohol dependence," is a disease that includes four symptoms:

- Craving: A strong need, or compulsion, to drink.
- Loss of control: The inability to limit one's drinking on any given occasion.
- Physical dependence: Withdrawal symptoms, such as nausea, sweating, shakiness, and anxiety, occur when alcohol use is stopped after a period of heavy drinking.
- Tolerance: The need to drink greater amounts of alcohol in order to "get high."

SOURCE: Adapted from *FAQ for the General Public: 1. What Is Alcoholism?*, U.S. Department of Health and Human Services, National Institutes of Health, National Institute on Alcohol Abuse and Alcoholism, February 2007, http://www.niaaa.nih.gov/FAQs/General-English/default.htm#whatis (accessed December 8, 2008)

TABLE 2.4

Four symptoms of alcohol abuse

Alcohol abuse is defined as a pattern of drinking that results in one or more of the following situations within a 12-month period:

- Failure to fulfill major work, school, or home responsibilities;
- Drinking in situations that are physically dangerous, such as while driving a car or operating machinery;
- Having recurring alcohol-related legal problems, such as being arrested for driving under the influence of alcohol or for physically hurting someone while drunk; and
- Continued drinking despite having ongoing relationship problems that are caused or worsened by the drinking.

SOURCE: Adapted from "Module 4. Screening and Assessment: Alcohol Use Disorders," in *The ABCs of Bullying: Addressing, Blocking, and Curbing School Aggression*, U.S. Department of Health and Human Services, Substance Abuse and Mental Health Services Administration, Center for Substance Abuse Prevention, May 19, 2004, http://pathwayscourses.samhsa.gov/bully/bully_4_pg19.htm (accessed December 18, 2008)

The NIAAA defines alcohol abuse as "a recurring pattern of high-risk drinking that creates problems for the drinker, for others, or for society." The symptoms of alcohol abuse may be manifested by people who are alcohol dependent as well as by those not dependent on alcohol. The primary symptoms of alcohol abuse are listed in Table 2.4. Other characteristics of alcohol abuse include the need to drink before facing certain situations, frequent drinking sprees, a steady increase in intake, solitary drinking, early morning drinking, and the occurrence of blackouts. For heavy drinkers, blackouts are not episodes of passing out, but are periods drinkers cannot remember later, even though they appeared to be functioning at the time.

Prevalence of Alcohol Dependence, Alcohol Abuse, Binge Drinking, and Heavy Drinking

The NIAAA notes in *Five Year Strategic Plan FY09–14* that 18 million Americans—8.5% of the population aged 18 and older—have alcohol use disorders (AUD; alcohol abuse and alcohol dependence).

Figure 2.1 shows the percentages of people who engaged in alcohol use, binge drinking, and heavy alcohol use in 2007 by age group. The graph shows that people aged 21 to 25 are

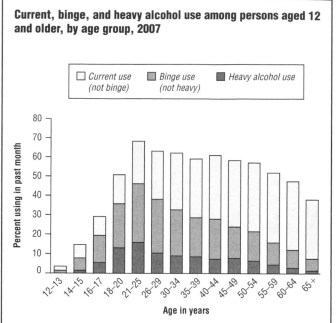

FIGURE 2.1

Current, binge, and heavy alcohol use among persons aged 12 and older, by age group, 2007

SOURCE: "Figure 3.1. Current, Binge, and Heavy Alcohol Use among Persons Aged 12 or Older, by Age: 2007," in *Results from the 2007 National Survey on Drug Use and Health: National Findings*, U.S. Department of Health and Human Services, Substance Abuse and Mental Health Services Administration, Office of Applied Studies, 2008, http://www.oas.samhsa.gov/nsduh/2k7nsduh/2k7Results.pdf (accessed December 8, 2008)

more likely to engage in binge drinking and heavy alcohol use than those in younger or older age groups. The rate of binge drinking and heavy alcohol use in this age group was about 46% in 2007. The graph also shows that as people grow older, the proportion of people who use alcohol without manifesting binge or heavy alcohol use increases.

Table 2.2 compares the rates of binge drinking and heavy alcohol use for males and females across all age groups. In 2006 and 2007 the rate of binge drinking in males was substantially higher than that of females. The percentage of males who binge drank in 2006 and 2007 was 31.2% and 31.7%, respectively, whereas the percentage of females who binge drank was about half that, at slightly over 15%. Heavy alcohol use was much more prevalent in males than in females. More than 10% of males were heavy alcohol users in 2006 and 2007, whereas only about 3% of females were.

ALCOHOL ABUSE AND ALCOHOLISM IN VARIOUS RACIAL AND ETHNIC GROUPS

The patterns of alcohol consumption vary across racial and ethnic groups. (See Table 2.2.) Low alcoholism rates occur in certain groups and individuals due to their customs or religion. Groups and individuals with multicultural backgrounds generally have fewer cultural or religious constraints regarding alcohol use and tend to have higher alcoholism rates. For example, alcohol is forbidden in Islam, so it is rare to find Muslims who engage in alcohol use. However, whites are a diverse population, both religiously and culturally. This group had the highest rate of alcohol use of all the groups listed in Table 2.2. Native Americans and Alaskan natives had the highest prevalence of binge alcohol use in 2006 and 2007.

Certain populations may be at a higher or lower risk for binge or heavy alcohol use because of the way their bodies metabolize (chemically process) alcohol. For example, many Asian-Americans have an inherited deficiency of aldehyde dehydrogenase, a chemical that breaks down ethyl alcohol in the body. Without it, toxic substances build up after drinking alcohol and rapidly lead to flushing, dizziness, and nausea. Therefore, many Asian-Americans experience warning signals very early on and are less likely to continue drinking. Conversely, research results suggest that Native Americans may lack these warning signals. They are less sensitive to the intoxicating effects of alcohol and are more likely to develop alcoholism. Table 2.2 shows that the prevalence of binge alcohol use and heavy alcohol use is low for Asian-Americans and high for Native Americans.

RISK FACTORS OF AUD

The development of AUD is the result of a complex mix of biological, psychological, and social factors including genetics, alcohol reactivity (sensitivity), and psychosocial factors. Genetics and alcohol reactivity are biological factors. The rest are psychosocial factors. Table 2.5 lists the factors involved in the development of AUD, which are discussed in the following sections.

Biological Factors

GENETICS. A variety of studies investigating family history, adopted versus biological children living in the same families, and twins separated and living in different families all indicate that genetics play a substantial role in some forms

TABLE 2.5

Factors involved in the development of alcohol use disorders

Biological
Genetics
Alcohol reactivity

Psychosocial
Social sanctions
Gender roles
Coping styles
Drinking motives and expectations
Depression
Sensation-seeking
Stress
Impulsivity
Interpersonal relationships
History of sexual assault or child abuse

SOURCE: Created by Sandra Alters for Gale, 2009

of AUD. For example, R. Dayne Mayfield, R. Adron Harris, and Marc A. Schuckit indicate in "Genetic Factors Influencing Alcohol Dependence" (*British Journal of Pharmacology*, vol. 154, 2008) that relatives of alcoholics have four times the risk of developing alcohol dependence than do nonrelatives of alcoholics, and that the twins of those dependent on alcohol have a higher risk of developing alcohol dependence than do fraternal twins or nontwin siblings. Most likely, many genes influence a range of characteristics that affect risk.

ALCOHOL REACTIVITY. Alcohol reactivity refers to the sense of intoxication one has when drinking alcohol. Susan Nolen-Hoeksema of the University of Michigan notes in "Gender Differences in Risk Factors and Consequences for Alcohol Use and Problems" (*Clinical Psychology Review*, vol. 24, no. 8, December 2004) that the research on this topic has been conducted primarily on sons of alcoholics and reveals that, in general, they have a lower reactivity to alcohol. That is, when given moderate amounts of alcohol, sons of alcoholics report a lower subjective sense of intoxication compared with sons of nonalcoholics. Sons of alcoholics also show fewer signs of intoxication on certain physiological indicators than do sons of nonalcoholics. Without early signals of intoxication, men with a low reactivity to alcohol may tend to drink more before they begin to feel drunk and thus may develop a high physiological tolerance for alcohol, which magnifies the problem. Nolen-Hoeksema also notes that "long-term studies of men with low reactivity to moderate doses of alcohol suggest they are significantly more likely to become alcoholics over time than are men with greater reactivity to moderate doses of alcohol."

Psychosocial Factors

SOCIAL SANCTIONS, GENDER ROLES, AND COPING STYLES. Social sanctions are a mechanism of social control for enforcing a society's standards. Social sanctions may be one factor explaining why men drink more alcohol than women. Besides social sanctions against women drinking as heavily as men, American culture appears to identify alcohol consumption as more of a part of the male gender role than of the female gender role. While discussing and reviewing the results of several studies, Nolen-Hoeksema finds "that people, particularly women, who endorse traditionally feminine traits (nurturance, emotional expressivity) report less quantity and frequency of alcohol use." In contrast, traits often associated with the male gender role, such as aggressiveness and overcontrol of emotions, have been associated with heavy and problem alcohol use in both men and women. In fact, heavy drinking may be a way that some people cope with stress and avoid emotions, a behavior called avoidant coping.

DRINKING MOTIVES, EXPECTATIONS, AND DEPRESSION/DISTRESS. People consume alcohol for various reasons: as part of a meal, to celebrate certain occasions, and to reduce anxiety in social situations. Nolen-Hoeksema comments that people also consume alcohol to cope with distress or depression or to escape from negative feelings. June M. Williams, Mary B. Ballard, and Hunter Alessi state in "Aging and Alcohol Abuse: Increasing Counselor Awareness" (*Adultspan Journal*, vol. 4, no. 1, Spring 2005) that depression, anxiety, and stress are frequently diagnosed in the elderly, who may self-medicate with alcohol to a level of abusing or becoming dependent on the drug.

People who drink alcohol expect that drinking will reduce tension, increase social or physical pleasure, and facilitate social interaction. Those who have positive expectations for their drinking, such as the belief that alcohol will reduce distress, tend to drink more than those who have negative expectancies, such as the belief that alcohol will interfere with the ability to cope with distress. In general, men have more positive expectations concerning alcohol consumption than women. These stronger motives to drink are more strongly associated with alcohol-related problems in men than in women, although Nolen-Hoeksema reports that the relationships among depression, general distress, and alcohol consumption are quite complex.

SELF-ESTEEM, IMPULSIVITY, SENSATION-SEEKING, BEHAVIORAL UNDERCONTROL, AND ANTISOCIALITY. Nolen-Hoeksema's review of the literature reveals that research results are inconclusive regarding the relationship between self-esteem and alcohol use disorders. However, impulsivity, sensation-seeking, and behavioral undercontrol (not controlling one's behavior well) are consistently associated with alcohol use and problems in men. This association is less clear in women and may be another factor determining why a higher percentage of men than women are alcohol dependent.

Antisociality is a personality disorder that includes a chronic disregard for the rights of others and an absence of remorse for the harmful effects of these behaviors on others. People with this disorder are usually involved in aggressive and illegal activities. They are often impulsive and reckless and are more likely to become alcohol dependent. Males are more likely than females to demonstrate antisociality.

INTERPERSONAL RELATIONSHIPS, SEXUAL ASSAULT, AND CHILD ABUSE. Married couples often have strongly similar levels of drinking. It is unclear whether men and women with problem drinking patterns seek out partners with similar drinking patterns or whether either is influenced by the other to drink during the marriage. However, marital discord is often present when spouses' drinking patterns differ significantly.

Being a victim of sexual assault and/or child abuse is a risk factor for AUD. Nolen-Hoeksema's literature review shows that women who have experienced a history of sexual assault, whether during childhood or as an adult, are at an increased risk for problem drinking and alcohol abuse. Daniel F. Becker and Carlos M. Grilo, in investigating the psychosocial factors of drug and alcohol abuse in adolescents, state in "Prediction of Drug and Alcohol Abuse in Hospitalized Adolescents: Comparisons by Gender and Substance Type" (*Behaviour Research and Therapy*, vol. 44, no. 10, 2006) that a history of child abuse is a risk factor for drug and alcohol abuse in both males and females.

EFFECTS OF PARENTAL ALCOHOLISM ON CHILDREN

Living with someone who has an alcohol problem affects every member of the family. Children often suffer many problems as a result. In the fact sheet "Children of Addicted Parents: Important Facts" (2008, http://www.nacoa.net/pdfs/addicted.pdf), the National Association for Children of Alcoholics (NACA) estimates that there are over 28 million children of alcoholics in the United States, including 11 million under the age of 18. As mentioned earlier, relatives of alcoholics have four times the risk of alcoholism than do nonrelatives. The NACA also notes that children of alcoholics are more likely to suffer from attention-deficit hyperactivity disorder, behavioral problems, and anxiety disorders. They tend to score lower on tests that measure cognitive and verbal skills. Furthermore, children of alcoholics are more likely to be truant, repeat grades, drop out of school, or be referred to a school counselor or psychologist.

SHORT-TERM EFFECTS OF ALCOHOL ON THE BODY

When most people think about how alcohol affects them, they think of a temporary light-headedness or a hangover the next morning. Many are also aware of the serious damage that continuous, excessive alcohol use can do to the liver. Alcohol, however, affects many organs of the body and has been linked to cancer, mental and/or physical retardation in newborns, heart disease, and other health problems.

Low to moderate doses of alcohol produce a slight, brief increase in heartbeat and blood pressure. Large doses can reduce the pumping power of the heart and produce irregular heartbeats. In addition, blood vessels within muscles constrict, but those at the surface expand, causing rapid heat loss from the skin and a flushing or reddening. Thus, large doses of alcohol decrease body temperature and, additionally, may cause numbness of the skin, legs, and arms, creating a false feeling of warmth. Figure 2.2 illustrates and describes in more detail the path alcohol takes through the body after it is consumed.

Alcohol affects the endocrine system (a group of glands that produce hormones) in several ways. One effect is increased urination. Urination increases not only because of fluid intake but also because alcohol stops the release of vasopressin (an antidiuretic hormone) from the pituitary gland. This hormone controls how much water the kidneys reabsorb from the urine as it is being produced and how much

FIGURE 2.2

The path alcohol takes after consumption

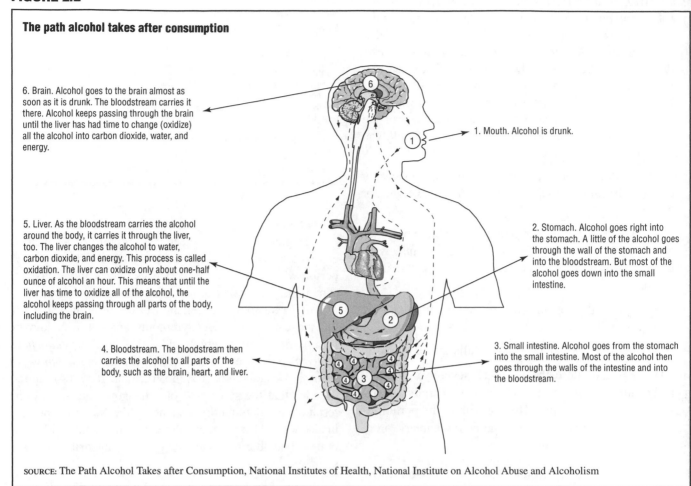

6. Brain. Alcohol goes to the brain almost as soon as it is drunk. The bloodstream carries it there. Alcohol keeps passing through the brain until the liver has had time to change (oxidize) all the alcohol into carbon dioxide, water, and energy.

1. Mouth. Alcohol is drunk.

5. Liver. As the bloodstream carries the alcohol around the body, it carries it through the liver, too. The liver changes the alcohol to water, carbon dioxide, and energy. This process is called oxidation. The liver can oxidize only about one-half ounce of alcohol an hour. This means that until the liver has time to oxidize all of the alcohol, the alcohol keeps passing through all parts of the body, including the brain.

2. Stomach. Alcohol goes right into the stomach. A little of the alcohol goes through the wall of the stomach and into the bloodstream. But most of the alcohol goes down into the small intestine.

4. Bloodstream. The bloodstream then carries the alcohol to all parts of the body, such as the brain, heart, and liver.

3. Small intestine. Alcohol goes from the stomach into the small intestine. Most of the alcohol then goes through the walls of the intestine and into the bloodstream.

SOURCE: The Path Alcohol Takes after Consumption, National Institutes of Health, National Institute on Alcohol Abuse and Alcoholism

water the kidneys excrete. Therefore, heavy alcohol intake can result in both dehydration and an imbalance in electrolytes, which are chemicals dissolved in body fluids that conduct electrical currents. Both of these conditions are serious health hazards.

Alcohol is sometimes believed to be an aphrodisiac (sexual stimulant). Whereas low to moderate amounts of alcohol can reduce fear and decrease sexual inhibitions, larger doses tend to impair sexual performance. Alcoholics sometimes report difficulties in their sex life.

Intoxication

The speed of alcohol absorption affects the rate at which one becomes intoxicated. Intoxication occurs when alcohol is absorbed into the blood faster than the liver can oxidize it (or break it down into water, carbon dioxide, and energy). In a 160-pound (72.6-kg) man, alcohol is metabolized (absorbed and processed by the body) at a rate of about one drink every two hours. The absorption of alcohol is influenced by several factors:

• Body weight—heavier people are less affected than lighter people by the same amount of alcohol because there is more blood and water in their system to dilute the alcohol intake. In addition, the greater the body muscle weight, the lower the blood alcohol concentration (BAC) for a given amount of alcohol.

• Speed of drinking—the faster alcohol is drunk, the faster the BAC level rises.

• Presence of food in the stomach—eating while drinking slows down the absorption of alcohol by increasing the amount of time it takes the alcohol to get from the stomach to the small intestine.

• Drinking history and body chemistry—the longer a person has been drinking, the greater his or her tolerance (in other words, the more alcohol it takes him or her to get drunk). An individual's physiological functioning or "body chemistry" may also affect his or her reactions to alcohol. Women are more easily affected by alcohol regardless of weight because women metabolize alcohol differently than men. Women are known to have less body water than men of the same body weight, so equivalent amounts of alcohol result in higher concentrations of alcohol in the blood of women than men.

As a person's BAC rises, there are somewhat predictable responses in behavior.

- At a BAC of about 0.05 grams (g) of alcohol per 1 deciliter (dL) of blood, thought processes, judgment, and restraint are more lax. The person may feel more at ease socially. Also, reaction time to visual or auditory stimuli slows down as the BAC rises. (It should be noted that a measurement of g/dL—a mass/volume measure—is approximately equal to a volume/volume—or a percentage—measurement when calculating BAC, and the two are often used interchangeably; so, a BAC of 0.05 g/dL can also mean a BAC of 0.05%.)

- At 0.10 g/dL, voluntary motor actions become noticeably clumsy. (It is illegal to drive with a BAC of 0.08 g/dL or higher.)

- At 0.20 g/dL, the entire motor area of the brain becomes significantly depressed. The person staggers, may want to lie down, may be easily angered, or may shout or weep.

- At 0.30 g/dL, the person generally acts confused or may be in a stupor.

- At 0.40 g/dL, the person usually falls into a coma.

- At 0.50 g/dL or more, the medulla is severely depressed, and death generally occurs within several hours, usually from respiratory failure. The medulla is the portion of the brainstem that regulates many involuntary processes, such as breathing.

Without immediate medical attention, a person whose BAC reaches 0.50 g/dL will almost certainly die. Death may even occur at a BAC of 0.40 g/dL if the alcohol is consumed quickly and in a large amount, causing the BAC to rise rapidly.

Sobering Up

Time is the only way to rid the body of alcohol. The more slowly a person drinks, the more time the body has to process the alcohol, so less alcohol accumulates in the bloodstream. In addition, having food in the stomach slows the absorption of alcohol there. Drinking slowly while eating and alternating nonalcoholic beverages with alcoholic beverages helps keep the BAC at lower levels than drinking more quickly on an empty stomach.

According to Brown University, in "Alcohol and Your Body" (December 15, 2008, http://www.brown.edu/Student _Services/Health_Services/Health_Education/atod/alc_aayb htm), five drinks consumed in quick succession by a 175-pound (79.4 kg) man will produce a BAC of 0.125 g/dL. In a 150-pound (68-kg) man this intake will produce a higher BAC of 0.145 g/dL. In a 125-pound (56.7-kg) woman it will produce an even higher BAC of 0.202 g/dL. It will take six hours for the BAC level of the 125-pound woman to drop to 0.112, which is still high above the legal driving limit of 0.08 g/dL.

TABLE 2.6

Symptoms of a hangover

Body aches
Diarrhea
Dizziness/lightheadedness
Dry mouth/thirst
Fatigue
Headache
Irritability
Lack of alertness/difficulty concentrating
Nausea

SOURCE: Created by Sandra Alters for Gale, 2009

Hangovers

Hangovers cause a great deal of misery as well as absenteeism and loss of productivity at school or work. A person with a hangover experiences two or more physical symptoms after drinking and fully metabolizing alcohol. The major symptoms of a hangover are listed in Table 2.6, but the causes of these symptoms are not well known. Results from Jeff Wiese et al.'s "Effect of *Opuntia ficus indica* on Symptoms of the Alcohol Hangover" (*Archives of Internal Medicine*, vol. 164, no. 12, June 28, 2004) support the idea that the symptoms of a hangover are largely the result of an inflammatory response of the body to impurities in alcohol and by-products of alcohol metabolism. Fluctuations in body hormones and dehydration intensify hangover symptoms.

There is no scientific evidence to support popular hangover cures, such as black coffee, raw egg, chili pepper, steak sauce, "alkalizers," and vitamins. To treat a hangover, health care practitioners usually prescribe bed rest as well as eating food and drinking nonalcoholic fluids.

LONG-TERM EFFECTS OF ALCOHOL ON THE BODY

The results of scientific research help health care practitioners and the general public understand both the positive and negative health consequences of drinking alcohol. Robin Room, Thomas Babor, and Jürgen Rehm summarize in "Alcohol and Public Health" (*Lancet*, vol. 365, no. 9458, February 2005) the major diseases and injury conditions related to alcohol use and the proportions attributable to alcohol worldwide. They note that about one-fifth of mouth and throat cancers are related to drinking alcohol. Nearly one-third of cancers of the esophagus (food tube) and one-fourth of cancers of the liver are linked to alcohol consumption as well. Alcohol consumption is also related to heart disease and stroke and is associated with cirrhosis of the liver, a condition in which the liver becomes scarred and dysfunctional. In addition, one-fifth of motor vehicle accidents are related to alcohol consumption.

Not all the effects of alcohol consumption are harmful to health, however. In "Alcohol on Trial: The Evidence"

(*Southern Medical Journal*, vol. 98, no. 1, 2005), Ronald Hamdy and Melissa McManama Aukerman list levels of alcohol consumption and the relative risk for total mortality (death) for a variety of diseases and conditions. Their data show that men aged 40 to 85 who drank up to, and possibly slightly over, two drinks per day had a lower total mortality risk than those who did not drink. That is, this level of drinking was good for the men's overall health and life expectancy.

Hamdy and Aukerman also compare alcohol consumption versus relative risk of hypertension (chronic high blood pressure) in women aged 25 to 42. Women in this age group who had up to one drink per day had a lower risk of hypertension than women in the same age group who did not drink alcohol. Drinking slightly more than 1 to 1.5 drinks per day put these drinkers at equal relative risk for hypertension as those who did not drink alcohol. Drinking more than 1.5 drinks per day was detrimental and put these heavier drinkers at a higher relative risk for hypertension than their nondrinking counterparts. Similar results were found with respect to dementia in adults aged 65 and older and alcohol consumption. Those consuming one to six drinks weekly had a lower risk of dementia than those who abstained from drinking. Those consuming 14 or more drinks per week had a higher risk of dementia than those who abstained.

According Hamdy and Aukerman, some diseases showed different patterns of protective and nonprotective effects of alcohol than the diseases/conditions discussed previously. For example, drinking two to four drinks per week reduced the risk of age-related macular degeneration (a disease of the retina of the eye), one drink per week had no protective effect, and five to six drinks per week appeared to raise the relative risk of this disease in men aged 40 to 85.

A study published in February 2009 in *American Journal of Clinical Nutrition* indicated that bone density can also benefit from alcohol consumption. As reported by Anne Harding in "Moderate Drinking May Help Bone Density" (Reuters, March 20, 2009, http://www.reuters.com:80/article/healthNews/idUSTRE52J2VX20090320), "People who enjoy a glass or two of wine or beer every day could be helping to keep their bones strong." The study cautioned, however, that "drinking more—and choosing hard liquor instead of wine or beer—may actually weaken bones."

With so many studies and so many health-related factors to take into account, how does a person know how much alcohol is beneficial and how much is too much? The World Cancer Research Fund and the American Institute for Cancer Research state in *Food, Nutrition, Physical Activity, and the Prevention of Cancer: A Global Perspective* (2007, http://www.dietandcancerreport.org/downloads/summary/english.pdf): "If alcoholic drinks are consumed,

limit consumption to no more than two drinks a day for men and one drink a day for women." Their justification for this statement is as follows: "The evidence on cancer justifies a recommendation not to drink alcoholic drinks. Other evidence shows that modest amounts of alcoholic drinks are likely to reduce the risk of coronary heart disease."

In "Alcohol, Wine, and Cardiovascular Disease" (2009, http://www.americanheart.org/presenter.jhtml?identifier=4422), the American Heart Association states that "if you drink alcohol, do so in moderation. This means an average of one to two drinks per day for men and one drink per day for women.... Drinking more alcohol increases such dangers as alcoholism, high blood pressure, obesity, stroke, breast cancer, suicide and accidents. Also, it's not possible to predict in which people alcoholism will become a problem. Given these and other risks, the American Heart Association cautions people NOT to start drinking... if they do not already drink alcohol. Consult your doctor on the benefits and risks of consuming alcohol in moderation."

EFFECTS OF ALCOHOL ON SEX AND REPRODUCTION

Alcohol consumption can affect sexual response and reproduction in profound ways. Many alcoholics suffer from erectile dysfunction (impotence) and/or reduced sexual drive. Some studies, such as Jane Y. Polsky et al.'s "Smoking and Other Lifestyle Factors in Relation to Erectile Dysfunction" (*BJU International*, vol. 96, no. 9, 2005), suggest that alcohol consumption, even at low levels, is associated with a greater risk of erectile dysfunction. Many alcoholics suffer from depression, which may further impair their sexual function. In addition, Jerrold S. Greenberg, Clint E. Bruess, and Sarah C. Conklin report in *Exploring the Dimensions of Human Sexuality* (2007) that alcohol use is associated with poor sperm quality in men.

In premenopausal women chronic heavy drinking can contribute to a variety of reproductive disorders. According to Greenberg, Bruess, and Conklin, these disorders include the cessation of menstruation, irregular menstrual cycles, failure to ovulate, early menopause, increased risk of spontaneous miscarriages, and lower rates of conception. Some of these disorders can be caused directly by the interference of alcohol with the hormonal regulation of the reproductive system. They may also be caused indirectly through other disorders associated with alcohol abuse, such as liver disease, pancreatic disease, malnutrition, or fetal abnormalities.

Fetal Alcohol Spectrum Disorders

Alcohol consumption during pregnancy can result in severe harm to the fetus (unborn child). The development of such defects can begin early in pregnancy when the mother-to-be may not even know she is pregnant, and such defects are likely to be exacerbated by binge drinking. For example, Lisa A. DeRoo et al. reveal in "First-Trimester

"Maternal Alcohol Consumption and the Risk of Infant Oral Clefts in Norway: A Population-Based Case-Control Study" (*American Journal of Epidemiology*, vol. 168, no. 6, September 2008) that women who binge drank in their first trimester of pregnancy were twice as likely as nondrinkers to give birth to an infant having a cleft lip, cleft palate, or both.

Drinking during pregnancy can also cause fetal alcohol spectrum disorders (FASD). As Edward P. Riley and Christie L. McGee note in "Fetal Alcohol Spectrum Disorders: An Overview with Emphasis on Changes in Brain and Behavior" (*Experimental Biology and Medicine*, vol. 230, no. 6, 2005), "The term FASD is…an umbrella term that describes the range of effects that can occur in an individual whose mother drank alcohol during pregnancy. These effects can be physical, mental, or behavioral, with possible lifelong implications."

The key facial characteristics of a child born with FASD are shown in Figure 2.3. These characteristics are the most pronounced in fetal alcohol syndrome (FAS), the most recognizable form of FASD. Children with FASD also exhibit a complex pattern of behavioral and cognitive dysfunctions, which are listed in Table 2.7. Besides these characteristics and dysfunctions, results of studies, such as Maria de Los Angeles Avaria et al.'s "Peripheral Nerve Conduction Abnormalities in Children Exposed to Alcohol in Utero" (*Journal of Pediatrics*, vol. 144, no. 3, 2004), show that prenatal alcohol exposure is associated with abnormalities in the electrical properties of nerves.

In "Fetal Alcohol Spectrum Disorders" (May 2, 2006, http://www.cdc.gov/ncbddd/fas/fasask.htm), the Centers for Disease Control and Prevention (CDC) shows that FAS rates range from 0.2 to 1.5 per 1,000 live births. In addition, the CDC reports that other prenatal alcohol-related conditions less severe than FAS, such as alcohol-related neurodevelopmental disorder (ARND) and alcohol-related birth defects (ARBD), occur approximately three times as often as FAS. ARND and ARBD were formerly and collectively known as fetal alcohol effects. Now all prenatal alcohol-related conditions are collectively known as FASD.

In February 2005 the U.S. surgeon general Richard Carmona (1949–) issued an advisory on alcohol use in pregnancy. Key points of the advisory are listed in Table 2.8. As noted in the advisory, there is no known safe level of alcohol consumption during pregnancy. The CDC emphasizes, along with the surgeon general, that FAS and other prenatal alcohol-related disorders are 100% preventable if a woman does not drink alcohol while she is pregnant or if she is of reproductive age and is not using birth control. Yet, data show that some women who might become pregnant, or who are pregnant, consume alcohol and put themselves at risk for having a child with FASD.

Table 2.9 shows that 11.6% of pregnant women consumed alcohol in the past month in 2006–07 when questioned for the annual National Survey on Drug Use and Health. This figure was down from 12.1% in the 2004–05

FIGURE 2.3

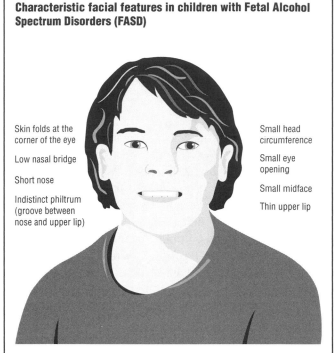

Characteristic facial features in children with Fetal Alcohol Spectrum Disorders (FASD)

Skin folds at the corner of the eye

Low nasal bridge

Short nose

Indistinct philtrum (groove between nose and upper lip)

Small head circumference

Small eye opening

Small midface

Thin upper lip

SOURCE: "Fetal Alcohol Syndrome," in "Alcohol's Damaging Effects on the Brain," *Alcohol Alert*, no. 63, Department of Health and Human Services, National Institutes of Health, National Institute on Alcohol Abuse and Alcoholism, October 2004, http://pubs.niaaa.nih.gov/publications/aa63/aa63.pdf (accessed August 12, 2008)

TABLE 2.7

Cognitive and behavioral characteristics typical of Fetal Alcohol Spectrum Disorders (FASD)

Low IQ
Attention deficit
Slow reaction time
Delayed motor development
Disruptive and impulsive behavior
Difficulties in learning and in abstract thinking

SOURCE: Created by Sandra Alters for Gale, 2006

period. In 2004–05 and 2006–07 approximately one-fifth (20.6% and 17.6%, respectively) of pregnant women drank during their first trimester of pregnancy, a time when all the organ systems of the fetus are developing. Fewer women drank during their second and third trimesters.

ALCOHOL'S INTERACTION WITH OTHER DRUGS

Because alcohol is easily available and such an accepted part of American social life, people often forget that it is a drug. When someone takes a medication while drinking alcohol, he or she is taking two drugs. Alcohol consumed with other drugs—for example, an illegal drug such as cocaine, an over-the-counter (without a prescription) drug

TABLE 2.8

Key points in the U.S. Surgeon General's advisory on alcohol use during pregnancy, 2005

Based on the current, best science available we now know the following:

- Alcohol consumed during pregnancy increases the risk of alcohol related birth defects, including growth deficiencies, facial abnormalities, central nervous system impairment, behavioral disorders, and impaired intellectual development.
- No amount of alcohol consumption can be considered safe during pregnancy.
- Alcohol can damage a fetus at any stage of pregnancy. Damage can occur in the earliest weeks of pregnancy, even before a woman knows that she is pregnant.
- The cognitive deficits and behavioral problems resulting from prenatal alcohol exposure are lifelong.
- Alcohol-related birth defects are completely preventable.

For these reasons:

1. A pregnant woman should not drink alcohol during pregnancy.
2. A pregnant woman who has already consumed alcohol during her pregnancy should stop in order to minimize further risk.
3. A woman who is considering becoming pregnant should abstain from alcohol.
4. Recognizing that nearly half of all births in the United States are unplanned, women of childbearing age should consult their physician and take steps to reduce the possibility of prenatal alcohol exposure.
5. Health professionals should inquire routinely about alcohol consumption by women of childbearing age, inform them of the risks of alcohol consumption during pregnancy, and advise them not to drink alcoholic beverages during pregnancy.

SOURCE: Adapted from "Surgeon General's Advisory on Alcohol Use in Pregnancy," in *News Release: U.S. Surgeon General Releases Advisory on Alcohol Use in Pregnancy*, U.S. Department of Health and Human Services, February 21, 2005, http://www.hhs.gov/surgeongeneral/pressreleases/sg02222005.html (accessed August 12, 2008)

such as cough medicine, or a prescription drug such as an antibiotic—may make the combination harmful or even deadly or may counteract the effectiveness of a prescribed medication.

To promote the desired chemical or physical effects, a medication must be absorbed into the body and must reach its site of action. Alcohol may prevent an appropriate amount of the medication from reaching its site of action. In other cases alcohol can alter the drug's effects once it reaches the site. Alcohol interacts negatively with more than 150 medications. Table 2.10 shows some possible effects of combining alcohol and other types of drugs.

The U.S. Food and Drug Administration recommends that anyone who regularly has three alcoholic drinks per day should check with a physician before taking aspirin, acetaminophen, or any other over-the-counter painkiller. Combining alcohol with aspirin, ibuprofen, or related pain relievers may promote stomach bleeding. Combining alcohol with acetaminophen may promote liver damage.

ALCOHOL-RELATED DEATHS

In "Deaths: Final Data for 2005" (*National Vital Statistics Reports*, vol. 56, no. 10, April 24, 2008), Hsiang-Ching Kung et al. of the CDC report that 21,634 people in

---

TABLE 2.9

Percentage of past-month alcohol use among females aged 15–44, by pregnancy status, 2004–05 and 2006–07

| | Total[b] | | Pregnancy status | | | |
| | | | Pregnant | | Not pregnant | |
Demographic/pregnancy characteristic	2004–2005	2006–2007	2004–2005	2006–2007	2004–2005	2006–200
Total	51.4	51.4	12.1	11.6	53.1	53.2
Age						
15–17	27.6[a]	25.3	13.9	15.8	27.7[a]	25.4
18–25	55.7[a]	57.5	9.7	9.8	58.5[a]	60.5
26–44	53.4	53.1	13.5	12.5	55.0	54.9
Hispanic origin and race						
Not Hispanic or Latino	54.1	54.0	13.4	13.5	55.7	55.8
White	58.9	58.8	13.8	14.5	60.7	60.6
Black or African American	40.5	42.5	13.4	15.7	41.6	43.8
American Indian or Alaska Native	44.3	41.4	*	*	45.0	42.3
Native Hawaiian or other Pacific Islander	*	34.5	*	*	*	35.9
Asian	31.2	31.1	*	*	32.4	32.6
Two or more races	60.5	55.1	*	*	61.8	56.4
Hispanic or Latino	37.4	38.3	6.8	4.1	39.1	40.1
Trimester[c]						
First	N/A	N/A	20.6	17.6	N/A	N/A
Second	N/A	N/A	10.2	8.2	N/A	N/A
Third	N/A	N/A	6.7	8.0	N/A	N/A

Note: Difference between estimate and 2006–2007 estimate is statistically significant.
*Low precision; no estimate reported.
N/A: Not applicable.
[a]Difference between estimate and 2006–2007 estimate is statistically significant.
[b]Estimates in the total column are for all females aged 15 to 44, including those with unknown pregnancy status.
[c]Pregnant females aged 15 to 44 not reporting trimester were excluded.

SOURCE: "Table 7.74B. Alcohol Use in the Past Month among Females Aged 15 to 44, by Pregnancy Status and Demographic Characteristics: Percentages, Annual Averages Based on 2004–2005 and 2006–2007," in *2007 National Survey on Drug Use and Health: Detailed Tables*, U.S. Department of Health and Human Services, Substance Abuse and Mental Health Services Administration, Office of Applied Studies, September 2008, http://www.oas.samhsa.gov/NSDUH/2k7NSDUH/tabs/Sect7peTabs59to115.htm#Tab7.74B (accessed December 8, 2008)

TABLE 2.10

Interactions between alcohol and medications

Medications	Interactions when taken with alcohol.
Antidepressants	Increase in the sedative effects of some antidepressants.
Antibiotics	Nausea, vomiting, headache, and possibly convulsions may occur with some antibiotics. Effectiveness of antibiotics may be reduced.
Antihistamines	Increase in the sedative effects of some antihistamines Dizziness and excessive sedation may occur in the elderly.
Cardiovascular medications	Dizziness or fainting upon standing may occur. Effect of some cardiovascular medications may be reduced.
Narcotic pain relievers (e.g. morphine, codeine, Darvon, Demerol)	Increase in the sedative effects of both alcohol and narcotics. Risk of death increased from overdose.
Non-narcotic pain relievers (e.g. Aspirin, acetominaphen [Tylenol], ibuprofen	Stomach bleeding and liver damage may occur. Blood clotting may be inhibited. Alcohol effects may be increased.
Sedatives/hypnotics (e.g. sleeping pills)	Great increase in the sedative effects of both drugs. May result in reduced heartbeat and breathing rates. May lead to coma and death.

SOURCE: Created by Sandra Alters for Gale, 2009

the United States died of alcohol-induced causes in 2005. This category included deaths from dependent use of alcohol, nondependent use of alcohol, and accidental alcohol poisoning. It excluded accidents, homicides, and other causes indirectly related to alcohol use, as well as deaths because of fetal alcohol syndrome. The age-adjusted death rate for males was 3.2 times the rate for females. In 2005, 12,928 people died from alcoholic liver disease.

MOTOR VEHICLE AND PEDESTRIAN ACCIDENTS

In "Traffic Safety Facts 2007 Data" (2008, http://www.nhtsa.dot.gov/portal/site/nhtsa/menuitem.6a6eaf83cf719ad24ec86e10dba046a0/), the National Highway Traffic Safety Administration (NHTSA) of the U.S. Department of Transportation defines a fatal traffic crash as alcohol related if either the driver or an involved pedestrian had a BAC of 0.01 g/dL or greater. People with a BAC of 0.08 g/dL or higher are considered intoxicated. The NHTSA defines a nonfatal traffic crash as alcohol involved or alcohol related if police note in their incident report that alcohol was present. Neither definition means that alcohol was necessarily the cause of the accident.

The NHTSA reports that 41,059 people were killed in traffic accidents in 2007, with 15,387 of them in alcohol-related crashes. (See Table 2.11.) These alcohol-related traffic deaths represented 37% of all car crash fatalities in 2007. The percentage of alcohol-related traffic fatalities has declined somewhat steadily from a high of 55% in 1982, and leveled out from about the mid-1990s to 2007. The peak number of fatalities occurred in 1988, when 47,087 traffic accident deaths, including both alcohol-related accidents (46%) and nonalcohol-related accidents (53%), were recorded.

A number of important factors have contributed to the decline of drunk driving fatalities. Mothers against Drunk Driving was founded in 1980. This organization's most significant achievement was lobbying to get the legal drinking age raised to 21 in all states, which occurred in 1988. There were also successful campaigns such as "Friends Don't Let Friends Drive Drunk." The use of seat belts has also helped reduce deaths in motor vehicle accidents.

As of August 2005, all states, the District of Columbia, and Puerto Rico had lowered the BAC limit for drunk driving from 0.1 g/dL to 0.08 g/dL. According to the Insurance Institute for Highway Safety, in "DUI/DWI Laws" (February 2009, http://www.iihs.org/laws/dui.aspx), 41 states and the District of Columbia also had administrative license revocation laws, which require prompt, mandatory suspension of drivers' licenses for failing or refusing to take the BAC test. This immediate suspension, before conviction and independent of criminal procedures, is invoked immediately after arrest.

In both 1997 and 2007 drivers aged 21 to 44 were the most likely to be involved in fatal crashes in which the driver had a BAC of 0.08 g/dL or higher. (See Table 2.12.) The percentage of drivers within the 21- to 24-year-old age group increased from 30% in 1997 to 35% in 2007, as did the percentage for drivers in the 25- to 34-year-old age group, from 27% to 29%. By contrast, the percentage in the 35- to 44-year-old group decreased slightly from 26% to 25%.

In 2007 the percentage of male drivers involved in fatal crashes who had a BAC of 0.08 g/dL or greater was 12% higher than female drivers involved in fatal crashes (25% versus 13%, respectively). (See Table 2.12.) When compared with 1997, the percentage of drunk male and female drivers in fatal accidents in 2007 increased by 1%, from 24% to 25% for males, and from 12% to 13% for females; thus the gap between the two groups remained the same over the decade.

Alcohol was related to a higher percentage of fatal crashes by motorcycles (27%) in 2007 than for crashes involving automobiles (23%) and light trucks (23%). (See Table 2.12.) Fatal crashes involving large trucks were very unlikely to be alcohol related (1%).

In 1997 over half of all pedestrians aged 25 to 44 who were killed in a traffic accident had a BAC of 0.08 g/dL or higher. (See Table 2.13.) In 2007 the age of this group declined; over half of all pedestrians aged 21 to 34 who were killed in a traffic accident had a BAC of 0.08 g/dL or higher.

ALCOHOL-RELATED OFFENSES

Table 2.14 shows arrest trends for alcohol-related offenses and driving under the influence from 1970 to 2006. Arrests were the highest for alcohol-related offenses from 1975 to 1992, with 1981 being the peak year. Arrests for

TABLE 2.11

Fatalities in motor vehicle accidents, by blood alcohol concentration (BAC) at time of crash, 1982–2007

Year	BAC=.00 Alcohol not consumed		BAC=.01–.07 Impaired		Alcohol-impaired driving fatalities (BAC=.08+) Intoxicated		BAC=.01+		Total fatalities	
	Number	Percent	Number	Percent	Number	Percent	Number	Percent	Number	Percent
1982	19,771	45	2,912	7	21,113	48	24,025	55	43,945	100
1983	19,787	46	2,588	6	20,051	47	22,639	53	42,589	100
1984	21,429	48	3,007	7	19,638	44	22,645	51	44,257	100
1985	22,589	52	2,974	7	18,125	41	21,098	48	43,825	100
1986	22,896	50	3,487	8	19,554	42	23,041	50	46,087	100
1987	24,186	52	3,238	7	18,813	41	22,051	48	46,390	100
1988	25,164	53	3,156	7	18,611	40	21,767	46	47,087	100
1989	25,152	55	2,793	6	17,521	38	20,314	45	45,582	100
1990	23,823	53	2,901	7	17,705	40	20,607	46	44,599	100
1991	23,025	55	2,480	6	15,827	38	18,307	44	41,508	100
1992	22,726	58	2,352	6	14,049	36	16,401	42	39,250	100
1993	23,979	60	2,300	6	13,739	34	16,039	40	40,150	100
1994	24,948	61	2,236	5	13,390	33	15,626	38	40,716	100
1995	25,768	62	2,416	6	13,478	32	15,893	38	41,817	100
1996	26,052	62	2,415	6	13,451	32	15,866	38	42,065	100
1997	26,902	64	2,216	5	12,757	30	14,973	36	42,013	100
1998	26,477	64	2,353	6	12,546	30	14,899	36	41,501	100
1999	26,798	64	2,235	5	12,555	30	14,790	35	41,717	100
2000	26,082	62	2,422	6	13,324	32	15,746	38	41,945	100
2001	26,334	62	2,441	6	13,290	31	15,731	37	42,196	100
2002	27,080	63	2,321	5	13,472	31	15,793	37	43,005	100
2003	27,328	64	2,327	5	13,096	31	15,423	36	42,884	100
2004	27,413	64	2,212	5	13,099	31	15,311	36	42,836	100
2005	27,423	63	2,404	6	13,582	31	15,985	37	43,510	100
2006	26,633	62	2,479	6	13,491	32	15,970	37	42,708	100
2007	25,555	62	2,388	6	12,998	32	15,387	37	41,059	100

Notes: Total fatalities include those in which there was no driver or motorcycle rider present. The National Highway Traffic Safety Administration (NHTSA) estimates alcohol involvement when alcohol test results are unknown.

SOURCE: "Table 13. Persons Killed, by Highest Blood Alcohol Concentration (BAC) in the Crash, 1982–2007," in *Traffic Safety Facts 2007 Early Edition*, U.S. Department of Transportation, National Center for Statistics and Analysis, National Highway Traffic Safety Administration, http://www.nhtsa .dot.gov/portal/site/nhtsa/menuitem.6a6eaf83cf719ad24ec86e10dba046a0/ (accessed January 7, 2009)

driving under the influence were the highest from 1977 to 1996, with 1983 being the peak year. In 2007 there were 2.5 million alcohol-related arrests; slightly more than 1 million of those arrests were for driving under the influence.

Doris J. James of the Bureau of Justice Statistics (BJS) mentions in *Profile of Jail Inmates, 2002* (July 2004, http://www.ojp.usdoj.gov/bjs/pub/pdf/pji02.pdf) that in 2002, 33.4% of convicted jail inmates reported that they had been under the influence of alcohol alone (not in combination with any other drug) when they committed their offenses. This figure had decreased since 1996. A higher percentage of jail inmates used alcohol when committing a violent offense than did those committing other types of crimes, such as property or drug offenses. As of February 2009, these data were the most recent from the BJS.

TABLE 2.12

Drivers with a blood alcohol concentration (BAC) of 0.08 or higher involved in motor vehicle crashes, by age, gender, and vehicle type, 1997 and 2007

	Total drivers involved in fatal crashes						Change in percentage with BAC=.08+ 1997–2007
	1997			2007			
		BAC=.08+			BAC=.08+		
Drivers involved in fatal crashes	Total number of drivers	Number	Percent of total	Total number of drivers	Number	Percent of total	
Total	56,668	11,579	20%	55,681	12,068	22%	+22%
Drivers by age group (years)							
16–20	7,719	1,321	17%	6,851	1,205	18%	+1%
21–24	5,705	1,704	30%	6,256	2,160	35%	+5%
25–34	12,453	3,406	27%	10,692	3,118	29%	+2%
35–44	10,904	2,787	26%	9,862	2,418	25%	−1%
45–54	7,522	1,296	17%	8,982	1,829	20%	+3%
55–64	4,394	479	11%	6,011	734	12%	+1%
65–74	3,401	259	8%	3,025	227	8%	0%
75+	3,314	141	4%	2,855	117	4%	0%
Drivers by gender							
Male	40,954	9,624	24%	40,804	10,015	25%	+1%
Female	14,954	1,824	12%	14,099	1,855	13%	+1%
Drivers by vehicle type							
Passenger cars	29,896	6,460	22%	22,621	5,154	23%	+1%
Light trucks	18,502	4,173	23%	21,591	5,033	23%	0%
Large trucks	4,859	83	2%	4,551	40	1%	−1%
Motorcycles	2,159	699	32%	5,286	1,431	27%	−5%

Note: Numbers shown for groups of drivers do not add to the total number of drivers due to unknown or other data not included.

SOURCE: "Table 3. Drivers in Fatal Crashes with a BAC of 0.08 or Higher, by Age, Gender, and Vehicle Type, 1997 and 2007," in *Traffic Safety Facts 2007 Data Alcohol-Impaired Driving*, National Highway Traffic Safety Administration, National Center for Statistics and Analysis, 2008, http://www.nhtsa.dot.gov/portal/site/nhtsa/menuitem.6a6eaf83cf719ad24ec86e10dba046a0/ (accessed January 7, 2009)

TABLE 2.13

Pedestrians killed in motor vehicle crashes, by age group and percent BAC, 1997 and 2007

| | 1997 | | | | | 2007 | | | | |
Age (years)	Number of fatalities	% with BAC=.00	% with BAC=.01–.07	% with BAC=.08+	% with BAC=.01+	Number of fatalities	% with BAC=.00	% with BAC=.01–.07	% with BAC=.08+	% with BAC=.01+
16–20	301	71	4	25	29	287	69	5	26	31
21–24	253	48	7	45	52	296	43	5	51	57
25–34	762	41	4	55	59	606	45	5	51	55
35–44	932	43	4	53	57	754	47	6	47	53
45–54	700	55	5	40	45	916	47	4	49	53
55–64	499	68	4	28	32	494	66	4	30	34
65–74	507	82	2	15	18	382	80	4	16	20
75–84	465	91	3	6	9	387	89	2	9	11
85+	202	92	3	5	8	134	90	5	5	10
Total*	4,621	61	4	35	39	4,256	58	5	37	42

*Excludes pedestrians under 16 years old and pedestrians of unknown age.
BAC =Blood Alcohol Concentration.

SOURCE: "Table 4. Alcohol Involvement for Pedestrians Killed in Fatal Crashes by Age, 1997 and 2007," in *Traffic Safety Facts 2007 Data: Pedestrians*, U.S. Department of Transportation, National Center for Statistics and Analysis, National Highway Traffic Safety Administration, http://www.nhtsa.dot.gov/portal/site/nhtsa/menuitem.6a6eaf83cf719ad24ec86e10dba046a0/ (accessed December 8, 2008)

TABLE 2.14

Arrests for alcohol-related offenses and driving under the influence, 1970–2006

[In thousands]

	Alcohol-related offenses	Driving under the influence
1970	2,849	424
1971	2,914	490
1972	2,835	604
1973	2,539	654
1974	2,297	617
1975	3,044	909
1976	2,790	838
1977	3,303	1,104
1978	3,406	1,205
1979	3,455	1,232
1980	3,535	1,304
1981	3,745	1,422
1982	3,640	1,405
1983	3,729	1,613
1984	3,153	1,347
1985	3,418	1,503
1986	3,325	1,459
1987	3,248	1,410
1988	2,995	1,294
1989	3,180	1,333
1990	3,270	1,391
1991	3,000	1,289
1992	3,061	1,320
1993	2,886	1,229
1994	2,698	1,080
1995	2,578	1,033
1996	2,677	1,014
1997	2,510	986
1998	2,451	969
1999	2,238	931
2000	2,218	916
2001	2,224	947
2002	2,401	1,020
2003	2,301	1,006
2004	2,373	1,014
2005	2,374	997
2006	2,463	1,039

Note: This table presents data from all law enforcement agencies submitting complete reports for 12 months. Alcohol-related offenses include driving under the influence, liquor law violations, drunkenness, disorderly conduct, and vagrancy.

SOURCE: Ann L. Pastore and Kathleen Maguire, eds. "Table 4.27.2006. Arrests for Alcohol-Related Offenses and Driving under the Influence, United States, 1970–2006," in *Sourcebook of Criminal Justice Statistics Online*, U.S. Department of Justice, Bureau of Justice Statistics, University at Albany School of Criminal Justice, Hindelang Criminal Justice Research Center, 2008, http://www.albany.edu/sourcebook/pdf/t4272006.pdf (accessed August 18, 2008)

CHAPTER 3
TOBACCO

In the mid-20th century smoking in the United States was often associated with romance, relaxation, and adventure; movie stars oozed glamour on screen while smoking, and movie tough guys were never more masculine than when lighting up. Songs such as "Smoke Gets in Your Eyes" topped the hit parade. Smoking became a rite of passage for many young males and a sign of increasing independence for women.

Since the 1990s, however, there has been an increase of opposition to tobacco use. Health authorities warn of the dangers of smoking and chewing tobacco, and nonsmokers object to secondhand smoke—because of both the smell and the health dangers of breathing smoke from other people's cigarettes. In the first decade of the 21st century, a smoker is more likely to ask for permission before lighting up, and the answer is often "no." Because of health concerns, smoking has been banned on airplanes, in hospitals, and in many workplaces, restaurants, and bars. In 2008, 82% of respondents to a Gallup poll believed that cigarette smoking was very harmful to adults who smoke. (See Figure 3.1.)

PHYSICAL PROPERTIES OF NICOTINE

Tobacco is a plant native to the Western Hemisphere. It contains nicotine, a drug classified as a stimulant, although it has some depressive effects as well. Nicotine is a poisonous alkaloid that is the major psychoactive (mood-altering) ingredient in tobacco. (Alkaloids are carbon- and nitrogen-containing compounds that are found in some families of plants. They have both poisonous and medicinal properties.)

Nicotine's effects on the body are complex. The drug affects the brain and central nervous system as well as the hypothalamus and pituitary glands of the endocrine (hormone) system. Nicotine easily crosses the blood-brain barrier (a series of capillaries and cells that controls the flow of substances from the blood to the brain), and it accumulates in the brain—faster than caffeine or heroin, but slower than diazepam (a sedative medicine used to treat anxiety). In the brain nicotine imitates the actions of the hormone epinephrine (adrenaline) and the neurotransmitter acetylcholine, both of which heighten awareness. Nicotine also triggers the release of dopamine, which enhances feelings of pleasure, and endorphins, which have a calming effect.

As noted earlier, nicotine acts as both a stimulant and a depressant. By stimulating certain nerve cells in the spinal cord, nicotine relaxes the nerves and slows some reactions, such as the knee-jerk reflex. Small amounts of nicotine stimulate some nerve cells, but these cells are depressed by large amounts of nicotine. In addition, nicotine stimulates the brain cortex (the outer layer of the brain) and affects the functions of the heart and lungs.

TRENDS IN TOBACCO USE
Cigarettes

CONSUMPTION DATA. According to the Centers for Disease Control and Prevention (CDC), in "The National Tobacco Control Program" (*Chronic Disease Notes and Reports*, vol. 14, no. 3, Fall 2001), the consumption of cigarettes, the most widely used tobacco product, has decreased over the past generation among adults. After increasing rather consistently for 60 years, the per capita (per person) consumption of cigarettes peaked in the 1960s at well over 4,000 cigarettes per year. The steady decline in smoking came shortly after 1964, when the *Smoking and Health: Report of the Advisory Committee to the Surgeon General of the Public Health Service* (1964, http://profiles.nlm.nih.gov/NN/B/B/M/Q/_/nnbbmq.pdf) concluded that cigarette smoking is a cause of lung and laryngeal cancer in men, a probable cause of lung cancer in women, and the most important cause of chronic bronchitis in both genders.

By 2006 the annual per capita consumption of cigarettes for those aged 18 and older was 1,691. (See Table 3.1.) These data are taken from *Tobacco Outlook* (September 26, 2006, http://usda.mannlib.cornell.edu/usda/ers/TBS//2000s/2006

FIGURE 3.1

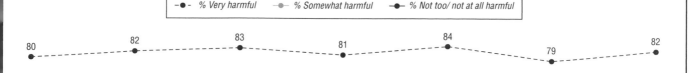

Public opinion on the harmfulness of smoking, 2003–08

IN GENERAL, HOW HARMFUL DO YOU FEEL SMOKING IS TO ADULTS WHO SMOKE?

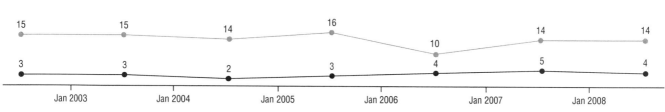

-●- % Very harmful   -●- % Somewhat harmful   -●- % Not too/ not at all harmful

SOURCE: Lymari Morales, "In General, How Harmful Do You Feel Smoking Is to Adults Who Smoke?" in *Most Americans Consider Smoking Very Harmful*, The Gallup Organization, July 28, 2008, http://www.gallup.com/poll/109129/Most-Americans-Consider-Smoking-Very-Harmful.aspx? version=print (accessed August 25, 2008). Copyright © 2008 by The Gallup Organization. Reproduced by permission of The Gallup Organization.

TABLE 3.1

Per capita consumption of tobacco products, 1996–2006

	Per capita 16 years and over	Per capita 18 years and over			Per male 18 years and over		
		Cigarettes[a]	Snuff[b]	All tobacco products	Large cigars & cigarillos	Smoking tobacco[b]	Chewing tobacco[b]
Year	Number	Number	Pounds		Number	Pounds	
1996	2,355	2,445	4.1	0.31	4.83	31.9	0.52	0.12	0.63
1997	2,290	2,422	4.1	0.31	4.85	37.3	0.61	0.11	0.60
1998	2,190	2,275	3.6	0.31	4.32	37.1	0.61	0.12	0.53
1999	2,022	2,101	3.5	0.32	4.23	38.5	0.63	0.13	0.51
2000	1,974	2,049	3.4	0.33	4.10	38.0	0.62	0.13	0.48
2001	1,976	2,051	3.5	0.34	4.30	41.2	0.68	0.15	0.47
2002	1,909	1,982	3.4	0.34	4.16	41.8	0.68	0.16	0.43
2003	1,820	1,890	3.2	0.35	3.97	44.5	0.73	0.16	0.40
2004	1,747	1,814	3.1	0.36	3.87	47.9	0.79	0.15	0.37
2005	1,675	1,716	2.9	0.36	3.69	46.9	0.77	0.16	0.36
2006[c]	1,650	1,691	2.9	0.38	3.69	47.8	0.78	0.15	0.37

[a]Unstemmed processing weight.
[b]Finished product weight.
[c]Preliminary.

SOURCE: Tom Capehart, "Table 2. Per Capita Consumption of Tobacco Products in the United States (including Overseas Forces), 1996–2006," in *Tobacco Outlook*, U.S. Department of Agriculture, Economic Research Service, September 26, 2006, http://usda.mannlib.cornell.edu/usda/ers/TBS//2000s/2006/TBS-09-26-2006.pdf (accessed December 17, 2008)

TBS-09-26-2006.pdf) by Tom Capehart of the Economic Research Service (ERS). This was the final report provided by the ERS on this topic because the ERS discontinued this publication along with another tobacco-related publication, the *Tobacco Briefing Room*, after a tobacco buyout was formalized by the U.S. Department of Agriculture (USDA)

TABLE 3.2

Percentage of lifetime, past-year, and past-month cigarette users, by age group, gender, and ethnicity, 2006 and 2007

| | Time period | | | | | |
| | Lifetime | | Past year | | Past month | |
Demographic characteristic	2006	2007	2006	2007	2006	2007
Total	66.3	65.3	29.1	28.5	25.0	24.2
Age						
12–17	25.8	23.7	17.0	15.7	10.4	9.8
18–25	66.6	64.7	47.0	45.1	38.4	36.2
26 or older	71.7	70.9	27.7	27.3	24.7	24.1
Gender						
Male	71.0	70.4	32.5	31.8	27.8	27.1
Female	61.7	60.5	26.0	25.3	22.4	21.5
Hispanic origin and race						
Not Hispanic or Latino	68.2	67.5	29.4	29.0	25.4	24.8
White	72.1	71.8	30.2	29.9	26.1	25.6
Black or African American	54.6	53.3	27.5	26.9	24.4	23.2
American Indian or Alaska Native	73.2	72.2	44.5	41.4	38.1	34.4
Native Hawaiian or other Pacific Islander	*	*	*	*	*	
Asian	42.7	38.6	18.0	17.5	14.6	14.2
Two or more races	67.7	65.6	33.8	33.4	30.5	29.9
Hispanic or Latino	53.8	51.2	27.4	25.4	22.4	20.5

*Low precision; no estimate reported.

SOURCE: "Table 2.22B. Cigarette Use in Lifetime, Past Year, and Past Month among Persons Aged 12 or Older, by Demographic Characteristics: Percentages, 2006 and 2007," in *2007 National Survey on Drug Use and Health: Detailed Tables*, U.S. Department of Health and Human Services, Substance Abuse and Mental Health Services Administration, Office of Applied Studies, September 2008, http://oas.samhsa.gov/NSDUH/2k7NSDUH/tabs/Sect2peTabs1to42 .htm#Tab2.42B (accessed December 8, 2008)

in February 2005. The tobacco buyout is a part of the Fair and Equitable Tobacco Reform Act of 2004 and is formally known as the Tobacco Transition Payment Program. (See Chapter 7.) Several USDA agencies discontinued their tobacco programs after the buyout.

Each year the Substance Abuse and Mental Health Services Administration surveys U.S. households on drug use for the National Survey on Drug Use and Health (NSDUH). According to the NSDUH, in *Results from the 2007 National Survey on Drug Use and Health: National Findings* (September 2008, http://www.oas.samhsa.gov/nsduh/2k7nsduh/ 2k7Results.pdf), 65.3% of the U.S. population in 2007 had smoked cigarettes at some point in their life and 24.2% were current smokers (meaning they had smoked within the month before the survey). (See Table 3.2.)

In 2007 men (27.1%) were more likely than women (21.5%) to be current smokers. (See Table 3.2.) Additionally, whites (25.6%) were more likely to be current smokers than African-Americans (23.2%), Hispanics (20.5%), or Asian-Americans (14.2%). Those aged 18 to 25 had the highest rate of current smoking at 36.2%, compared with 9.8% for 12- to 17-year-olds and 24.1% for those aged 26 and older. Rates of cigarette smoking declined from 2006 to 2007.

The National Health Interview Survey (NHIS), which is conducted annually by the National Center for Health Statistics, reports findings similar to those of the NSDUH. In *Early Release of Selected Estimates Based on Data from the 2007 National Health Interview Survey* (June 25, 2008, http://www.cdc.gov/nchs/data/nhis/earlyrelease/200806_08 .pdf), the NHIS indicates that 19.7% of adults in the United States were current smokers in 2007, down from 24.7% in 1997. (See Figure 3.2.) Like the NSDUH, the NHIS finds that men are more likely than women to smoke. Just over 22% of adult men and 17% of adult women were current smokers. (See Figure 3.3.) Women were more likely than men to have never smoked.

Even though the NHIS uses different age groups than the NHSDA, the results of both surveys show that younger people smoked at a higher rate than older people in 2007. Figure 3.4 shows that those aged 18 to 44 were slightly more likely to smoke than those aged 45 to 64. The rate of smoking in the 65 and older age group was dramatically lower than in either of the two younger groups. Men in all age categories were more likely than women in the same age group to smoke.

Furthermore, the NHIS finds that the prevalence of current smoking among various races and ethnicities was highest for non-Hispanic whites (22%) in 2007. (See Figure 3.5.) Non-Hispanic African-Americans (19%) were less likely to smoke than whites, whereas Hispanics (13%) were the least likely to smoke among the three groups.

Cigars, Pipes, and Other Forms of Tobacco

According to the NSDUH, 3.2% of those aged 12 and older were current users of smokeless tobacco (chewing

FIGURE 3.2

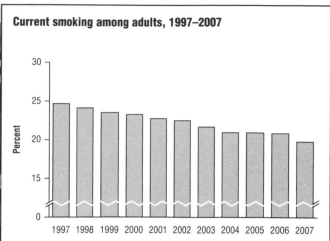

Current smoking among adults, 1997–2007

Notes: Current smokers were defined as those who smoked more than 100 cigarettes in their lifetime and now smoke every day or some days. The analyses excluded persons with unknown smoking status (about 2% of respondents each year). Beginning with the 2003 data, the National Health Interview Survey (NHIS) transitioned to weights derived from the 2000 census. In this early release, estimates for 2000–2002 were recalculated using weights derived from the 2000 census.

SOURCE: "Figure 8.1. Prevalence of Current Smoking among Adults Aged 18 Years and over: United States, 1997–2007," in *Early Release of Selected Estimates Based on Data from the 2007 National Health Interview Survey*, U.S. Department of Health and Human Services, Centers for Disease Control and Prevention, National Center for Health Statistics, June 25, 2008, http://www.cdc.gov/nchs/data/nhis/earlyrelease/200806_08.pdf (accessed August 18, 2008)

FIGURE 3.4

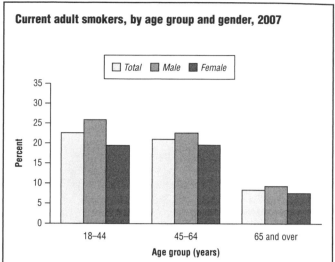

Current adult smokers, by age group and gender, 2007

Notes: Current smokers were defined as those who smoked more than 100 cigarettes in their lifetime and now smoke every day or some days. The analyses excluded 393 persons (1.7%) with unknown smoking status.

SOURCE: "Figure 8.3. Prevalence of Current Smoking among Adults Aged 18 Years and over, by Age Group and Sex: United States, 2007," in *Early Release of Selected Estimates Based on Data from the 2007 National Health Interview Survey*, U.S. Department of Health and Human Services, Centers for Disease Control and Prevention, National Center for Health Statistics, June 25, 2008, http://www.cdc.gov/nchs/data/nhis/earlyrelease/200806_08.pdf (accessed August 18, 2008)

FIGURE 3.3

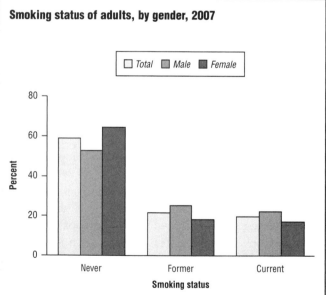

Smoking status of adults, by gender, 2007

Notes: Current smokers were defined as those who smoked more than 100 cigarettes in their lifetime and now smoke every day or some days. The analyses excluded 393 persons (1.7%) with unknown smoking status.

SOURCE: "Figure 8.2. Percent Distribution of Smoking Status among Adults Aged 18 Years and over, by Sex: United States, 2007," in *Early Release of Selected Estimates Based on Data from the 2007 National Health Interview Survey*, U.S. Department of Health and Human Services, Centers for Disease Control and Prevention, National Center for Health Statistics, June 25, 2008, http://www.cdc.gov/nchs/data/nhis/earlyrelease/200806_08.pdf (accessed August 18, 2008)

FIGURE 3.5

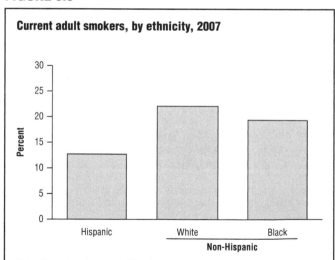

Current adult smokers, by ethnicity, 2007

Notes: Current smokers were defined as those who smoked more than 100 cigarettes in their lifetime and now smoke every day or some days. The analyses excluded 393 persons (1.7%) with unknown smoking status. Estimates are age-sex adjusted using the projected 2000 U.S. population as the standard population and using five age groups: 18–24 years, 25–34 years, 35–44 years, 45–64 years, and 65 years and over.

SOURCE: "Figure 8.4. Age-Sex-Adjusted Prevalence of Current Smoking among Adults Aged 18 Years and over, by Race/Ethnicity: United States, 2007," in *Early Release of Selected Estimates Based on Data from the 2007 National Health Interview Survey*, U.S. Department of Health and Human Services, Centers for Disease Control and Prevention, National Center for Health Statistics, June 25, 2008, http://www.cdc.gov/nchs/data/nhis/earlyrelease/200806_08.pdf (accessed August 18, 2008)

FIGURE 3.6

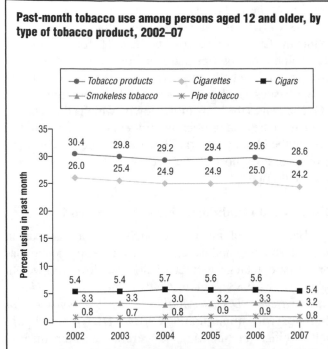

Past-month tobacco use among persons aged 12 and older, by type of tobacco product, 2002–07

SOURCE: "Figure 4.1. Past Month Tobacco Use among Persons Aged 12 or Older: 2002–2007," in *Results from the 2007 National Survey on Drug Use and Health: National Findings*, U.S. Department of Health and Human Services, Substance Abuse and Mental Health Services Administration, Office of Applied Studies, 2008, http://www.oas.samhsa.gov/nsduh/2k7nsduh/2k7Results.pdf (accessed December 8, 2008)

tobacco and/or snuff) and 5.4% were current users of cigars in 2007. (See Figure 3.6.) Only 0.8% smoked pipes. These percentages remained relatively constant from 2002 to 2007.

In 2006 the per capita consumption of large cigars and small, narrow cigars called cigarillos by males aged 18 and older was 47.8. (See Table 3.1.) This figure is much higher than in 1996, when the per capita consumption of cigars and cigarillos among this group was 31.9. The use of snuff has increased as well, although not as much as cigars. The per capita consumption of snuff rose from 0.31 of a pound (0.14 kg) in 1996 to 0.38 of a pound (0.17 kg) in 2006. Snuff is powdered tobacco that is inhaled through the nose.

ADDICTIVE NATURE OF NICOTINE

Is tobacco addictive? In *The Health Consequences of Smoking—Nicotine Addiction: A Report of the Surgeon General* (1988, http://profiles.nlm.nih.gov/NN/B/B/Z/D/_/nnbbzd.pdf), researchers examine this question. They determine that the pharmacological (chemical and physical) effects and behavioral processes that contribute to tobacco addiction are similar to those that contribute in the addiction to drugs such as heroin and cocaine. Many researchers consider nicotine to be as potentially addictive as cocaine and heroin and note that it can create dependence quickly in some users. After more than 20 years since the surgeon general's

report—with study after study confirming the addictive nature of nicotine while also zeroing in on characteristics that increase the likelihood for addiction, such as genetics, ethnicity, and even tobacco additives like menthol—the National Institute on Drug Abuse states conclusively (April 17, 2009, http://www.drugabuse.gov/drugpages/nicotine.html) that nicotine is not only "highly addictive" but also "one of the most heavily used addictive drugs" in the United States.

Cigarette smoking results in the rapid distribution of nicotine throughout the body, reaching the brain within 10 seconds of inhalation. However, the intense effects of nicotine disappear in a few minutes, causing smokers to continue smoking frequently throughout the day to maintain its pleasurable effects and to prevent withdrawal. Tolerance develops after repeated exposure to nicotine, and higher doses are required to produce the same initial stimulation. Because nicotine is metabolized fairly quickly, disappearing from the body in a few hours, some tolerance is lost overnight. Smokers often report that the first cigarette of the day is the most satisfying. The more cigarettes smoked during the day, the more tolerance develops, and the less effect subsequent cigarettes have.

Is There a Genetic Basis for Nicotine Addiction?

Smoking is influenced by both environment and genetics, as are all addictions. (See Chapter 1.) The results of many scientific studies, such as those detailed in Viba Malaiyandi, Edward M. Sellers, and Rachel F. Tyndale's "Implications of CYP2A6 Genetic Variation for Smoking Behaviors and Nicotine Dependence" (*Clinical Pharmacology and Therapeutics*, vol. 77, no. 3, March 2005), show that about 60% of the initiation of nicotine dependence and about 70% of the maintenance of dependent smoking behavior is genetically influenced.

In "Co-occurring Risk Factors for Alcohol Dependence and Habitual Smoking" (*Alcohol Research and Health*, vol. 24, no. 4, 2000), Laura Jean Bierut et al. report on the results of the Collaborative Study on the Genetics of Alcoholism. The researchers note the hypothesis that some common genetic factors are involved in the susceptibility for developing both alcohol and nicotine addiction. Moreover, studies of twins support the role of common genetic factors in the development of both disorders. More recent results of the Collaborative Study are reported by Richard A. Grucza and Laura J. Bierut of the Washington University School of Medicine in St. Louis, Missouri, in "Co-occurring Risk Factors for Alcohol Dependence and Habitual Smoking Update on Findings from the Collaborative Study on the Genetics of Alcoholism" (*Alcohol Research and Health*, vol. 29, no. 3, 2006). The researchers reveal that alcohol and nicotine dependence are not only linked by many common genes but are also individually influenced by drug-specific genes. In "The Genetics of Alcohol and Other Drug Dependence" (*Alcohol Research and Health*, vol. 31, no. 2,

2008), Danielle M. Dick and Arpana Agrawal state that genes involved in alcohol, nicotine, and other drug dependence have been found to regulate the metabolism of alcohol, the transmission of signals among nerve cells, and the gradations of nerve cell activity.

Nicotine May Not Be the Only Substance in Cigarettes Linked to Addiction

Research results suggest that nicotine may not be the only ingredient in tobacco involved with addiction. Various compounds called monoamine oxidase (MAO) inhibitors are found in high concentrations in cigarette smoke. MAO is an enzyme responsible for breaking down the brain chemical dopamine. The decrease in MAO results in higher dopamine levels and may be another reason that smokers continue to smoke—to sustain the high dopamine levels that result in pleasurable effects and the desire for repeated cigarette use.

One issue that complicates any efforts by a longtime smoker to quit is nicotine withdrawal, which is often referred to as craving. This urge for nicotine is not well understood by researchers. Withdrawal may begin within a few hours after the last cigarette. According to the National Institute on Drug Abuse, high levels of craving may persist six months or longer. Besides craving, withdrawal can include irritability, attention deficits, interruption of thought processes, sleep disturbances, and increased appetite.

Some researchers also point out the behavioral aspects involved in smoking. The purchasing, handling, and lighting of cigarettes may be just as pleasing psychologically to the user as the chemical properties of tobacco itself.

HEALTH CONSEQUENCES OF TOBACCO USE

Respiratory System Effects

Cigarette smoke contains almost 4,000 different chemical compounds, many of which are toxic, mutagenic (capable of increasing the frequency of mutation, or change, in the genetic material), and carcinogenic (cancer causing). At least 43 carcinogens have been identified in tobacco smoke. Besides nicotine, the most damaging substances are tar and carbon monoxide (CO). Smoke also contains hydrogen cyanide and other chemicals that can damage the respiratory system. These substances and nicotine are absorbed into the body through the linings of the mouth, nose, throat, and lungs. About 10 seconds later they are delivered by the bloodstream to the brain.

Tar, which adds to the flavor of cigarettes, is released by the burning of tobacco. As it is inhaled, it enters the alveoli (air cells) of the lungs. There, the tar hampers the action of cilia (small, hairlike extensions of cells that clean foreign substances from the lungs), allowing the substances in cigarette smoke to accumulate.

CO affects the blood's ability to distribute oxygen throughout the body. CO is chemically similar to carbon dioxide (CO_2), which bonds with the hemoglobin in blood so that the CO_2 can be carried to the lungs for elimination. Hemoglobin has two primary functions: to carry oxygen to all parts of the body and to remove excess CO_2 from the body's tissues. CO bonds to hemoglobin more tightly than CO_2 and leaves the body more slowly, which allows CO to build up in the hemoglobin, in turn reducing the amount of oxygen the blood can carry. The lack of adequate oxygen is damaging to most of the body's organs, including the heart and brain.

Diseases and Conditions Linked to Tobacco Use

The results of medical research show an association between smoking and cancer, as well as heart and circulatory disease, fetal growth retardation, and low birth weight babies. The 1983 *Health Consequences of Smoking—Cardiovascular Disease: Report of the Surgeon General* (http://profiles.nlm.nih.gov/NN/B/B/T/D/_/nnbbtd.pdf) linked cigarette smoking to cerebrovascular disease (strokes) and associated it with cancer of the uterine cervix. Two 1992 studies showed that people who smoke double their risk of forming cataracts, the leading cause of blindness. Recent research links smoking to unsuccessful pregnancies, increased infant mortality, and peptic ulcer disease. In 2004 the U.S. surgeon general Richard Carmona (1949–) released *The Health Consequences of Smoking: A Report of the Surgeon General* (http://www.cdc.gov/Tobacco/sgr/sgr_2004/index .htm), which revealed for the first time that cigarette smoking causes diseases in nearly every organ of the body. Table 3.3 lists diseases—including cancers—and other adverse health effects for which cigarette smoking is identified as a cause.

The National Cancer Institute notes in "Questions and Answers about Cigar Smoking and Cancer" (March 7, 2000, http://www.cancer.gov/cancertopics/factsheet/Tobacco/cigars) that cigar smoking is associated with cancers of the lip, tongue, mouth, throat, larynx (voice box), lungs, and esophagus (food tube). Those who smoke cigars daily and inhale the smoke have an increased risk for developing heart and lung disease.

Smokeless tobacco, which includes chewing tobacco and snuff, also creates health hazards for its users. The 1979 *Smoking and Health: A Report of the Surgeon General* (http://profiles.nlm.nih.gov/NN/B/C/M/D/_/nnbcmd.pdf) noted that smokeless tobacco was associated with oral cancers; and the 1986 *Health Consequences of Involuntary Smoking: A Report of the Surgeon General* (http://profiles .nlm.nih.gov/NN/B/C/P/M/_/nnbcpm.pdf) concluded that it was a cause of cancers of the lip, gum, and mouth and not a safer alternative to smoking. The nicotine in smokeless tobacco is absorbed into the bloodstream through the lining of the mouth and, along with causing oral cancers,

TABLE 3.3

Diseases and other adverse health effects caused by cigarette smoking, 2004

Disease	Highest level conclusion from previous Surgeon General's reports (year)	Conclusion from the 2004 Surgeon General's report
Cancer		
Bladder cancer	"Smoking is a cause of bladder cancer; cessation reduces risk by about 50 percent after only a few years, in comparison with continued smoking." (1990)	"The evidence is sufficient to infer a causal relationship between smoking and . . . bladder cancer."
Cervical cancer	"Smoking has been consistently associated with an increased risk for cervical cancer." (2001)	"The evidence is sufficient to infer a causal relationship between smoking and cervical cancer."
Esophageal cancer	"Cigarette smoking is a major cause of esophageal cancer in the United States." (1982)	"The evidence is sufficient to infer a causal relationship between smoking and cancers of the esophagus."
Kidney cancer	"Cigarette smoking is a contributory factor in the development of kidney cancer in the United States. The term 'contributory factor' by no means excludes the possibility of a causal role for smoking in cancers of this site." (1982)	"The evidence is sufficient to infer a causal relationship between smoking and renal cell, [and] renal pelvis . . . cancers."
Laryngeal cancer	"Cigarette smoking is causally associated with cancer of the lung, larynx, oral cavity, and esophagus in women as well as in men. . . ." (1980)	"The evidence is sufficient to infer a causal relationship between smoking and cancer of the larynx."
Leukemia	"Leukemia has recently been implicated as a smoking-related disease . . . but this observation has not been consistent." (1990)	"The evidence is sufficient to infer a causal relationship between smoking and acute myeloid leukemia."
Lung cancer	"Additional epidemiological, pathological, and experimental data not only confirm the conclusion of the Surgeon General's 1964 report regarding lung cancer in men but strengthen the causal relationship of smoking to lung cancer in women." (1967)	"The evidence is sufficient to infer a causal relationship between smoking and lung cancer."
Oral cancer	"Cigarette smoking is a major cause of cancers of the oral cavity in the United States." (1982)	"The evidence is sufficient to infer a causal relationship between smoking and cancers of the oral cavity and pharynx."
Pancreatic cancer	"Smoking cessation reduces the risk of pancreatic cancer, compared with continued smoking, although this reduction in risk may only be measurable after 10 years of abstinence." (1990)	"The evidence is sufficient to infer a causal relationship between smoking and pancreatic cancer."
Stomach cancer	"Data on smoking and cancer of the stomach . . . are unclear." (2001)	"The evidence is sufficient to infer a causal relationship between smoking and gastric cancers."
Cardiovascular diseases		
Abdominal aortic aneurysm	"Death from rupture of an atherosclerotic abdominal aneurysm is more common in cigarette smokers than in nonsmokers." (1983)	"The evidence is sufficient to infer a causal relationship between smoking and abdominal aortic aneurysm."
Atherosclerosis	"Cigarette smoking is the most powerful risk factor predisposing to atherosclerotic peripheral vascular disease." (1983)	"The evidence is sufficient to infer a causal relationship between smoking and subclinical atherosclerosis."
Cerebrovascular disease	"Cigarette smoking is a major cause of cerebrovascular disease (stroke), the third leading cause of death in the United States." (1989)	"The evidence is sufficient to infer a causal relationship between smoking and stroke."
Coronary heart disease	"In summary, for the purposes of preventive medicine, it can be concluded that smoking is causally related to coronary heart disease for both men and women in the United States." (1979)	"The evidence is sufficient to infer a causal relationship between smoking and coronary heart disease."
Respiratory diseases		
Chronic obstructive pulmonary disease	"Cigarette smoking is the most important of the causes of chronic bronchitis in the United states, and increases the risk of dying from chronic bronchitis." (1964)	"The evidence is sufficient to infer a causal relationship between active smoking and chronic obstructive pulmonary disease morbidity and mortality."
Pneumonia	"Smoking cessation reduces rates of respiratory symptoms such as cough, sputum production, and wheezing, and respiratory infections such as bronchitis and pneumonia, compared with continued smoking." (1990)	"The evidence is sufficient to infer a causal relationship between smoking and acute respiratory illnesses, including pneumonia, in persons without underlying smoking-related chronic obstructive lung disease."
Respiratory effects in utero	"In utero exposure to maternal smoking is associated with reduced lung function among infants. . . ." (2001)	"The evidence is sufficient to infer a causal relationship between maternal smoking during pregnancy and a reduction of lung function in infants."
Respiratory effects in childhood and adolescence	"Cigarette smoking during childhood and adolescence produces significant health problems among young people, including cough and phlegm production, an increased number and severity of respiratory illnesses, decreased physical fitness, an unfavorable lipid profile, and potential retardation in the rate of lung growth and the level of maximum lung function." (1994)	"The evidence is sufficient to infer a causal relationship between active smoking and impaired lung growth during childhood and adolescence." "The evidence is sufficient to infer a causal relationship between active smoking and the early onset of lung function decline during late adolescence and early adulthood." "The evidence is sufficient to infer a causal relationship between active smoking and respiratory symptoms in children and adolescents, including coughing, phlegm, wheezing, and dyspnea." "The evidence is sufficient to infer a causal relationship between active smoking and asthma-related symptoms (i.e., wheezing) in childhood and adolescence."
Respiratory effects in adulthood	"Cigarette smoking accelerates the age-related decline in lung function that occurs among never smokers. With sustained abstinence from smoking, the rate of decline in pulmonary function among former smokers returns to that of never smokers." (1990)	"The evidence is sufficient to infer a causal relationship between active smoking in adulthood and a premature onset of and an accelerated age-related decline in lung function." "The evidence is sufficient to infer a causal relationship between active sustained cessation from smoking and a return of the rate of decline in pulmonary function to that of persons who had never smoked."
Other respiratory effects	"Smoking cessation reduces rates of respiratory symptoms such as cough, sputum production, and wheezing, and respiratory infections such as bronchitis and pneumonia, compared with continued smoking." (1990)	"The evidence is sufficient to infer a causal relationship between active smoking and all major respiratory symptoms among adults, including coughing, phlegm, wheezing, and dyspnea." "The evidence is sufficient to infer a causal relationship between active smoking and poor asthma control."

TABLE 3.3

Diseases and other adverse health effects caused by cigarette smoking, 2004 [CONTINUED]

Disease	Highest level conclusion from previous Surgeon General's reports (year)	Conclusion from the 2004 Surgeon General's report
Reproductive effects		
Fetal death and stillbirths	"The risk for perinatal mortality—both stillbirth and neonatal deaths—and the risk for sudden infant death syndrome (SIDS) are increased among the offspring of women who smoke during pregnancy." (2001)	"The evidence is sufficient to infer a causal relationship between sudden infant death syndrome and maternal smoking during and after pregnancy."
Fertility	"Women who smoke have increased risks for conception delay and for both primary and secondary infertility." (2001)	"The evidence is sufficient to infer a causal relationship between smoking and reduced fertility in women."
Low birth weight	"Infants born to women who smoke during pregnancy have a lower average birth weight . . . than . . . infants born to women who do not smoke." (2001)	"The evidence is sufficient to infer a causal relationship between maternal active smoking and fetal growth restriction and low birth weight."
Pregnancy complications	"Smoking during pregnancy is associated with increased risks for preterm premature rupture of membranes, abruptio placentae, and placenta previa, and with a modest increase in risk for preterm delivery." (2001)	"The evidence is sufficient to infer a casual relationship between maternal active smoking and premature rupture of the membranes, placenta previa, and placental abruption." "The evidence is sufficient to infer a causal relationship between maternal active smoking and preterm delivery and shortened gestation."
Other effects		
Cataract	"Women who smoke have an increased risk for cataract." (2001)	"The evidence is sufficient to infer a causal relationship between smoking and nuclear cataract."
Diminished health status/morbidity	"Relationships between smoking and cough or phlegm are strong and consistent; they have been amply documented and are judged to be causal. . . ." (1984)	"The evidence is sufficient to infer a causal relationship between smoking and diminished health status that may be manifest as increased absenteeism from work and increased use of medical care services."
	"Consideration of evidence from many different studies has led to the conclusion that cigarette smoking is the overwhelmingly most important cause of cough, sputum, chronic bronchitis, and mucus hypersecretion." (1984)	"The evidence is sufficient to infer a causal relationship between smoking and increased risks for adverse surgical outcomes related to wound healing and respiratory complications."
Hip fractures	"Women who currently smoke have an increased risk for hip fracture compared with women who do not smoke." (2001)	"The evidence is sufficient to infer a causal relationship between smoking and hip fractures."
Low bone density	"Postmenopausal women who currently smoke have lower bone density than do women who do not smoke." (2001)	"In postmenopausal women, the evidence is sufficient to infer a causal relationship between smoking and low bone density."
Peptic ulcer disease	"The relationship between cigarette smoking and death rates from peptic ulcer, especially gastric ulcer, is confirmed. In addition, morbidity data suggest a similar relationship exists with the prevalence of reported disease from this cause." (1967)	"The evidence is sufficient to infer a causal relationship between smoking and peptic ulcer disease in persons who are helicobacter pylori positive."

SOURCE: "Table 1.1. Diseases and Other Adverse Health Effects for Which Smoking Is Identified As a Cause in the Current Surgeon General's Report," in *The Health Consequences of Smoking: A Report of the Surgeon General*, U.S. Department of Health and Human Services, Centers for Disease Control and Prevention, National Center for Chronic Disease Prevention and Health Promotion, Office on Smoking and Health, 2004, http://www.cdc.gov/tobacco/data_statistics/sgr/sgr_2004/chapters.htm (accessed August 19, 2008)

has been linked to periodontal (gum) disease. In addition, smokeless tobacco use can lead to nicotine addiction and may, therefore, lead to smoking.

Premature Aging

Smoking cigarettes contributes to premature aging in a variety of ways. The results of research conducted over nearly four decades, such as Akimichi Morita's "Tobacco Smoke Causes Premature Skin Aging" (*Journal of Dermatological Science*, vol. 48, no. 3, 2007), show that smoking enhances facial aging and skin wrinkling. Additionally, smoking has been associated with a decline in overall fitness in women.

Interactions with Other Drugs

Smoking can have adverse effects when combined with over-the-counter (without a prescription) and prescription medications that a smoker may be taking. In many cases tobacco smoking reduces the effectiveness of medications, such as pain relievers (acetaminophen), antidepressants, such as pain relievers (acetaminophen), antidepressants, tranquilizers, sedatives, ulcer medications, and insulin. With estrogen and oral contraceptives, tobacco smoking may increase the risk of heart and blood vessel disease and can cause strokes and blood clots.

SMOKING AND PUBLIC HEALTH

A study in the 1920s found that men who smoked two or more packs of cigarettes per day were 22 times more likely than nonsmokers to die of lung cancer. At the time, these results surprised researchers and medical authorities alike. Some 40 years ago, the U.S. government first officially recognized the negative health consequences of smoking. In 1964 the Advisory Committee to the Surgeon General released a groundbreaking survey of studies on tobacco use. In *Smoking and Health: Report of the Advisory Committee to the Surgeon General of the Public Health Service*, the U.S. surgeon general Luther L. Terry (1911–1985) reported that cigarette smoking increased overall mortality in men and caused lung and laryngeal cancer, as well as chronic bronchitis. The report concluded, "Cigarette smoking is a health hazard of sufficient importance in the United States to warrant appropriate remedial action," but what action should be taken was left unspecified at that time.

TABLE 3.4

Surgeon General's reports on smoking and health, 1964–2008

1964	Smoking and Health: Report of the Advisory Committee to the Surgeon General of the Public Health Service
1967	The Health Consequences of Smoking: A Public Health Service Review
1968	The Health Consequences of Smoking: 1968 Supplement to the 1967 Public Health Service Review
1969	The Health Consequences of Smoking: 1969 Supplement to the 1967 Public Health Service Review
1971	The Health Consequences of Smoking
1972	The Health Consequences of Smoking
1973	The Health Consequences of Smoking
1974	The Health Consequences of Smoking
1975	The Health Consequences of Smoking
1976	The Health Consequences of Smoking: A Reference Edition
1979	The Health Consequences of Smoking, 1977–1978
1979	Smoking and Health
1980	The Health Consequences of Smoking for Women
1981	The Health Consequences of Smoking: The Changing Cigarette
1982	The Health Consequences of Smoking: Cancer
1983	The Health Consequences of Smoking: Cardiovascular Disease
1984	The Health Consequences of Smoking: Chronic Obstructive Lung Disease
1985	The Health Consequences of Smoking: Cancer and Chronic Lung Disease in the Workplace
1986	The Health Consequences of Involuntary Smoking
1988	The Health Consequences of Smoking: Nicotine Addiction
1989	Reducing the Health Consequences of Smoking: 25 Years of Progress
1990	Smoking and Health: A National Status Report
1990	The Health Benefits of Smoking Cessation
1992	Smoking and Health in the Americas
1994	SGR 4 KIDS: The Surgeon General's Report for Kids About Smoking
1995	Preventing Tobacco Use among Young People
1998	Tobacco Use among U.S. Racial/Ethnic Minority Groups
2000	Reducing Tobacco Use
2001	Women and Smoking
2004	The Health Consequences of Smoking
2006	The Health Consequences of Involuntary Exposure to Tobacco Smoke
2007	Children and Secondhand Smoke Exposure: Excerpts from the Health Consequences of Involuntary Exposure to Tobacco Smoke

SOURCE: Created by Sandra Alters for Gale, 2009

Later surgeons general issued additional reports on the health effects of smoking and the dangers to nonsmokers of secondhand smoke. Besides general health concerns, the reports have addressed specific health consequences and populations. Table 3.4 shows a listing of reports of the surgeons general and the years in which they were published. The later reports concluded that smoking increases the morbidity (proportion of diseased people in a particular population) and mortality (proportion of deaths in a particular population) of both men and women.

In 1965 Congress passed the Federal Cigarette Labeling and Advertising Act, which required the following health warning on all cigarette packages: "Caution: Cigarette smoking may be hazardous to your health." The Public Health Cigarette Smoking Act of 1969 strengthened the warning to read: "Warning: The Surgeon General has determined that cigarette smoking is dangerous to your health." Still later acts resulted in four different health warnings to be used in rotation.

In "Ten Great Public Health Achievements—United States, 1900–1999" (*Morbidity and Mortality Weekly Report*, vol. 48, no. 12, April 2, 1999), the CDC includes "recognition of tobacco use as a health hazard" as one of the country's 10 greatest public health achievements of the 20th century, along with vaccination, motor-vehicle safety, safer workplaces, control of infectious diseases, decline in deaths from coronary heart disease and stroke, safer and healthier foods, healthier mothers and babies, family planning, and fluoridation of drinking water. These 10 accomplishments were chosen based on their contributions to prevention and their impact on illness, disability, and death in the United States.

DEATHS ATTRIBUTED TO TOBACCO USE

According to the 2004 *Health Consequences of Smoking*, cigarette smoking is the leading cause of preventable death in the United States and produces substantial health-related economic costs to society. The report notes that smoking caused an estimated 440,100 deaths in the United States each year from 1995 to 1999. Nationwide, smoking kills more people each year than alcohol, drug abuse, car crashes, murders, suicides, fires, and acquired immune deficiency syndrome (AIDS) combined.

From 2001 through 2006 diseases linked to smoking accounted for four of the top five leading causes of death in the United States. (See Figure 3.7.) The death rates for heart disease, cancer, and cerebrovascular disease declined from 2001 to 2006, whereas the rates for chronic lower respiratory diseases, such as emphysema and chronic bronchitis, stayed about the same. Heart disease death rates declined from 248 deaths per 100,000 people in 2001 to 199 per 100,000 in 2006, a drop of 19.5%. Cancer death rates declined from 196 to 181 deaths per 100,000 during this same period, a drop of 7.8%.

In *Cancer Facts and Figures, 2008* (2008, http://www.cancer.org/downloads/STT/2008CAFFfinalsecured.pdf) the American Cancer Society estimates that 161,840 Americans died of lung and bronchus cancer in 2008. Even though not all lung and bronchus cancer deaths are directly attributable to smoking, a large proportion of them are. Lung cancer is the leading cause of cancer mortality in both men and women in the United States. It has been the leading cause of cancer deaths among men since the early 1950s and, in 1987, it surpassed breast cancer to become the leading cause of cancer deaths in women.

SECONDHAND SMOKE

Secondhand smoke, also known as environmental tobacco smoke or passive smoke, is a health hazard for nonsmokers who live or work with smokers. The National Cancer Institute (2008, http://www.cancer.gov/Templates/db_alpha.aspx?CdrID=46431) defines secondhand smoke as "smoke that comes from the burning of a tobacco product and smoke that is exhaled by smokers. Inhaling environmental tobacco smoke is called involuntary or passive smoking."

FIGURE 3.7

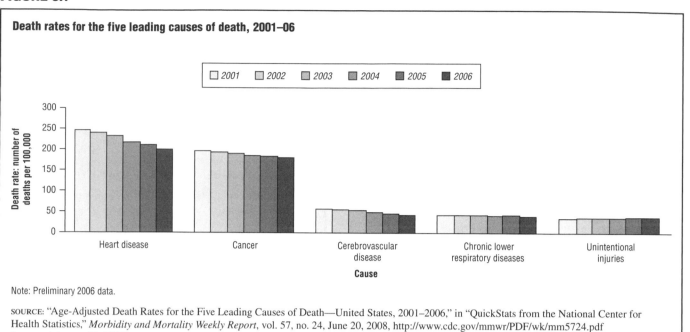

Death rates for the five leading causes of death, 2001–06

Note: Preliminary 2006 data.

SOURCE: "Age-Adjusted Death Rates for the Five Leading Causes of Death—United States, 2001–2006," in "QuickStats from the National Center for Health Statistics," *Morbidity and Mortality Weekly Report*, vol. 57, no. 24, June 20, 2008, http://www.cdc.gov/mmwr/PDF/wk/mm5724.pdf (accessed August 19, 2008)

The article "Non-smoking Wives of Heavy Smokers Have a Higher Risk of Lung Cancer: A Study from Japan" (*British Medical Journal*, vol. 282, no. 6259, January 17, 1981) by Takeshi Hirayama of the National Cancer Centre Research Institute was the first scientific paper on the harmful effects of secondhand smoke. Hirayama studied 91,540 nonsmoking wives of smoking husbands and a similarly sized group of women married to nonsmokers. He discovered that nonsmoking wives of husbands who smoked faced a 40% to 90% elevated risk of lung cancer (depending on how frequently their husbands smoked) compared with the wives of nonsmoking husbands.

Other studies followed. The U.S. Environmental Protection Agency (EPA) concluded in *Respiratory Health Effects of Passive Smoking: Lung Cancer and Other Disorders* (December 1992, http://cfpub2.epa.gov/ncea/cfm/recordisplay.cfm?deid=2835) that the "widespread exposure to environmental tobacco smoke (ETS) in the United States presents a serious and substantial public health impact." In Elizabeth T. Fontham et al.'s "Environmental Tobacco Smoke and Lung Cancer in Nonsmoking Women: A Multicenter Study" (*Journal of the American Medical Association*, vol. 271, no. 22, June 8, 1994), a large case-control study on secondhand smoke, compelling links were found between passive smoke and lung cancer. In 2000 the Environmental Health Information Service's *Ninth Report on Carcinogens* classified secondhand smoke as a Group A (human) carcinogen. According to the EPA, there is no safe level of exposure to such Group A toxins.

In 2005 more evidence accumulated on the risks of secondhand smoking. In "Environmental Tobacco Smoke and Risk of Respiratory Cancer and Chronic Obstructive Pulmonary Disease in Former Smokers and Never Smokers in the EPIC Prospective Study" (*British Medical Journal*, vol. 330, no. 7486, February 5, 2005), Paolo Vineis et al. revealed that those who had been exposed to secondhand smoke during childhood for many hours each day had more than triple the risk of developing lung cancer compared to people who were not exposed. In addition, Sarah M. McGhee et al. showed in "Mortality Associated with Passive Smoking in Hong Kong" (*British Medical Journal*, vol. 330, no. 7486, February 5, 2005) that there is a correlation between an increased risk of dying from various causes (including lung cancer and other lung diseases, heart disease, and stroke) and the number of smokers in the home. The risk increased by 24% when one smoker lived in the home and by 74% with two smokers in the household.

In 2006 the 29th report of the surgeon general on smoking—*The Health Consequences of Involuntary Exposure to Tobacco Smoke* (http://www.surgeongeneral.gov/library/secondhandsmoke/report/fullreport.pdf)—was published. The report noted that:

With regard to the involuntary exposure of nonsmokers to tobacco smoke, the scientific evidence now supports the following major conclusions:

1. Secondhand smoke causes premature death and disease in children and in adults who do not smoke.

2. Children exposed to secondhand smoke are at an increased risk for sudden infant death syndrome (SIDS), acute respiratory infections, ear problems, and more severe asthma. Smoking by parents causes respiratory symptoms and slows lung growth in their children.

3. Exposure of adults to secondhand smoke has immediate adverse effects on the cardiovascular system and causes coronary heart disease and lung cancer.

4. The scientific evidence indicates that there is no risk-free level of exposure to secondhand smoke.

5. Many millions of Americans, both children and adults, are still exposed to secondhand smoke in their homes and workplaces despite substantial progress in tobacco control.

6. Eliminating smoking in indoor spaces fully protects nonsmokers from exposure to secondhand smoke. Separating smokers from nonsmokers, cleaning the air, and ventilating buildings cannot eliminate exposures of nonsmokers to secondhand smoke.

In 2007 an excerpt of this report was published: *Children and Secondhand Smoke Exposure, Excerpts from The Health Consequences of Involuntary Exposure to Tobacco Smoke* (http://www.surgeongeneral.gov/library/smokeexposure/report/fullreport.pdf). The purpose of the publication was to highlight the serious consequences of secondhand smoke exposure on the health of children, to emphasize that they are more heavily exposed to secondhand smoke than are adults, and to urge that children be protected from this unnecessary threat to their health.

A MOVEMENT TO BAN SMOKING

Many efforts have been initiated over the years to control public smoking or to separate smokers and nonsmokers. In 1975 the Clean Indoor Air Act in Minnesota became the nation's first statewide law to require the separation of smokers and nonsmokers. The purpose of the law was to protect public health, public comfort, and the environment by banning smoking in public places and at public meetings, except in designated smoking areas.

Other states soon followed Minnesota. In 1977 Berkeley became the first community in California to limit smoking in restaurants and other public places. In 1990 San Luis Obispo, California, became the first city to ban smoking in all public buildings, bars, and restaurants. In 1994 smoking was restricted in many government buildings in California. In that same year the fast-food giant McDonald's banned smoking in all of its establishments. In 1995 New York City banned smoking in the dining areas of all restaurants with more than 35 seats. As of July 2003, all public and workplaces in New York City became smoke-free, including bars and restaurants. Laws vary from state to state and from city to city, but by 2005 smoking was banned in most workplaces, hospitals, government buildings, museums, schools, theaters, and many restaurants throughout the United States.

According to Lydia Saad of the Gallup Organization, in *Many Americans Still Downplay Risk of Passive Smoking* (July 21, 2006, http://www.gallup.com/poll/23851/Many-Americans-Still-Downplay-Risk-Passive-Smoking.aspx), a Gallup poll on secondhand smoke was conducted following the release of the 2006 surgeon general's report on the subject. Saad notes that the report had "little immediate impact on public attitudes about the risks" of passive smoking. A 2008 Gallup poll showed that only 56% of those surveyed in 2006 perceived the risk of secondhand smoke to be very harmful. (See Figure 3.8.) This percentage remained the same in 2007. Another 30% believed secondhand smoke is somewhat harmful and 13% thought it is not too harmful or not at all harmful. In general, these percentages have declined from the 1990s, whereas the percentages of those thinking that secondhand smoke is very harmful to adults have risen slightly.

STOPPING SMOKING

In "Cigarette Smoking among Adults—United States, 2007" (*Morbidity and Mortality Weekly Report*, vol. 57, no. 45, November 14, 2008), the CDC estimates that there were 43.4 million current smokers in 2007. This number seems high, but the CDC notes that there has been a slow decline over the past 40 years in the percentage of the U.S. adult population who smoke and that declines have been seen in all racial and socioeconomic groups.

Many current cigarette smokers report they are trying to stop smoking—or would at least like to. In *Tobacco and Smoking* (2008, http://www.gallup.com/poll/1717/Tobacco-Smoking.aspx), the Gallup Organization asked smokers if they would like to give up smoking. Seventy-four percent answered yes. This figure is down from 82% in 2004 but up from 63% in 1989. (See Table 3.5.)

Global Efforts to Reduce Tobacco Use

According to the World Health Organization (WHO) in *Tobacco: Deadly in Any Form or Disguise* (2006, http://www.who.int/tobacco/communications/events/wntd/2006/Tfi_Rapport.pdf), an estimated 1.3 billion adults around the world use tobacco. The WHO states in *WHO Report on the Global Tobacco Epidemic, 2008: The MPOWER Package* (2008, http://www.who.int/tobacco/mpower/mpower_report_full_2008.pdf) the results of this high level of worldwide tobacco use: "In the 20th century, the tobacco epidemic killed 100 million people worldwide.... During the 21s century, it could kill one billion."

The WHO is working diligently to curb smoking around the world. In May 2003 member states of the WHO adopted the world's first international public health treaty for global cooperation in reducing the negative health consequences of tobacco use. The WHO Framework Convention on Tobacco Control (2005, http://www.who.int/tobacco/framework/WHO_FCTC_english.pdf) was designed to reduce tobacco-related deaths and disease worldwide. In February 2005 the treaty came into force after being ratified by 40 member countries. Each of the other 128 countries that signed the treaty but did not ratify it was to work toward thi

FIGURE 3.8

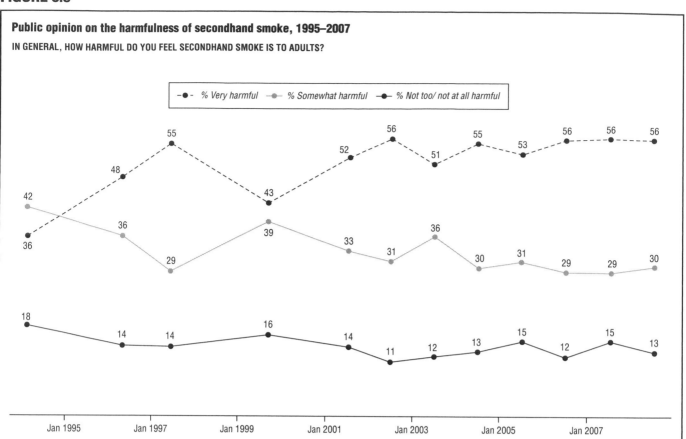

Public opinion on the harmfulness of secondhand smoke, 1995–2007

IN GENERAL, HOW HARMFUL DO YOU FEEL SECONDHAND SMOKE IS TO ADULTS?

SOURCE: Lymari Morales, "In General, How Harmful Do You Feel Secondhand Smoke Is to Adults?" in *Most Americans Consider Smoking Very Harmful*, The Gallup Organization, July 28, 2008, http://www.gallup.com/poll/109129/Most-Americans-Consider-Smoking-Very-Harmful.aspx?version= print (accessed August 25, 2008). Copyright © 2008 by The Gallup Organization. Reproduced by permission of The Gallup Organization.

goal in their country. The WHO (January 15, 2009, http://www.who.int/fctc/signatories_parties/en/index.html) notes that the United States signed the treaty in May 2004, indicating its general acceptance, but as of April 2009 it had not yet ratified (become bound by) the treaty. The treaty has many measures, which include requiring countries to impose restrictions on tobacco advertising, sponsorship, and promotion; establishing new packaging and labeling of tobacco products; establishing clean indoor air controls; and promoting taxation as a way to cut consumption and fight smuggling.

According to the article "WHO Finds Anti-smoking Efforts Fall Short" (Reuters, February 7, 2008), the treaty's measures were only slowly being implemented around the world in 2007, and only 5% of the world's people lived in countries in which the recommendations were being fully practiced. This news report was released at about the same time that the WHO unveiled *Report on the Global Tobacco Epidemic, 2008: The MPOWER Package*. In this document the primary measures of the treaty are configured into the acronym MPOWER, which stands for: "Monitor tobacco use and prevention policies; Protect people from tobacco smoke; Offer help to quit tobacco use; Warn about the dangers of tobacco; Enforce bans on tobacco advertising, promotion and sponsorship; and Raise taxes on tobacco." The WHO emphatically states that the tobacco epidemic is growing worldwide, especially in third-world countries, primarily among young females who are being targeted by tobacco companies. In many countries women traditionally do not smoke, and the WHO suggests that tobacco companies are working to weaken this cultural taboo in their "advertising, promotion and sponsorship, including charitable donations to women's causes." It also notes that many poorer nations, in which tobacco controls are weak, rely on income from the tobacco business for revenue. The state-owned China National Tobacco Corporation is given as one example of this fiscal reliance.

The 2008 WHO report was partially funded by Bloomberg Philanthropies, an organization developed by the New York mayor Michael Bloomberg (1942–). Bloomberg has funded antismoking initiatives for many years and in July 2008 teamed with fellow billionaire Bill Gates (1955–) to help stop smoking worldwide. In "Pledging $500 Million, Bloomberg and Gates Take Aim at Smoking" (*New York Times*, July 24, 2008), Donald G. McNeil Jr. indicates that the money their foundations donate will help fund the

TABLE 3.5

Percentage of cigarette smokers who would like to give up smoking, selected years 1977–2008

ALL THINGS CONSIDERED, WOULD YOU LIKE TO GIVE UP SMOKING, OR NOT?

[Based on smokers]

	Yes	No	No opinion
	%	%	%
2008 Jul 10–13	74	24	2
2007 Jul 12–15	81	17	1
2006 Jul 6–9	75	22	3
2005 Jul 7–10	76	22	2
2004 Jul 8–11	82	17	1
2003 Jul 7–9	82	17	1
2002 Jul 9–11	79	18	3
2000 Nov 13–15	82	16	2
1999 Sep 23–26	76	23	1
1997 Jun 26–29	74	24	2
1997 Jun 23–24	64	34	2
1996 May 9–12	73	26	1
1994 Mar 11–13	70	28	2
1991 Nov 7–10	76	22	2
1990 Jul 6–8	74	24	2
1989 May 15–18	63	33	4
1988 Jul 1–7	68	27	5
1987 Mar 14–18	77	20	3
1986 Jun 9–16	75	22	3
1981 Jun 26–29	66	30	4
1977 Aug 19–22	66	29	5

SOURCE: "All Things Considered, Would You Like to Give up Smoking, or Not?" in *Tobacco and Smoking*, The Gallup Organization, 2008, http://www.gallup.com/poll/1717/Tobacco-Smoking.aspx#1 (accessed December 18, 2008). Copyright © 2008 by The Gallup Organization. Reproduced by permission of The Gallup Organization.

MPOWER program and will coordinate efforts with other antismoking Bloomberg initiatives.

Benefits of Stopping

The 1990 *Health Benefits of Smoking Cessation: A Report of the Surgeon General* (http://profiles.nlm.nih.gov/NN/B/B/C/T/_/nnbbct.pdf) noted that quitting offers major and immediate health benefits for both sexes and for all ages. This first comprehensive report on the benefits of quitting showed that many of the ill effects of smoking can be reversed. The surgeon general's report *Health Consequences of Smoking* revealed that deaths attributable to smoking can be reduced dramatically if the prevalence of smoking is cut.

According to Melonie P. Heron et al. of the CDC, in "Deaths: Preliminary Data for 2006" (*National Vital Statistics Reports*, vol. 56, no. 16, June 11, 2008), heart disease was the number-one killer of Americans in 2006 and cancer was the number-two killer. Of all cancers, the American Cancer Society states in *Cancer Facts and Figures, 2008* that lung and bronchial cancer was the number-one killer of both men and women in 2008. People who quit smoking in middle age or before middle age avoid more than 90% of the lung cancer risk attributable to tobacco. The results of Richard Peto et al.'s "Smoking, Smoking Cessation, and Lung Cancer in the UK since 1950: Combination of National Statistics with Two Case-Control Studies" (*British Medical Journal*, vol. 321, no. 7257, August 5, 2000) reveal the extent to which smoking cessation lowers lung cancer risk. For men who stopped smoking at age 60, 50, 40, and 30, the cumulative risks of lung cancer by the age of 75 were 10%, 6%, 3%, and 2%, respectively. These results were supported by the findings of Anna Crispo et al., in "The Cumulative Risk of Lung Cancer among Current, Ex- and Never-Smokers in European Men" (*British Journal of Cancer*, vol. 91, no. 7, October 4, 2004), which led to the conclusion that, for long-term smokers, giving up smoking in middle age allows people to avoid most of the subsequent risk of lung cancer.

For smokers who quit, the risk of heart disease drops rapidly after smoking cessation. After one year's abstinence from smoking, the risk of heart disease is reduced by about 50% and continues to decline gradually. After five to ten years of smoking cessation, the risk has declined to that of a person who has never smoked. In addition, Gay Sutherland of London University reports in "Smoking: Can We Really Make a Difference?" (*Heart*, vol. 89, May 2003) that stopping smoking reduces the risk of stroke to that of a nonsmoker after five years of smoking cessation. The American Cancer Society in 2007 further confirmed the benefits of quitting (October 16, 2007, http://www.cancer.org/docroot/subsite/greatamericans/content/Why_Quit.asp), stating "People who stop smoking before age 50 cut their risk of dying in the next 15 years in half compared with those who continue to smoke. Ex-smokers enjoy a higher quality of life with fewer illnesses from cold and flu viruses, better self-reported health, and reduced rates of bronchitis and pneumonia."

Quitting and Pregnancy

In *Results from the 2007 National Survey on Drug Use and Health*, the NSDUH finds that 16.4% of pregnant women smoked cigarettes in the month before the survey, which took place in 2006–07. This percentage of smokers is lower than among women who were not pregnant (28.4%) and down from 18% in 2003–04. (See Figure 3.9.) The report also notes that in the 15- to 17-year-old group a higher percentage of pregnant girls smoked than nonpregnant girls, 24.3% versus 16%, respectively. In addition, the smoking rate for pregnant girls in this age group was higher than for pregnant women aged 18 to 25 or 26 to 44.

Smoking during pregnancy can compromise the health of the developing fetus (unborn child). The surgeon general's 2004 report *Health Consequences of Smoking* notes that evidence suggests the possibility of a causal relationship between maternal smoking and ectopic pregnancy, a situation in which the fertilized egg implants in the fallopian tube rather than in the uterus. This situation is quite serious and is life-threatening to the mother. Smoking by pregnant women is also linked to an increased risk of miscarriage, stillbirth,

FIGURE 3.9

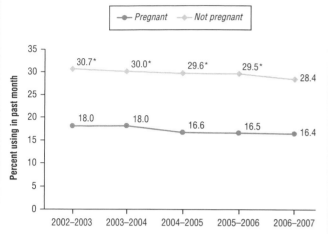

Percentage of past-month cigarette use among females aged 15–44, by pregnancy status, 2002–03 to 2006–07

*Difference between this estimate and the 2006–2007 estimate is statistically significant.

SOURCE: "Figure 4.5. Past Month Cigarette Use among Women Aged 15 to 44, by Pregnancy Status: Combined Years 2002–2003 to 2006–2007," in *Results from the 2007 National Survey on Drug Use and Health: National Findings*, U.S. Department of Health and Human Services, Substance Abuse and Mental Health Services Administration, Office of Applied Studies, 2008, http://www.oas.samhsa.gov/nsduh/2k7nsduh/2k7Results.pdf (accessed December 8, 2008)

premature delivery, and SIDS, and is a cause of low birth weight in infants. A woman who stops smoking before pregnancy or during her first trimester (three months) of pregnancy significantly reduces her chances of having a low birth weight baby. Additionally, it takes smokers longer to get pregnant than nonsmokers, but women who quit are as likely to get pregnant as those who have never smoked.

Complaints about Quitting

A major side effect of smoking cessation is nicotine withdrawal. The short-term consequences of nicotine withdrawal may include anxiety, irritability, frustration, anger, difficulty concentrating, and restlessness. Possible long-term consequences are urges to smoke and increased appetite. Nicotine withdrawal symptoms peak in the first few days after quitting and subside during the following weeks. Improved self-esteem and an increased sense of control often accompany long-term abstinence.

One of the most common complaints among former smokers is that they gain weight when they stop smoking. Many reasons explain this weight gain, but two primary reasons are the metabolism changes when nicotine is withdrawn from the body and the use of food by many former smokers in attempts to manage their withdrawal cravings. To combat weight gain, some former smokers start exercise programs.

Ways to Stop Smoking

Nicotine replacement treatments can be effective for many smokers. Nicotine patches and gum are two types of nicotine replacement therapy (NRT). The nicotine in a patch is absorbed through the skin, and the nicotine in gum is absorbed through the mouth and throat. NRT helps a smoker cope with nicotine withdrawal symptoms that discourage many smokers from trying to stop. Nicotine patches and gum are available over the counter. Other NRT products are the nicotine nasal spray and the nicotine inhaler, which are available by prescription.

Another product marketed to combat the use of cigarettes—electronic cigarettes, or e-cigarettes—drew scrutiny in 2009. E-cigarettes, plastic devices fashioned to look like cigarettes, contain liquid nicotine that is warmed by a battery activated when the user inhales through the device. According to the Web site Medical News Today ("Lautenberg Urges FDA to Remove Electronic Cigarettes from the Market Until Proven Safe," March 24, 2009, http://www.medicalnewstoday.com/articles/143429.php), "Manufacturers and retailers of these products claim that electronic cigarettes are safe, and even that these products can help smokers quit traditional cigarettes. However, no clinical studies have proven these products are effective in helping smokers quit smoking, nor have any studies considered the safety of these products' long-term health effects. While the [Food and Drug Administration] has indicated it will evaluate electronic cigarettes on a case-by-case basis, it has not taken any enforcement action against these products, which are currently being sold in mall kiosks across the country and on the Internet."

The nonnicotine therapy bupropion (an antidepressant drug) is also available by prescription for the relief of nicotine withdrawal symptoms. In addition, behavioral treatments, such as smoking-cessation programs, are useful for some smokers who want to quit. Behavioral methods are designed to create an aversion to smoking, develop self-monitoring of smoking behavior, and establish alternative coping responses.

Quitting smoking is not easy. Sutherland notes that the expected one-year success rate of quitting smoking varies among stop-smoking interventions. Only 1% to 2% of smokers trying to quit will remain smoke-free for a year with no advice or support from a doctor or other health care professional and no treatment (NRT or bupropion). Five percent of those who receive three minutes' advice from a health care professional to help them quit will remain smoke-free for a year. Advice plus treatment raises the percentage of those who remain smoke free to 10%. Intensive behavioral support from a specialist plus treatment can lead to a 25% success rate.

CHAPTER 4
ILLICIT DRUGS

Illegal drugs are those with no currently accepted medical use in the United States, such as heroin, lysergic acid diethylamide (LSD), and marijuana. (Some states and local jurisdictions have decriminalized certain uses of certain amounts of marijuana, but federal laws supersede these state and local marijuana decriminalization laws. See Chapter 9.) Controlled substances are legal drugs whose sale, possession, and use are restricted because they are psychoactive (mood- or mind-altering) drugs that have the potential for abuse. These drugs are medications, such as certain narcotics, depressants, and stimulants, that physicians prescribe for various conditions. The term *illicit drugs* is used by the Substance Abuse and Mental Health Services Administration (SAMHSA) to mean both illegal drugs and controlled substances that are used illegally.

WHO USES ILLICIT DRUGS?

The National Survey on Drug Use and Health (NSDUH) is an annual survey conducted by SAMHSA, and its 2007 survey results are published in *Results from the 2007 National Survey on Drug Use and Health: National Findings* (September 2008, http://www.oas.samhsa.gov/nsduh/2k7nsduh/2k7Results.pdf). The NSDUH reveals that an estimated 19.9 million Americans aged 12 and older were current illicit drug users in 2007. By "current" SAMHSA means the people who were surveyed about their drug use and who had taken an illicit drug during the month before participating in the survey. (Current users are "past month" users.) This figure represented 8% of the U.S. population in 2007.

Table 4.1 presents a demographic profile of this population of drug users. In 2007, 19.7% of those aged 18 to 25 were current illicit drug users, and 9.5% of those aged 12 to 17 were. In contrast, only 5.8% of those aged 26 and older were current illicit drug users.

Figure 4.1 shows a more detailed look at current illicit drug use by age. In 2007 18- to 20-year-olds accounted for the highest percentage of illicit drug users. At 21.6% of their population, over one out of every five young people aged 18 to 20 were current illicit drug users in that year. Twenty-one- to 25-year-olds (18.5%) were the second highest current illicit drug users, followed by 16- and 17-year-olds (16%).

Regarding other demographics of illicit drug use, Table 4.1 shows that a higher proportion of males than females were current, past-year, or lifetime illicit drug users from 2006 to 2007. (Past-year users took a specific drug in the 12 months before taking the SAMHSA survey. Lifetime users took a specific drug at least once in their lifetime.) Those of Native American and Alaskan native heritage had the highest percentage of current illicit drug users in their population (12.6%). Those of two or more races were next (11.8%), followed by African-Americans (9.5%). Asian-Americans (4.2%) had the lowest percentage of current illicit drug users in their population.

WHICH ILLICIT DRUGS ARE USED MOST FREQUENTLY?

Figure 4.2 shows the types of illicit drugs used in 2007 and how many people used those drugs in that year. Nearly three-quarters (72%) of current illicit drug users used marijuana—14.4 million people of the 19.9 million illicit drug users. According to the NSDUH, those who only used marijuana made up more than half the population of current illicit drug users in 2007.

From 2002 to 2007, 5.8% of people aged 12 and older had used marijuana in the month prior to being surveyed. (See Figure 4.3.) Psychotherapeutics was the next most used group of illicit drugs, ranging from 2.5% to 2.9% of the population from 2002 to 2007. Psychotherapeutics is a group of drugs that include pain relievers, tranquilizers, stimulants (including methamphetamine), and sedatives. This group does not include over-the-counter (without a prescription) drugs. The next most used illicit drugs were pain relievers (used illicitly by about 2.1% of the population) and cocaine (used by 0.8% of the population).

TABLE 4.1

Use of illicit drugs among persons aged 12 and older, by time of use and demographic characteristics, 2006–07

| | Time period | | | | | |
| | Lifetime | | Past year | | Past month | |
Demographic characteristic	2006	2007	2006	2007	2006	2007
Total	45.4	46.1	14.5	14.4	8.3	8.0
Age						
12–17	27.6	26.2	19.6	18.7	9.8	9.5
18–25	59.0	57.4	34.4	33.2	19.8	19.7
26 or older	45.5	46.8	10.4	10.6	6.1	5.8
Gender						
Male	50.3	50.6	17.4	17.4	10.5	10.4
Female	40.9	41.8	11.8	11.6	6.2	5.8
Hispanic origin and race						
Not Hispanic or Latino	47.1	48.0	14.8	14.8	8.5	8.2
White	49.0	50.3	14.8	14.9	8.5	8.2
Black or African American	42.9	43.1	16.4	16.0	9.8	9.5
American Indian or Alaska Native	58.8	54.6	20.1	18.4	13.7	12.6
Native Hawaiian or other Pacific Islander	40.9	*	13.4	13.3	7.5	*
Asian	23.7	22.8	8.9	7.2	3.6	4.2
Two or more races	55.4	51.5	18.1	22.1	8.9	11.8
Hispanic or Latino	35.0	34.2	13.1	12.2	6.9	6.6

*Low precision; no estimate reported.

Note: Illicit drugs include marijuana/hashish, cocaine (including crack), heroin, hallucinogens, inhalants, or prescription-type psychotherapeutics used nonmedically, based on data from original questions not including methamphetamine items added in 2005 and 2006.

SOURCE: "Table 1.19B. Illicit Drug Use in Lifetime, Past Year, and Past Month among Persons Aged 12 or Older, by Demographic Characteristics: Percentages, 2006 and 2007," in *2007 National Survey on Drug Use and Health: Detailed Tables*, U.S. Department of Health and Human Services, Substance Abuse and Mental Health Services Administration, Office of Applied Studies, September 2008, http://oas.samhsa.gov/NSDUH/2k7NSDUH/tabs/Sect1peTabs1to46 htm#Tab1.19B (accessed December 8, 2008)

FIGURE 4.1

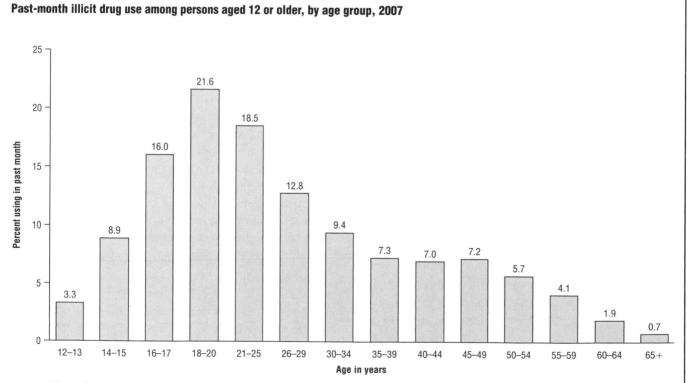

Past-month illicit drug use among persons aged 12 or older, by age group, 2007

SOURCE: "Figure 2.4. Past Month Illicit Drug Use among Persons Aged 12 or Older, by Age: 2007," in *Results from the 2007 National Survey on Drug Use and Health: National Findings*, U.S. Department of Health and Human Services, Substance Abuse and Mental Health Services Administration, Office of Applied Studies, 2008, http://www.oas.samhsa.gov/nsduh/2k7nsduh/2k7Results.pdf (accessed December 8, 2008)

FIGURE 4.2

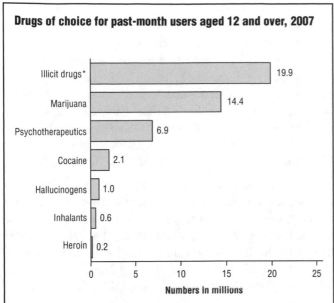

Drugs of choice for past-month users aged 12 and over, 2007

*Illicit drugs include marijuana/hashish, cocaine (including crack), heroin, hallucinogens, inhalants, or prescription-type psychotherapeutics used nonmedically.

SOURCE: "Figure 2.1. Past Month Illicit Drug Use among Persons Aged 12 or Older: 2007," in *Results from the 2007 National Survey on Drug Use and Health: National Findings*, U.S. Department of Health and Human Services, Substance Abuse and Mental Health Services Administration, Office of Applied Studies, 2008, http://www.oas.samhsa.gov/nsduh/2k7nsduh/2k7Results.pdf (accessed December 8, 2008)

FIGURE 4.3

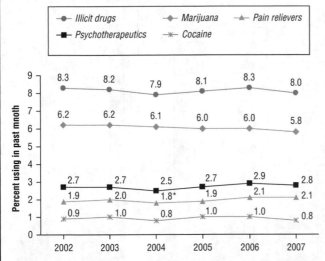

Past-month use of selected illicit drugs among persons aged 12 or older, 2002–07

*Difference between this estimate and the 2007 estimate is statistically significant.

SOURCE: "Figure 2.2. Past Month Use of Selected Illicit Drugs among Persons Aged 12 or Older: 2002–2007," in *Results from the 2007 National Survey on Drug Use and Health: National Findings*, U.S. Department of Health and Human Services, Substance Abuse and Mental Health Services Administration, Office of Applied Studies, 2008, http://www.oas.samhsa.gov/nsduh/2k7nsduh/2k7Results.pdf (accessed December 8, 2008)

DRUG-RELATED DEATHS

Sherry L. Murphy of the Centers for Disease Control and Prevention (CDC) reports in "Deaths: Final Data for 1998" (*National Vital Statistics Reports*, vol. 48, no. 11, July 24, 2000) that there were 16,926 drug-related deaths in 1998. Hsiang-Ching Kung et al. of the CDC note in "Deaths: Final Data for 2005" (*National Vital Statistics Reports*, vol. 56, no. 10, April 24, 2008) that by 2005 the number of drug-related deaths doubled to 33,541. In this annual CDC report, drug-related deaths include those due directly to the use of either legal or illegal drugs but exclude deaths due indirectly to drug use, such as unintentional injuries or homicides.

CANNABIS AND MARIJUANA

Cannabis sativa, the hemp plant from which marijuana is made, grows wild throughout most of the world's tropic and temperate regions, including Mexico, the Middle East, Africa, and India. For centuries its therapeutic potential has been explored, including uses as an analgesic (painkiller) and anticonvulsant. However, with the advent of new, synthetic drugs and the passage of the Marijuana Tax Act of 1937, interest in marijuana—even for medicinal purposes—faded. In 1970 the Controlled Substances Act (CSA) classified marijuana as a Schedule I drug, because it has "no currently accepted medical use in treatment in the United States," though this classification is debated by those in favor of using it for medical and recreational purposes. (See Chapter 9.)

Besides regular marijuana, there are two alternate forms: ditchweed and sinsemilla. All three are tobacco-like substances produced by drying the leaves and flowery tops of cannabis plants. The Office of National Drug Control Policy (ONDCP) explains in *National Drug Control Strategy: Data Supplement 2008* (October 2008, http://www.whitehouse drugpolicy.gov/publications/policy/ndcs08_data_supl/ndcs _suppl08.pdf) that potency varies considerably among the three, depending on how much of the chemical THC (delta-9-tetrahydrocannabinol) is present. Ditchweed, or wild U.S marijuana, is the least potent form of marijuana and generally has a THC content of less than 0.5%. Sinsemilla is the most potent form of marijuana. The name is Spanish for "without seed" and refers to the unpollinated, and therefore seedless, female cannabis plant. Sinsemilla can contain over 14% THC. Generally, the marijuana cultivated in the United States has a THC content of about 3%, whereas the marijuana from other countries has a higher potency of up to 7%.

Effects of Marijuana

Marijuana is usually smoked in the form of loosely rolled cigarettes called joints, in hollowed-out commercial cigars called blunts, or in water pipes called bongs. Sometimes it is ingested. The effects are felt within minutes, usually peaking in 10 to 30 minutes and lingering for two to three hours. Low doses induce restlessness and an increasing sense of well-being, followed by a dreamy state of relaxation and, frequently, hunger. Changes in sensory perception—a more vivid sense of sight, smell, touch, taste, and hearing—may occur, with subtle alterations in thought formation and expression. However, the U.S. Drug Enforcement Administration (DEA) reports in *Drugs of Abuse* (2005, http://www.usdoj.gov/dea/pubs/abuse/doa-p.pdf) that along with the pleasant side effects of smoking marijuana come some not-so-pleasant effects with extended use: short-term memory loss, lung damage, adverse effects on reproductive function, suppression of the immune system, apathy, impairment of judgment, and loss of interest in personal appearance and pursuit of goals.

The immediate physical effects of marijuana include a faster heartbeat (by as much as 50%), bloodshot eyes, and a dry mouth and throat. It can alter one's sense of time and reduce concentration and coordination. Some users experience lightheadedness and giddiness, whereas others feel depressed and sad. Many users have also reported experiencing severe anxiety attacks.

Even though the immediate effects of marijuana usually disappear in about four to six hours, it takes about three days for 50% of the drug to be broken down and eliminated from the body. It takes three weeks to completely excrete the THC from one marijuana cigarette. If a user smokes two joints per week, it takes months for all traces of the THC to disappear from the body.

Hashish and Hash Oil

Two other drugs besides marijuana come from the cannabis plant: hashish and hash oil. Hashish is made from the THC-rich, tar-like material that can be collected from the cannabis plant. This resin is dried and compressed into a variety of forms, including balls and cakes. Larger pieces are broken into smaller pieces and smoked. Most hashish comes from the Middle East, North Africa, Pakistan, and Afghanistan. According to the DEA, in 2005's *Drugs of Abuse*, the THC content of hashish in the United States hovered around 5% during the 1990s. Demand in the United States is limited.

Despite the name, hash oil is not directly related to hashish. It is produced by extracting the cannabinoids from the cannabis plant with a solvent. The color and odor of hash oil depend on the solvent used. The DEA indicates that seized hash oil ranges from amber to dark brown with about 15% THC. In terms of effect, a drop or two of hash oil on a cigarette is equal to a single joint of marijuana.

Prevalence of Use of Marijuana

Figure 4.4 shows the lifetime, annual, and 30-day (current) use of marijuana among 18- to 45-year-olds in 2007. Current and annual use generally drops with age—younger

FIGURE 4.4

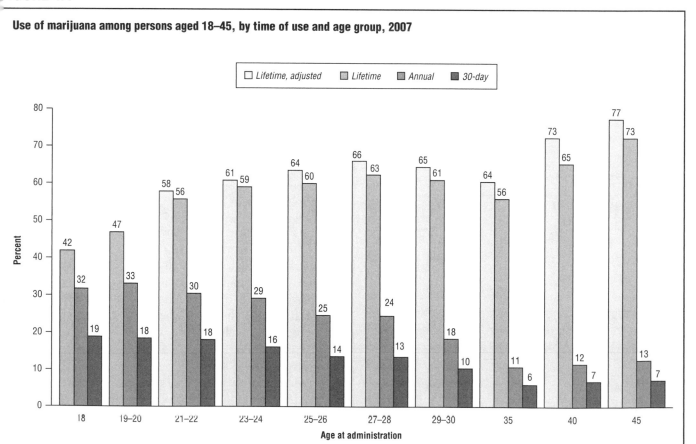

Use of marijuana among persons aged 18–45, by time of use and age group, 2007

Note: Lifetime prevalence estimates were adjusted for inconsistency in self-reports of drug use over time.

SOURCE: Lloyd D. Johnston et al., "Figure 4-3. Marijuana: Lifetime, Annual, and Thirty-Day Prevalence among Respondents of Modal Ages 18 through 45 by Age Group, 2007," in *Monitoring the Future National Survey Results on Drug Use, 1975–2007: Volume 2, College Students and Adults Ages 19–45*, National Institute on Drug Abuse, 2008, http://www.monitoringthefuture.org/pubs/monographs/vol2_2007.pdf (accessed December 8, 2008)

FIGURE 4.5

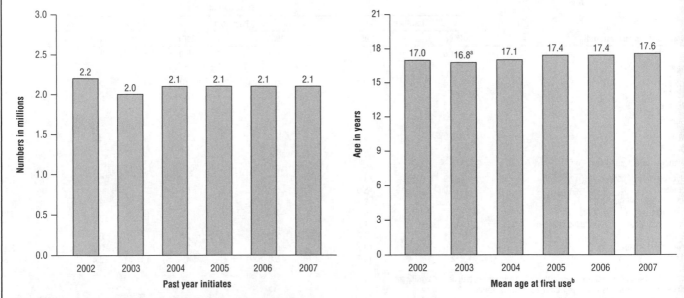

New users of marijuana over age 12 and the mean age at first use among those aged 12–49, 2002–07

[a]Difference between this estimate and the 2007 estimate is statistically significant.
[b]Mean-age-at-first-use estimates are for recent initiates aged 12 to 49.

SOURCE: "Figure 5.4. Past Year Marijuana Initiates among Persons Aged 12 or Older and Mean Age at First Use of Marijuana among Past Year Marijuana Initiates Aged 12 to 49: 2002–2007," in *Results from the 2007 National Survey on Drug Use and Health: National Findings*, U.S. Department of Health and Human Services, Substance Abuse and Mental Health Services Administration, Office of Applied Studies, 2008, http://www.oas.samhsa.gov/nsduh/2k7nsduh/2k7Results.pdf (accessed December 8, 2008)

people are more likely to have used marijuana during the past year or past month than older people. However, by the age of 45, about three-quarters of the U.S. population in 2007 had tried marijuana at sometime in their lives.

In 2007, 19% of 18-year-olds were current users of marijuana. Use rates dropped to 18% each for 19- to 20-year-olds and 21- to 22-year-olds. By the age of 30, 10% were current users of marijuana, and by the age of 45, this figure had dropped to 7%. (See Figure 4.4.)

For each year from 2002 to 2007 approximately 2 million people over the age of 12 tried marijuana for the first time. (See Figure 4.5.) The average age of those first-timers ranged from 16.8 years in 2003 to 17.6 years in 2007, indicating in general that the average age at which people tried marijuana for the first time is about 17.

PSYCHOTHERAPEUTICS

Psychotherapeutics, a group of drugs that includes pain relievers, tranquilizers, stimulants (including methamphetamine), and sedatives, was the second most used group of illicit drugs from 2002 to 2007. (See Figure 4.3.) During those years the use of psychotherapeutics among people aged 12 and older ranged from 2.5% to 2.9% of this population.

Figure 4.3 shows that 2.8% of the population aged 12 and older were current users of prescription-type psychother-

apeutic drugs for nonmedical reasons in 2007. According to the NSDUH, in 2007 pain relievers were the most used and sedatives were the least used psychotherapeutics. Of the 6.9 million users of illicit psychotherapeutics, 5.2 million used pain relievers, 1.8 million used tranquilizers, 1.1 million used stimulants, and 346,000 used sedatives. These estimates were similar to the 2006 estimates for pain relievers, tranquilizers, and sedatives, but the number of those who illicitly used stimulants decreased from 2006 to 2007.

Pain Relievers

Table 4.2 shows the percentages of people aged 12 and older who used prescription pain relievers for nonmedical reasons in their lifetime, during the past year, and during the past month in 2006 and 2007. Current users made up 2.1% of the population for both 2006 and 2007. Approximately 5% of people had used painkillers for nonmedical reasons within the past year, and 13.6% had tried them at least once in their lifetime in 2006, decreasing slightly to 13.3% in 2007.

Most current users of illicit pain relievers in 2006 and 2007 were young adults aged 18 to 25 (4.9% in 2006 and 4.6% in 2007). (See Table 4.2.) Those aged 12 to 17 were the next most likely to take these drugs (2.7% in both 2006 and 2007). Only 1.5% of those aged 26 and older were current illicit users of prescription pain relievers in 2006, and 1.6% in 2007.

TABLE 4.2

Nonmedical use of pain relievers among persons aged 12 and older, by time of use and demographic characteristics, 2006 and 2007

	Lifetime		Past year		Past month	
Demographic characteristic	2006	2007	2006	2007	2006	2007
Total	13.6	13.3	5.1	5.0	2.1	2.1
Age						
12–17	10.4	9.7	7.2	6.7	2.7	2.7
18–25	25.5	24.8	12.4	12.1	4.9	4.6
26 or older	12.0	11.8	3.6	3.6	1.5	1.6
Gender						
Male	16.0[a]	15.0	6.1	5.7	2.5	2.6
Female	11.3	11.7	4.3	4.4	1.7	1.7
Hispanic origin and race						
Not Hispanic or Latino	13.9	13.8	5.2	5.1	2.1	2.1
White	15.0	15.0	5.5	5.4	2.1	2.2
Black or African American	10.1	9.1	3.8	4.1	2.0	1.9
American Indian or Alaska Native	15.7	15.1	7.4	6.5	4.1	4.2
Native Hawaiian or other Pacific Islander	12.9	11.2	3.4	5.8	0.6	[b]
Asian	6.1	6.0	3.0	2.5	0.9	1.3
Two or more races	15.5	19.3	6.7	8.0	3.2	3.1
Hispanic or Latino	12.0	10.7	5.0	4.4	2.4	1.8

Note: Difference between estimate and 2007 estimate is statistically significant.
Difference between estimate and 2007 estimate is statistically significant.
Low precision; no estimate reported.

SOURCE: "Table 1.54B. Nonmedical Use of Pain Relievers in Lifetime, Past Year, and Past Month among Persons Aged 12 or Older, by Demographic Characteristics: Percentages, 2006 and 2007," in *2007 National Survey on Drug Use and Health: Detailed Tables*, U.S. Department of Health and Human Services, Substance Abuse and Mental Health Services Administration, Office of Applied Studies, September 2008, http://oas.samhsa.gov/NSDUH/2k7NSDUH/tabs/Sect1peTabs47to92.htm#Tab1.54B (accessed December 10, 2008)

The percentage of current users of illicit pain relievers among whites and African-Americans was approximately 2% of each population in 2006 and 2007. (See Table 4.2.) In 2006 the Native Hawaiian and other Pacific Islander group had a very low current rate of use at 0.6%. The Native American and Alaskan native group had a very high percentage of current users at 4.1% in 2006 and 4.2% in 2007, figures that were double the national average of 2.1% in both years.

NARCOTICS: OXYCODONE, HYDROCODONE, AND MORPHINE. Two prescription pain relievers that have been popular with users of illicit prescription drugs are oxycodone and hydrocodone, both of which are strong narcotic pain relievers. Narcotics are addictive drugs, such as morphine, codeine, and opium, that reduce pain, alter mood and behavior, and usually induce sleep. Whereas morphine, codeine, and opium are natural narcotics extracted from the juice of the opium poppy, oxycodone and hydrocodone are semi-synthetic narcotics; that is, they are made in the laboratory from codeine.

Hydrocodone and oxycodone are two of the most commonly prescribed narcotic painkillers in the United States. Even though they are designed to have a less euphoric effect than morphine, they are still highly sought after by recreational users and addicts. Like morphine, these drugs have enough potential for abuse that they are classified as Schedule II substances.

Oxycodone is the active ingredient in many narcotic pain relievers, including those manufactured as time-release caplets or those containing other pain relievers such as aspirin and acetaminophen. Illicit users of oxycodone crush, chew, or dissolve and inject the drug so that they receive all the oxycodone at once, giving them a heroin-like high. Emergency rooms have reported serious injuries and deaths from the abuse of oxycodone, often by teenagers and young adults.

According to the NSDUH, in 2007 there were 554,000 new nonmedical users of oxycodone aged 12 and older. In *Monitoring the Future: National Survey Results on Drug Use, 1975–2007, Volume I: Secondary School Students* (September 2008, http://www.monitoringthefuture.org/pubs/monographs/vol1_2007.pdf), Lloyd D. Johnston et al. of the University of Michigan report that 3% of high school seniors had tried oxycodone at least once in the past year. The less dangerous drug, hydrocodone, showed an annual rate of use of 5.8% for high school seniors in 2007.

Morphine is extracted from opium and is one of the most effective drugs known for pain relief. It is marketed in the form of oral solutions, sustained-release tablets, and injectable preparations. Morphine is used legally only in hospitals or hospice care, usually to control the severe pain resulting from illnesses such as cancer. Tolerance and dependence develop rapidly in the morphine abuser. According to Johnston et al., the annual prevalence rate of morphine use for high school seniors in 2007 was 1.8%.

Tranquilizers

A tranquilizer is a calming medication that relieves tension and anxiety. Tranquilizers are central nervous system depressants and include a group of drugs called benzodiazepines. They are also known as sleeping pills, downers, or tranks. Benzodiazepines have a relatively slow onset but long duration of action. They also have a greater margin of safety than other depressants. According to the DEA, in *Drugs of Abuse*, benzodiazepines account for 20% of prescriptions in the United States.

Johnston et al. note that most illicit tranquilizer use reported in recent years involved the drugs diazepam and alprazolam. In 2007, 2.4% of high school seniors had taken diazepam during the previous year and 3.3% had taken alprazolam.

Prolonged use of excessive doses of tranquilizers may result in physical and psychological dependence. Because benzodiazepines are eliminated from the body slowly, withdrawal symptoms generally develop slowly, usually seven to ten days after continued high doses are stopped. When these drugs are used illicitly, they are often taken with alcohol or marijuana to achieve a euphoric high.

FLUNITRAZEPAM—THE DATE RAPE DRUG. Flunitrazepam, another benzodiazepine, has become increasingly popular among young people. Manufactured as a short-term treatment for severe sleeping disorders, the drug is not marketed legally in the United States and must be smuggled in. It is widely known as a date rape drug because would-be rapists have been known to drop it secretly into a victim's drink to facilitate sexual assault. In a sufficiently large dose it can leave a victim physically incapacitated and cause amnesia that may prevent him or her from recalling an assault. Responding to pressure from the U.S. government, Roche, the Mexican producer of flunitrazepam, began putting a blue dye in the pill so that it can be seen when dissolved in a drink. Johnston et al. state that in 2007, 1% of high school seniors used flunitrazepam at least once during the year before their being surveyed.

Synthetic Stimulants

Stimulants (uppers) are drugs that produce a sense of euphoria or wakefulness. They are used to increase alertness, boost endurance and productivity, and suppress the appetite. Examples of stimulants are caffeine, nicotine, amphetamine, methamphetamine, and cocaine.

Potent stimulants, such as amphetamine and methamphetamine, make users feel stronger, more decisive, and self-possessed. Chronic users often develop a pattern of using uppers in the morning and depressants (downers), such as alcohol or sleeping pills, at night. Such manipulation interferes with normal body processes and can lead to mental and physical illness.

Large doses of stimulants can produce paranoia and auditory and visual hallucinations. Overdoses can also produce dizziness, tremors, agitation, hostility, panic, headaches, flushed skin, chest pain with palpitations, excessive sweating, vomiting, and abdominal cramps. When withdrawing from stimulants, chronic high-dose users exhibit depression, apathy, fatigue, and disturbed sleep.

AMPHETAMINE AND METHAMPHETAMINE. In *Drugs of Abuse*, the DEA notes that amphetamine has been used to treat sleeping disorders and during World War II (1939–1945) to keep soldiers awake. Abuse of amphetamine was noticed in the 1960s. It was used by truckers to help them stay alert during long hauls, by athletes to help them train longer, and by many people to lose weight. An intravenous form of amphetamine, methamphetamine, was abused by a subculture of people dubbed "speed freaks."

In 1965 the federal government realized that amphetamine products had tremendous potential for abuse, so it amended food and drug laws to place stricter controls on their distribution and use. All amphetamines are now Schedule II drugs, in the same category as morphine and cocaine.

Methamphetamine is a powerful stimulant that is relatively easy for drug traffickers to synthesize in homemade labs, so its illegal synthesis, distribution, and sale developed after new laws made amphetamine more difficult to get. Two products that come out of these clandestine labs are the injectable form of methamphetamine (meth) and the crystallized form (crystal meth or ice) that is smoked. The DEA explains in "Methamphetamine" (August 2006, http://www.dea.gov/concern/meth.html) that both forms are highly addictive and toxic. Chronic abuse results in a schizophrenic-like mental illness characterized by paranoia, picking at the skin, and hallucinations.

Figure 4.6 shows data on past-year meth initiates and meth use during the past year from 2002 to 2007. In 2007, 157,000 people aged 12 and older began using methamphetamine. This figure was down significantly from 259,000 initiates the previous year. In addition, Figure 4.6 shows that the average age at which meth users first used the drug ranged from 18.6 to 22.2 from 2002 to 2007. Johnston et al. note that in 2007 annual methamphetamine use was highest among 23- to 24-year-olds at 3%. (See Figure 4.7). Annual use of this drug ranged from 1% to 2% in all other age groups.

Sedatives

Like tranquilizers, sedatives are calming, soothing drugs. They relieve tension and anxiety. Also, like tranquilizers, sedatives are central nervous system depressants, but they include a group of drugs called barbiturates, which are generally stronger than tranquilizers. Barbiturates have many street names, including barbs, yellows, and reds.

Small therapeutic doses of sedatives calm nervous conditions; larger doses cause sleep within a short period.

FIGURE 4.6

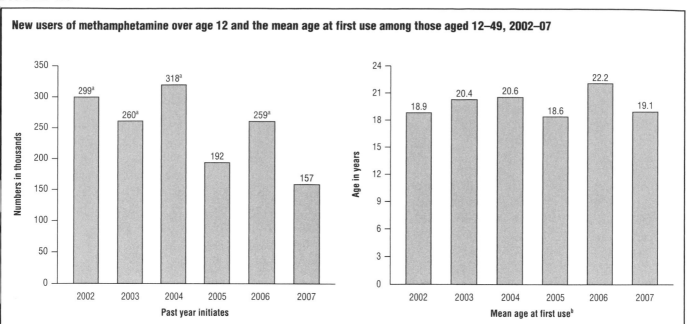

New users of methamphetamine over age 12 and the mean age at first use among those aged 12–49, 2002–07

[a]Difference between this estimate and the 2007 estimate is statistically significant.
[b]Mean-age-at-first-use estimates are for recent initiates aged 12 to 49.

SOURCE: "Figure 5.6. Past Year Methamphetamine Initiates among Persons Aged 12 or Older and Mean Age at First Use of Methamphetamine among Past Year Methamphetamine Initiates Aged 12 to 49: 2002–2007," in *Results from the 2007 National Survey on Drug Use and Health: National Findings*, U.S. Department of Health and Human Services, Substance Abuse and Mental Health Services Administration, Office of Applied Studies, 2008, http://www.oas.samhsa.gov/nsduh/2k7nsduh/2k7Results.pdf (accessed December 8, 2008)

FIGURE 4.7

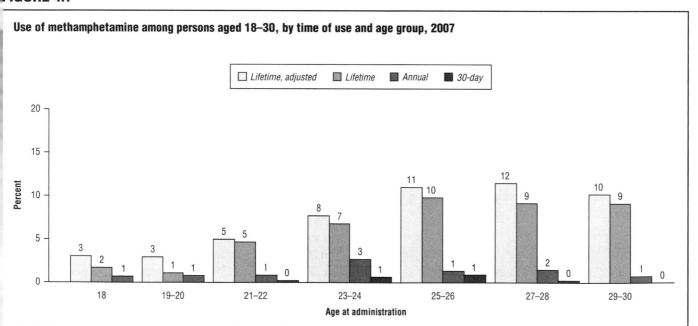

Use of methamphetamine among persons aged 18–30, by time of use and age group, 2007

Note: Lifetime prevalence estimates were adjusted for inconsistency in self-reports of drug use over time.

SOURCE: Lloyd D. Johnston et al., "Figure 4-5. Methamphetamine: Lifetime, Annual, and 30-Day Prevalence among Respondents of Modal Ages 18 through 30 by Age Group, 2007," in *Monitoring the Future National Survey Results on Drug Use, 1975–2007: Volume 2, College Students and Adults Ages 19–45*, National Institute on Drug Abuse, 2008, http://www.monitoringthefuture.org/pubs/monographs/vol2_2007.pdf (accessed December 8, 2008)

A feeling of excitement precedes the sedation. The primary danger of sedatives is that too large a dose can bring a person through stages of sedation, sleep, and coma and ultimately cause death via respiratory failure and cardiovascular complications. According to Johnston et al., the annual prevalence of use of sedatives by high school seniors has slowly risen since the 1990s, from 2.8% in 1992 to 6.2% in 2007.

COCAINE

After marijuana, psychotherapeutics, and pain relievers, cocaine was the next most used illicit drug in 2007. (See Figure 4.3.) Cocaine, a powerful stimulant, is extracted from the leaves of the coca plant (*Erythroxylon coca*). These plants have been cultivated in the Andean highlands of South America since prehistoric times. In these regions of South America, coca leaves are frequently chewed for refreshment and relief from fatigue—in much the same way some North Americans chew tobacco.

According to the ONDCP, in "Cocaine" (2008, http://www.whitehousedrugpolicy.gov/drugfact/cocaine/index.html), pure cocaine was first used in the 1880s as a local anesthetic in eye, nose, and throat surgeries. It was also used in dental procedures. Since then, other drugs, such as lidocaine and novocaine, have replaced it as an anesthetic.

Illicit cocaine is distributed as a white crystalline powder, often contaminated (cut) with sugars or local anesthetics. The drug is commonly snorted through the nasal passages. Less commonly, it is mixed with water and injected, which brings a more intense high because the drug reaches the brain more rapidly.

Cocaine produces a short but extremely powerful rush of energy and confidence. Because the pleasurable effects are so intense, cocaine can lead to severe mental dependency, destroying a person's life as the need for the drug supersedes any other considerations. Physically, cocaine users risk permanent damage to their nose by exposing the cartilage and dissolving the nasal septum (membrane), resulting in a collapsed nose. Cocaine significantly increases the risk of heart attack in the first hour after use. Heavy use (2 grams or more per week) impairs memory, decision making, and manual dexterity.

Freebasing is the smoking of purified cocaine prepared using a method that frees the cocaine base from impurities. Freebase is prepared by mixing cocaine with ether and sodium hydroxide or baking powder (sodium bicarbonate). The salt base dissolves, leaving granules of pure cocaine. Next, these granules are collected, dried, and heated in a pipe filled with water or rum until they vaporize. The vapor is inhaled directly into the lungs, causing an immediate high that lasts about 10 minutes.

There is a danger of being badly burned if the open flame gets too close to the ether or the rum, causing them to flare up as they burn. When the late actor-comedian Richard Pryor (1940–2005) set himself on fire while freebasing in 1980, many users started to search for a safer way to achieve the same high. The dangers inherent in freebasing may have been the catalyst for the development of crack cocaine.

Crack Cocaine

Cocaine hydrochloride, the powdered form of cocaine, is soluble in water, can be injected, and is fairly insensitive to heat. Crack cocaine is processed by mixing cocaine with baking soda and heating it to remove the hydrochloride. The resultant chips or rocks of pure cocaine are usually smoked in a pipe or added to a cigarette or marijuana joint. The name comes from the crackling sound made when the mixture is smoked.

Inhaling the cocaine fumes produces a rapid, intense, and short-lived effect. This incredible intensity is followed within minutes by an abnormally disconcerting and anxious crash, which leads almost inevitably to the need for more of the drug—and a great likelihood of addiction.

Prevalence of Cocaine Use

Figure 4.3 shows that about 1% of the population aged 12 and older were current users of cocaine from 2002 to 2007. Narrowing the survey population from 18 through 45 gives a clearer picture of actual use, because most users are within this age range. Figure 4.8 shows that in 2007 between 1% and 3% of 18- through 28-year-olds were current users and about 5% to 7% were annual users. For 29- to 45-year-olds, 1% to 2% were current users and 2% to 4% were annual users.

HALLUCINOGENS

According to the NSDUH, after marijuana, psychotherapeutics, and cocaine, hallucinogenic drugs were the next most used illicit drugs in 2007. (See Figure 4.2.) Hallucinogens, also known as psychedelics, are natural or synthetic substances that distort the perceptions of reality. They cause excitation, which can vary from a sense of well-being to severe depression. Time may appear to stand still, and forms and colors seem to change and take on new meaning. Typically, the heart rate increases, blood pressure rises, and the pupils dilate. The experience may be pleasurable or extremely frightening. The effects of hallucinogens vary from use to use and cannot be predicted.

The most common danger of using hallucinogens is impaired judgment, which can lead to rash decisions and accidents. Long after hallucinogens have been eliminated from the body, users may experience flashbacks, in the form of perceived intensity of color, the apparent motion of fixed objects, or illusions that present one object when another one is present. Some hallucinogens are present in plants (e.g., mescaline in the peyote cactus), whereas others (e.g., LSD) are synthetic.

Peyote and Mescaline

Mescaline is a psychoactive chemical found naturally in the peyote cactus (*Lophophora williamsii*), which is a small, spineless plant native to Mexico and the U.S. Southwest. The top of the cactus, often called the crown, consists of disk-shaped buttons that can be cut off and dried. These buttons

FIGURE 4.8

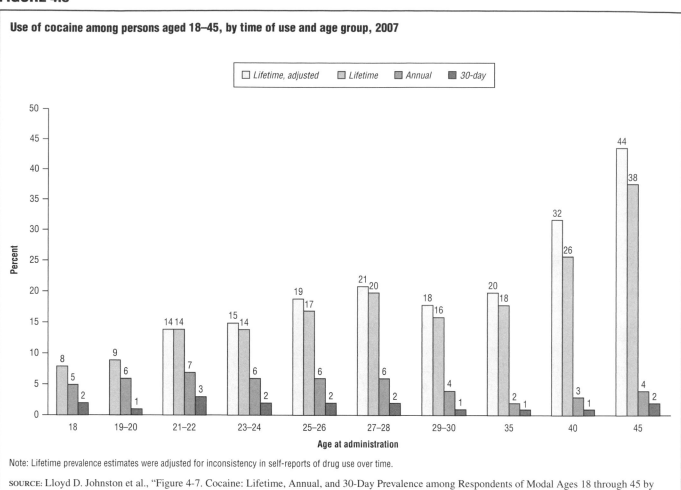

Use of cocaine among persons aged 18–45, by time of use and age group, 2007

Note: Lifetime prevalence estimates were adjusted for inconsistency in self-reports of drug use over time.

SOURCE: Lloyd D. Johnston et al., "Figure 4-7. Cocaine: Lifetime, Annual, and 30-Day Prevalence among Respondents of Modal Ages 18 through 45 by Age Group, 2007," in *Monitoring the Future National Survey Results on Drug Use, 1975–2007: Volume 2, College Students and Adults Ages 19–45*, National Institute on Drug Abuse, 2008, http://www.monitoringthefuture.org/pubs/monographs/vol2_2007.pdf (accessed December 8, 2008)

are generally chewed or soaked in water to produce an intoxicating liquid. A dose of 350 to 500 milligrams produces hallucinations lasting from 5 to 12 hours. Mescaline can be extracted from peyote or produced synthetically.

Peyote and mescaline have long been used by Native Americans in religious ceremonies. The legality of the use of peyote in these ceremonies is decided by individual states.

MDMA and Other Designer Drugs

Designer drugs are those that are produced in a laboratory by making minor modifications to the chemical structure of existing drugs, resulting in new substances with similar effects. DOM (4-methyl-2,5-dimethoxyamphetamine), DOB (4-bromo-2,5-dimethoxyamphetamine), MDA (3,4-methyle nedioxyamphetamine), MDMA (3,4-methylenedioxy-methamphetamine), and other designer drugs are chemical variations of mescaline and amphetamine that have been synthesized in the laboratory. Designer drugs differ from one another in speed of onset, duration of action, and potency. They are usually taken orally, but they can also be snorted or injected intravenously. Because they are produced illegally, designer drugs are seldom pure. Dosage quantity and quality vary considerably.

The most noted designer drug is MDMA (3,4-methylenedioxy-methamphetamine; also called ecstasy). It acts as both a stimulant and a psychedelic and is noted for enhancing a user's sense of touch. It was first banned by the DEA in 1985. The Anti-drug Abuse Act of 1986 made all designer drugs illegal. Widespread abuse placed MDMA in Schedule I of the CSA.

Designer drugs such as MDMA are often used at raves—large, all-night dance parties once held in unusual places such as warehouses or railroad yards. Even though many raves became mainstream events that are professionally organized and held at public venues, the underground style and culture of raves remains an alluring draw to many teenagers. Part of the allure is drug use. For this reason, such drugs are also called club drugs. (Club drugs include MDMA, flunitrazepam, LSD, and methamphetamine, among others.)

Users of MDMA have been known to suffer serious psychological effects—including confusion, depression, sleep problems, drug craving, severe anxiety, and paranoia—both during and sometimes weeks after taking the drug. Physical symptoms include muscle tension, involuntary teeth clenching, nausea, blurred vision, rapid eye movement, faintness, and chills or sweating. MDMA can also interfere with the body's ability to regulate temperature, and severe dehydration, particularly among users who dance for hours while under the drug's influence, is a serious hazard.

According to Johnston et al., past-year MDMA use by high school seniors rose from 3.6% in 1998 to 9.2% in 2001. Since then a dramatic decline in MDMA use in this group occurred. By 2007 only 4.5% of high school seniors used MDMA in the past year. Similar declines occurred among college students and young adults. Johnston et al. suggest the decline is due in large part to educational campaigns on the adverse effects of MDMA and the decreasing novelty of all-night raves.

LSD

LSD is one of the most potent mood-changing chemicals in existence. Odorless, colorless, and tasteless, it is produced from a substance derived from ergot fungus or from a chemical found in morning glory seeds. Both chemicals are found in Schedule III of the CSA, whereas LSD itself is a Schedule I substance.

LSD is usually sold in tablets, thin squares of gelatin, or impregnated paper. It can also be taken in a liquid form dropped on the tongue or in the eyes with an eye dropper. The effects of doses higher than 30 to 50 micrograms can persist for 10 to 12 hours, severely impairing judgment and decision making. Tolerance develops rapidly, and more of the drug is needed to achieve the desired effect. It is, however, nonaddictive.

Because of its structural similarity to a chemical present in the brain, LSD was originally used as a research tool to study the mechanism of mental illness. It was later adopted by the drug culture of the 1960s. LSD use dropped in the 1980s, showed a resurgence in the 1990s, and then dropped again through 2007. Johnston et al. note that the annual prevalence of use of LSD in 2007 was 2.1% for high school seniors, 1.3% for college students, and 1.1% for young adults.

Phencyclidine and Related Drugs

Many drug-treatment professionals believe that phencyclidine (PCP) poses greater risks to the user than any other drug. In the United States most PCP is manufactured in clandestine laboratories and sold on the black market. This drug is sold under at least 50 different names, many of which reflect its bizarre and volatile effects. It is often sold to users who think they are buying mescaline or LSD.

Because PCP is an anesthetic, it produces an inability to feel pain, which can lead to serious bodily injury. Unlike other hallucinogens, PCP produces depression in some

individuals. Regular use often impairs memory, perception, concentration, motor movement, and judgment. PCP can also produce a psychotic state in many ways indistinguishable from schizophrenia, or it can lead to hallucinations, mood swings, paranoia, and amnesia.

Because of the extreme psychic disorders associated with repeated use, or even one dose, of PCP and related drugs, Congress passed the Psychotropic Substances Act of 1978. The penalties imposed for the manufacture or possession of these chemicals are the stiffest of any non-narcotic violation under the CSA.

In its pure form PCP is a white crystalline powder that readily dissolves in water. It can also be taken in tablet or capsule form. It can be swallowed, snorted, smoked, or injected. It is commonly applied to a leafy material, such as parsley, mint, oregano, or marijuana, and smoked. According to Johnston et al., the annual prevalence of use of PCP in 2007 was only 0.9% for high school seniors and 0.3% for young adults. No figure was available for college students.

Prevalence of Hallucinogen Use

According to the NSDUH, about one million people aged 12 and older used hallucinogens in the past month in 2007. (See Figure 4.2.) In 2007 current users were concentrated among 18- to 26-year-olds, while annual use persisted up into the 29- to 30-year-old group. (See Figure 4.9.) Johnston et al. indicate that the annual prevalence for hallucinogen use other than LSD in 2007 was 4.8% for high school seniors, 4.7% for college students, and 3.6% for young adults.

INHALANTS

Inhalants were the least used group of illicit drugs in 2007. (See Figure 4.2.) Inhalants are volatile liquids, such as cleaning fluids, glue, gasoline, paint, and turpentine, the vapors of which are inhaled. Sometimes the sprays of aerosols are inhaled, such as those of spray paints, spray deodorants, hair spray, or fabric protector spray. According to the NSDUH, an estimated 775,000 people tried inhalants for the first time in 2007. As in past years, this group was dominated by those aged 18 and under, representing 66.3% of new users. The NSDUH also reports that in 2007, 1.2% of people aged 12 to 17 were current inhalant users, as were 0.4% of those aged 18 to 25 and 0.1% of those aged 26 and older.

OTHER ILLICIT DRUGS
Heroin

Heroin is a narcotic, as are oxycodone, hydrocodone, and morphine. Heroin, however, is not used as a medicine, so it is not included with the psychotherapeutics.

Heroin is extracted from morphine, which is extracted from opium. This drug was not used extensively until the Bayer Company of Germany began commercial production in 1898. It was widely accepted as a painkiller for years

FIGURE 4.9

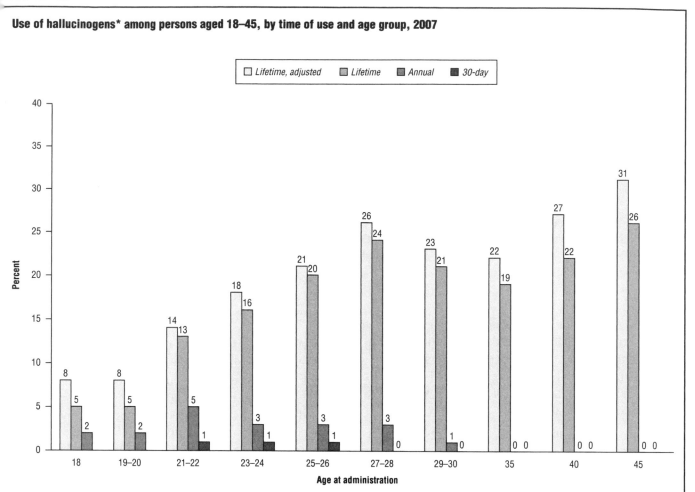

Use of hallucinogens* among persons aged 18–45, by time of use and age group, 2007

Note: Lifetime prevalence estimates were adjusted for inconsistency in self-reports of drug use over time.
*Unadjusted for the possible underreporting of PCP.

SOURCE: Lloyd D. Johnston et al., "Figure 4-10. Hallucinogens: Lifetime, Annual, and 30-Day Prevalence among Respondents of Modal Ages 18 through 45 by Age Group, 2007," in *Monitoring the Future National Survey Results on Drug Use, 1975–2007: Volume 2, College Students and Adults Ages 19–45*, National Institute on Drug Abuse, 2008, http://www.monitoringthefuture.org/pubs/monographs/vol2_2007.pdf (accessed December 8, 2008)

with the medical profession largely unaware of its potential for addiction. However, by 1914 the Harrison Narcotic Act established control of heroin in the United States.

Pure heroin, a bitter white powder, is usually dissolved and injected. Street-quality heroin may vary in color from white to dark brown, depending on the amount of impurities left from the extraction process or the presence of additives, such as food coloring, cocoa, or brown sugar.

Black tar heroin is popular in the western United States. A crudely processed form of heroin, black tar is manufactured illegally in Mexico and derives its name from its sticky, dark brown or black appearance. Black tar is often sold on the street in its tar-like state and can be diluted with substances such as burned cornstarch or converted into a powder.

In the past heroin was usually injected—intravenously (the preferred method), subcutaneously, or intramuscularly. The increased availability of high-purity heroin, however,

meant that users could snort or smoke the drug, which contributed to an increase in heroin use. Snorting or smoking is more appealing to users who fear contracting the human immunodeficiency virus (HIV) and hepatitis through needles shared with potentially infected users. Users who smoke or snort heroin also avoid the stigma attached to heroin use: the marks of the needle left on one's skin. Once hooked, however, many abusers who started by snorting or smoking the drug shift to intravenous use.

Symptoms and signs of heroin use include euphoria, drowsiness, respiratory depression, constricted pupils, and nausea. Withdrawal symptoms include watery eyes, runny nose, yawning, loss of appetite, tremors, panic, chills, sweating, nausea, diarrhea, muscle cramps, and insomnia. Elevations in blood pressure, pulse, respiratory rate, and temperature occur as withdrawal progresses. Because heroin abusers are often unaware of the actual strength of the drug and its true contents, they are at risk of overdose. Symptoms of overdose, which may result in death, include shallow breathing, clammy skin, convulsions, and coma. The NSDUH reports that 153,000 Americans aged 12 and older were current heroin users in 2007. This is a decrease from 338,000 current heroin users in 2006.

Anabolic Steroids

Anabolic steroids are drugs derived from the male sex hormone testosterone. They are used illegally by some athletes, including weight lifters, bodybuilders, long-distance runners, cyclists, and others who believe these drugs can give them a competitive advantage or improve their physical appearance. When used in combination with exercise training and a high-protein diet, anabolic steroids can lead to increased size and strength of muscles, improved endurance, and shorter recovery time between workouts.

Steroids are taken orally or by intramuscular injection. Most are smuggled into the United States and sold at gyms and competitions or by mail-order companies. In 1991 concerns about anabolic steroids led Congress to place them into Schedule III of the CSA.

There is growing evidence of serious health problems from taking anabolic steroids, including cardiovascular and liver damage and harm to reproductive organs. The U.S. Department of Justice and the DEA's Diversion Control Program list the effects of steroids in "Anabolic Steroids—Hidden Dangers" (March 2008, http://www.deadiversion.usdoj.gov/pubs/brochures/steroids/hidden/hiddendangers.pdf). Physical side effects are many and include elevated LDL (bad) cholesterol levels and reduced HDL (good) cholesterol levels, severe acne, premature balding, mood swings, and atrophying of the testicles. Males may develop breasts, whereas females may experience a deepening of the voice, increased body-hair growth, fewer menstrual cycles, and diminished breast size. Some of these effects can be irreversible. In adolescents, bone development may stop, causing stunted growth. Some users become violently aggressive.

By the turn of the 21st century a few professional sports agencies had begun to acknowledge that widespread steroid use was taking place in their ranks. In 2005 Major League Baseball (MLB) initiated regular testing of players for steroid use. New York Yankees shortstop Alex Rodriguez in early 2009 was accused of using steroids back in 2003 when he played for the Texas Rangers, joining a long list of other record-breaking, award-winning MLB players implicated in the use of performance-enhancing drugs that included Roger Clemens, Mark McGwire, and Barry Bonds. Derek Kravitz in the Washingtonpost.com (February 10, 2009, http://voices.washingtonpost.com/washingtonpostinvestigations/2009/02/fact_and_fiction_in_baseballs_steroids.html) stated, "Since steroids became a full-blown scandal in Major League Baseball five years ago, some of the game's most famous players have testified before Congress, held news conferences pro-claiming their innocence (or sometimes guilt) and dealt with the fallout any way they could."

Steroid use is not limited to professional athletes, however. Danice K. Eaton et al. report in "Youth Risk Behavior Surveillance—United States, 2007" (*Morbidity and Mortality Weekly Report*, vol. 57, no. SS-4, June 6, 2008) that in 2007, 5.6% of male high school students and 1.9% of female students had used illegal steroids by the time they were seniors. Johnston et al. determine the annual prevalence rates for androstenedione, a precursor to anabolic steroids, which was available over the counter until early 2005: among males, annual prevalence rates of this drug in 2007 were 0.9%, 0.9%, and 1.2% in 8th, 10th, and 12th grades, respectively. The rates among females in 2007 were lower than among males: 0.8%, 0.2%, and 0.4% in 8th, 10th, and 12th grades, respectively.

ILLICIT DRUG USE DURING PREGNANCY

Illicit drug use during pregnancy places both mother and the fetus (unborn child) at risk for serious health problems. For example, a fetus may become addicted to heroin in its mother's womb—provided the fetus reaches full term and is born (fetal death is a possibility). Cocaine use by the pregnant mother carries similar risks to the fetus and may kill the mother as well. LSD use may lead to birth defects. PCP users may have smaller-than-normal babies who later turn out to have poor muscle control. Learning disabilities are associated with children born to women using cocaine and MDMA while pregnant. Smoking marijuana may prevent an embryo from attaching to the uterine wall and halt pregnancy.

The NSDUH surveyed pregnant women as to their illicit drug use. Results from this 2007 survey, as well as from those conducted in 2004, 2005, and 2006, are shown in Table 4.3. A smaller percentage of pregnant women took illicit drugs than did women who were not pregnant. However, illicit drug use did occur. In 2006–07, 5.2% of pregnant women took illicit drugs. The most prevalent illicit drug use during pregnancy was smoking marijuana and hashish: 3.8% in 2006–07, up from 2.8% in 2004–05. Even though smoking marijuana may seem safe to some pregnant women, it is not. In *NIDA Research Report Series: Marijuana Abuse* (July 2005, http://www.drugabuse.gov/PDF/RRMarijuana.pdf), the National Institute on Drug Abuse lists many of the effects of marijuana abuse during pregnancy, all of which relate to detrimental effects on the developing brain and other parts of the nervous system of the fetus.

The next most used illicit drugs during pregnancy are psychotherapeutics taken for nonmedical reasons. (See Table 4.3.) Over 1% of pregnant women in 2004–05 and 2006–07 took these prescription drugs, such as pain relievers, tranquilizers, stimulants, and sedatives. Of the psychotherapeutics, pain relievers were taken the most often. The percentage of pregnant women who used heroin, hallucinogens, or inhalants during their pregnancy was low.

TABLE 4.3

Percentage of past-month illicit drug use among females aged 15–44, by pregnancy status, 2004–05 and 2006–07

Drug	Total[c]		Pregnancy status			
			Pregnant		Not pregnant	
	2004–2005	2006–2007	2004–2005	2006–2007	2004–2005	2006–2007
Illicit drugs[d]	9.6	9.5	3.9	5.2	9.9	9.7
Marijuana and hashish	6.9	6.7	2.8	3.8	7.1	6.8
Cocaine	1.1	1	0.3	0.4	1.1	1
Crack	0.3	0.2	0.1	0.3	0.3[a]	0.2
Heroin	0.1	0.1	0.1	0.1	0.1	0.1
Hallucinogens	0.4[a]	0.6	0.2	0.1	0.4[a]	0.6
LSD	0	0.1	0.1	0	0	0.1
PCP	0	0	*	0	0	0
Ecstasy	0.3[a]	0.4	0.1	0.1	0.3[a]	0.4
Inhalants	0.2	0.3	0.1	0.3	0.2	0.3
Nonmedical use of psychotherapeutics3[e,f]	3.8	3.6	1.4	1.2	3.9	3.7
Pain Relievers	2.7	2.6	1.2	0.8	2.8	2.7
OxyContin®	0.2	0.2	0.1	0	0.2	0.2
Tranquilizers	1.1	1.1	0.3	0.3	1.1	1.1
Stimulants[f]	0.9	0.8	0.2	0.4	0.9	0.8
Methamphetamine[f]	0.4	0.3	0.1	0.1	0.4	0.3
Sedatives	0.2	0.2	0	0	0.2	0.2
Illicit drugs other than marijuana[d]	4.7	4.7	1.6	1.9	4.9	4.8

*Low precision; no estimate reported.
[a]Difference between estimate and 2006–2007 estimate is statistically significant.
[b]Difference between estimate and 2006–2007 estimate is statistically significant.
[c]Estimates in the total column are for all females aged 15 to 44, including those with unknown pregnancy status.
[d]Illicit drugs include marijuana/hashish, cocaine (including crack), heroin, hallucinogens, inhalants, or prescription-type psychotherapeutics used nonmedically. Illicit drugs other than marijuana include cocaine (including crack), heroin, hallucinogens, inhalants, or prescription-type psychotherapeutics used nonmedically. The estimates for nonmedical use of psychotherapeutics, stimulants, and methamphetamine incorporated in these summary estimates do not include data from the methamphetamine items added in 2005 and 2006.
[e]Nonmedical use of prescription-type psychotherapeutics includes the nonmedical use of pain relievers, tranquilizers, stimulants, or sedatives and does not include over-the-counter drugs.
[f]Estimates of nonmedical use of psychotherapeutics, stimulants, and methamphetamine in the designated rows include data from methamphetamine items added in 2005 and 2006 and are not comparable with estimates presented in prior NSDUH reports.

SOURCE: "Table 7.69B. Types of Illicit Drug Use in the Past Month among Females Aged 15 to 44, by Pregnancy Status: Percentages, Annual Averages Based on 2004–2005 and 2006–2007," in *2007 National Survey on Drug Use and Health: Detailed Tables*, U.S. Department of Health and Human Services, Substance Abuse and Mental Health Services Administration, Office of Applied Studies, September 2008, http://oas.samhsa.gov/NSDUH/2k7NSDUH/tabs/Sect7peTabs59to115.htm#Tab7.69B (accessed December 10, 2008)

DRUG ABUSE ARRESTS

Tina L. Dorsey, Doris J. James, and Priscilla Middleton of the Bureau of Justice Statistics (BJS) estimate in *Drugs and Crime Facts* (August 14, 2008, http://www.ojp.usdoj.gov/bjs/pub/pdf/dcf.pdf) that there were nearly 1.9 million arrests for drug abuse violations in 2006. The estimated number of arrests for drug abuse violations has been increasing rather steadily since the early 1990s. (See Figure 4.10.) The researchers also note that drug arrests increased as a percentage of all arrests, from 7.4% in 1987 to 13.1% in 2006. Drug abuse violations topped the list of the seven leading arrest offenses in the United States in 2006. That year more people were arrested for drug abuse violations (1.9 million) than were arrested for driving under the influence (1.5 million), simple assault (1.3 million), larceny/theft (1.1 million), disorderly conduct (703,000), liquor laws (645,000), or drunkenness (553,000).

Possession versus Sale

Most people arrested for drug offenses are charged with possession (carrying some kind of drug) rather than with trafficking (the sale or manufacture of drugs). Dorsey, James, and Middleton state that in 2006 more than four-

FIGURE 4.10

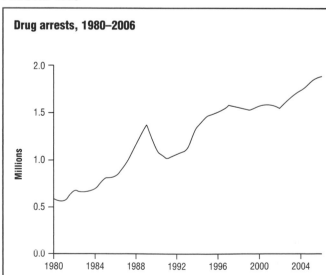

Drug arrests, 1980–2006

SOURCE: Tina L. Dorsey, Doris J. James, and Priscilla Middleton, "Drug Abuse Violation Arrests, 1980–2006," in *Drugs and Crime Facts*, U.S. Department of Justice, Bureau of Justice Statistics, August 14, 2008, http://www.ojp.usdoj.gov/bjs/dcf/enforce.htm (accessed August 19, 2008)

fifths of those arrested for drug law violations were for possession.

ARRESTEE DRUG USE

The National Institute of Justice operated the Arrestee Drug Abuse Monitoring (ADAM) Program from 1987 to 2004 and published an annual report that summarized the previous year's data. The most recent report, *Drug and Alcohol Use and Related Matters among Arrestees, 2003* (April 2003, http://www.ncjrs.gov/nij/adam/ADAM2003 .pdf) by Zhiwei Zhang of the National Opinion Research Center, analyzes data gathered through 2003. The ADAM Program ended in 2004 in response to budgetary consider-ations, with plans of being resumed when funding became available. As of spring 2009, the program had not been reinstituted.

In 2003 the ADAM Program surveyed arrestees in 39 urban sites about drug use in the past year and conducted urinalyses to determine if any of nine drugs (barbiturates, benzodiazepines, cocaine, marijuana, methadone, metham-phetamine, opiates, PCP, and propoxyphene) or alcohol had been used recently. Zhang notes that in half of the sites surveyed, urinalysis revealed that over 67% of adult male arrestees in 2003 had used at least one of five drugs: marijuana, cocaine, methamphetamine, opiates, or PCP. Use ranged from a low of 41.6% of arrestees in Woodbury, Iowa, to a high of 86% in Chicago, Illinois. In half the sites at least 23% tested positive for multiple drugs, with a low of 10.3% in Woodbury and a high of 38.1% in Chicago.

Arrests and Race

Enforcing the official public policy on drugs has a sig-nificant impact on the nation's justice system: local policing, the courts, and the state and federal corrections systems. A relatively small percentage of total users are arrested, but at increasing rates. Sentencing policies have changed to require mandatory incarceration of those who possess, not just those who sell, drugs. As a consequence, prison populations have swollen, thereby putting pressure on prison capacities. The number of people in state correctional facilities for drug offenses escalated from 19,000 in 1980 to 250,000 in 2005. (See Figure 4.11.) Of the inmate population under state jurisdiction in 2005, 253,300 (19.5%) were incarcerated for drug offenses. (See Table 4.4.)

The proportion of state prison inmates incarcerated on drug charges differ for whites, African-Americans, and His-panics. In 2005, 72,300 (out of 253,300, or 28.5%) of state drug offense arrestees were white, 113,500 (44.8%) were African-American, and 51,100 (20.2%) were Hispanic. (See Table 4.4.) The remainder were people of other races and ethnicities.

CONVICTION AND SENTENCING TRENDS

According to Dorsey, James, and Middleton, drug pros-ecutions account for an increasing proportion of the federal

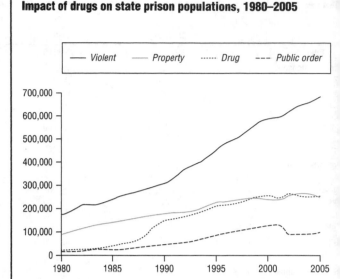

FIGURE 4.11

Impact of drugs on state prison populations, 1980–2005

SOURCE: Tina L. Dorsey, Doris J. James, and Priscilla Middleton, "State Prison Population by Offense Type, 1980–2004," in *Drugs and Crime Facts*, U.S. Department of Justice, Bureau of Justice Statistics, August 14, 2008, http://www.ojp.usdoj.gov/bjs/dcf/correct.htm#State (accessed August 19, 2008)

criminal caseload, growing from 21% of defendants in 1982 to 35% in 2004. Similarly, the number of convictions of drug defendants increased from 76% in 1981 to 92% in 2004. Along with higher conviction rates came more and longer prison sentences for drug offenses. The proportion of drug offenders sentenced to federal prison rose from 79% in 1988 to 93% in 2004. Table 4.5 shows that the duration of sen-tences fluctuated in the twenty years between 1988 and 2007, increasing from 78 months in 1988 to 95.7 months in 1991, then generally decreasing to a low of 73.8 months in 2001 before steadily increasing to 88.9 months in 2007.

Convictions and Race

Dorsey, James, and Middleton note that of the 282,592 adults arrested at the state level for drug trafficking in 2004, 201,760 were convicted. Of those convicted, 83% were male, 51% were white, and 47% were African-American. In absolute numbers, more whites are arrested and convicted for drug violations than African-Americans, but African-Americans are much more likely not only to be arrested but also to be convicted in proportion to their representation in the population. According the U.S. Census Bureau (August 13, 2008, http://www.census.gov/population/www/projections/usinterimproj/usproj2000-2050.xls), in 2004 the U.S. pop-ulation was 80.3% (235,250,847 of 292,800,571) white and 12.8% (37,594,748) African-American.

The Human Rights Watch (HRW), an independent nongovernmental organization dedicated to protecting the human rights of people around the world, documents racial disparities in the incarceration of state drug offenders

TABLE 4.4

Number of sentenced offenders in state prisons, by race, gender, and offense, 2005

	All inmates	Male	Female	White[a]	Black[a]	Hispanic
Total	1,296,700	1,208,500	88,200	470,700	504,700	240,100
Violent offenses	687,700	656,400	31,200	235,800	275,700	131,500
Murder[b]	166,700	156,800	9,800	49,300	72,100	32,200
Manslaughter	16,700	15,100	1,700	6,900	6,500	2,300
Rape	60,800	60,300	500	30,000	20,900	6,800
Other sexual assault	103,800	102,300	1,500	58,000	21,200	21,500
Robbery	177,900	170,300	7,600	38,700	95,200	30,700
Assault	129,200	121,400	7,700	40,500	48,100	32,000
Other violent	32,500	30,200	2,400	12,400	11,700	6,000
Property offenses	248,900	223,700	25,200	114,700	81,300	38,800
Burglary	124,400	118,800	5,600	54,500	42,900	20,500
Larceny	45,200	38,200	7,100	20,500	16,200	5,700
Motor vehicle theft	22,400	21,100	1,300	9,100	5,500	6,700
Fraud	32,100	22,800	9,200	17,900	9,600	2,400
Other property	24,800	22,800	2,100	12,800	7,200	3,500
Drug offenses	253,300	228,000	25,300	72,300	113,500	51,100
Public-order offenses[c]	98,700	93,400	5,300	44,200	31,600	17,500
Other/unspecified[d]	8,100	7,100	1,100	3,700	2,600	1,300

Note: Data are for inmates sentenced to more than 1 year under the jurisdiction of state correctional authorities. The estimates for gender were based on jurisdiction counts at yearend. The estimates by race and Hispanic origin were based on data from 2005 Survey of Inmates in State Correctional Facilities and updated by yearend jurisdiction counts; estimates within offense categories were based on offense distributions from the National Corrections Reporting Program, 2005, updated by yearend jurisdiction counts. All estimates were rounded to the nearest 100. Detail may not add to total due to rounding.

[a]Excludes Hispanics and persons identifying two or more races.

[b]Includes negligent manslaughter.

[c]Includes weapons, drunk driving, court offenses, commercialized vice, morals and decency offenses, liquor law violations, and other public-order offenses.

[d]Includes juvenile offenses and other unspecified offense categories.

SOURCE: Heather C. West and William J. Sabol, "Appendix Table 10. Estimated Number of Sentenced Prisoners under State Jurisdiction, by Offense, Gender, Race, and Hispanic Origin, Yearend 2005," in *Prisoners in 2007*, U.S. Department of Justice, Office of Justice Programs, Bureau of Justice Statistics, December 2008, http://www.ojp.usdoj.gov/bjs/pub/pdf/p07.pdf (accessed December 26, 2008)

The HRW considers crime rates, law enforcement priorities, and sentencing legislation as factors that contribute to creating racial disparities in incarceration. It contends that African-Americans have been disproportionately affected by the war on drugs, which largely aims to arrest, prosecute, and imprison street-level drug offenders from inner-city areas. Bolstering its claims, the HRW discusses in "US: World's Leading Jailer, New Numbers Show" (December 11, 2008, http://www.hrw.org/en/news/2008/12/10/us-world-s-leading-jailer-new-numbers-show/) these racial disparities and notes that African-American males are jailed at a rate 6.5 times that of white males.

THE BROADER RELATIONSHIP BETWEEN ILLICIT DRUGS AND CRIME

The relationship between illicit drugs and crime goes beyond the fact that illicit drug use is inherently illegal. There are strong correlations between drug use and a variety of nondrug crimes. There are usually three reasons given for this correlation:

• Drugs may reduce inhibitions or stimulate aggression and interfere with the ability to earn a legitimate income.

• People who develop a dependence on an illegal drug need a substantial income to pay for it and may commit crimes to fund their habit.

• Drug trafficking may lead to crimes such as extortion, aggravated assault, and homicide. For example, the Department of Justice reports in *Drug Use and Crime* (August 14, 2008, http://www.ojp.usdoj.gov/bjs/dcf/duc.htm) that 4.9% to 7.4% of homicides committed each year between 1987 and 2006 were drug related.

In *Drug Use and Dependence, State and Federal Prisoners, 2004* (October 2006, http://www.ojp.usdoj.gov/bjs/pub/pdf/dudsfp04.pdf), Christopher J. Mumola and Jennifer C. Karberg of the BJS discuss the drug use of state and federal prisoners by the type of offense they committed in 2004. (As of spring 2009 the BJS had not yet updated these data.) Overall, more than half of state and federal prisoners (56% and 50.2%, respectively) reported using illicit drugs in the month before their offense. Unsurprisingly, a high percentage of those in state prison for drug offenses (71.9%) had used drugs in the month before their offense. The correlation between drug use and nondrug crimes can be seen, however, in the fact that 64% of state prisoners who committed property offenses and 49.6% of those who committed violent offenses had used drugs in the month before their offense. The percentages for federal prisoners were lower but still substantial, with 57.3% of drug offenders, 49.1% of violent offenders, and 27.7% of property offenders reporting drug use in the month before their offense. Furthermore, more than a quarter of state and

TABLE 4.5

Sentences for violation of drug laws, by type and length of sentence, U.S. District Courts, 1945–2007

		Type of sentence									Average sentence to imprisonment (in months)[d]	Average sentence to probation (in months)
		Imprisonment										
		Regular sentences[a]										
	Total	Total regular	1 through 12 months	13 through 35 months	36 through 60 months	Over 60 months	Life sentences	Other[b]	Probation	Fine and other[c]		
1945	861	X	308	360	140	53	NA	X	287	37	22.2	NA
1946	949	X	430	377	108	34	NA	X	369	20	18.7	NA
1947	1,128	X	471	452	161	44	NA	X	504	38	19.7	NA
1948	1,048	X	488	408	122	30	NA	X	411	23	18.6	NA
1949	1,187	X	541	451	152	43	NA	X	398	13	18.9	NA
1950	1,654	X	595	736	218	105	NA	X	471	11	21.9	NA
1951	1,659	X	473	671	328	187	NA	X	345	24	27.1	NA
1952	1,551	X	221	652	402	276	NA	X	312	6	35.2	NA
1953	1,586	X	108	789	358	331	NA	X	403	14	38.4	NA
1954	1,483	X	72	681	360	370	NA	X	411	16	41.3	NA
1955	1,457	X	47	648	360	402	NA	X	329	17	43.5	NA
1956	1,258	X	30	511	341	376	NA	X	250	13	45.8	NA
1957	1,432	X	16	326	248	842	NA	X	220	2	66.0	NA
1958	1,351	X	25	167	141	1,018	NA	X	282	8	69.4	NA
1959	1,151	X	43	126	95	887	NA	X	224	3	74.2	NA
1960	1,232	X	33	145	148	906	NA	X	271	3	72.8	NA
1961	1,258	X	42	126	105	985	NA	X	252	5	74.0	NA
1962	1,173	X	38	129	106	900	NA	X	217	13	70.5	NA
1963	1,085	X	39	144	113	789	NA	X	304	17	70.1	NA
1964	1,076	X	28	142	157	749	NA	X	309	23	63.7	NA
1965	1,257	X	53	186	197	821	NA	X	480	18	60.3	NA
1966	1,272	X	85	154	276	757	NA	X	589	13	61.3	NA
1967	1,180	X	83	139	245	713	NA	X	620	22	62.0	NA
1968	1,368	X	93	141	293	841	NA	X	728	33	64.4	NA
1969	1,581	X	110	179	500	892	NA	X	1,110	18	63.7	NA
1970	1,283	X	101	166	276	740	NA	X	1,156	22	64.8	NA
1971	1,834	X	249	300	428	857	NA	X	1,258	70	58.5	NA
1972	3,050	X	882	396	789	983	NA	X	2,068	130	46.4	NA
1973	5,097	X	1,445	744	1,343	1,565	NA	X	2,591	126	45.5	NA
1974	5,125	X	1,547	792	1,390	1,396	NA	X	3,039	81	43.7	NA
1975	4,887	X	1,366	706	1,441	1,374	NA	X	3,209	55	45.3	NA
1976	5,039	X	1,221	790	1,544	1,484	NA	X	2,927	75	47.6	NA
1977	5,223	X	1,505	886	1,366	1,466	NA	X	2,324	88	47.3	NA
1978	4,119	3,605	885	623	956	1,141	NA	514	1,630	68	51.3	38.6
1979	3,641	2,820	369	614	868	969	NA	821	1,379	47	50.8	37.8
1980	3,479	2,547	281	565	792	909	NA	932	1,232	38	54.5	38.7
1981	3,856	2,865	403	578	748	1,136	NA	991	1,371	119	55.5	36.6
1982	4,586	3,516	383	729	966	1,438	NA	1,070	1,617	133	61.4	34.1
1983	5,449	4,150	447	890	1,011	1,802	NA	1,299	1,893	148	63.8	33.7
1984	5,756	4,306	354	845	1,173	1,934	NA	1,450	1,584	119	65.7	43.2
1985	6,786	5,207	411	1,103	1,459	2,234	NA	1,579	2,039	238	64.8	36.2
1986	8,152	6,601	506	1,271	1,808	3,016	NA	1,551	2,353	259	70.0	38.7
1987	9,907	8,188	613	1,491	2,049	4,035	NA	1,719	2,680	112	73.0	39.9
1988	9,983	8,560	708	1,466	1,577	4,809	NA	1,423	3,042	137	78.0	33.4
1989	11,626	10,838	1,270	2,343	1,844	5,381	NA	788	2,358	155	73.8	32.8
1990	13,838	13,462	1,490	3,047	1,801	7,124	NA	376	2,135	215	79.3	32.3
1991	14,382[f]	14,286	1,687	2,828	3,063	6,708	34	61	1,896	68	95.7	53.4
1992	16,040	15,775	1,810	3,423	3,397	7,145	80	185	2,011	194	87.8	38.7
1993	16,995[f]	16,639	2,097	3,383	4,128	7,031	186	169	1,943	310	83.2	35.8
1994	15,623	15,130	1,836	3,074	3,798	6,422	238	255	1,908	73	84.3	34.4
1995	14,157	13,734	1,606	2,716	3,311	6,101	150	273	1,597	107	88.7	33.6
1996	18,333	16,684	1,643	3,334	4,025	7,113	197	372	1,534	112	82.5	35.0
1997	18,231[f]	17,456	1,687	4,166	4,445	7,158	228	546	1,523	79	79.3	34.9
1998	19,809	19,062	2,100	4,443	4,517	8,002	180	567	1,629	91	78.0	34.9
1999	22,443[f]	21,513	2,670	5,074	5,240	8,529	205	724	1,719	85	74.6	34.2
2000	23,120	22,207	2,523	5,095	5,452	9,137	148	765	1,591	75	75.7	35.1
2001	24,011	23,127	2,780	5,350	5,670	9,327	122	762	1,671	133	73.8	34.5
2002	25,031	23,838	2,825	5,250	5,727	10,036	168	1,025	1,947	148	75.9	33.4
2003	25,060	23,937	2,632	4,781	5,967	10,557	157	966	1,781	145	80.2	32.2

federal prisoners (32.1% and 26.4%, respectively) reported they were using illicit drugs at the time of their offense.

Table 4.6 shows drug use in the month before the offense by selected characteristics of state and federal prisoners, comparing results from 1997 and 2004. For state prisoners the likelihood that they used drugs in the month before the offense stayed the same from 1997 to 2004, at approximately 56%. The likelihood that federal prisoners used drugs in the month before their offense rose from 44.8% in 1997 to 50.2% in 2004. For state prisoners women were more likely than men to have used drugs in the month before their offense in both years. Federal prisoners showed the opposite trend—men were

TABLE 4.5

Sentences for violation of drug laws, by type and length of sentence, U.S. District Courts, 1945–2007 [CONTINUED]

		Type of sentence										Average sentence to imprisonment (in months)[d]	Average sentence to probation (in months)[e]
		Imprisonment											
		Regular sentences[a]											
	Total	Total regular	1 through 12 months	13 through 35 months	36 through 60 months	Over 60 months	Life sentences	Other[b]	Probation	Fine and other[c]		
2004	23,920	22,984	2,581	4,181	5,553	10,669	146	790	1,598	184		82.5	28.4
2005	24,786	23,831	2,389	4,296	5,719	11,427	151	804	1,508	294		85.7	32.7
2006	26,488[g]	25,437	2,035	4,438	6,159	12,805	195	853	1,548	275		87.9	31.8
2007	25,520	24,439	2,132	4,017	5,962	12,328	171	910	1,344	250		88.9	31.0

Notes: Data for 1945–91 are reported for the 12-month period ending June 30. Beginning in 1992, data are reported for the federal fiscal year, which is the 12-month period ending September 30.

Includes sentences of more than 6 months that are to be followed by a term of probation (mixed sentences). Beginning in 1991, includes sentences of at least 1 month that may be followed by a term of probation.

From 1978–88, "other" includes split sentences, indeterminate sentences, and Youth Corrections Act and youthful offender sentences. In 1989 and 1990, the category includes split sentences and indeterminate sentences. Beginning in 1991, "other" includes deportation, suspended and sealed sentences, imprisonment of 4 days or less, and no sentence.

Includes supervised release, probation of 4 days or less, suspended sentences, sealed sentences, and no sentence.

From 1978–90, split sentences, Youth Corrections Act and youthful offender sentences, and life sentences were not included in computing average sentence. Beginning in 1991, life sentences, death sentences, deportation, suspended and sealed sentences, imprisonment of 4 days or less, and no sentence also are not included in computing average sentence.

From 1986–90, split sentences, indeterminate sentences, and Youth Corrections Act and youthful offender sentences were not included in computing average sentence. Beginning in 1991, supervised release, probation of 4 days or less, suspended sentences, sealed sentences, and no sentence also are not included in computing average sentence.

Includes one death sentence.

Includes three death sentences.

SOURCE: Ann L. Pastore and Kathleen Maguire, eds., "Table 5.38.2007. Defendants Sentenced for Violation of Drug Laws in U.S. District Courts," in *Sourcebook of Criminal Justice Statistics Online*, U.S. Department of Justice, Bureau of Justice Statistics, University at Albany School of Criminal Justice, Hindelang Criminal Justice Research Center, 2008, http://www.albany.edu/sourcebook/pdf/t5382007.pdf (accessed August 19, 2008)

TABLE 4.6

Drug use among state and federal prisoners in the month before their offense, by demographic characteristics, 1997 and 2004

	State		Federal	
Characteristic	2004	1997	2004	1997
All prisoners	56.0%	56.5%	50.2%	44.8%
Gender				
Male	55.7%	56.1%	50.4%	45.4%
Female	59.3	62.4	47.6	36.7
Race/Hispanic origin				
White[a]	57.7%	55.2%	58.2%	49.4%
Black[a]	56.0	58.3	52.7	47.2
Hispanic	53.5	55.0	38.4	37.5
Other[a, b]	52.9	52.7	48.4	38.5
Age				
24 or younger	66.2%	63.2%	62.0%	57.2%
25–34	60.9	60.0	56.7	48.5
35–44	54.9	56.5	47.9	46.8
45–54	47.4	40.4	44.9	35.2
55 or older	19.2	18.4	20.9	24.3

Excludes persons of Hispanic origin.

Includes Asians, American Indians, Alaska Natives, Native Hawaiians, other Pacific Islanders, and inmates who specified more than one race.

SOURCE: Christopher J. Mumola and Jennifer C. Karberg, "Table 3. Drug Use in the Month before the Offense, by Selected Characteristics of State and Federal Prisoners, 1997 and 2004," in *Drug Use and Dependence, State and Federal Prisoners, 2004*, U.S. Department of Justice, Office of Justice Programs, Bureau of Justice Statistics, October 2006, http://www.ojp.usdoj.gov/bjs/pub/pdf/dudsfp04.pdf (accessed December 10, 2008)

more likely than women to have used drugs in the month before their offense in both years.

For both state and federal prisoners, people aged 24 and younger were the most likely to have used drugs in the month before the offense in both years. (See Table 4.6.) The likelihood of drug use fell with age in both years and for both sets of prisoners. In general, whites were slightly more likely than African-Americans to have used drugs in the month before their offense in both years. Hispanics were the least likely of the three racial groups to have used drugs in the month before their offense. In 2004 the incidence of drug use was over half for whites (58.2%) and African-Americans (52.7%) in federal prison. Only 38.4% of Hispanic federal prisoners used drugs in the month before their offense.

CHAPTER 5
ALCOHOL, TOBACCO, ILLICIT DRUGS, AND YOUTH

"What do you think is the most important problem facing people your age today?" According to Joseph Carroll of the Gallup Organization, in *Drugs, Smoking, Alcohol Most Important Problem Facing Teens* (February 17, 2006, http://www.gallup.com/poll/21517/Drugs-Smoking-Alcohol-Most-Important-Problem-Facing-Teens.aspx), this question was asked of 480 teenagers aged 13 to 17 in a survey conducted between December 5, 2005, and January 16, 2006. The results show that 31% of this teenaged population placed the consumption of alcohol, tobacco, and drugs at the top of their list of concerns. The next most important problem cited by only 17% of the teens was peer pressure/fitting in/looks/popularity. Sexual issues, such as teen pregnancy, abortion, and sexually transmitted diseases, shared the number-three spot with education; 14% of the teens thought these were the top problems faced by people their age.

Gallup pollsters then separated the teens into two response groups: 13- to 15-year-olds and 16- to 17-year-olds. In both groups the top problem was the same: the consumption of alcohol, tobacco, and drugs, although the younger teens mentioned this problem more frequently (35%) than did the older teens (26%). When separated by sex, male and female teens responded in near-equal percentages (32% and 31%, respectively) that the consumption of alcohol, tobacco, and drugs was the top problem facing people their age.

PROBLEM BEHAVIORS BEGIN EARLY IN LIFE
Risk and Protective Factors

Figure 5.1 shows the risk factors associated with drug addiction. The illustration points out that drug addiction is not due to a single factor but to a variety of interacting factors. A person's heredity and environment act together to influence his or her behavior. More specifically, the National Institute on Drug Abuse (NIDA) notes in *Drugs, Brains, and Behavior: The Science of Addiction* (February 2008, http://www.drugabuse.gov/ScienceofAddiction/sciofaddiction.pdf) that

genetic factors account for about half of an individual's risk for addiction. In addition, certain environmental factors, such as having parents or close friends who use drugs, being a victim of abuse, and being an underachiever in school, raise the risk that an individual will use and become addicted to drugs. Figure 5.1 notes that early use of drugs is also a risk factor for drug addiction.

Protective factors are those that lower the risk for drug addiction. According to the NIDA, these factors include positive relationships with peers and parents, success in schoolwork, self-control, and a strong neighborhood attachment.

Early Use of Alcohol, Tobacco, and Marijuana

Danice K. Eaton et al. of the Centers for Disease Control and Prevention state in "Youth Risk Behavior Surveillance—United States, 2007" (*Morbidity and Mortality Weekly Report*, vol. 57, no. SS-4, June 6, 2008) that high school students were asked if they had smoked a whole cigarette, had drunk alcohol, or had tried marijuana before the age of 13. The results are shown in Table 5.1 and Table 5.2.

A higher percentage of younger students than older students reported having initiated cigarette, alcohol, or marijuana use before age 13. The most frequently reported behavior in 2007 was drinking alcohol before the age of 13. Nearly one-third (30.9%) of 9th graders reported they had done so, as had a quarter (24.4%) of 10th graders and nearly one-fifth of both 11th graders (19.6%) and 12th graders (18%). (See Table 5.1.) Males (27.4%) throughout all grades were more likely to report having had a drink before age 13 than females (20%). Hispanics (29%) were the most likely ethnic group to report having an alcoholic drink before the age of 13, followed by African-Americans (26.7%) and whites (21.5%).

Table 5.1 shows that the next most frequently reported behavior in 2007 was smoking an entire cigarette before the age of 13. Once again, males (16.4%) throughout all grades were more likely than females (11.9%) to report having

FIGURE 5.1

Risk factors for drug addiction

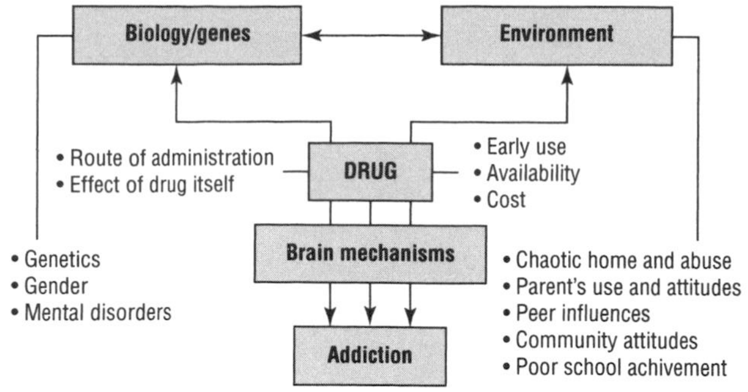

SOURCE: "Risk Factors," in *Drugs, Brains, and Behavior: the Science of Addiction*, National Institutes of Health, U.S. Department of Health and Human Services, National Institute on Drug Abuse, February 2008, http://www.drugabuse.gov/ScienceofAddiction/sciofaddiction.pdf (accessed August 20, 2008)

TABLE 5.2

Percentage of high school students who tried marijuana before age 13, by gender, ethnicity, and grade, 2007

Category	Female %	Male %	Total %
Race/ethnicity			
White*	4.4	10.0	7.2
Black*	4.9	14.2	9.5
Hispanic	7.1	12.4	9.8
Grade			
9	6.1	13.3	9.8
10	5.7	11.7	8.7
11	4.2	10.1	7.2
12	4.2	9.1	6.6
Total	**5.2**	**11.2**	**8.3**

*Non-Hispanic.

SOURCE: Danice K. Eaton et al., "Table 53. Percentage of High School Students Who Tried Marijuana for the First Time before Age 13 Years, by Sex, Race/Ethnicity, and Grade—United States, Youth Risk Behavior Survey, 2007," in "Youth Risk Behavior Surveillance—United States, 2007," *Morbidity & Mortality Weekly Report*, vol. 57, no. SS-4, June 6, 2008, http://www.cdc.gov/HealthyYouth/yrbs/pdf/yrbss07_mmwr.pdf (accessed August 19, 2008)

TABLE 5.1

Percentage of high school students who drank alcohol and smoked cigarettes before age 13, by gender, ethnicity, and grade, 2007

Category	Smoked a whole cigarette before age 13 years Female %	Male %	Total %	Drank alcohol before age 13 years Female %	Male %	Total %
Race/ethnicity						
White*	12.2	16.5	14.4	17.8	25.0	21.5
Black*	10.5	14.6	12.5	22.7	30.7	26.7
Hispanic	11.9	16.8	14.3	24.2	33.6	29.0
Grade						
9	13.2	19.2	16.3	27.1	34.5	30.9
10	12.9	15.7	14.3	22.2	26.6	24.4
11	9.2	14.6	12.0	13.8	25.1	19.6
12	11.5	15.2	13.3	14.8	21.2	18.0
Total	**11.9**	**16.4**	**14.2**	**20.0**	**27.4**	**23.8**

Note: Other than a few sips.
*Non-Hispanic.

SOURCE: Danice K. Eaton et al., "Table 51. Percentage of High School Students Who Smoked a Whole Cigarette and Who Drank Alcohol for the First Time before Age 13 Years, by Sex, Race/Ethnicity, and Grade—United States, Youth Risk Behavior Survey, 2007," in "Youth Risk Behavior Surveillance—United States, 2007," *Morbidity & Mortality Weekly Report*, vol. 57, no. SS-4, June 6, 2008, http://www.cdc.gov/HealthyYouth/yrbs/pdf/yrbss07_mmwr.pdf (accessed August 19, 2008)

smoked a cigarette before age 13. Whites (14.4%) and Hispanics (14.3%) were the groups most likely to report having smoked before their teens. African-Americans (12.5%) reported this behavior slightly less frequently.

The same pattern between males (11.2%) and females (5.2%) emerged with the least frequently reported behavior in 2007 of trying marijuana before the age of 13. (See Table 5.2.) Hispanics (9.8%) were the most likely to report this early behavior, followed closely by African-Americans (9.5%) and whites (7.2%).

ALCOHOL AND YOUTH

Age of First Use

The data in the previous section clearly show that the use of alcohol, tobacco, and marijuana often begins early in life, especially alcohol use. Elizabeth J. D'Amico and Denis M. McCarthy explain in "Escalation and Initiation of Younger Adolescents' Substance Use: The Impact of Perceived Peer Use" (*Journal of Adolescent Health*, vol. 39, no. 4, October 2006) that the middle school years are peak years for the first-time use of alcohol, tobacco, and marijuana.

Even though the precise reasons for alcohol and drug use at young ages have not yet been pinpointed, Drew W. Edwards and Mark S. Gold speculate in "Facts about Marijuana Use" (February 6, 2001, http://psychcentral.com/library/sa_factsm.htm) that a variety of factors contribute to young ages of first use. These include media and other cultural influences that minimize the dangers and glamorize the use of illegal drugs; increasing parental expectations and acceptance of a certain amount of experimentation with illegal drugs; and easy access to alcohol, tobacco, and marijuana. Furthermore, in "Middle Childhood and Early Adolescence: Growth and Change" (2004, http://www.childrenssummit.umn.edu/docs/growthandchange.pdf), the 2004 Minnesota Children's Summit: Staying Strong through Challenge and Change cites less face-to-face contact with working parents and limited parental monitoring of behavior; reduced access to after-school programs; safety concerns that limit children's ability for unstructured outdoor play, which has increased time spent home alone and unsupervised; and greater access to undesirable content via television, music, and the Internet.

The Substance Abuse and Mental Health Services Administration conducts the annual National Survey on Drug Use and Health (NSDUH), and its 2007 survey results are published in *Results from the 2007 National Survey on Drug Use and Health: National Findings* (September 2008, http://www.oas.samhsa.gov/nsduh/2k7 nsduh/2k7Results.pdf). According to the NSDUH, 4.6 million people used alcohol for the first time in 2007. The number of initiates (first-timers) increased from 3.9 million in 2002 and from 4.1 million in 2003. Most (85.9%) of the 4.6 million alcohol initiates in 2007 were younger than the age of 21 when they took their first drink.

Influences on the Decision to Drink

According to the *GfK Roper Youth Report, 2008* (2008, http://alcoholstats.com/mm/docs/6221.pdf), a 2008 nationwide survey of 13- to 17-year-olds, 74% of respondents cited parents as the most influential factor in their decision whether to drink. Best friends (6%) were the second-most important factor influencing a young person's decision to drink (after "don't know" at 13%). The attitudes of one's peer group can hold sway over a young person's alcohol choices, though parents seem the exert the most influence by a large margin.

Current Use of Alcohol in High School Students

It is illegal for high school students to purchase alcoholic beverages, yet Eaton et al. indicate that in 2007, 44.7% of high school students had consumed alcohol at least once in the 30 days before being surveyed. (See Table 5.3.) These

TABLE 5.3

Percentage of high school students who drank alcohol, by gender, ethnicity, and grade, 2007

	Lifetime alcohol use[a]			Current alcohol use[b]		
	Female	Male	Total	Female	Male	Total
Category	%	%	%	%	%	%
Race/ethnicity						
White[c]	76.4	75.8	76.1	47.1	47.4	47.3
Black[c]	70.0	68.4	69.1	34.9	34.1	34.5
Hispanic	79.3	76.5	77.9	47.5	47.7	47.6
Grade						
9	66.1	65.0	65.5	37.2	34.3	35.7
10	74.6	74.9	74.7	42.3	41.4	41.8
11	79.1	79.7	79.4	46.5	51.5	49.0
12	85.2	80.2	82.8	54.2	55.6	54.9
Total	**75.7**	**74.3**	**75.0**	**44.6**	**44.7**	**44.7**

[a]Had at least one drink of alcohol on at least 1 day during their life.
[b]Had at least one drink of alcohol on at least 1 day during the 30 days before the survey.
[c]Non-Hispanic.

SOURCE: Danice K. Eaton et al., "Table 35. Percentage of High School Students Who Drank Alcohol, by Sex, Race/Ethnicity, and Grade—United States, Youth Risk Behavior Survey, 2007," in "Youth Risk Behavior Surveillance—United States, 2007," *Morbidity & Mortality Weekly Report*, vol. 57, no. SS-4, June 6, 2008, http://www.cdc.gov/HealthyYouth/yrbs/pdf/yrbss07_mmwr.pdf (accessed August 19, 2008)

students are considered current users. Lloyd D. Johnston e al. of the University of Michigan, in *Monitoring the Future National Survey Results on Drug Use, 1975–2007, Volume 1: Secondary School Students* (September 2008, http://www .monitoringthefuture.org/pubs/monographs/vol1_2007.pdf) provide data on current alcohol use among 8th, 10th, and 12th graders. Data from Johnston et al.'s survey and Eaton et al.'s survey overlap in current drinking data for 10th and 12th graders. Comparing the "total" figures in Table 5.3 and Table 5.4 for these grades, Eaton et al. show a higher prevalence of current drinking for 12th graders (54.9% compared with 44.4% by Johnston et al.) and for 10th graders (41.8% compared with 33.4% by Johnston et al.).

The NSDUH also collected data on alcohol use in 2007 It reports that an estimated 10.7 million people aged 12 to 20 (27.9% of this age group) used alcohol in the month before the survey. The NSDUH presents rates of current alcohol use in 2007 among various age groups: 3.5% among 12- to 13-year-olds (7th and 8th grades), 14.7% of 14- to 15-year olds (9th and 10th grades), 29% of 16- to 17-year-olds (11th and 12th grades), and 50.7% of 18- to 20-year-olds. The peak age of current alcohol use was 21 to 25 years at 68.3% of this population.

What can be gleaned from all these studies? Looking at all the data presented here, each study shows 2007 current rates of alcohol use in high school students rising with grade level. As students grew older, they drank more Looking at the studies together, the percentage of 10th graders who were current alcohol users in 2007 ranged from about 15% to 42%. The percentage of 12th graders who were current alcohol users in 2007 ranged from about 29% to 55%. Taken separately or together, data from these surveys present a picture of a high percentage of teen who use alcohol, which can cause bodily harm, serious diseases, and possibly death. (See Chapter 2.) Concerning the teens who reported to Carroll that alcohol was one of the most important problems facing young people today they appear to understand the state of current alcohol use of high school students.

Alcohol Use among College Students and Other Young Adults

The NSDUH indicates that 50.7% of 18- to 20-year olds and 68.3% of 21 to 25-year-olds (the peak age group used alcohol in 2007. These college-aged students and recent graduates are a part of the youth of this nation; many of them are using a potentially dangerous drug, and those under 21 are using it illegally.

In *Monitoring the Future National Survey Results on Drug Use, 1975–2007, Volume 2: College Students and Adult Ages 19–45* (2008, http://www.monitoringthefuture.org/pubs monographs/vol2_2007.pdf), Johnston et al. report the drug use results for college students and adults. Table 5.5 shows the annual prevalence of the use of alcohol and flavored alcoholic

TABLE 5.4

Past-month use of alcohol by eighth, tenth, and twelfth graders, 2007

[Entries are percentages]

	Alcohol			Been drunk			Flavored alcoholic beverages		
Grade	8th	10th	12th	8th	10th	12th	8th	10th	12th
Total	**15.9**	**33.4**	**44.4**	**5.5**	**18.1**	**28.7**	**12.2**	**21.8**	**29.1**
Gender									
Male	15.6	33.4	47.1	5.3	18.9	31.7	10.4	18.8	25.4
Female	16.0	33.3	41.4	5.6	17.4	25.7	13.4	24.7	32.8
College plans									
None or under 4 years	33.5	47.4	48.6	16.3	28.9	30.6	23.8	32.0	37.0
Complete 4 years	14.3	31.7	43.3	4.6	16.8	28.2	11.1	20.6	27.5
Region									
Northeast	12.9	36.2	51.8	3.5	20.5	32.6	9.7	23.2	36.0
Midwest	15.5	34.4	47.9	5.7	19.6	32.0	12.0	21.2	28.5
South	17.1	31.2	43.1	6.1	16.3	26.5	14.0	20.0	28.8
West	15.9	32.9	36.6	5.7	16.9	26.0	10.9	23.6	24.9
Population density									
Large MSA	14.8	31.8	47.1	4.8	16.3	29.8	10.6	21.5	30.8
Other MSA	16.1	33.3	42.1	5.6	18.5	27.6	12.4	21.4	27.8
Non-MSA	16.8	36.2	45.2	6.4	20.0	29.4	14.2	23.0	29.5
Parental education*									
1.0–2.0 (Low)	26.1	36.5	38.3	10.6	17.7	19.7	21.1	25.5	34.0
2.5–3.0	20.3	37.0	46.0	7.9	19.9	31.6	17.5	25.8	32.4
3.5–4.0	16.9	35.6	43.6	6.0	19.1	26.8	12.3	23.1	29.9
4.5–5.0	11.6	31.5	45.0	3.1	16.8	28.4	9.8	19.7	27.6
5.5–6.0 (High)	11.2	28.8	47.6	3.1	17.7	33.0	7.1	16.9	25.3

*Parental education is an average score of mother's education and father's education reported on the following scale: (1) Completed grade school or less, (2) Some high school, (3) completed high school, (4) Some college, (5) Completed college, (6) Graduate or professional school after college. Missing data were allowed on one of the two variables.
MSA = Metropolitan Statistical Areas.

SOURCE: Adapted from Lloyd D. Johnston et al., "Table 4-7. Thirty-Day Prevalence of Use of Various Drugs by Subgroups: 8th, 10th, and 12th Graders, 2007," in *Monitoring the Future National Survey Results on Drug Use, 1975–2007: Volume 1, Secondary School Students*, National Institute on Drug Abuse, 2008, http://www.monitoringthefuture.org/pubs/monographs/vol1_2007.pdf (accessed December 10, 2008)

TABLE 5.5

Annual prevalence of alcohol use by full-time college students vs. other young adults 1–4 years beyond high school, 2007

[Entries are percentages]

	Total		Males		Females	
	Full-time college	Others	Full-time college	Others	Full-time college	Others
Alcohol	80.9	79.3	80.1	77.1	81.4	80.9
Been drunk	64.8	60.9	61.9	61.6	66.7	60.5
Flavored alcoholic bvg.	62.6	63.5	55.2	58.5	67.0	67.3

SOURCE: Adapted from Lloyd D. Johnston et al., "Table 8–2. Annual Prevalence of Use for Various Types of Drugs, 2007: Full-Time College Students vs. Others among Respondents 1 to 4 Years beyond High School," in *Monitoring the Future National Survey Results on Drug Use, 1975–2007: Volume 2, College Students and Adults Ages 19–45*, National Institute on Drug Abuse, 2008, http://www.monitoringthefuture.org/pubs/monographs/vol2_2007.pdf (accessed December 8, 2008)

noncollege students of the same age), but college students have the higher rate of use. Female college students were slightly more likely to have consumed alcohol in the past year (81.4%) than male college students (80.1%). The same is true for noncollege students one to four years beyond high school; females (80.9%) were more likely than males (77.1%) to have consumed alcohol in the past year.

Table 5.6 shows the trend of lifetime prevalence of alcohol use from 1987 to 2007 among those aged 19 to 28 years. From 1987 to 1991 the annual prevalence of alcohol use for this group remained relatively steady at around 94% to 95%. Throughout the rest of the 1990s the annual prevalence fell; by 1999 the annual prevalence of alcohol use for this group was 90.2%. In 2007 the lifetime prevalence reached a low of 87.9%. The lifetime prevalence of drinking flavored alcoholic beverages (the data for which have only recently been gathered) for 19- to 28-year-olds remained about 84% from 2005 through 2007.

Table 5.7 shows the trend of lifetime prevalence of alcohol use among college students one to four years beyond high school. The lifetime prevalence of alcohol use in this group (83.1% in 2007) is lower than that for the 19- to 28-year-old group (87.9% in 2007).

beverages for college students and noncollege students who are one to four years beyond high school. The results indicate that both groups had a high annual prevalence of alcohol use in 2007 (80.9% for full-time college students and 79.3% for

TABLE 5.6

Trends in lifetime prevalence of alcohol use among young adults aged 19–28, selected years, 1987–2007

[Entries are percentages]

	1987	1989	1991	1993	1995	1997	1999	2001	2003	2005	2007	2006–2007 change
Alcohol	94.9	94.5	94.1	92.1	91.6	90.7	90.2	89.9	89.3	89.1	87.9	−1.0
Been drunk	N/A	N/A	82.9	81.4	82.1	81.4	81.6	81.1	80.9	79.9	80.1	−0.8
Flvd. alcoholic bvg.	N/A	N/A	N/A	N/A	N/A	N/A	N/A	N/A	N/A	84.6	84.0	−0.4

N/A indicates data not available.

SOURCE: Adapted from Lloyd D. Johnston et al., "Table 5-1. Trends in Lifetime Prevalence of Various Types of Drugs among Respondents of Modal Ages 19–28," in *Monitoring the Future National Survey Results on Drug Use, 1975–2007: Volume 2, College Students and Adults Ages 19–45*, National Institute on Drug Abuse, 2008, http://www.monitoringthefuture.org/pubs/monographs/vol2_2007.pdf (accessed December 8, 2008)

TABLE 5.7

Trends in lifetime prevalence of alcohol use among college students 1–4 years beyond high school, selected years, 1987–2007

[Entries are percentages]

	1987	1989	1991	1993	1995	1997	1999	2001	2003	2005	2007	2006–2007 change
Alcohol	94.1	93.7	93.6	89.3	88.5	87.3	88.0	86.1	86.2	86.6	83.1	−1.5
Been drunk	N/A	N/A	79.6	76.4	76.6	77.0	75.1	76.1	74.9	72.9	71.6	−1.5
Flavored alcoholic beverages	N/A	N/A	N/A	N/A	N/A	N/A	N/A	N/A	N/A	84.5	80.6	−0.2

N/A indicates data not available.

SOURCE: Adapted from Lloyd D. Johnston et al., "Table 9-1. Trends in Lifetime Prevalence of Various Types of Drugs among College Students 1 to 4 Years beyond High School," in *Monitoring the Future National Survey Results on Drug Use, 1975–2007: Volume 2, College Students and Adults Ages 19–45*, National Institute on Drug Abuse, 2008, http://www.monitoringthefuture.org/pubs/monographs/vol2_2007.pdf (accessed December 8, 2008)

Heavy Drinking, Binge Drinking, and Drunkenness

Merriam-Webster's Collegiate Dictionary defines the term *drunk* as "having the faculties impaired by alcohol." According to Johnston et al., in *Monitoring the Future National Survey Results on Drug Use, 1975–2007, Volume 1*, the rates of occurrences of drunkenness within the past 30 days among high school students generally declined between 2000 and 2007 after the increases of the 1990s. The highest rate for 8th graders occurred in 1996, when 9.6% reported having been drunk in the past 30 days. The highest rate for 10th graders came in 2000, when the rate hit 23.5%. The highest rate for 12th graders was 34.2% in 1997. In 2007, 5.5% of 8th graders, 18.1% of 10th graders, and 28.7% of 12th graders reported being drunk during the previous month. (See Table 5.4.)

The National Institute on Alcohol Abuse and Alcoholism defines binge drinking as the consumption of five or more drinks of alcoholic beverages on at least one occasion during the past month. Heavy drinking is an average of more than one drink per day for women and more than two drinks per day for men. (There is a male-female difference because the same amount of alcohol affects women more than it does men. Women's bodies have less water than men's bodies, so a given amount of alcohol becomes more highly concentrated in a woman's body than in a man's.)

Eaton et al. use the term *episodic heavy drinking* and define it using the same definition as binge drinking, rather than asking students if they had "been drunk" (with no definition) as Johnston et al. do. According to Eaton et al., 26% of high school students were current binge drinkers in 2007. The incidence of binge drinking increased with grade level: 17% in 9th grade, 23.7% in 10th grade, 29.9% in 11th grade, and 36.5% in 12th grade. (See Table 5.8.)

Demographic Factors in Youth Alcohol Use

GENDER, RACIAL, AND ETHNIC DIFFERENCES. In 2007 high school males (44.7%) were as likely to be current alcohol users as females (44.6%). (See Table 5.3.) However, males (27.8%) were more likely than females (24.1%) to engage in episodic heavy drinking. (See Table 5.8.)

Similarly, Johnston et al. show in *Monitoring the Future National Survey Results on Drug Use, 1975–2007, Volume 1* close percentages of current alcohol use for males and females in grades 8 and 10 in 2007. (See Table 5.4.) However, the data indicate that 12th-grade males (47.1%) were more likely to have been current drinkers in 2007 than females (41.4%). The results that Johnston et al. report for

TABLE 5.8

Percentage of high school students who had five or more drinks in a row and who usually bought alcohol at a store, by gender, ethnicity, and grade, 2007

Category	Episodic heavy drinking			Bought alcohol in a store		
	Female	Male	Total	Female	Male	Total
	%	%	%	%	%	%
Race/ethnicity						
White*	27.9	31.8	29.8	2.2	6.9	4.6
Black*	10.7	14.5	12.5	3.8	8.1	5.9
Hispanic	25.3	28.3	26.8	3.6	9.8	6.7
Grade						
9	17.2	17.0	17.0	1.1	5.1	3.1
10	21.8	25.5	23.7	2.6	4.6	3.6
11	26.7	33.1	29.9	2.0	9.1	5.6
12	32.8	40.4	36.5	5.0	11.1	8.0
Total	**24.1**	**27.8**	**26.0**	**2.7**	**7.6**	**5.2**

Notes: Five or more drinks within a couple of hours on at least 1 day during the 30 days before the survey. Purchased at a liquor store, convenience store, supermarket, discount store, or gas station. Percentages based on the 44.7% of students who currently drank alcohol during the 30 days before thesurvey.
*Non-Hispanic.

SOURCE: Danice K. Eaton et al., "Table 37. Percentage of High School Students Who Had Five or More Drinks of Alcohol in a Row and Who Usually Obtained the Alcohol They Drank by Buying It in a Store, by Sex, Race/Ethnicity, and Grade—United States, Youth Risk Behavior Survey, 2007," in "Youth Risk Behavior Surveillance—United States, 2007," *Morbidity & Mortality Weekly Report*, vol. 57, no. SS-4, June 6, 2008, http://www.cdc.gov/ HealthyYouth/yrbs/pdf/yrbss07_mmwr.pdf (accessed August 19, 2008)

being drunk are similar to the results that Eaton et al. report for binge drinking: males in grades 10 (18.9%) and 12 (31.7%) were more likely than females in those grades (17.4% and 25.7%, respectively) to have been drunk. Nonetheless, the data for 8th grade show females (5.6%) slightly more likely than males (5.3%) to have been drunk.

Johnston et al. also provide data for males and females among full-time college students versus others one to four years beyond high school. (See Table 5.5.) The 2007 annual prevalence rates for alcohol use show gender differences. Females of both groups were slightly more likely than males to have been drunk. Full-time college females (67%) were more likely to drink flavored alcoholic beverages than full-time college males (55.2%). The same was true for non-college students in the same age group: females (67.3%) were more likely than males (58.5%) to drink flavored alcoholic beverages. A female preference for these drinks was also seen among 8th, 10th, and 12th graders. (See Table 5.4.)

Table 5.3 also shows that in 2007 Hispanic (77.9%) high school students were more likely than white (76.1%) or African-American (69.1%) high school students to have consumed alcohol in their lifetime. However, whites (29.8%) were more likely to have engaged in episodic heavy drinking than African-Americans (12.5%) and Hispanics (26.8%). (See Table 5.8.) White (47.3%) and Hispanic (47.6%) high

school students were equally likely to be current drinkers in 2007, and African-Americans (34.5%) were less likely to be current drinkers. (See Table 5.3.)

WHERE STUDENTS LIVE. In *Monitoring the Future National Survey Results on Drug Use, 1975–2007, Volume 1,* Johnston et al. look at population density as a factor in student drinking patterns. (See Table 5.4.) They use the category metropolitan statistical area (MSA), which means the area contains at least one town that has more than 50,000 inhabitants. Large MSAs are the biggest cities in the United States, such as New York City, New York; Los Angeles, California; Chicago, Illinois; Philadelphia, Pennsylvania; and Boston, Massachusetts. Eighth and 10th graders who lived in non-MSA areas were more likely to be current drinkers than students of the same grades living in larger metropolitan districts, but 12th graders in large MSAs were more likely to be current alcohol users than 12th graders living in smaller metropolitan areas or non-MSAs. Sophomore and senior high school students who lived in the Northeast were more likely to be current alcohol users than same-aged students who lived in other parts of the country.

PARENTAL EDUCATION. Table 5.4 shows an inverse relationship between current alcohol use in 8th graders and parental education: the less parental education, the more likely 8th graders were to drink. This relationship is not as strong in 10th graders and is reversed in 12th graders, who were more likely to drink the more educated their parents were. In addition, students in all three grades who had no college plans were more likely to be current drinkers, to have been drunk in the past 30 days, and to drink flavored alcoholic beverages than those with plans to complete four years of college.

Perception of Harmfulness of Alcohol Use

The PRIDE Survey (formerly the Parents Resource Institute for Drug Education) also asks adolescents and teenagers questions about drug and alcohol use. Figure 5.2 shows the results from the *PRIDE Surveys Questionnaire Report for Grades 6 to 12, 2007–08 National Survey.* The report reveals that 48.6% of 6th graders perceived alcohol as having "great risk" with regular use. The perception of regular alcohol use having "great risk" decreased with increasing grade level. Only 34% of 12th graders perceived regular alcohol use as having great risk. Thus, when the perception of risk decreased, the use of alcohol increased. (See Table 5.3 and Table 5.4.)

The PRIDE Survey also notes that easy access to alcohol increases the probability that adolescents and teenagers will drink. The survey results show that access to alcohol increased as grade level increased. As grade level increased from grade 9 to grade 12, the percentage of students (underage drinkers) who purchased alcohol in a store in 2007 increased from 3.1% to 8%. (See Table 5.8.)

FIGURE 5.2

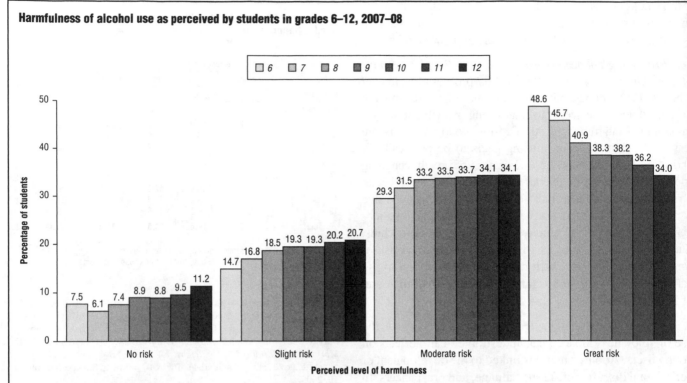

Harmfulness of alcohol use as perceived by students in grades 6–12, 2007–08

SOURCE: Adapted from "Perception of Risk—Regular Alcohol Use," in *PRIDE Surveys Questionnaire Report for Grades 6 to 12, 2007–08 National Summary—Grades 6 thru 12*, September 19, 2008, http://www.pridesurveys.com/customercenter/us07ns.pdf (accessed December 13, 2008)

Drinking and Young Drivers

In *Traffic Safety Facts, 2007 Data—Young Drivers* (2008, http://www-nrd.nhtsa.dot.gov/Pubs/811001.PDF), the National Highway Traffic Safety Administration (NHTSA) reports that in 2007 a total of 6,982 drivers aged 15 to 20 were involved in fatal crashes—a 12% decrease from the 7,936 drivers involved in 1997. Twenty-six percent of the drivers 15 to 20 years of age who were killed in crashes were intoxicated (had a blood alcohol level of 0.08 grams per deciliter [g/dL] or higher). For young male drivers aged 15 to 20, fatalities dropped 14.6% between 1997 and 2007, compared with a 2.6% decrease for females.

As of July 2004 all states, the District of Columbia, and Puerto Rico had lowered the legal BAC limit for driving to 0.08 g/dL. The NHTSA estimates that between 1975 and 2007 the minimum drinking age laws have reduced traffic fatalities involving drivers aged 18 to 20 by 13%, saving approximately 26,333 lives.

All states and the District of Columbia have zero-tolerance laws for drinking drivers under the age of 21. It is illegal for drivers under the age of 21 to drive with BAC levels of 0.02 g/dl or greater. According to Matthew Gever, in "Environmental Strategies for Preventing Underage Drinking" (September 30, 2006, http://www.ncsl.org/programs/health/forum/uderagedrinking.htm), early evidence on the results of the law is encouraging. Heavy episodic drinking for both males and females has been reduced by 13% to 18%.

Also, the number of drinks consumed in a month by males ha decreased by 20%. Among the various laws in various state created to prevent underage drinking and driving, four wer determined by researcher James C. Fell et al. in "The Impac of Underage Drinking Laws on Alcohol-Related Fatal Crashe of Young Drivers," (*Alcoholism: Clinical and Experimenta Research*, July 2009) to be most effective in reducing fatal ities. As reported by ScienceDaily (April 8, 2009, http://www .sciencedaily.com/releases/2009/04/090407174626.htm), Fel and his colleagues analyzed driving- and alcohol-related dat from 1982 to 2004, concluding: "Four of the six underag drinking laws that we examined were effective in reducin the rate of drinking drivers aged 20 and younger in fata crashes . . . while controlling for many other factors that coul have accounted for the decrease. Collectively, these fou laws—possession [by minors], purchase [by minors], us [alcohol] and lose [one's driver's license], and zero toler ance—save an estimated 864 lives each year."

TOBACCO AND YOUTH

Health Consequences of Early Tobacco Use

In "Polyphenol Associated-DNA Adducts in Lung an Blood Mononuclear Cells from Lung Cancer Patients" (*Can cer Letters*, vol. 236, no. 1, May 8, 2006), Andrea Várkonyi e al. indicate that the age at which smoking is initiated is significant factor in the risk of developing lung cance Smoking in the teen years appears to cause permanent geneti changes in the lungs, increasing the risk of lung cancer—even if the smoker quits. The younger a person starts smoking, the more lasting damage is done to his or her lungs. Such damage is less likely among smokers who start in their twenties.

Preventing Tobacco Use among Young People: A Report of the Surgeon General (1994, http://profiles.nlm.nih.gov/NN/B/C/L/Q/_/nnbclq.pdf) indicated that cigarette smoking during adolescence seems to retard lung growth and reduce maximum lung function. As a result, young smokers are less likely than their nonsmoking peers to be physically fit and more likely to experience shortness of breath, coughing spells, wheezing, and overall poorer health. These health problems pose a clear risk for developing other chronic conditions in adulthood, such as chronic obstructive pulmonary disease, including emphysema and chronic bronchitis. Early smoking has also been linked to an increased risk of cardiovascular diseases, such as high cholesterol and triglyceride levels, atherosclerosis (arterial plaque), and early onset of heart disease.

The surgeon general's report also points out that the use of smokeless tobacco has undesirable health effects on young users. Adolescent use is linked to the development of periodontal disease, soft-tissue damage, and oral cancers. In addition, young people who use smokeless tobacco are more likely than their nonusing peers to become cigarette smokers.

Age of First Use

Even though these health effects of early tobacco use are known, most cigarette smokers begin their habit early in life. According to Johnston et al., in *Monitoring the Future National Survey Results on Drug Use, 1975–2007, Volume 1*, 10.6% of the 8th graders surveyed in 2007 said they had their first cigarette in the 6th and 7th grades, and 8.8% said they had their first cigarette even earlier. Twenty-two percent of the 12th graders who were surveyed responded they had their first cigarette by the 8th grade.

Johnston et al. reveal that smokeless tobacco use begins early in life as well. Smokeless tobacco is chewing tobacco or finer-cut tobacco that is inhaled (snuff). The highest rates of initiation in smokeless tobacco use are in grades 7 through 11. In 2007, 4% of the 8th graders surveyed reported they began using smokeless tobacco by the 6th grade, and 6.1% started by the 8th grade.

Current Use of Tobacco by High School Students

The NSDUH indicates that in 2007, 12.4% of students aged 12 to 17 used various tobacco products in the month before the survey; that is, they were current users. The use of tobacco products among this age group declined from 15.2% in 2002. This decline was due primarily to the decrease in the use of cigarettes. In 2002, 13% of students aged 12 to 17 were current cigarette smokers, and by 2007, 9.8% were. Use of other tobacco products (cigars, smoke-

TABLE 5.9

Percentage of high school students who smoked cigars and who used tobacco, by gender, ethnicity, and grade, 2007

	Current cigar use			Current tobacco use		
	Female	Male	Total	Female	Male	Total
Category	%	%	%	%	%	%
Race/ethnicity						
White*	7.4	22.0	14.8	24.3	35.3	29.9
Black*	6.7	13.2	10.0	12.1	19.9	16.0
Hispanic	9.0	16.3	12.7	16.4	23.9	20.1
Grade						
9	6.1	13.5	9.9	14.4	22.6	18.6
10	7.9	16.9	12.5	21.0	28.5	24.8
11	7.6	23.2	15.5	21.8	34.5	28.2
12	9.2	26.2	17.6	28.6	38.3	33.4
Total	**7.6**	**19.4**	**13.6**	**21.0**	**30.3**	**25.7**

Notes: Smoked cigars, cigarillos, or little cigars on at least 1 day during the 30 days before the survey. Current cigarette use, current smokeless tobacco use, or current cigar use.
*Non-Hispanic.

SOURCE: Danice K. Eaton et al., "Table 33. Percentage of High School Students Who Currently Smoked Cigars and Who Currently Used Tobacco, by Sex, Race/Ethnicity, and Grade—United States, Youth Risk Behavior Survey, 2007," in "Youth Risk Behavior Surveillance—United States, 2007," *Morbidity & Mortality Weekly Report*, vol. 57, no. SS-4, June 6, 2008, http://www.cdc.gov/HealthyYouth/yrbs/pdf/yrbss07_mmwr.pdf (accessed August 19, 2008)

less tobacco, and pipe tobacco) remained relatively steady. In 2007, 4.2% of students aged 12 to 17 were current cigar smokers, 2.4% were smokeless tobacco users, and 0.7% were pipe tobacco users.

Eaton et al. focus on students in grades 9 through 12, not students aged 12 to 17 as the NSDUH does. The researchers note that 25.7% of high school students in 2007 reported current tobacco use. (See Table 5.9.) The NSDUH results are lower (12.4% of 12- to 17-year-olds), but it includes younger students, who are less likely to use tobacco, and it does not include 18-year-olds, who are more likely to use tobacco and who are likely present in Eaton et al.'s cohort of high school seniors. Eaton et al. find that 13.6% of high school students in 2007 were current cigar smokers (the NSDUH reports 4.2%) and 7.9% were current smokeless tobacco users (the NSDUH reports 2.4%). (See Table 5.9 and Table 5.10.) Eaton et al.'s results also show that, in general, tobacco use increases with grade level.

Trends in Prevalence of Cigarette Use in High School Students

Eaton et al. look for trends in the prevalence of cigarette smoking in high school students from 1991 to 2007. Their results reveal that in 2007, 20% of high school students were current cigarette smokers. This rate is down from the 1991 rate of 27.5%. Current cigarette smoking rates rose from 1991 to 1997, however, to a high of 36.4% in 1997 before falling in ensuing years to the 2007 level.

TABLE 5.10

Percentage of high school students who used smokeless tobacco and who usually bought cigarettes at a store or gas station, by gender, ethnicity, and grade, 2007

	Bought cigarettes in a store or gas station			Current smokeless tobacco use		
	Female	Male	Total	Female	Male	Total
Category	%	%	%	%	%	%
Race/ethnicity						
White[a]	10.9	20.4	15.9	2.5	18.0	10.3
Black[a]	—[b]	22.6	19.3	0.5	2.0	1.2
Hispanic	9.9	17.1	13.8	2.7	6.7	4.7
Grade						
9	7.0	11.8	9.7	2.0	10.4	6.3
10	9.4	20.2	15.0	2.8	14.4	8.7
11	13.6	20.9	17.8	2.0	13.3	7.6
12	17.0	34.8	25.6	2.2	15.9	8.9
Total	**11.3**	**20.0**	**16.0**	**2.3**	**13.4**	**7.9**

Notes: During the 30 days before the survey, among the 16.1% of students nationwide who were aged <18 years and who currently smoked cigarettes. Used chewing tobacco, snuff, or dip on at least 1 day during the 30 days before the survey.
[a]Non-Hispanic.
[b]Not available.

SOURCE: Danice K. Eaton et al., "Table 31. Percentage of High School Students Who Usually Obtained Their Own Cigarettes by Buying Them in a Store or Gas Stationand Who Currently Used Smokeless Tobacco, by Sex, Race/Ethnicity, and Grade—United States, Youth Risk Behavior Survey, 2007," in "Youth Risk Behavior Surveillance—United States, 2007," *Morbidity & Mortality Weekly Report*, vol. 57, no. SS-4, June 6, 2008, http://www.cdc.gov/HealthyYouth/yrbs/pdf/yrbss07_mmwr.pdf (accessed August 19, 2008)

What are the causes of the general decrease in current smoking rates among high school students after 1997? In *Monitoring the Future National Survey Results on Drug Use, 1975–2007, Volume 1*, Johnston et al. provide a possible answer to this question: "We think that the extensive adverse publicity generated by the state attorneys general, the President, and Congress in the debate over a possible legal settlement with the tobacco companies contributed importantly to this turnaround by influencing youth attitudes toward cigarette companies and their products. Substantial price increases, the removal of some forms of advertising (such as billboard advertising and the Joe Camel campaign), the implementation of vigorous antismoking advertising (particularly that launched by the American Legacy Foundation and some of the states), and strong prevention programs in some states all may have contributed."

According to Eaton et al., lifetime cigarette use among high school students was also lower in 2007 than in 1991. In 1991, 70.1% of all high school students had tried smoking. The lifetime rates did not begin to fall, however, until 2001. The percentage of high school students who were current, frequent users of cigarettes in 2007 was also down from 1991 (12.7% versus 8.1%), as was the percentage of students who smoked more than 10 cigarettes per day (18% in 1991 versus 10.7% in 2007).

Tobacco Use among College Students and Other Young Adults

In *Monitoring the Future National Survey Results on Drug Use, 1975–2007, Volume 2*, Johnston et al. report on the prevalence of drug use for college students and adults aged 19 to 30. In 2007 the rates of current cigarette smoking for young adults was lowest for 19- to 20-year-olds (22.6%) and 29- to 30-year olds (22.9%). More of those in the 21- to 28-year-old range were current smokers—26.6% to 27.8%. Johnston et al. note that smoking rates of people in their early twenties used to be about the same rate as among high school seniors and then those rates would drop with age, because most smokers began using tobacco in high school. Beginning in 2005, however, smoking rates among high school seniors—as well as among high school students in general—dropped. This lower rate was reflected in the 19- to 20-year-olds in 2007.

Johnston et al. examine the trends in current cigarette smoking among college students and noncollege students who were one to four years beyond high school. In 2007 noncollege students (26.2%) had a higher rate of current cigarette use than college students (19.9%), opposite the results of alcohol use described earlier in this chapter. This difference in current cigarette use between college and noncollege students of the same age has been documented since 1980.

Demographic Factors in Youth Tobacco Use

GENDER, RACIAL, AND ETHNIC DIFFERENCES. In 2007 high school males (30.3%) were much more likely to currently use various tobacco products than females (21%). (See Table 5.9.) They were also much more likely to be current cigar smokers (19.4% for males versus 7.6% for females) and current smokeless tobacco users (13.4% for males versus 2.3% for females). (See Table 5.10.) According to Johnston et al., in *Monitoring the Future National Survey Results on Drug Use, 1975–2007, Volume 1*, there were similar differences in current smokeless tobacco use in 2007 between males and females in grades 8 (4.7% for males versus 1.7% for females), 10 (10.2% versus 2%), and 12 (11.9% versus 1.2%).

Looking at current cigarette use alone, Johnston et al. indicate that male rates of cigarette smoking were higher than that of females in all three grades: 8th grade (7.5% for males versus 6.4% for females), 10th grade (14.6% versus 13.3%), and 12th grade (23.1% versus 19.6%).

In *Monitoring the Future National Survey Results on Drug Use, 1975–2007, Volume 2*, Johnston et al. note that in 2007 male college students had a higher rate of current cigarette smoking than females (22% versus 19% respectively), but it has not always been that way. From 1980 to 1994 female college students were more likely to be current smokers than male college students. In 1994 their current rates of smoking were the same—nearly 25%. The rates for both increased during the mid- to late 1990s, with males generally leading females, but then both rates dropped to the 1994 level again in 2005, and dropped even further by 2007.

According to Eaton et al., in 2007 white (29.9%) high school students were more likely than Hispanic (20.1%) or African-American (16%) high school students to be current tobacco users. (See Table 5.9.) This pattern persisted with current cigar smoking (14.8% of whites, 12.7% of Hispanics, and 10% of African-Americans) and with current smokeless tobacco use (10.3% of whites, 4.7% of Hispanics, and 1.2% of African-Americans). (See Table 5.10.)

WHERE STUDENTS LIVE. In *Monitoring the Future National Survey Results on Drug Use, 1975–2007, Volume 1*, Johnston et al. look at population density as a factor in student patterns of tobacco use. Eighth, 10th, and 12th graders who lived in the largest cities in the United States in 2007 (large MSAs such as Boston, New York, and Los Angeles) were the least likely to be current smokers. Those who lived in smaller cities (other MSAs) were somewhat more likely to be current smokers, and those who lived in rural areas (non-MSAs) were the most likely to be current smokers. In "Prevalence and Trends in Smoking: A National Rural Study" (*Journal of Rural Health*, vol. 22, no. 2, April 2006), Mark P. Doescher et al. determine that "the higher prevalence of smoking in rural areas compared to urban areas … can be explained, in part, by lower levels of income and education attainment among rural residents and by the greater likelihood of rural residents being white or American Indian; both groups have high rates of smoking. Additionally, people with lower levels of income and education who reside in rural counties smoke at slightly higher rates than their urban counterparts."

PARENTAL EDUCATION. Johnston et al. note in *Monitoring the Future National Survey Results on Drug Use, 1975–2007, Volume 1* an inverse relationship between current daily cigarette use in 8th graders and parental education: the less parental education, the more likely 8th graders were to be current daily smokers in 2007. This relationship is the same for 10th and 11th graders except for the lowest parental educational level. In addition, students in all three grades who had no college plans or had plans to complete less than four years of college were much more likely to be current smokers and to have used smokeless tobacco than those with plans to complete four years of college.

Perception of Harmfulness of Tobacco Use

Figure 5.3 shows results from the *PRIDE Surveys Questionnaire Report for Grades 6 to 12, 2007–08 National Survey*. The report reveals that 70.3% of 6th graders perceived the use of tobacco as "very harmful." The perception of tobacco

FIGURE 5.3

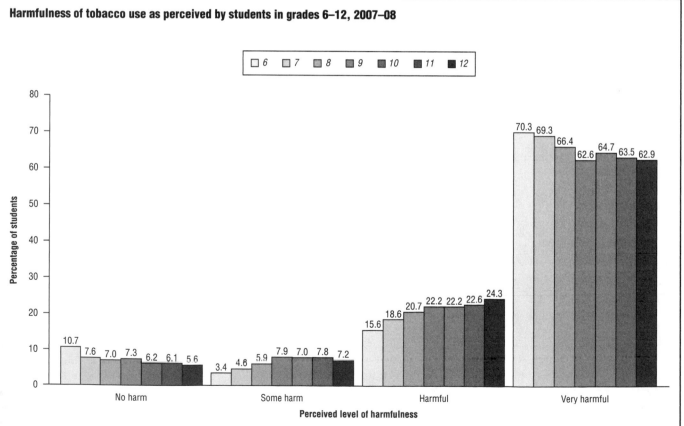

Harmfulness of tobacco use as perceived by students in grades 6–12, 2007–08

SOURCE: Adapted from "Perception of Risk—Any Tobacco," in *PRIDE Surveys Questionnaire Report for Grades 6 to 12, 2007–08 National Summary—Grades 6 thru 12*, September 19, 2008, http://www.pridesurveys.com/customercenter/us07ns.pdf (accessed December 13, 2008)

being "very harmful" decreased with increasing grade level to about grade 9. From 62.6% to 64.7% of 9th, 10th, 11th, and 12th graders perceived tobacco use as being "very harmful." Thus, a much higher percentage of students in grades 6 through 12 perceived tobacco use as harmful than the percentage who perceived alcohol use as harmful. (See Figure 5.2.) Even though the perception of risk of tobacco use stayed relatively steady in grades 9 through 12, the use of tobacco increased in these grades as the grade level increased. (See Table 5.9.) The report also notes that, as with alcohol, easy access to tobacco increases the probability that adolescents and teenagers will use tobacco. Table 5.10 shows that access to tobacco increased as the grade level increased.

ILLICIT DRUGS AND YOUTH

Age of First Use

The use of alcohol and tobacco often begins early in life; the initiation data are presented previously in this chapter. Regarding the initiation of other drugs, Johnston et al. reveal in *Monitoring the Future National Survey Results on Drug Use, 1975–2007, Volume 1* that inhalants and marijuana are the drugs next most likely to be initiated early in life. Peak initiation rates for illicit drugs other than marijuana generally do not occur until grades 9 through 11 in high school, and initiation rates for cocaine and crack generally occur in grades 10 through 12. Johnston et al. state:

> Of all 12th graders who reported prior use of any drug, the proportion reporting an initial use of that drug *by the end of grade 9* is presented here. This listing is a good indicator of the order of age initiation (with some exceptions):

- cigarettes (66%)
- inhalants (58%)
- alcohol (57%)
- marijuana (55%)
- sedatives (barbiturates) (53%)
- PCP (48%)
- been drunk (48%)
- heroin (47%)
- daily cigarette smoking (47%)
- tranquilizers (46%)
- smokeless tobacco (44%)
- amphetamines (38%)
- narcotics other than heroin (36%)
- LSD (35%)
- crack (34%)
- hallucinogens (32%)

- hallucinogens other than LSD (30%)
- cocaine (27%)
- other forms of cocaine (25%)

Trends in Annual Prevalence of Drug Use in Youth

TRENDS ACROSS FIVE POPULATIONS. Annual prevalence means that a person has tried a particular drug at least once during the year before being surveyed about its use. Figure 5.4 compares trends in the annual prevalence of drug use across five populations: 8th-, 10th-, and 12th-grade students, full-time college students aged 19 to 22, and all young adults through the age of 28 who are high school graduates (a group that includes college students and is referred to in Figure 5.4 as "adults"). In the early 1980s the rates of drug use decreased, and college students had a higher rate of drug use than high school seniors. By the mid 1980s the annual prevalence of drug use of these two groups was somewhat equivalent. In the late 1980s, when data for young adults were added, the annual prevalence rates of drug use in all three groups declined dramatically. The annual prevalence of drug use by college students and 12th graders was about the same during those years, and the annual prevalence of drug use by young adults was slightly lower.

In 1991 data for 8th and 10th graders were added. The annual prevalence of drug use rose dramatically for high school students for several years, but the increase was less dramatic for college students. The annual prevalence of drug use increase for adults was minor. Thus, the annual prevalence of drug use for 12th and 10th graders became higher than the annual prevalence for college students and adults. Around 1998 the annual prevalence of drug use for 12th graders began to slowly drop. It dropped, then rose, then dropped again for 10th graders, and it dropped dramatically for 8th graders. However, the annual prevalence rates continued to slowly climb for college students and adults. Thus, in 2005 the annual prevalence rate of drug use was highest for 12th graders at nearly 40%, followed by college students at about 38%, adults at about 33%, 10th graders at about 30%, and 8th graders at about 17%. By 2007 rates for all three groups of high school students continued to drop. As of early 2009, 2007 data for college students and adults were not available.

TRENDS IN INHALANT USE IN HIGH SCHOOL STUDENTS. Inhalants have an early high rate of initiation. According to Johnston et al., in *Monitoring the Future National Survey Results on Drug Use, 1975–2007, Volume 1*, of all the 12th graders who reported prior use of inhalants in 2007, 58% reported an initial use of this drug by the end of 9th grade. Inhalants are volatile liquids, such as cleaning fluids, glue, gasoline, paint, and turpentine, the vapors of which are inhaled. Sometimes the sprays of aerosols are inhaled, such as those of spray paints, spray deodorants, hair spray, or fabric protector spray. These products are legal and easily accessible.

FIGURE 5.4

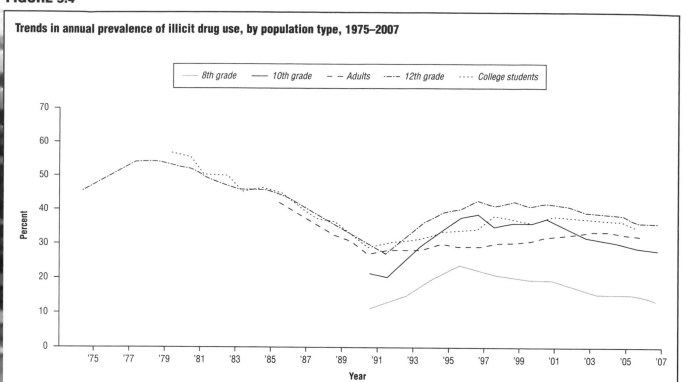

Trends in annual prevalence of illicit drug use, by population type, 1975–2007

Note: "Illicit drug use index" includes any use of marijuana, LSD, other hallucinogens, crack, other cocaine, or heroin; or any use which is not under a doctor's orders of other opiates, stimulants, sedatives (barbiturates), methaqualone (excluded since 1990), or tranquilizers. Beginning in 1982, the question about stimulant use (i.e., amphetamines) was revised to get respondents to exclude the inappropriate reporting of nonprescription stimulants. The prevalence rate dropped slightly as a result of this methodological change. 2007 data not yet available for college students and adults.

SOURCE: Lloyd D. Johnston et al., "Figure 2-1. Trends in Annual Prevalence of an Illicit Drug Use Index across 5 Populations," in *Monitoring the Future National Survey Results on Drug Use, 1975–2007: Volume 2, College Students and Adults Ages 19–45*, National Institute on Drug Abuse, 2008, http://www.monitoringthefuture.org/pubs/monographs/vol2_2007.pdf (accessed December 8, 2008)

Figure 5.5 shows trends in annual prevalence of inhalant use for 8th, 10th, and 12th graders. Since 1991, when data collection began for all three of these grade levels, 8th graders have had the highest annual prevalence of inhalant use, followed by 10th graders and then 12th graders. Between 1991 and 1995 the annual prevalence of inhalant use rose by more than one-third among 8th and 10th graders to reach 12.8% and 9.6%, respectively, and rose by about one-fifth in 12th graders to reach 8%. The annual prevalence rates for inhalant use then fell through 2002 for 8th graders to 7.7%, and through 2003 for 10th and 12th graders to 5.4% and 4.5%, respectively. Rates rose quite steeply for 8th graders from 2002 until 2004, reaching 9.6%, then steadying in 2005 at 9.5%, and dropping to 8.3% by 2007. Rates rose less dramatically through 2005 for 10th and 12th graders to 6% and 5.4%, respectively. Rates continued to rise for 10th graders through 2007, reaching 6.6%, but they dropped for 12th graders to 3.7% in 2007.

TRENDS IN MARIJUANA USE IN HIGH SCHOOL STUDENTS. Besides inhalants, marijuana is one of the first drugs tried by school students. Figure 5.6 shows results from the *PRIDE Surveys Questionnaire Report for Grades 6 to 12, 2007–08 National Survey.* The report reveals that 44.7% to 79.4% of students in all grades perceived the use of marijuana as "very harmful." Only a small proportion of students (from 9.6% to 17.1%) thought that marijuana use posed "no harm" to the individual. Johnston et al. indicate in *Monitoring the Future National Survey Results on Drug Use, 1975–2007, Volume 1* that even though the perception of risk of illicit drug use was high, of all the 12th graders who reported prior use of marijuana in 2007, 55% reported an initial use of this drug by the end of 9th grade. Figure 5.6 shows that 60.8% of 9th graders believed marijuana use to be "very harmful."

Figure 5.7 shows trends in annual prevalence rates of marijuana use for 8th, 10th, and 12th graders. Since 1991, when data collection began for all three of these grade levels, 12th graders have had the highest annual prevalence of marijuana use, followed by 10th graders and then 8th graders. The annual prevalence rates of marijuana use for 8th graders rose from 1991 to 1996, reaching 18.3%. These rates then dropped steadily to 11.8% in 2004 and to 10.3% in 2007. For 10th and 12th graders the annual prevalence rates of marijuana use rose from 1992 to 1997, reaching 35% and 39%, respectively. The rates for both held relatively steady from 1998 through 2001 and then dropped to the 2007 levels of 24.6% and 31.7%, respectively.

FIGURE 5.5

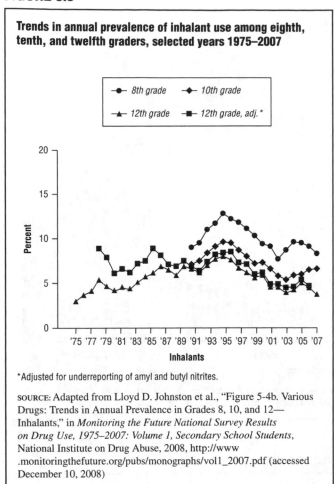

Trends in annual prevalence of inhalant use among eighth, tenth, and twelfth graders, selected years 1975–2007

Inhalants

*Adjusted for underreporting of amyl and butyl nitrites.

SOURCE: Adapted from Lloyd D. Johnston et al., "Figure 5-4b. Various Drugs: Trends in Annual Prevalence in Grades 8, 10, and 12—Inhalants," in *Monitoring the Future National Survey Results on Drug Use, 1975–2007: Volume 1, Secondary School Students*, National Institute on Drug Abuse, 2008, http://www.monitoringthefuture.org/pubs/monographs/vol1_2007.pdf (accessed December 10, 2008)

TRENDS IN TRANQUILIZER USE IN HIGH SCHOOL STUDENTS. In *Monitoring the Future National Survey Results on Drug Use, 1975–2007, Volume 1*, Johnston et al. state that of all the 12th graders who reported prior use of tranquilizers in 2007, 46% reported an initial use of this type of drug by the end of 9th grade. Tranquilizers are drugs prescribed by physicians to relieve a patient's tension and anxiety. Drugs such as diazepam, chlordiazepoxide, and alprazolam are tranquilizers. This type of illicit drug does not have a high rate of early initiation as inhalants and marijuana do.

Figure 5.8 shows trends in annual prevalence rates of illicit tranquilizer use for 8th, 10th, and 12th graders. Since 1991, when data collection began for all three of these grade levels, 10th and 12th graders have had the highest prevalence of use. Eighth graders have had a lower annual prevalence rate of tranquilizer use. The annual prevalence rates for 8th graders rose slowly from 1.8% in 1991 to 3.3% in 1996. The rates then declined slightly to 2.9% in 1997 and then leveled off. The 2007 annual prevalence rate for tranquilizer use by 8th graders was 2.4%.

For 10th graders, the annual prevalence rates remained fairly steady from 1991 to 1994. (See Figure 5.8.) These rates then rose steadily from 3.3% in 1994 to 7.3% in 2001, then declined to 4.8% in 2005, and then rose again to 5.3% in 2007. For 12th graders, the annual prevalence rate fell from 3.6% in 1991 to 2.8% in 1992. The rate then rose steadily from 1992, reaching 7.7% in 2002. It then declined in 2003, rose in 2004, and declined again in 2005. The 2007 annual prevalence rate of tranquilizer use in 12th graders was 6.2%.

TRENDS IN AMPHETAMINE USE IN HIGH SCHOOL STUDENTS. Johnston et al. explain in *Monitoring the Future National Survey Results on Drug Use, 1975–2007, Volume 1* that of all the 12th graders who reported prior use of amphetamines in 2007, 38% reported an initial use of this type of drug by the end of 9th grade. Amphetamines are stimulants (uppers), drugs that produce a sense of euphoria or wakefulness. They are used to increase alertness, boost endurance and productivity, and suppress the appetite. Other stimulants include caffeine, nicotine, methamphetamine, and cocaine.

Figure 5.9 shows trends in annual prevalence rates of amphetamine use for 8th, 10th, and 12th graders. Since 1991, when data collection began for all three of these grade levels, 10th and 12th graders have had the highest rate of use. From 1992 through 2001, 10th-grade annual prevalence rates were higher than 12th-grade rates. From 1991 through 2007 8th-grade annual prevalence rates were consistently lower than those of their older classmates.

The annual prevalence rate for 8th graders rose from 6.2% in 1991 to 9.1% in 1996. (See Figure 5.9.) The rate then declined to 6.9% in 1999 and then declined in short plateaus to 4.2% by 2007. For 10th graders, the annual prevalence rate rose from 8.2% in 1991 to 11.7% in 2001, and then declined to 8% in 2007. For 12th graders, the annual prevalence rate of amphetamine use generally rose throughout the 1990s and after 2000 in a slight up-and-down fashion, from 7.1% in 1991 to 11.1% in 2002. Since 2002 the annual prevalence rate of amphetamine use in 12th graders declined to 7.5% in 2007.

TRENDS IN HALLUCINOGEN USE IN HIGH SCHOOL STUDENTS. In *Monitoring the Future National Survey Results on Drug Use, 1975–2007, Volume 1*, Johnston et al. note that of all the 12th graders who reported prior use of hallucinogens in 2007, 32% reported an initial use of this drug by the end of 9th grade, and 30% the use of hallucinogens other than LSD by the end of 9th grade. Hallucinogens, also known as psychedelics, distort the perception of reality. They cause excitation, which can vary from a sense of well-being to severe depression. The experience may be pleasurable or quite frightening. The effects of hallucinogens vary from use to use and cannot be predicted.

Figure 5.10 shows trends in the annual prevalence rates of hallucinogen use for 8th, 10th, and 12th graders. Since 1991, when data collection began for all three of these

FIGURE 5.6

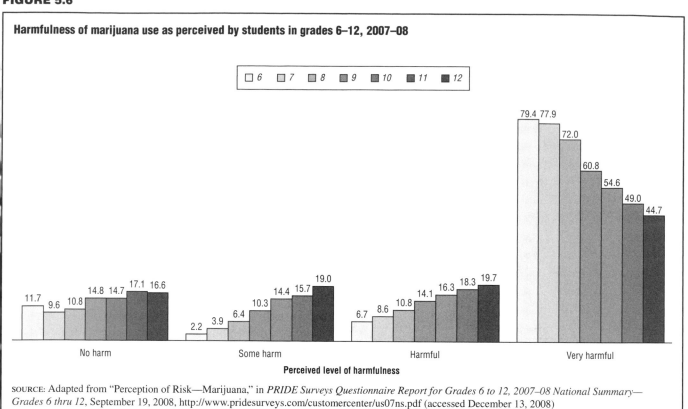

Harmfulness of marijuana use as perceived by students in grades 6–12, 2007–08

Legend: ☐ 6 ☐ 7 ☐ 8 ☐ 9 ☐ 10 ■ 11 ■ 12

No harm: 11.7, 9.6, 10.8, 14.8, 14.7, 17.1, 16.6

Some harm: 2.2, 3.9, 6.4, 10.3, 14.4, 15.7, 19.0

Harmful: 6.7, 8.6, 10.8, 14.1, 16.3, 18.3, 19.7

Very harmful: 79.4, 77.9, 72.0, 60.8, 54.6, 49.0, 44.7

Perceived level of harmfulness

SOURCE: Adapted from "Perception of Risk—Marijuana," in *PRIDE Surveys Questionnaire Report for Grades 6 to 12, 2007–08 National Summary—Grades 6 thru 12*, September 19, 2008, http://www.pridesurveys.com/customercenter/us07ns.pdf (accessed December 13, 2008)

FIGURE 5.7

Trends in annual prevalence of marijuana use among eighth, tenth, and twelfth graders, selected years 1975–2007

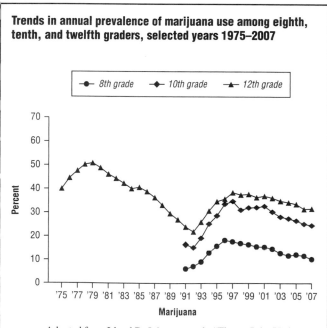

Legend: ● 8th grade ◆ 10th grade ▲ 12th grade

Marijuana

SOURCE: Adapted from Lloyd D. Johnston et al., "Figure 5-4a. Various Drugs: Trends in Annual Prevalence in Grades 8, 10, and 12—Marijuana," in *Monitoring the Future National Survey Results on Drug Use, 1975–2007: Volume 1, Secondary School Students*, National Institute on Drug Abuse, 2008, http://www.monitoringthefuture.org/pubs/monographs/vol1_2007.pdf (accessed December 10, 2008)

FIGURE 5.8

Trends in annual prevalence of tranquilizer use among eighth, tenth, and twelfth graders, selected years 1975–2007

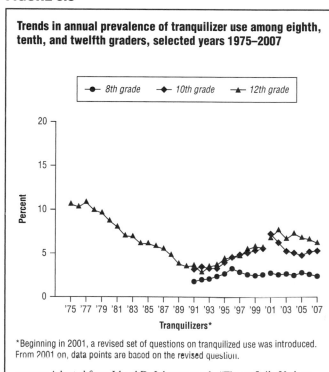

Legend: ● 8th grade ◆ 10th grade ▲ 12th grade

Tranquilizers*

*Beginning in 2001, a revised set of questions on tranquilized use was introduced. From 2001 on, data points are based on the revised question.

SOURCE: Adapted from Lloyd D. Johnston et al., "Figure 5-4b. Various Drugs: Trends in Annual Prevalence in Grades 8, 10, and 12—Tranquilizers," in *Monitoring the Future National Survey Results on Drug Use, 1975–2007: Volume 1, Secondary School Students*, National Institute on Drug Abuse, 2008, http://www.monitoringthefuture.org/pubs/monographs/vol1_2007.pdf (accessed December 10, 2008)

FIGURE 5.9

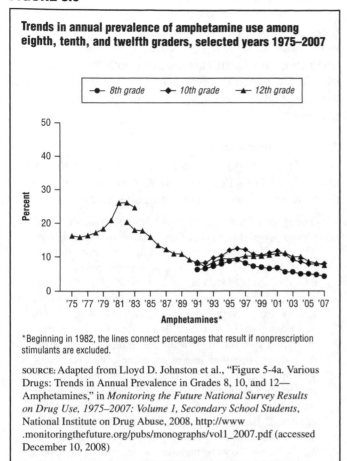

Trends in annual prevalence of amphetamine use among eighth, tenth, and twelfth graders, selected years 1975–2007

● 8th grade ◆ 10th grade ▲ 12th grade

Amphetamines*

*Beginning in 1982, the lines connect percentages that result if nonprescription stimulants are excluded.

SOURCE: Adapted from Lloyd D. Johnston et al., "Figure 5-4a. Various Drugs: Trends in Annual Prevalence in Grades 8, 10, and 12— Amphetamines," in *Monitoring the Future National Survey Results on Drug Use, 1975–2007: Volume 1, Secondary School Students*, National Institute on Drug Abuse, 2008, http://www .monitoringthefuture.org/pubs/monographs/vol1_2007.pdf (accessed December 10, 2008)

FIGURE 5.10

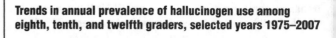

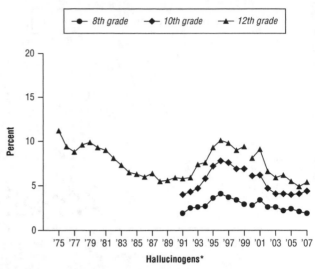

Trends in annual prevalence of hallucinogen use among eighth, tenth, and twelfth graders, selected years 1975–2007

● 8th grade ◆ 10th grade ▲ 12th grade

Hallucinogens*

*In 2001, a revised set of questions on other hallucinogen use was introduced. Data for hallucinogens were affected by these change. From 2001 on, data points are based on the revised questions.

SOURCE: Adapted from Lloyd D. Johnston et al., "Figure 5-4d. Various Drugs: Trends in Annual Prevalence in Grades 8, 10, and 12— Hallucinogens," in *Monitoring the Future National Survey Results on Drug Use, 1975–2007: Volume 1, Secondary School Students*, National Institute on Drug Abuse, 2008, http://www .monitoringthefuture.org/pubs/monographs/vol1_2007.pdf (accessed December 10, 2008)

grade levels, 12th graders have had the highest annual prevalence of hallucinogen use, followed by 10th graders and then 8th graders.

The annual prevalence rates of hallucinogen use for 8th graders rose from 1.9% in 1991 to 4.1% in 1996. (See Figure 5.10.) The rate declined to 2.2% in 2004 and then slightly rose in 2005 to 2.4%. The rate declined through 2007 to 1.9%. The trend patterns of annual prevalence rates of hallucinogen use for 10th and 12th graders were similar to that of 8th graders and to each other. The annual prevalence rates rose from 4% in 1991 to 7.8% in 1996 for 10th graders and from 5.8% in 1991 to 10.1% in 1996 for 12th graders. The rates for both grades then declined through 2003 to 4.1% and 5.9%, respectively. For 10th graders, the rate stayed steady through 2006 and rose slightly in 2007 to a rate of 4.4%. For 12th graders, the rate rose slightly in 2004, dropped through 2006, and then rose slightly again in 2007 to 5.4%.

TRENDS IN MDMA USE IN HIGH SCHOOL STUDENTS. MDMA (3,4-methylenedioxy-methamphetamine), or ecstasy, is a mind-altering drug with hallucinogenic properties. It is related to amphetamine and is made in laboratories by making minor modifications in the chemical structure of this drug. Thus, it is called a designer drug and is one of the most popular of this type of drug.

Figure 5.11 shows trends in the annual prevalence rates of ecstasy use for 8th, 10th, and 12th graders. Since 1996, when data collection began for this drug, 12th graders have had the highest annual prevalence of ecstasy use, followed by 10th graders and then 8th graders.

The annual prevalence rate of MDMA use for 8th graders declined initially from 2.3% in 1996 and 1997 to 1.7% in 1999. (See Figure 5.11.) The rate then peaked in 2001 at 3.5% but then dropped significantly through 2006 to 1.4%, and rose very slightly in 2007 to 1.5%. The trend patterns of annual prevalence rates of MDMA use for 10th and 12th graders were similar to that of 8th graders and to each other, with an initial drop, a sharp peak in 2001, a drop through 2004 and 2005, and then an increase. The peak annual prevalence rate for ecstasy use for 10th graders was 6.2% and for 12th graders, 9.2%, both in 2001. The annual prevalence rates for 10th and 12th graders in 2007 were 3.5% and 4.5%, respectively.

Current, Past-Year, and Lifetime Use of Illicit Drugs in Youth

The NSDUH indicates that in 2007 young people had the highest rate of current illicit drug use in the U.S. population. The rate of current drug use starting with 12-year-olds

FIGURE 5.11

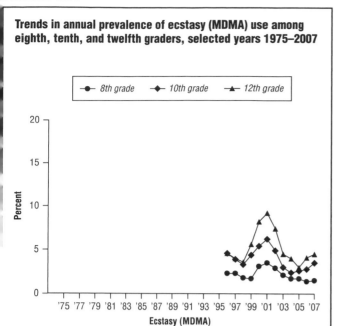

Trends in annual prevalence of ecstasy (MDMA) use among eighth, tenth, and twelfth graders, selected years 1975–2007

SOURCE: Adapted from Lloyd D. Johnston et al., "Figure 5-4h. Various Drugs: Trends in Annual Prevalence in Grades 8, 10, and 12—Ecstasy (MDMA)," in *Monitoring the Future National Survey Results on Drug Use, 1975–2007: Volume 1, Secondary School Students,* National Institute on Drug Abuse, 2008, http://www.monitoringthefuture.org/pubs/monographs/vol1_2007.pdf (accessed December 10, 2008)

increased with age, peaking with 18- to 20-year-olds, who had a current drug use rate of 21.6%. The rate of illicit drug use then generally declined with age.

The NSDUH also compares age groups 12 to 17, 18 to 25, and 26 and older regarding their past month (current), past-year, and lifetime prevalence of drug use. Those aged 18 to 25 showed the highest rates of illicit drug use in all categories in both 2006 and 2007. (See Table 4.1 in Chapter 4.) Those aged 12 to 17 had the next highest prevalence rate for past-year and current use.

A Youth Phenomenon

In *Monitoring the Future National Survey Results on Drug Use, 1975–2007, Volume 1*, Johnston et al. sum up the situation of drugs and youth quite well:

> Young people are often at the leading edge of social change—and this has been particularly true of drug use. The massive upsurge in illicit drug use during the last 35 to 40 years has proven to be a youth phenomenon, and this study documented that the "relapse" in the drug epidemic in the early 1990s initially occurred almost exclusively among adolescents. Adolescents and young adults in their 20s fall into the age groups at highest risk for illicit drug use; moreover, for some drug users, use that begins in adolescence continues well into adulthood. The original epidemic began on the nation's college campuses and then spread downward in age, but the more recent relapse phase in the epidemic first manifested itself among secondary school students and then started moving upward in age as those cohorts matured. From one year to the next, particular drugs rise or fall in popularity, and related problems occur for youth, their families, governmental agencies, and society as a whole.

CHAPTER 6
DRUG TREATMENT

DRUG ABUSE AND ADDICTION
Psychiatric Definition

Though not all experts agree on a single definition of drug addiction, the *Diagnostic and Statistical Manual of Mental Disorders-IV Text Revision* (*DSM-IV-TR*; 2000) is the most widely used reference for diagnosing and treating mental illness and substance-related disorders. In the *DSM-IV-TR*, the nation's psychiatrists draw a distinction between the terms *substance abuse* and *substance dependence*. They stress these terms should not be used interchangeably.

As mentioned in Chapter 1, the *DSM-IV-TR* requires that at least one of the following conditions be met within the year prior before a person can be diagnosed as a substance abuser:

- The person has repeatedly failed to live up to major obligations, such as on the job, at school, or in the family, because of drug use

- The person has used the substance in dangerous situations, such as before driving

- The person has had multiple legal problems because of drug use

- The person continues to use drugs in the face of interpersonal problems, such as arguments or fights caused by substance use

The *DSM-IV-TR* requires that at least three of the following conditions be met in the previous year before a person can be said to be substance dependent (drug addicted):

- Increased tolerance, withdrawal, loss of control over the quantity or duration of use

- An ongoing wish or inability to decrease use

- Inordinate amounts of time spent procuring or consuming drugs or recovering from substance use

- Important goals or activities given up because of substance use

- Substance use continued despite knowledge experiencing damaging effects

The National Institute on Drug Abuse Definition

In *Drugs, Brains, and Behavior: The Science of Addiction* (February 2008, http://www.drugabuse.gov/Scienceof Addiction/sciofaddiction.pdf), the National Institute on Drug Abuse (NIDA) answers the question "What is drug addiction?" the following way: "Addiction is defined as a chronic, relapsing brain disease that is characterized by compulsive drug seeking and use, despite harmful consequences. It is considered a brain disease because drugs change the brain—they change its structure and how it works. These brain changes can be long lasting, and can lead to the harmful behaviors seen in people who abuse drugs.... Addiction is similar to other diseases, such as heart disease. Both disrupt the normal, healthy functioning of the underlying organ, have serious harmful consequences, are preventable, treatable, and if left untreated, can last a lifetime."

Disease Model of Addiction

Beginning in the 1980s advances in neuroscience led to a new understanding of how people become addicted and why they stay that way. As reflected in the NIDA definition, most psychiatric and medical researchers espouse the disease model of addiction. Addicts, they say, respond to drugs differently than people who are not addicted. Much of the difference is associated with differences in brain functioning and can be linked to genetic factors. According to George R. Uhl et al., in "Molecular Genetics of Addiction and Related Heritable Phenotypes" (*Annals of the New York Academy of Sciences*, vol. 1141, October 2008), drug addiction is a disease that is linked to the effects of many genes as well as to environmental factors. Approaches to treatment

FIGURE 6.1

Components of comprehensive drug abuse treatment

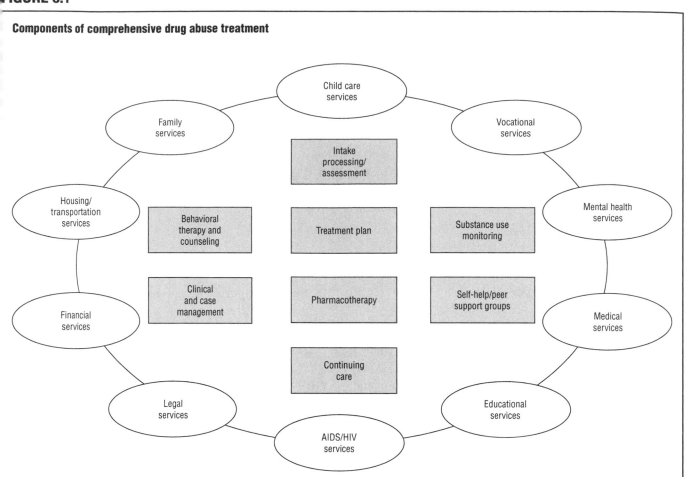

SOURCE: "Components of Comprehensive Drug Abuse Treatment," in *Principles of Drug Addiction Treatment: A Research-Based Guide*, National Institutes of Health, National Institute on Drug Abuse, July 2000, http://www.drugabuse.gov/PODAT/PODATIndex.html (accessed August 20, 2008)

emphasize that addiction must be treated in the same way as other chronic diseases.

In "Evidence-Based Treatments of Addiction" (*Philosophical Transactions of the Royal Society*, vol. 363, no. 1507, October 12, 2008), Charles P. O'Brien of the University of Pennsylvania points out that modern definitions of addiction (such as the NIDA definition) emphasize "uncontrolled drug use rather than tolerance and physiological dependence as essential features of the disorder." He adds that "it is generally recognized that addiction has strong hereditary influences and once established, it behaves as a chronic brain disorder with relapses and remissions over the long term." To help understand this pattern of compulsive behavior and its importance, O'Brien suggests that one only need to think of a friend, relative, or acquaintance who has tried to give up smoking only to relapse at some later time, and probably multiple times, into compulsive smoking behavior while knowing full well the health consequences of his or her actions.

An Integrated Approach to Treatment

The modern approach to treatment has come to reflect the complexity of the drug abuse-addiction spectrum and combines medical approaches, behavior modification, education, and social support functions intended to redress imbalances in the patient's total environment. Components of a comprehensive drug treatment approach are shown in Figure 6.1. Arrayed in the center are categories of treatment used alone or in combination and, on the periphery, social service functions that may have to be deployed to solve some of the patient's problems that led to drug use or addiction in the first place.

HOW MANY PEOPLE ARE BEING TREATED?
N-SSATS/UFDS Data

The Substance Abuse and Mental Health Services Administration (SAMHSA) has been collecting data on substance abuse facilities since 1976. One of its current programs is the National Survey of Substance Abuse Treatment Services (N-SSATS). N-SSATS numbers represent a snapshot of the treatment units on a particular day and do not indicate how many people were being treated over the course of the entire year. Another program is the Uniform Facility Data Set (UFDS) survey, which reports data on the gender, racial, ethnic, and age characteristics of people in treatment. Data on these breakdowns of admissions will be discussed later in this chapter.

As of March 31, 2006, N-SSATS reported in the *National Survey of Substance Abuse Treatment Services (N-SSATS): 2006—Data on Substance Abuse Treatment Facilities* (October 2007, http://wwwdasis.samhsa.gov/06nssats/nssats2k6web.pdf) that the number of people in the treatment facilities who responded to the survey stood at approximately 1.1 million. (See Table 6.1.)

NSDUH Data

To collect data from people who seek and receive substance abuse treatment, SAMHSA included questions about treatment in its 2007 National Survey on Drug Use and Health (NSDUH) and published its findings in *Results from the 2007 National Survey on Drug Use and Health: National Findings* (2008, http://www.oas.samhsa.gov/nsduh/2k7nsduh/2k7Results.pdf). Figure 6.2 shows the results of asking recipients where they received treatment for substance use in the past year at any location. People could report receiving treatment at more than one location. (This definition of treatment location is different from the specific treatment facilities reporting to SAMHSA for the N-SSATS.) The NSDUH determines that self-help groups, outpatient rehabilitation facilities, inpatient rehabilitation facilities, outpatient mental health centers, and hospital inpatient facilities are where people say they most commonly receive treatment.

The NSDUH also asked substance abusers why they did not receive the treatment they needed. SAMHSA data show that 7.5 million people needed treatment in 2007, but only a fraction of those people (approximately 1.3 million) received treatment at a specialty facility. Of the 6.2 million who needed but did not receive treatment, most (35.9%) cited financial reasons for not receiving treatment. (See Figure 6.3.) One out of four (26.6%) admitted they were not yet ready to give up drugs.

Treatment Episode Data Set Data

Another source of data for the drug-treatment population comes from SAMHSA's Treatment Episode Data Set (TEDS). This program counts admissions over the period of a year rather than the number of people in treatment on a particular day during the year. When the same person is admitted twice during the same year, he or she is counted twice, whereas in the N-SSATS survey individuals are counted only once. As reported in *Treatment Episode Data Set (TEDS) 1996–2006: National Admissions to Substance Abuse Treatment Services* (July 2008, http://wwwdasis.samhsa.gov/teds06/teds2k6aweb508.pdf), there were 1.8 million TEDS admissions in 2006.

CHARACTERISTICS OF THOSE ADMITTED

TEDS data from 1996 to 2006 on admissions by sex, race and ethnicity, and age are presented in Table 6.2 and Table 6.3.

Gender

Males represented most of those admitted for drug and/or alcohol treatment, although the percentage of men dropped slightly between 1996 and 2006 (from 70.5% to 68.2%) and that of women increased (from 29.5% to 31.8%). (See Table 6.2.) The number of males admitted for treatment in 2006 was over 1.2 million versus 571,574 female admissions. (See Table 6.3.) These results and data reflect that a greater proportion of men abuse drugs than women in the United States. According to Table 4.1 in Chapter 4, 10.5% of males were past-month users in 2006 and 10.4% in 2007, compared with 6.2% of females in 2006 and 5.8% in 2007.

Race and Ethnicity

Most of those admitted to substance abuse treatment facilities in 2006 were white (59.5%), and whites were admitted in the greatest numbers (1.1 million). (See Table 6.2 and Table 6.3.) They were followed by African-Americans at 21.3% (381,425). Compared with data from 1996, whites decreased slightly from 59.8% but increased in number from 973,808, and African-Americans decreased both in percentage and number from 25.7% (418,514). Hispanics increased their proportion of admissions to drug treatment facilities from 10.4% (169,285) in 1996 to 13.9% (248,436) in 2006. Native Americans and Alaskan natives dropped in share of those treated from 2.5% to 2.3% during this period. Asian-Americans and Pacific Islanders increased from 0.6% (40,082) of the total admissions in 1996 to 1% (40,629) in 2006.

Age

In 1996, 25- to 34-year-olds (33.9% of total) accounted for the largest percentage receiving substance abuse treatment, followed by those aged 35 to 44 years (31%). (See Table 6.2.) Ten years later, these were still the two largest groups receiving treatment, but the order was reversed: those aged 35 to 44 were in the group having the highest percentage receiving substance abuse treatment and those aged 25 to 34 were in the group having the second-highest percentage. The percentage of the younger group decreased to 25.3% in 2006. Even though the percentage of the older group decreased as well (to 27%), the decrease was not as dramatic, thus resulting in the reversal. Those aged 65 and older were the least represented (after those under the age of 12), accounting for 0.7% in 1996 and 0.6% in 2006.

TYPES OF TREATMENT

The disease model of addiction described in the beginning of this chapter, which views drug addiction as a chronic disease, views long-term treatment as necessary.

TABLE 6.1

Persons admitted into substance abuse treatment, by state or region and type of care received, as of March 31, 2006

Number of clients — Type of care offered

State or jurisdiction*	Total	Outpatient — Total outpatient	Regular	Intensive	Day treatment or partial hospitalization	Detox	Methadone maintenance	Non-hospital residential — Total residential	Short term	Long term	Detox	Hospital inpatient — Total hospital inpatient	Treatment	Detox
Total	1,130,881	1,008,915	589,542	128,706	24,039	12,579	254,049	107,790	22,234	79,069	6,487	14,176	8,956	5,220
Alabama	14,953	13,855	2,623	5,031	330	64	5,807	992	390	552	50	106	58	48
Alaska	2,683	2,355	1,740	424	73	25	93	318	21	276	21	10	5	5
Arizona	26,913	24,958	16,510	3,399	158	510	4,381	1,599	320	1,187	92	356	217	139
Arkansas	3,624	3,041	2,185	318	125	68	345	540	236	266	38	43	24	19
California	138,342	118,840	67,933	16,933	3,893	3,740	26,341	18,429	1,951	15,566	912	1,073	711	362
Colorado	33,264	31,591	28,254	1,835	114	60	1,328	1,567	246	1,195	126	106	71	35
Connecticut	22,809	20,896	8,993	1,468	474	352	9,609	1,607	338	1,147	122	306	149	157
Delaware	4,042	3,754	1,877	200	103	26	1,548	245	51	139	55	43	22	21
District of Columbia	4,310	3,682	933	336	278	81	2,054	587	100	403	84	41	3	38
Florida	52,734	44,602	27,834	3,390	2,137	297	10,944	7,309	1,124	5,734	451	823	580	243
Georgia	17,848	14,963	6,911	1,738	1,490	226	4,598	2,288	336	1,802	150	597	360	237
Guam	54	43	25	15	‡	3	‡	11	‡	11	‡	‡	‡	2
Hawaii	3,787	3,284	1,597	862	223	55	547	459	22	413	24	44	42	2
Idaho	3,824	3,546	2,500	1,034	6	6	‡	176	76	90	10	102	78	24
Illinois	43,724	39,900	21,524	5,853	660	220	11,643	3,436	852	2,338	246	388	188	200
Indiana	28,045	26,698	16,246	4,804	375	191	5,082	898	194	628	76	449	327	122
Iowa	7,229	6,660	5,241	1,011	111	10	287	540	184	343	13	29	13	16
Kansas	10,470	9,578	7,541	1,280	26	47	684	872	330	462	80	20	–	20
Kentucky	19,510	17,995	15,234	1,109	151	70	1,431	1,251	281	850	120	264	201	63
Louisiana	9,280	7,667	3,934	1,102	184	109	2,338	1,365	367	899	99	248	117	131
Maine	7,833	7,474	5,023	407	181	160	1,703	281	45	236	–	78	40	38
Maryland	35,224	32,683	16,140	3,280	183	516	12,564	2,501	789	1,596	116	40	14	26
Massachusetts	39,065	34,904	21,084	1,063	672	806	11,279	3,374	487	2,564	323	787	389	398
Michigan	45,290	41,962	31,742	2,537	311	569	6,803	3,120	996	1,926	198	208	137	71
Minnesota	10,078	7,246	1,838	2,823	553	19	2,013	2,731	908	1,649	174	101	80	21
Mississippi	5,912	4,035	3,386	344	149	–	156	1,534	181	1,328	25	343	182	161
Missouri	20,163	18,221	11,007	4,229	784	20	2,181	1,771	1,008	604	159	171	143	28
Montana	3,047	2,809	2,243	500	33	–	33	196	87	94	15	42	42	–
Nebraska	4,893	4,042	2,910	784	100	–	248	807	254	496	57	44	38	6
Nevada	7,248	6,747	5,051	412	24	87	1,173	450	83	308	59	51	29	22
New Hampshire	4,083	3,706	2,506	69	–	185	946	332	101	186	45	45	40	5
New Jersey	30,106	26,699	8,797	4,148	825	830	12,099	2,643	434	2,111	98	764	601	163
New Mexico	12,634	11,908	8,379	1,021	54	157	2,297	634	129	400	105	92	58	34
New York	118,892	104,790	46,862	13,490	3,982	463	39,993	11,894	1,476	9,947	471	2,208	1,320	888
North Carolina	25,855	23,411	12,966	2,824	360	85	7,176	2,049	351	1,586	112	395	285	110
North Dakota	2,301	1,837	1,159	300	258	83	37	398	164	213	21	66	46	20
Ohio	34,988	32,001	23,585	4,439	397	246	3,334	2,529	384	2,043	102	458	316	142
Oklahoma	11,804	10,144	8,147	759	144	108	986	1,545	385	1,086	74	115	78	37
Oregon	22,353	21,150	14,067	3,655	245	172	3,011	1,182	203	893	86	21	9	12
Palau	37	36	36	–	–	–	‡	–	–	‡	‡	1	1	–
Pennsylvania	44,349	39,286	18,475	6,415	755	118	13,523	4,582	1,862	2,395	325	481	353	128
Puerto Rico	13,724	9,548	2,319	418	159	105	6,547	3,897	69	3,518	310	279	127	152
Rhode Island	6,415	6,026	2,770	210	131	43	2,872	326	10	288	28	63	43	20
South Carolina	13,469	12,791	8,578	1,298	120	77	2,718	394	97	258	39	284	133	151
South Dakota	2,314	1,751	1,219	479	53	–	‡	516	161	320	35	47	43	4

TABLE 6.1

Persons admitted into substance abuse treatment, by state or region and type of care received, as of March 31, 2006 [CONTINUED]

							Number of clients							
							Type of care offered							
		Outpatient							Non-hospital residential				Hospital inpatient	
State or jurisdiction*	Total	Total outpatient	Regular	Intensive	Day treatment or partial hospitalization	Detox	Methadone maintenance	Total residential	Short term	Long term	Detox	Total hospital inpatient	Treatment	Detox
Tennessee	15,053	13,348	7,663	1,518	323	239	3,605	1,380	608	645	127	325	220	105
Texas	34,099	28,311	12,441	5,132	624	178	9,936	5,085	1,582	3,316	187	703	454	249
Utah	12,977	11,191	7,089	1,455	264	154	2,229	1,699	134	1,438	77	87	60	27
Vermont	3,726	3,476	2,663	221	53	20	519	137	67	65	5	113	88	25
Virgin Islands	173	156	87	46	1	1	21	17	—	17	—	‡	‡	‡
Virginia	22,847	21,311	15,277	1,595	577	148	3,714	1,375	317	915	143	161	50	111
Washington	42,701	40,480	27,315	8,347	156	508	4,154	2,039	969	968	102	182	122	60
West Virginia	8,691	8,075	2,683	277	71	218	4,826	486	179	279	28	130	98	32
Wisconsin	17,846	16,558	12,028	1,578	559	100	2,293	1,081	225	799	57	207	119	88
Wyoming	3,246	2,894	2,372	491	27	4	—	316	20	281	15	36	32	4

*Facilities operated by federal agencies are included in the states in which the facilities are located.

—Quantity is zero.

‡ No facilities in this category.

SOURCE: "Table 6.23a. Clients in Treatment, According to Type of Care Received, by State or Jurisdiction: March 31, 2006, Number," in *National Survey of Substance Abuse Treatment Services (N-SSATS): 2006. Data on Substance Abuse Treatment Facilities*, U.S. Department of Health and Human Services, Substance Abuse and Mental Health Services Administration, Office of Applied Studies, 2007, http://wwwdasis.samhsa.gov/06nssats2k6web.pdf (accessed December 15, 2008)

FIGURE 6.2

Where persons aged 12 and over received substance abuse treatment, 2007

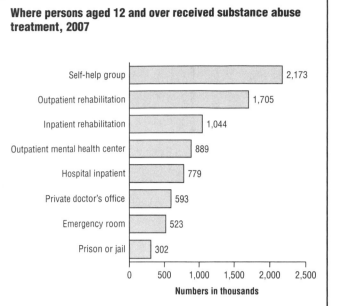

SOURCE: "Figure 7.5. Locations Where Past Year Substance Use Treatment Was Received among Persons Aged 12 or Older: 2007," in *Results from the 2007 National Survey on Drug Use and Health: National Findings*, U.S. Department of Health and Human Services, Substance Abuse and Mental Health Services Administration, Office of Applied Studies, 2008, http://www.oas.samhsa.gov/nsduh/2k7nsduh/2k7Results.pdf (accessed December 8, 2008)

FIGURE 6.3

Reasons persons aged 12 and over gave for not receiving the substance abuse treatment they sought, 2004–07 combined

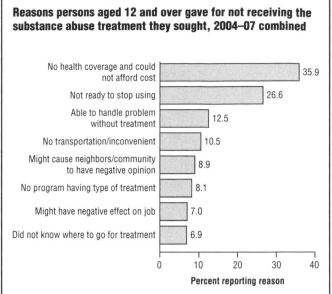

SOURCE: "Figure 7.8. Reasons for Not Receiving Substance Use Treatment among Persons Aged 12 or Older Who Needed and Made an Effort to Get Treatment but Did Not Receive Treatment and Felt They Needed Treatment: 2004–2007 Combined," in *Results from the 2007 National Survey on Drug Use and Health: National Findings*, U.S. Department of Health and Human Services, Substance Abuse and Mental Health Services Administration, Office of Applied Studies, 2008, http://www.oas.samhsa.gov/nsduh/2k7nsduh/2k7Results.pdf (accessed December 8, 2008)

TABLE 6.2

Percentage of persons admitted into substance abuse treatment, by gender, ethnicity, and age at admission, 1996–2006

Gender, race/ethnicity, and age at admission	Treatment Episode Data Set (TEDS) admissions											U.S. population
	1996	1997	1998	1999	2000	2001	2002	2003	2004	2005	2006	2006
Gender												
Male	70.5	70.4	70.5	70.5	70.1	69.8	69.8	69.1	68.4	68.2	68.2	49.3
Female	29.5	29.6	29.5	29.5	29.9	30.2	30.2	30.9	31.6	31.8	31.8	50.7
Total	100.0	100.0	100.0	100.0	100.0	100.0	100.0	100.0	100.0	100.0	100.0	100.0
Race/ethnicity												
White (non-Hispanic)	59.8	59.6	59.5	59.2	58.2	58.8	58.6	58.6	59.9	59.1	59.5	66.4
Black (non-Hispanic)	25.7	25.3	24.9	24.3	25.1	24.5	24.2	24.0	22.7	22.3	21.3	12.3
Hispanic origin	10.4	10.9	11.3	12.0	12.1	12.2	12.8	12.8	12.7	13.6	13.9	14.2
American Indian/Alaska Native	2.5	2.4	2.4	2.4	2.2	2.1	2.1	1.9	1.9	2.1	2.3	0.8
Asian/Pacific Islander	0.6	0.7	0.7	0.8	0.8	0.8	0.9	1.0	0.9	1.0	1.0	4.4
Other	1.0	1.1	1.2	1.4	1.6	1.5	1.4	1.6	1.9	1.7	2.0	1.9
Total	100.0	100.0	100.0	100.0	100.0	100.0	100.0	100.0	100.0	100.0	100.0	100.0
Age at admission												
Under 12 years	0.2	0.2	0.2	0.2	0.2	0.2	0.2	0.2	0.3	0.1	0.1	16.1
12 to 17 years	7.9	8.2	8.1	8.0	7.9	8.2	8.4	8.4	8.5	7.6	7.6	8.5
18 to 24 years	13.4	13.8	14.4	15.0	15.8	16.7	17.1	17.5	18.2	18.5	18.4	9.8
25 to 34 years	33.9	32.2	30.3	28.4	27.0	25.9	25.1	24.8	24.7	25.1	25.3	13.5
35 to 44 years	31.0	31.6	32.2	32.6	32.5	31.9	31.0	30.2	28.8	28.1	27.0	14.6
45 to 54 years	10.3	10.8	11.5	12.4	13.2	13.8	14.7	15.2	15.0	15.5	17.3	14.5
55 to 64 years	2.5	2.5	2.6	2.7	2.8	2.7	2.9	3.1	3.2	3.5	3.7	10.6
65 years and older	0.7	0.7	0.7	0.7	0.7	0.6	0.6	0.6	0.6	0.6	0.6	12.4
Total	100.0	100.0	100.0	100.0	100.0	100.0	100.0	100.0	100.0	100.0	100.0	100.0

SOURCE: "Table 2.9b. Admissions by Gender, Race/Ethnicity, and Age at Admission: TEDS 1996–2006 and U.S. Population 2006 Percent Distribution," in *Treatment Episode Data Set (TEDS) 1996–2006. National Admissions to Substance Abuse Treatment Services*, U.S. Department of Health and Human Services, Substance Abuse and Mental Health Services Administration, Office of Applied Studies, 2008, http://wwwdasis.samhsa.gov/teds06/teds2k6aweb508.pdf (accessed December 15, 2008)

TABLE 6.3

Persons admitted into substance abuse treatment, by gender, ethnicity, and age at admission, 1996–2006

Gender, race/ethnicity, and age at admission	1996	1997	1998	1999	2000	2001	2002	2003	2004	2005	2006
Total	1,639,064	1,607,957	1,712,268	1,725,885	1,759,417	1,781,018	1,898,412	1,864,614	1,889,859	1,859,039	1,799,239
Gender											
Male	1,151,527	1,128,154	1,202,608	1,212,676	1,229,040	1,242,188	1,325,014	1,288,197	1,291,914	1,267,789	1,227,189
Female	481,191	474,350	502,961	507,136	525,258	536,425	572,511	575,770	596,836	590,637	571,574
No. of admissions	1,632,718	1,602,504	1,705,569	1,719,812	1,754,298	1,778,613	1,897,525	1,863,967	1,888,750	1,858,426	1,798,763
Race/ethnicity											
White (non-Hispanic)	973,808	948,992	1,004,115	1,008,503	1,013,439	1,038,978	1,104,411	1,085,397	1,124,362	1,086,467	1,063,871
Black (non-Hispanic)	418,514	402,619	419,784	413,754	436,375	433,463	456,384	444,277	425,594	410,437	381,425
Hispanic origin	169,285	173,347	191,484	203,750	211,559	215,197	240,854	237,200	238,414	250,534	248,436
American Indian/Alaska Native	40,082	38,333	40,511	40,138	37,982	37,904	39,527	35,870	36,440	38,882	40,625
Asian/Pacific Islander	10,197	10,893	11,515	13,610	14,672	14,133	16,474	17,766	16,276	19,250	18,111
Other	16,606	18,263	20,351	23,467	27,835	26,161	26,984	30,535	35,438	31,311	36,414
No. of admissions	1,628,492	1,592,447	1,687,760	1,703,222	1,741,862	1,765,836	1,884,634	1,851,045	1,876,524	1,836,881	1,788,886
Age at admission											
Under 12 years	3,469	3,704	3,390	2,987	3,506	3,011	3,125	3,395	5,233	1,974	1,889
12 to 17 years	129,858	131,194	139,129	137,596	137,844	145,924	158,299	156,957	160,587	141,244	136,658
18 to 24 years	219,406	220,714	245,508	258,208	277,757	296,245	324,540	325,757	343,183	343,430	331,001
25 to 34 years	555,300	516,346	517,297	488,394	473,246	460,986	474,962	460,748	466,282	466,476	454,348
35 to 44 years	507,067	506,624	549,754	559,649	570,618	566,141	588,041	561,607	543,610	521,306	484,854
45 to 54 years	167,899	173,335	197,211	213,538	231,065	244,984	278,503	283,802	294,741	306,997	310,153
55 to 64 years	41,377	40,736	44,096	46,299	48,302	48,534	55,762	57,671	60,356	64,303	67,218
65 years and older	11,535	11,381	11,611	11,652	11,838	11,065	11,169	11,128	11,169	11,227	10,769
No. of admissions	1,635,911	1,604,034	1,707,996	1,718,323	1,754,176	1,776,890	1,894,401	1,861,065	1,885,161	1,856,957	1,796,890

SOURCE: "Table 2.9a. Admissions by Gender, Race/Ethnicity, and Age at Admission: TEDS 1996–2006, Number," in *Treatment Episode Data Set (TEDS) 1996–2006. National Admissions to Substance Abuse Treatment Services*, U.S. Department of Health and Human Services, Substance Abuse and Mental Health Services Administration, Office of Applied Studies, 2008, http://wwwdasis.samhsa.gov/teds06/teds2k6aweb508.pdf (accessed December 15, 2008)

O'Brien notes that "as is the case with other chronic diseases, when the treatment is ended, relapse eventually occurs in most cases."

Detoxification is usually a precursor to rehabilitation because that process cannot begin until the individual's body has been cleared of the drug and a certain physiological equilibrium has been established. Drug rehabilitation refers to processes that assist a drug-addicted person in discontinuing drug use and returning to a drug-free life.

Detoxification

Drug-addicted individuals must usually undergo medical detoxification (detox) in an outpatient facility, a residential center, or a hospital. Medical help, including sedation, is provided to manage the painful physical and psychological symptoms of withdrawal. The detox of many drugs can be achieved with minimal discomfort by replacing the drug of dependence with a less risky drug in the same pharmacological category (e.g., replacing heroin with methadone) and gradually reducing the dose. People addicted to nicotine can accomplish detox on their own by using gradually decreasing doses of nicotine patches. Rehabilitation usually follows detox.

Rehabilitation

Rehabilitation (rehab) has many forms, but it is always designed to change the behavior of the drug abuser. Changed behavior—achieving independence of drugs or alcohol—requires understanding the circumstances that led to dependence, building the confidence that the individual can succeed, and changing the individual's lifestyle so that the individual avoids occasions that produce drug-using behavior. Individual counseling, interaction with support groups, and formal education are used in combination with close supervision, incentives, and disincentives. Certain individuals require a new socialization that is achieved by living for an extended period in a structured and supportive environment in which new life skills can be acquired. Treatment may involve guiding the individual to seek help from other social agencies to reorder his or her life. (See Figure 6.1.)

Individuals, of course, may be mentally ill and will then receive, as part of drug rehab, mental health services in outpatient or hospital settings. Most treatment takes place in outpatient settings, with the individual reporting daily, weekly, or less frequently for periodic treatment and assessment.

Distribution of Patients

On March 31, 2006, 1 million (89.2%) out of 1.1 million patients were receiving outpatient care. (See Table 6.1.) Of the remainder, 107,790 (9.5%) were in residential facilities and 14,176 (1.3%) received hospital inpatient treatment. Of those under outpatient treatment but not in detox, the majority were receiving what SAMHSA calls regular, or nonintensive, treatment.

Of the total treatment population, 24,286 individuals (2.1% of all patients) were undergoing detox, most in outpatient settings (12,579), the rest in residential facilities (6,487) and hospitals (5,220). (See Table 6.1.) Among all patients under treatment, 254,049 (22.5%) were receiving methadone.

STATISTICS ON ADMITTED PATIENTS

Admissions by Substance

Data on admissions by the primary substance of abuse provided by TEDS for 2006 are shown in Table 6.4. In that year alcohol alone or in combination with a secondary substance accounted for the largest number of people receiving treatment (714,032, or 39.7% of all admissions), followed by opiates (320,734, or 17.8%, mainly heroin), marijuana (289,988, or 16.1%), cocaine (250,135, or 13.9%), and stimulants (156,486, or 8.7%, primarily methamphetamine).

The 2006 admissions for alcohol abuse (either alone or in combination with a secondary substance) of 39.7% is down from 50.7% reported by TEDS in 1996. Total alcohol-related admissions have been declining annually, largely accounting for the decreasing trend in total admissions.

The category showing the largest growth has been stimulants. In 1996 stimulants accounted for 3.2% of all admissions, whereas in 2006 they accounted for 8.7%. (See Table 6.4.) Within the stimulant category, admissions caused by amphetamine (particularly methamphetamine) accounted for the vast majority. Methamphetamine is addictive and is produced in makeshift laboratories around the country. Marijuana-related admissions have had the second-most rapid growth, representing 16.1% of cases in 2006, up from 11.7% in 1996.

Opiate-related admissions have been growing, whereas cocaine-related admissions have been declining. In 1996 opiate-related admissions were 14.7% and cocaine-related admissions were 16.1% of the total; 10 years later their order was reversed, with opiates accounting for 17.8% and cocaine for 13.9% of admissions. (See Table 6.4.)

Demographics by Substance

A detailed examination of admissions in 2006 is provided in Table 6.4, which shows the distribution of people admitted by major drug categories, gender, race and ethnicity, and age at admission.

GENDER. As noted previously in this chapter, the total male admissions (68.2%) were higher than the total female admissions (31.8%) in 2006. (See Table 6.2.) This trend held in all but two substance categories: sedatives (57.3% females versus 42.7% males) and tranquilizers (53.6% females versus 46.4% males). (See Table 6.4.) The greatest male-female differences were noted in alcohol-only admissions (74.6% males versus 25.4% females), marijuana-related admissions (73.8% males versus 26.2% females), and alcohol admissions with a secondary drug (73.7% males versus 26.3% females).

RACE AND ETHNICITY. In 2006 whites made up 59.4% of the substance abuse treatment admissions; African-Americans, 21.3%; Hispanics, 14%; Native Americans, 2.2%; and Asian-Americans and Pacific Islanders, 1%. (See Table 6.4.) Whites had the highest admission rates for all drug categories except smoked cocaine and phencyclidine (PCP). African-Americans had the highest smoked-cocaine admissions (48.8%) and PCP-related admissions (57.9%). African-Americans were second in admission rates for alcohol with a secondary drug, cocaine other than smoked, marijuana, other stimulants, hallucinogens, and other. Hispanics were second in admission rates for alcohol only, heroin, methamphetamine/amphetamine, sedatives, PCP, and inhalants. African-Americans and Hispanics were both admitted in nearly equal percentages for other opiates. It should be noted that the Hispanics category is treated as an ethnicity rather than as a race and includes both white and black individuals of Hispanic origin.

It is important, however, to consider these rates of substance abuse treatment by race in the context of the overall racial composition of the United States. The 2006 TEDS data indicate that the population consisted of 66.4% whites, 14.2% Hispanics, and 12.3% African-Americans in that year. When substance abuse treatment rates are compared with these population statistics, whites were underrepresented in treatment (59.5% in treatment versus 66.4% of the population), the proportion of Hispanics in treatment was comparable to Hispanics in the population (13.9% in treatment versus 14.2% of the population), and African-Americans were disproportionately admitted for treatment (21.3% in treatment versus 12.3% of the population).

AGE AT ADMISSION. The 2006 TEDS data show that 74.2% of people admitted for alcohol-only abuse that year were between the ages of 20 and 49. The average age of admission for alcohol-only abuse that year was 39 years. Crack (smoked) cocaine treatment recipients clustered in the 30- to 49-year-old age group (71.2%) and had an average age of 38 years. In contrast, 43.2% of those admitted for using inhalants were aged 17 or younger and had an average age of 25 years. Those being treated for marijuana abuse were another young group. Nearly three-quarters (72.6%) were between the ages of 15 and 29. The marijuana treatment group had an average age of 24 years.

Type of Treatment

In 2006, 62.9% of those admitted to treatment were admitted into ambulatory (nonresidential) treatment facilities; of the remainder, 19.9% went into residential-type (24-hour) detox and 17.1% went into residential facilities. (See Table 6.5.)

TABLE 6.4

Percentage of persons admitted into substance abuse treatment, by gender, ethnicity, and primary substance abused, 2006

Primary substance at admission

Gender and race/ethnicity	All admissions	Alcohol		Opiates		Cocaine		Mari-juana/hashish	Stimulants		Tranquilizers	Sedatives	Hallu-cinogens	PCP	Inhalants	Other/none specified
		Alcohol only	With secondary drug	Heroin	Other opiates	Smoked cocaine	Other route		Metham-phetamine/amphetamine	Other stimulants						
Total	1,800,717	393,810	320,222	245,984	74,750	178,475	71,660	289,988	155,643	843	8,011	3,866	1,510	2,777	1,034	52,144
Gender																
Male	68.2	74.6	73.7	68.3	53.8	58.4	65.0	73.8	54.2	59.8	46.4	42.7	72.7	71.1	67.0	61.3
Female	31.8	25.4	26.3	31.7	46.2	41.6	35.0	26.2	45.8	40.2	53.6	57.3	27.3	28.9	33.0	38.7
Total	100.0	100.0	100.0	100.0	100.0	100.0	100.0	100.0	100.0	100.0	100.0	100.0	100.0	100.0	100.0	100.0
No. of admissions	1,800,241	393,736	320,166	245,944	74,731	178,440	71,650	289,927	155,550	843	8,008	3,864	1,508	2,777	1,034	52,063
Race/ethnicity																
White (non-Hispanic)	59.4	69.3	60.0	51.7	88.3	40.5	53.9	51.5	67.5	57.6	85.9	81.5	65.8	16.3	65.3	65.0
Black (non-Hispanic)	21.3	11.3	23.7	21.6	4.2	48.8	24.8	29.3	3.2	21.8	5.0	6.9	18.4	57.9	6.5	17.7
Hispanic origin	14.0	12.7	10.8	23.7	4.1	7.9	17.9	13.7	19.3	12.7	6.4	8.3	9.4	22.2	17.2	12.7
Mexican	5.8	6.7	3.5	5.4	1.4	2.5	6.7	6.4	14.5	8.8	1.7	4.2	3.1	10.4	10.9	0.9
Puerto Rican	3.8	1.5	3.5	12.7	1.0	2.7	5.6	3.1	0.4	0.8	2.3	1.1	2.6	6.4	1.7	2.0
Cuban	0.4	0.4	0.4	0.9	0.3	0.4	0.7	0.3	0.1	0.2	0.5	0.8	0.5	0.5	0.9	0.5
Other/not specified	3.9	4.1	3.4	4.7	1.4	2.3	4.9	3.9	4.2	2.9	2.0	2.1	3.2	4.9	3.7	9.3
Other	5.3	6.7	5.5	3.1	3.4	2.8	3.4	5.4	10.0	7.8	2.7	3.3	6.4	3.6	10.9	4.6
Alaska Native	0.1	0.1	0.1	0.1	0.1	0.1	0.1	0.1	0.1	--	0.1	0.1	0.1	—	—	*
American Indian	2.2	3.9	3.0	0.5	1.5	0.7	0.8	1.7	2.5	2.4	0.8	1.0	1.9	0.6	6.7	2.1
Asian/Pacific Islander	1.0	0.9	0.7	0.5	0.6	0.6	0.7	1.2	3.2	1.6	0.5	0.7	1.6	0.6	0.9	0.7
Other	2.0	1.7	1.7	2.0	1.2	1.4	1.9	2.4	4.2	3.8	1.3	1.6	2.7	2.4	3.3	1.7
Total	100.0	100.0	100.0	100.0	100.0	100.0	100.0	100.0	100.0	100.0	100.0	100.0	100.0	100.0	100.0	100.0
No. of admissions	1,790,362	391,202	318,635	245,033	74,325	177,813	71,309	288,393	154,916	833	7,977	3,830	1,494	2,758	1,023	50,821

*Less than 0.05 percent.
—Quantity is zero.

source: "Table 3.1a. Admissions by Primary Substance of Abuse, According to Gender and Race/Ethnicity: TEDS 2006, Column Percent Distribution," in *Treatment Episode Data Set (TEDS) 1996–2006. National Admissions to Substance Abuse Treatment Services*, U.S. Department of Health and Human Services, Substance Abuse and Mental Health Services Administration, Office of Applied Studies, 2008, http://wwwdasis.samhsa.gov/teds06/teds2k6aweb508.pdf (accessed December 15, 2008)

TABLE 6.5

Percentage of persons admitted into substance abuse treatment, by primary substance of abuse and type of care received, 2006

Primary substance at admission

Type of service and opioid therapy	All admissions	Alcohol		Opiates		Cocaine		Mari- juana/ hashish	Stimulants		Tran- quilizers	Sedatives	Hallu- cinogens	PCP	Inhalants	Other/ none specified
		Alcohol only	With secondary drug	Heroin	Other opiates	Smoked cocaine	Other route		Metham- phetamine/ amphetamine	Other stimulants						
Total	**1,800,717**	**393,810**	**320,222**	**245,984**	**74,750**	**178,475**	**71,660**	**289,988**	**155,643**	**843**	**8,011**	**3,866**	**1,510**	**2,777**	**1,034**	**52,144**
Type of service																
Ambulatory	62.9	59.4	58.7	50.7	59.6	51.7	66.0	84.3	67.2	69.2	51.9	59.5	67.6	67.0	69.5	81.8
Outpatient	50.0	48.2	46.5	39.3	44.4	37.4	50.3	67.8	53.8	53.1	38.6	44.3	52.3	52.3	52.0	76.9
Intensive outpatient	11.7	10.0	11.8	6.1	11.7	13.9	15.3	16.5	13.2	15.8	12.1	13.5	14.7	14.5	16.1	4.8
Detoxification	1.3	1.2	0.4	5.4	3.4	0.3	0.4	0.1	0.1	0.2	1.1	1.7	0.6	0.2	1.5	0.2
Detoxification (24-hour service)	19.9	29.6	22.7	34.4	24.4	18.0	10.3	2.2	8.1	22.5	29.6	19.5	6.4	6.4	11.0	9.6
Free-standing residential	15.6	24.6	16.1	23.9	19.3	16.6	8.8	2.0	7.8	21.7	21.0	14.4	5.8	6.1	9.6	5.6
Hospital inpatient	4.3	5.1	6.6	10.5	5.1	1.4	1.5	0.2	0.4	0.8	8.7	5.1	0.6	0.3	1.5	4.0
Rehabilitation/residential	17.1	10.9	18.6	14.9	16.1	30.4	23.7	13.5	24.7	8.3	18.5	21.0	26.0	26.6	19.4	8.6
Short-term (<31 days)	9.4	6.9	11.6	7.4	10.7	16.3	13.4	7.1	9.5	4.5	12.2	14.8	14.2	10.8	9.8	5.2
Long-term (31+ days)	7.2	3.5	6.5	7.1	4.9	13.6	9.9	6.1	14.8	3.4	5.5	5.0	10.7	15.4	8.6	2.6
Hospital (non-detox)	0.5	0.6	0.5	0.4	0.5	0.5	0.5	0.3	0.4	0.4	0.9	1.1	1.1	0.3	1.1	0.7
Total	**100.0**	**100.0**	**100.0**	**100.0**	**100.0**	**100.0**	**100.0**	**100.0**	**100.0**	**100.0**	**100.0**	**100.0**	**100.0**	**100.0**	**100.0**	**100.0**
No. of admissions	1,800,717	393,810	320,222	245,984	74,750	178,475	71,660	289,988	155,643	843	8,011	3,866	1,510	2,777	1,034	52,144

SOURCE: Adapted from "Table 3.6. Admissions by Primary Substance of Abuse, According to Type of Service and Opioid Therapy: TEDS 2006, Percent Distribution," in *Treatment Episode Data Set (TEDS) 1996–2006. National Admissions to Substance Abuse Treatment Services*, U.S. Department of Health and Human Services, Substance Abuse and Mental Health Services Administration, Office of Applied Studies, 2008, http://www.dasis.samhsa.gov/teds06/teds2k6aweb508.pdf (accessed December 15, 2008)

Among those going into residential-type detox, the largest percentages had been admitted for heroin (34.4%), alcohol only (29.6%), and tranquilizer (29.6%) use. (See Table 6.5.) Those using marijuana had the highest percentage entering ambulatory care (84.3%). The largest proportion of substance abusers assigned to residential treatment were cocaine users (54.1%).

Referring Source

Table 6.6 shows the source of referral of patients to substance abuse treatment in 2006. One-third (32.8%) of all people admitted came to get treatment at their own volition. The largest referral source (sending 38% of individuals) was the criminal justice system, referring people for drug use or driving under the influence of alcohol. Much of the remaining third of all referrals came from substance abuse treatment providers and other health care agencies (10.1% and 6.5% of referrals, respectively), referring individuals for specific services. Other referrals came from schools, employers, and community agencies.

Regarding the source of referral based on the drug of abuse, most heroin users (59.3%) and other opiate users (51.9%) sought treatment of their own accord. (See Table 6.6.) Justice system sources sent over half of marijuana users (58%), methamphetamine/amphetamine users (54.9%), and PCP users (57.6%), along with nearly half of hallucinogen users (46.9%) and alcohol-only users (43.3%), to treatment.

HOW EFFECTIVE IS TREATMENT?

During the 1960s there was an opioid epidemic in the United States, and the federal government released substantial funds to substance abuse treatment programs. This funding has continued over the decades and is supplemented by state governments and private sources. According to the Office of National Drug Control Policy, in *National Drug Control Strategy: FY 2009 Budget Summary* (February 2008, http://www.whitehousedrugpolicy.gov/publications/policy/09budget/fy09budget.pdf), the 2009 federal budget request for drug abuse treatment was $2.8 billion, and the request for treatment research was $601.8 million.

With so much money devoted to substance abuse treatment, there has been considerable research conducted on the effectiveness of the programs. The bulk of this research began in the late 1960s and extended into the 1990s.

In press release "New Research Documents Success of Drug Abuse Treatments" (December 15, 1997, http://www.nih.gov/news/pr/dec97/nida-15.htm), the National Institutes of Health notes that the first major study of drug-treatment effectiveness was the Drug Abuse Reporting Program (DARP), which studied more than 44,000 clients in 52 treatment centers from 1969 to 1973. Program staff then studied a smaller group of these clients 6 and 12 years after their treatment. A second important study was the Treatment Outcome Prospective Study (TOPS), which followed 11,000 clients admitted to 41 treatment centers between 1979 and 1981. Both DARP and TOPS found major reductions in both drug abuse and criminal activity after treatment.

Services Research Outcomes Study

SAMHSA's Services Research Outcomes Study (SROS, September 1998, http://www.oas.samhsa.gov/sros/toc.htm) confirmed that both drug use and criminal behavior are reduced after drug treatment. Because it conducted a five-year follow-up on initial data in the Drug Services Research Survey (DSRS; http://www.oas.sam hsa.gov/dsrs.htm), the SROS provided the first nationally representative data to answer the question: "Does treatment work?" This study, although now over a decade old and reporting on even older data, has not been repeated.

In this nationally representative sample, alcohol use decreased 14% and drug use declined 21%, leading to the following conclusion in the SROS report: "A nationally representative survey of 1,799 persons confirms that both drug use and criminal behavior are reduced following inpatient, outpatient and residential treatment for drug abuse."

According to the SROS report, decreases varied from drug to drug, with heroin use decreasing the least. It went down 13.2%, suggesting that heroin use continued for 86.8% of users. Crack use declined 16.4%, but those treated for snorting cocaine powder did better: 45.4% had abandoned the drug after treatment and continued to do so five years later—but 54.6% were still snorting cocaine. Among marijuana users 28% had given up the drug, whereas 72% continued. Results were better in all the other drug categories, but these are also the drugs of limited use by the study sample (and the population at large). The study also showed that success of treatment is higher when users are older. The exception was crack cocaine.

TYPE AND LENGTH OF TREATMENT. According to the SROS report, results by type of treatment were variable. Overall results for any illicit drug show that best results (25% decrease in drug use) were obtained by inpatient (hospital) treatment, followed by residential treatment. Outpatient methadone treatment had less favorable results (10% decrease) than outpatient drug-free treatment (19%). Outpatient methadone treatment consists of receiving methadone during visits to a treatment center; the center may also provide other services, such as counseling. Outpatient drug-free treatment consists of counseling, group therapy, and other services.

On average, the best results for decreasing use of all drugs, especially cocaine, were achieved with treatment that lasted six months or more; this length of treatment

TABLE 6.6

Percentage of persons admitted into substance abuse treatment, by primary substance of abuse, source of referral, and number of prior treatment episodes, 2006

Source of referral to treatment and number of prior treatment episodes	All admissions	Alcohol		Opiates		Cocaine		Marijuana/ hashish	Stimulants		Tranquilizers	Sedatives	Hallu- cinogens	PCP	Inhalants	Other/none specified
		Alcohol only	With secondary drug	Heroin	Other opiates	Smoked cocaine	Other route		Metham- phetamine/ amphetamine	Other stimulants						
Total	1,800,717	393,810	320,222	245,984	74,750	178,475	71,660	289,988	155,643	843	8,011	3,866	1,510	2,777	1,034	52,1144
Source of referral to treatment																
Criminal justice/DUI	38.0	43.3	35.6	14.2	16.7	27.8	35.7	58.0	54.9	34.6	21.6	25.8	46.9	57.6	30.3	33.0
Self- or individual	32.8	28.4	32.1	59.3	51.9	37.7	30.4	15.1	21.4	26.7	42.1	38.5	25.6	20.6	32.2	38.0
Alcohol/drug abuse care provider	10.1	8.1	12.2	14.5	13.6	14.8	11.9	5.6	5.3	9.9	13.6	12.8	8.4	8.2	8.2	4.4
Other health care provider	6.5	8.0	7.8	5.1	9.0	7.0	6.8	4.2	3.4	6.0	12.6	9.3	6.5	3.4	11.7	8.8
School (educational)	1.1	0.7	0.8	0.1	0.2	0.1	0.4	3.5	0.4	5.3	0.4	1.3	1.7	0.2	4.3	4.0
Employer/EAP	0.7	0.9	0.9	0.2	0.8	0.5	1.5	0.9	0.3	0.4	0.6	1.1	0.3	0.1	0.7	0.6
Other community referral	10.9	10.5	10.7	6.7	7.9	12.1	13.4	12.6	14.2	17.1	9.1	11.3	10.6	9.9	12.7	11.3
Total	**100.0**	**100.0**	**100.0**	**100.0**	**100.0**	**100.0**	**100.0**	**100.0**	**100.0**	**100.0**	**100.0**	**100.0**	**100.0**	**100.0**	**100.0**	**100.0**
No. of admissions	1,768,402	388,160	315,700	242,041	73,439	175,591	70,413	284,929	152,982	830	7,899	3,769	1,459	2,706	1,010	47,474
No. of prior treatment episodes																
None	47.8	53.0	43.5	25.9	45.1	38.4	50.7	61.6	51.2	56.1	44.8	60.8	49.8	46.0	58.7	73.9
1	21.3	20.5	22.4	18.0	23.7	21.6	22.2	22.0	24.6	23.2	20.3	18.7	23.8	23.0	18.6	11.9
2	11.2	9.6	12.2	14.3	12.7	13.8	11.7	8.5	11.8	9.1	11.9	8.4	11.7	13.0	9.1	5.3
3	6.2	5.1	7.0	9.9	6.8	8.4	5.7	3.4	5.5	3.2	6.4	4.4	6.2	7.1	3.5	2.7
4	3.6	2.9	4.1	6.7	3.8	5.1	3.2	1.6	2.7	3.3	3.9	2.3	2.6	3.8	2.6	1.4
5 or more	10.0	8.9	10.8	25.3	8.0	12.8	6.5	2.9	4.2	5.0	12.7	5.4	5.9	7.1	7.6	4.8
Total	**100.0**	**100.0**	**100.0**	**100.0**	**100.0**	**100.0**	**100.0**	**100.0**	**100.0**	**100.0**	**100.0**	**100.0**	**100.0**	**100.0**	**100.0**	**100.0**
No. of admissions	1,415,526	314,971	226,700	182,176	66,032	137,226	52,446	237,352	149,615	757	6,804	3,200	1,342	2,292	936	33,677

Notes: DUI = Driving Under the influence. EAP = Employee Assistance Program.

SOURCE: "Table 3.5. Admissions by Primary Substance of Abuse, According to Source of Referral to Treatment and Number of Prior Treatment Episodes: TEDS 2006, Percent Distribution," in *Treatment Episode Data Set (TEDS) 1996–2006. National Admissions to Substance Abuse Treatment Services,* U.S. Department of Health and Human Services, Substance Abuse and Mental Health Services Administration, Office of Applied Studies, 2008, http://wwwdasis.samhsa.gov/teds06/teds2k6aweb508.pdf (accessed December 15, 2008)

was also nearly the top category for marijuana use. In his review of addiction treatment, O'Brien concurs that long-term treatment is necessary due to the chronic nature of addiction and its tendency to recur when treatment is stopped. His literature review suggests that successful treatments for addictions last months to years.

CRIMINAL BEHAVIOR. The SROS report shows that treatment for substance abuse can significantly reduce crime. Criminal activities such as breaking and entering, drug sales, prostitution, driving under the influence, and theft/larceny decreased between 23% and 38% after drug treatment. However, incarceration and parole/probation violations actually increased, by 17% and 26%, respectively. Data in the study on those incarcerated or detained were less reliable than other data because of nonresponse to the survey.

More Studies on Effectiveness and Cost-Effectiveness of Treatment

Matilde P. Machado of the Universidad Carlos III de Madrid compares in "Substance Abuse Treatment, What Do We Know? An Economist's Perspective" (*European Journal of Health Economics*, vol. 6, no. 1, March 2005) the effectiveness and cost-effectiveness of substance abuse treatment programs by conducting a literature review and summarizing the results. Machado notes that there is no common definition of the term *effectiveness* but that three objectives represent most expectations about substance abuse treatment: reducing alcohol and/or drug use, improving personal and social functioning, and improving public health. Machado notes, "The evidence largely indicates that treatment is effective in each of these aspects."

Nonetheless, Machado suggests that not all treatment programs are equally effective. Some may work better for patients with certain characteristics. For example, "stable alcoholic patients do well in short inexpensive programs while patients with more serious conditions benefit from additional services and longer treatment."

In analyzing the cost-effectiveness of drug abuse treatment programs, Machado finds that most cost-effectiveness studies limited their analyses to treatment costs. She suggests that cost-effectiveness can only be determined by including all the resources needed to provide treatment, such as patient costs (e.g., transportation and day care) and societal costs (e.g., crime and unemployment).

Medications under Development for Treating Addiction

According to O'Brien, vaccines that trigger the development of antidrug antibodies in the drug user have been under development for decades. Vaccines have been under development and tested for morphine and cocaine. These vaccines are constructed by altering the molecular structure of the drugs so that when injected, the recipient

develops antimorphine or anticocaine antibodies. These antibodies reduce a person's response to the specific drug and lower the concentration of the drug in the brain. Research is still ongoing; as of spring 2009, antidrug vaccines were not yet ready for use in humans.

O'Brien explains that other types of medications to help drug addicts break their addiction are under development as well. This group of drugs is being designed to lessen an addict's craving and withdrawal symptoms during drug detox and rehab, with the hopes of increasing the percentage of drug-addicted people who successfully remain drug-free. The development of these new medications has been helped by research on how the brain reacts to the use of addictive drugs and the withdrawal from them.

DRUG COURTS

Drug courts are programs that use the court's authority to offer certain drug-addicted offenders to have their charges dismissed or their sentences reduced if they participate in drug court substance abuse treatment programs. Drug court programs vary across the nation, but most programs offer a range of treatment options and generally require one year of commitment from the defendant.

Figure 6.4 shows the increase in the use of drug courts nationwide. There were over 2,000 drug courts operating in the United States in 2007, and more were in the planning stages.

FIGURE 6.4

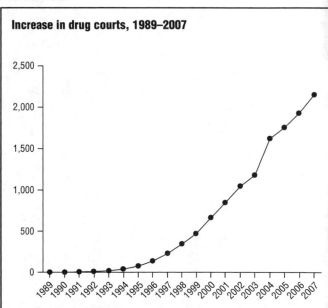

Increase in drug courts, 1989–2007

SOURCE: "Figure 15. The Number of Drug Courts Continues to Increase Nationwide (1989–2007)," in *National Drug Control Strategy: 2008 Annual Report*, Executive Office of the President, Office of National Drug Control Policy, February 2008, http://www.whitehousedrugpolicy.gov/publications/policy/ndcs08/2008ndcs.pdf (accessed August 20, 2008). Data from the National Drug Court Institute.

In *Adult Drug Courts: Evidence Indicates Recidivism Reductions and Mixed Results for Other Outcomes* (February 2005, http://www.gao.gov/new.items/d05219.pdf), the U.S. Government Accountability Office (GAO) notes that drug court programs reduce the recidivism rate (rate of reoffenses) during the time that drug abusers are enrolled in drug court treatment programs. The GAO does, however, find limited and mixed evidence of substance use relapse outcomes. Nonetheless, the GAO concludes that "overall, positive findings from relatively rigorous evaluations in relation to recidivism, coupled with positive net benefit results ... indicate that drug court programs can be an effective means to deal with some offenders. These programs appear to provide an opportunity for some individuals to take advantage of a structured program to help them reduce their criminal involvement and their substance abuse problems, as well as potentially provide a benefit to society in general."

C. West Huddleston III, Douglas B. Marlowe, and Rachel Casebolt assert in *Painting the Current Picture: A National Report Card on Drug Courts and Other Problem-Solving Court Programs in the United States* (May 2008, http://www.ndci.org/publications/PCPII1_web.pdf) that drug courts decrease criminal recidivism, save money, increase retention in treatment, and provide affordable treatment.

WHERE TO GO FOR HELP

Many organizations provide assistance for addicts, their families, and their friends. Most of the self-help groups are based on the Twelve Step program of Alcoholics Anonymous (AA). Whereas AA is a support group for problem drinkers, Al-Anon/Alateen is for friends and families of alcoholics. Families Anonymous provides support for family members and friends concerned about a loved one's problems with drugs and/or alcohol. Other organizations include Adult Children of Alcoholics, Cocaine Anonymous, and Narcotics Anonymous. For an addict, many of these organizations can provide immediate help. For families and friends, they can provide knowledge, understanding, and support. For contact information for some of these organizations, see the Important Names and Addresses section at the back of this book.

CHAPTER 7
HOW ALCOHOL, TOBACCO, AND DRUG USE AFFECT ECONOMICS AND GOVERNMENT

The alcohol and tobacco industries play large roles in the U.S. economy. Both industries not only provide jobs and income for those involved in growing, manufacturing, and selling these products but also contribute significant tax revenues to the federal, state, and local governments. The U.S. economy also feels the effects of alcohol, tobacco, and illicit drug use in other, less beneficial, ways. All these drugs can have significant health consequences, with associated health care costs. There are also costs in the form of loss of productivity—work that was never performed because of poor health, death, or imprisonment. The cost of enforcing drug laws, and incarcerating those convicted of breaking such laws, are significant as well.

U.S. ALCOHOL SALES AND CONSUMPTION

Retail sales of alcoholic beverages are divided into three groups: beer, wine, and distilled spirits. According to the Economic Research Service (ERS; March 15, 2008, http://www.ers.usda.gov/Data/FoodConsumption/spreadsheets/beverage.xls), of all the beverage categories in retail sales, such as bottled water, carbonated beverages, and coffee, carbonated beverages had the highest consumption at 50.6 gallons (191.5 L) per person in 2006. Bottled water was second at 27.6 gallons (104.5 L) per person and alcoholic beverages were third at 25.3 gallons (65.8 L) per person. Of the three alcoholic beverage categories, beer was consumed in the greatest quantity (21.6 gallons [81.8 L] per person in 2006), followed by wine (2.3 gallons [8.7 L] per person) and distilled spirits (1.4 gallons [5.3 L] per person).

Beer

The ERS notes that the per capita (per person) consumption of beer fell almost steadily through the 1980s and early 1990s. Beer consumption was 24.6 gallons (93.1 L) per person in 1981 and 21.6 (81.8 L) gallons per person in 2006, with the latter amount being relatively constant since the mid-1990s. According to the Beer Institute, in *Brewer's Almanac 2008* (September 1, 2008, http://www.beerinsti

tute.org/statistics.asp?bid=200), the beer industry grew by 2.2% in 2006 and by 1.3% in 2007.

The Beer Institute also notes that there were an estimated 1,572 domestic brewers in the United States in 2006, well over five times the number in 1990. Microbreweries and brewpubs (specialty brewers) account for this increase.

Wine

The Wine Institute reports in "2007 California Wine Sales Continue to Increase as Wine Expands Its Popularity among Americans" (2008, http://www.wineinstitute.org/resources/statistics/article122) that wine sales in the United States grew 4% in 2007 to 745 million gallons (2.8 billion L) for a retail sales value of $30 billion. In comparison, a total of 617 million gallons (2.3 billion L) of wine were sold in the United States in 2002, for a retail sales value of $21.8 billion, up from $20.3 billion in 2001. Nonetheless, the ERS notes that the per capita consumption of wine was at its peak of 2.4 gallons (9.1 L) a year in the mid-1980s before beginning a slow decline to 1.7 gallons (6.4 L) per capita in the early to mid-1990s. The per capita consumption rate then rose slowly; in 2006 it was 2.3 gallons (8.7 L) per person, having risen close to the peak consumption.

According to the Wine Institute, the California wine industry accounted for a 61% share of the U.S. wine market in 2007. Red wines held a 43% market share in 2007, white wines a 42% share, and blush wines a 15% share. Chardonnay was the leading varietal wine (a wine produced from a single variety of grape) followed by Cabernet Sauvignon, Merlot, and White Zinfandel, respectively.

Distilled Spirits

In *Distilled Spirits Council 2007 Industry Review* (January 25, 2008, http://www.discus.org/pdf/2007Review Brief.pdf), the Distilled Spirits Council of the United States indicates that the 2007 revenues from distilled spirits (e.g. whiskey, vodka, and rum) were $18.2 billion, an increase of

56% from the revenues of 2000. Each year from 2000 to 2007 industry revenues grew—on average—6.5%.

How Much Do Individuals and Families Spend on Alcohol?

The U.S. Bureau of Labor Statistics reports in *Consumer Expenditures in 2007* (November 2008, http://www.bls.gov/cex/2007/Standard/cucomp.pdf) that the average American family (or other consumer unit) spent $506 on alcoholic beverages in 2007. This figure represents 0.8% of the average annual expenditures for the American family.

The amount spent on alcohol varied in 2007, depending on the characteristics of the household. On average, single parents with at least one child under the age of 18 spent only $212 on alcoholic beverages in 2007, or about 0.6% of their average annual expenditures. Married couples with no children spent $559, which was 1% of their average annual expenditures. The percentage other groups spent on alcohol varied within a range of 0.6% to 0.8%, except for the "single person and other consumer units" group. This group spent the largest proportion of its average annual expenditures on alcohol: 1.2%.

U.S. TOBACCO PRODUCTION AND CONSUMPTION

Farming Trends

In 1881 James A. Bonsack (1859–1924) invented the cigarette-making machine, which made cigarettes cheaper and faster to manufacture. Thomas Capehart of the ERS notes in "Trends in U.S. Tobacco Farming" (November 2004, http://www.ers.usda.gov/publications/tbs/nov04/tbs25702/tbs25702.pdf) that tobacco production in the United States grew from 300 million pounds (136,078 t) in the mid-1860s to over 1 billion pounds (453,592 t) in 1909. In 1946, at the end of World War II (1939–1945), tobacco production was above 2 billion pounds (907,185 t). During the 1960s changes in tobacco preparation and the introduction of new machinery increased the amount of tobacco production per acre. Nonetheless, the number of tobacco farms dropped from about 512,000 in 1954 to 56,977 in 2002.

In general, the amount of land devoted to cultivating tobacco and the value of that crop has continued to decline in recent years. Table 7.1 shows that the acreage devoted to tobacco declined steadily from 1998 through 2005, but rose slightly in 2006 and 2007. The value of production declined through 2003, rose in 2004, declined again in 2005, and rose in 2006 and 2007.

In 2007 North Carolina led in tobacco production, followed by Kentucky, South Carolina, Virginia, Georgia, and Tennessee. (See Table 7.2.) Tobacco plays a major role in the agricultural economies of these leading tobacco-producing states.

Manufacturing

In *Tobacco Situation and Outlook Yearbook* (December 2005, http://usda.mannlib.cornell.edu/reports/erssor/specialty/tbs-bb/2005/tbs2005.pdf), Capehart estimates that in 2005 U.S. factories produced 481.9 billion cigarettes, of which 109.2 billion were shipped to other countries. This is down from a peak output of 754.5 billion cigarettes produced by U.S. factories in 1996. Exports were high that year as well: 243.9 billion cigarettes.

Tobacco Consumption

The ERS (January 9, 2008, http://www.ers.usda.gov/Briefing/Archive/Tobacco/) notes that cigarette smoking in the United States has been dropping almost every year since 1963, when per capita consumption reached a record high of 4,345 cigarettes. By 2006 the annual per capita

TABLE 7.1

Tobacco crops by area, yield, production, price, and value, 1998–2007

Year	Area harvested	Yield per acre	Production*	Marketing year average price per pound received by farmers	Value of production
	Acres	Pounds	1,000 pounds	Dollars	1,000 dollars
1998	717,620	2,062	1,479,891	1.828	2,700,925
1999	647,160	1,997	1,292,692	1.828	2,356,304
2000	469,420	2,244	1,053,264	1.910	2,001,811
2001	432,490	2,292	991,293	1.956	1,938,892
2002	427,310	2,039	871,122	1.936	1,686,809
2003	411,150	1,952	802,560	1.964	1,576,436
2004	408,050	2,161	881,875	1.984	1,749,856
2005	297,080	2,171	645,015	1.642	1,059,324
2006	338,000	2,146	727,347	1.665	1,210,978
2007	356,000	2,187	778,624	1.683	1,310,483

*Production figures are on farm-sales-weight basis.

SOURCE: "Table 2-37. Tobacco: Area, Yield, Production, Price, and Value, United States, 1998–2007," in *Agricultural Statistics 2008*, U.S. Department of Agriculture, National Agricultural Statistics Service, 2008, http://www.nass.usda.gov/Publications/Ag_Statistics/2008/Chap02.pdf (accessed August 20, 2008)

TABLE 7.2

Area, yield, and production of tobacco, by tobacco-growing state, 2005–07

State	Area harvested			Yield per harvested acre			Production		
	2005	**2006**	**2007ª**	**2005**	**2006**	**2007ª**	**2005**	**2006**	**2007ª**
	Acres	Acres	Acres	Pounds	Pounds	Pounds	1,000 pounds	1,000 pounds	1,000 pound
CT	2,450	2,500	2,900	1,598	1,549	1,647	3,916	3,873	4,775
FLᵇ	2,500	1,100	—	2,200	2,600	—	5,500	2,860	—
GA	16,000	17,000	18,500	1,735	1,770	2,150	27,760	30,090	39,775
KY	79,700	83,000	89,200	2,186	2,250	2,136	174,260	186,780	190,560
MA	1,190	1,150	1,320	1,550	1,558	1,650	1,845	1,792	2,178
MO	1,350	1,500	1,600	2,075	2,250	2,200	2,801	3,375	3,520
NC	126,000	158,900	170,000	2,213	2,080	2,255	278,900	330,580	383,420
OH	3,400	3,500	3,500	1,980	2,000	2,050	6,732	7,000	7,175
PA	5,000	7,900	7,900	2,140	2,056	2,177	10,700	16,240	17,200
SC	19,000	23,000	20,500	2,100	2,100	2,250	39,900	48,300	46,125
TN	22,950	19,800	19,980	2,251	2,482	1,934	51,670	49,135	38,636
VA	17,140	19,650	20,600	2,354	2,408	2,197	40,351	47,322	45,260
WVᶜ	400	—	—	1,700			680	—	—
US	297,080	339,000	356,000	2,171	2,146	2,187	645,015	727,347	778,624

ªPreliminary.
ᵇEstimates discontinued in 2007.
ᶜEstimates discontinued in 2006.

SOURCE: "Table 2-38. Tobacco: Area, Yield, and Production, by States, 2005–2007," in *Agricultural Statistics 2008*, U.S. Department of Agriculture, National Agricultural Statistics Service, 2008, http://www.nass.usda.gov/Publications/Ag_Statistics/2008/Chap02.pdf (accessed August 20, 2008)

consumption of cigarettes for those aged 18 and older was 1,691. These data are taken from *Tobacco Outlook* (September 26, 2006, http://usda.mannlib.cornell.edu/usda/ers/TBS//2000s/2006/TBS-09-26-2006.pdf) by Capehart. This was the final report provided by the ERS on this topic because the ERS discontinued this publication, along with another tobacco-related publication, the *Tobacco Briefing Room*, after a tobacco buyout was formalized by the U.S. Department of Agriculture (USDA) in February 2005. The tobacco buyout is part of the Fair and Equitable Tobacco Reform Act of 2004 and is formally known as the Tobacco Transition Payment Program. Several USDA agencies discontinued their tobacco programs after the buyout. However, the ERS will continue to conduct research on other, less-routine tobacco-related projects.

Capehart finds that the per capita consumption of all tobacco products generally decreased from 1996 to 2006, from 4.8 pounds (2.2 kg) in 1996 to 3.7 pounds (1.7 kg) in 2006. However, the per capita consumption of large cigars by males increased during this period, jumping from 31.9 large cigars and cigarillos (small cigars) per adult male in 1996 to 47.8 in 2006.

Consumer Spending on Tobacco

Americans spent an estimated $90.7 billion on tobacco products in 2006, more than double that of 1989 spending. (See Table 7.3.) The majority ($83.6 billion, or 92%) was spent on cigarettes. This was slightly less than 1% of all disposable personal income. Even though the per capita consumption of cigarettes has declined, expenditures (after adjustment for inflation) have increased because of increasing cigarette prices and an increase in the population of

people of smoking age. Table 7.4 shows that the average American family (or other consumer unit) spent $288 or tobacco products and smoking supplies in 2004, $319 in 2005, and $327 in 2006.

Exports

Capehart reports in *Tobacco Situation and Outlook Year book* that in 2005, 109.2 billion cigarettes were exported From 1996 to 2005 cigarette exports fell by about 135 billion cigarettes. Most of the cigarettes exported in 2005 went to Japan (60.9 billion), Saudi Arabia (7.4 billion), Iran (3. billion), and Lebanon (3.1 billion). Other major importers o American cigarettes were Kuwait (1.6 billion), Hong Kong (1.4 billion), the United Arab Emirates (1.4 billion), Israel (1.2 billion), and Taiwan (1.2 billion). Many of the importer in these countries export these cigarettes to other countries.

WORLD TOBACCO MARKETS

In *Agricultural Statistics, 2005* (2005, http://www.nass.usda.gov/Publications/Ag_Statistics/2005/agstats2005.pdf), the National Agricultural Statistics Service estimate the world production of tobacco in 2004 at 6.7 million metric tons (7.4 million tons), down from 6.9 million metric tons (7.6 million tons) in 2000. China produced 36% (abou 2.4 million metric tons [2.6 million tons]). Other leading tobacco producers included Brazil (890,500 metric ton [981,608 tons]), India (665,000 metric tons [733,037 tons] the United States (397,347 metric tons [438,000 tons] Indonesia (158,900 metric tons [175,157 tons]), Argentin (154,300 metric tons [170,086 tons]), and Turkey (153,75 metric tons [169,480 tons]).

TABLE 7.3

Personal spending for tobacco products, 1989–2006

Year	Total	Cigarettes	Cigars[a]	Other[b]	Disposable personal income	Percent of disposable personal income spent on tobacco products			
						All	Cigarettes	Cigars[a]	Other[b]
	Million dollars				Billion dollars	Percent			
1989	39,675	37,400	675	1,600	4,022	0.99	0.93	0.02	0.04
1990	41,920	39,500	695	1,725	4,286	0.98	0.92	0.02	0.04
1991	45,305	42,850	705	1,840	4,464	1.01	0.96	0.02	0.04
1992	48,470	45,790	715	1,965	4,751	1.02	0.96	0.02	0.04
1993	48,955	46,150	730	2,075	4,912	1.00	0.94	0.01	0.04
1994	47,297	44,544	766	1,987	5,152	0.92	0.86	0.01	0.04
1995	48,692	45,793	846	2,053	5,408	0.90	0.85	0.02	0.04
1996	50,363	47,233	1,012	2,118	5,689	0.89	0.83	0.02	0.04
1997	52,167	48,734	1,229	2,205	5,989	0.87	0.81	0.02	0.04
1998	57,273	53,236	1,607	2,430	6,396	0.90	0.83	0.03	0.04
1999	70,715	66,286	1,796	2,633	6,695	1.06	0.99	0.03	0.04
2000	77,705	72,945	1,926	2,833	7,194	1.08	1.01	0.03	0.04
2001	82,919	77,845	2,121	2,953	7,487	1.11	1.04	0.03	0.04
2002	89,136	83,789	2,270	3,077	7,830	1.14	1.07	0.03	0.04
2003	87,757	82,002	2,541	3,215	8,163	1.08	1.00	0.03	0.04
2004	86,252	79,895	2,935	3,422	8,682	0.99	0.92	0.03	0.04
2005[c]	88,695	81,964	3,061	3,669	9,036	0.98	0.91	0.03	0.04
2006[d]	90,665	83,659	3,166	3,840	9,535	0.95	0.88	0.03	0.04

Note: Expenditures exclude sales tax.
[a]Includes small cigars (cigarette-size).
[b]Smoking tobacco, chewing tobacco, and snuff.
[c]Subject to revision.
[d]Estimated.

SOURCE: Tom Capehart, "Table 21. Expenditures for Tobacco Products and Disposable Personal Income, 1989/2006," in *Tobacco Briefing Room*, U.S. Department of Agriculture, Economic Research Service, May 16, 2007, http://www.ers.usda.gov/Briefing/Archive/Tobacco/ (accessed August 20, 2008)

The Campaign for Tobacco-Free Kids reports in 'Tobacco Facts" (June 2005, http://www.tobaccofreekids.org/campaign/global/docs/1.pdf) how lucrative overseas markets can be for cigarette makers. In 2003 Philip Morris had global revenues of $81.8 billion, producing 887.3 billion cigarettes, or 16.5% of the total world cigarette production. Furthermore, in *WHO Report on the Global Tobacco Epidemic, 2008: The MPOWER Package* (2008, http://www.who.int/tobacco/mpower/mpower_report_full_2008.pdf), the World Health Organization (WHO) reveals that in 2008 nearly two-thirds of the world's smokers lived in 10 countries, with China being the top consumer of cigarettes. About 29% of the world's smokers lived in China, and about 11% lived in India, the world's second-largest consumer of cigarettes. Indonesia, the Russian Federation, and the United States were tied for third place. The remaining top 10 cigarette-consuming countries were Japan, Brazil, Bangladesh, Germany, and Turkey.

World Tobacco Control Treaty

On February 27, 2005, the world's first tobacco control treaty, the WHO's Framework Convention on Tobacco Control (2005, http://www.who.int/tobacco/framework/WHO_FCTC_english.pdf), became law in the 40 countries that ratified it (became bound by it). According to the WHO (January 15, 2009, http://www.who.int/fctc/signatories_parties/en/index.html), the United States signed the measure in May 2004, but as of spring 2009 it had still not ratified it. However, 168 other countries had ratified the treaty by that time. The goal of the treaty is to improve global health by reducing tobacco consumption. Nations that ratified the treaty obligate themselves to raise their taxes on tobacco products, ban tobacco advertising, pass laws requiring smoke-free workplaces and public places, and provide stronger health warnings about the dangers of smoking to their residents. (See Chapter 3 for further information on this effort and its progress.)

ALCOHOL AND TOBACCO ADVERTISING

Alcohol Advertising

The Center for Science in the Public Interest (CSPI) indicates in "Alcoholic-Beverage Advertising Expenditures" (October 2008, http://www.cspinet.org/booze/FactSheets/AlcAdExp.pdf) that the beer industry spent approximately $978.8 million in 2007 on advertising, down from over $1 billion spent each year from 2002 to 2006. The liquor industry spent $547 million in 2007, up from the $400 million per year range of expenditures from 2001 to 2006. The wine industry spent approximately $120.5 million in 2007, which was within its general range of advertising expenditures for the previous decade.

According to the CSPI, in 2006 the beer industry focused most of its advertising dollars on television. The wine industry targeted print media (magazines, newspapers, and billboards), with its spending for television advertising down considerably since the late 1990s. The liquor

TABLE 7.4

Average annual consumer spending and percent changes, by category, 2004–06

Item	2004	2005	2006	Percent change 2004–05	2005–0…
Number of consumer units (in thousands)	116,282	117,356	118,843		
Income before taxes	$54,453	$58,712	$60,533		
Averages					
Age of reference person	48.5	48.6	48.7		
Number of persons in consumer unit	2.5	2.5	2.5		
Number of earners	1.3	1.3	1.3		
Number of vehicles	1.9	2.0	1.9		
Percent homeowner	68	67	67		
Average annual expenditures	$43,395	$46,409	$48,398	6.9	4.3
Food	5,781	5,931	6,111	2.6	3.0
Food at home	3,347	3,297	3,417	−1.5	3.6
Cereals and bakery products	461	445	446	−3.5	.2
Meats, poultry, fish, and eggs	880	764	797	−13.1	4.3
Dairy products	371	378	368	2.0	−2.6
Fruits and vegetables	561	552	592	−1.7	7.2
Other food at home	1,075	1,158	1,212	7.7	4.7
Food away from home	2,434	2,634	2,694	8.2	2.3
Alcoholic beverages	459	426	497	−7.2	16.7
Housing	13,918	15,167	16,366	9.0	7.9
Shelter	7,998	8,805	9,673	10.1	9.9
Utilities, fuels, and public services	2,927	3,183	3,397	8.8	6.7
Household operations	753	801	948	6.3	18.4
Housekeeping supplies	594	611	640	2.9	4.7
Housefurnishings and equipment	1,646	1,767	1,708	7.4	−3.3
Apparel and services	1,816	1,886	1,874	3.8	−.6
Transportation	7,801	8,344	8,508	7.0	2.0
Vehicle purchases (net outlay)	3,397	3,544	3,421	4.3	−3.5
Gasoline and motor oil	1,598	2,013	2,227	26.0	10.6
Other vehicle expenses	2,365	2,339	2,355	−1.1	.7
Public transportation	441	448	505	1.6	12.7
Health care	2,574	2,664	2,766	3.5	3.8
Entertainment	2,218	2,388	2,376	7.7	−.5
Personal care products and services	581	541	585	−6.9	8.1
Reading	130	126	117	−3.1	−7.1
Education	905	940	888	3.9	−5.5
Tobacco products and smoking supplies	288	319	327	10.8	2.5
Miscellaneous	690	808	846	17.1	4.7
Cash contributions	1,408	1,663	1,869	18.1	12.4
Personal insurance and pensions	4,823	5,204	5,270	7.9	1.4
Life and other personal insurance	390	381	322	−2.3	−15.5
Pensions and Social Security	4,433	4,823	4,948	8.8	2.6

SOURCE: "Table A. Average Annual Expenditures of All Consumer Units and Percent Changes, Consumer Expenditure Survey, 2004–06," in *Consumer Expenditures in 2006*, U.S. Department of Labor, U.S. Bureau of Labor Statistics, October 2008, http://www.bls.gov/cex/csxann06.pdf (accessed December 15, 2008)

industry focused its advertising primarily on print media as well, but its spending on television and radio advertising rose substantially between 1999 and 2006 as a result of this industry's decision to lift its self-imposed ban on advertising in these media. The liquor industry's annual expenditure for television and radio advertising in 2007 was about the same as in 2006.

After the liquor industry lifted its ban, the National Broadcasting Company (NBC) also ended its ban on hard liquor advertising and became the first network television station to do so. The broadcaster's 2001 decision was met with nearly universal derision, and a short time later NBC returned to its ban on hard liquor advertisements. As a response, the liquor industry developed guidelines to restrict advertising to publications or television programs with at least 70% of readers or viewers being age 21 and older. Stuart Elliott reports in "Thanks to Cable, Liquor Ads Find a TV Audience" (*New York Times*, December 15, 2003) that by the end of 2003 hard liquor was being advertised on two dozen national cable networks, 14 local cable systems, and 420 local broadcast stations. In a subsequent article, "In a First, CNN Runs a Liquor Commercial" (*New York Times*, March 2, 2005), Elliott notes that CNN became the first national cable news network to air, in March 2005, ads for hard liquor with a commercial for Grey Goose vodka.

ALCOHOL ADVERTISING AND YOUTH. In "Effects of Alcohol Advertising Exposure on Drinking among Youth" (*Archives of Pediatric Adolescent Medicine*, vol. 160, January 2006), Leslie B. Snyder et al. state that their objective was "to test whether alcohol advertising expenditures and the degree of exposure to alcohol advertisements affect alcohol consumption by youth." Their results reveal that people aged 15 to 26 who reported seeing more alcohol advertisements drank more, on average, than those who reported seeing fewer or no alcohol advertisements. By analyzing data on alcohol advertising expenditures on television, radio, billboards, and newspapers with the rest of the data they collected, Snyder et al. determine that young people in markets with greater alcohol advertising expenditures drank more than those in markets with less alcohol advertising expenditures. These findings suggest that attempts to reduce youth drinking must involve limiting or changing alcohol advertising to lessen its effect on youth and/or countering alcohol advertising with public health campaigns to reduce youth drinking.

Tobacco Advertising

According to the U.S. Federal Trade Commission (FTC), in *Cigarette Report for 2004 and 2005* (2007, http://www.ftc.gov/reports/tobacco/2007cigarette2004-2005 pdf), cigarette sales in 2005 fell 2.4% from the previous year, to 351.6 billion cigarettes. Advertising expenditures in 2005 decreased from $15.1 billion 2003 to $13.1 billion in 2005, a decline of 13.2%, the most ever reported to the FTC.

The tobacco industry is forbidden by law to advertise on radio, television, and billboards. Where do the industry's advertising dollars go? The largest share (about $9.8 billion) of the approximately $13.1 billion spent in 2005 was used for price discounts, which are paid to cigarette retailers or wholesalers to discount the price of the cigarettes to the consumer. About $870.1 million was used for coupons and $725 million for promotional cigarettes given to consumers. These are all considered promotional activities and are the primary ways in which cigarettes are advertised.

TOBACCO ADVERTISING AND YOUTH. In *The Role of the Media in Promoting and Reducing Tobacco Use* (June 2008, http://cancercontrol.cancer.gov/tcrb/monographs/19/m19_complete.pdf), the National Cancer Institute (NCI) includes an examination of how the marketing efforts of the tobacco industry affect adolescent tobacco use. The NCI concludes that "much tobacco advertising targets the psychological needs of adolescents, such as popularity, peer acceptance, and positive self-image. Advertising creates the perception that smoking will satisfy these needs." It cites "strong and consistent evidence" that "exposure to cigarette advertising influences nonsmoking adolescents to initiate smoking and to move toward regular smoking." The NCI also discusses cigarette product placement in movies and concludes that seeing people smoke in films can influence attitudes toward smoking in positive ways, not only among adolescents but also among adults. Furthermore, based on a variety of scientific studies, the NCI determines that there is "a causal relationship between

exposure to movie smoking depictions and youth smoking initiation."

ALCOHOL AND TOBACCO TAXATION

Taxation is an age-old method by which the government raises money. Alcoholic beverages have been taxed since colonial times, and tobacco products have been taxed since 1863. The alcohol and tobacco industries contribute a great deal of tax money to federal, state, and local governments.

Alcohol Taxes

According to the Distilled Spirits Council of the United States, in "Distilled Spirits Taxes" (2007, http://www.discus.org/issues/taxes.asp), hard liquor is the most highly taxed consumer product in the nation. The council estimates that direct and indirect local, state, and federal taxes and fees accounted for 59% of the typical bottle price in 2005. Even though the beer and wine industries are taxed at lower levels, they still contribute a significant amount of tax revenue.

In fiscal year (FY) 2007 the federal government collected approximately $9.3 billion in excise taxes (monies paid on purchases of specific goods) on alcoholic beverages. (See Table 7.5.) Federal excise taxes on distilled spirits amounted to approximately half that total—about $4.7 billion, which included taxes on both domestic and imported distilled spirits. Distilled spirits are taxed by the proof gallon, which is a standard U.S. gallon of 231 cubic inches (3,785 cubic cm) containing 50% ethyl alcohol by volume, or 100 proof.

Excise taxes on wine and beer make up the other half of the excise taxes collected on alcoholic beverages. The calculation of wine taxes depends on several variables, such as alcohol content and the size of the winery. In 2007 federal excise taxes on wine totaled $874.4 million. (See Table 7.5.) Total beer excise taxes were much higher, at $3.7 billion. According to the Alcohol and Tobacco Tax and Trade Bureau, in "Beer" (TTB; 2008, http://www.ttb.gov/beer/tax.shtml), brewers who produce fewer than 2 million barrels (1 barrel equals 31 gallons [117.3 L]) get a reduced excise tax rate of $7 per barrel on the first 60,000 barrels. Those who produce more than 2 million barrels pay an excise tax of $18 per barrel. By FY 2008 the federal government, according to the TTB (March 26, 2009, http://www.ttb.gov/statistics/final08.pdf), collected a total of approximately $9.5 billion in excise taxes on alcoholic beverages.

Besides the federal excise taxes, the states levy sales taxes on alcohol. In "State Government Tax Collections: 2007" (February 29, 2008, http://www.census.gov/govs/statetax/0700usstax.html), U.S. Census Bureau indicates that the state sales tax collected on alcoholic beverages totaled $5.2 billion in 2007. The total state tax collections from alcohol include not only the sales tax but also pay-

TABLE 7.5

Federal government tax collections on alcohol and tobacco, October 2006–September 2007

[In thousands of dollars]

Revenue source	1st quarter	2nd quarter	3rd quarter	4th quarter	Cumulative 2007	2006
Excise tax, total	$4,154,644	$3,763,628	$4,469,766	$4,778,393	$17,166,431	$17,127,854
Alcohol tax, total	$2,259,685	$2,062,812	$2,451,384	$2,574,160	$9,348,041	$9,176,946
Distilled spirits tax, total	$1,225,029	$1,036,523	$1,241,468	$1,225,656	$4,728,676	$4,630,080
Domestic	$874,278	$743,114	$918,924	$907,939	$3,444,255	$3,394,734
Imported	$350,751	$293,409	$322,544	$317,717	$1,284,421	$1,235,346
Wine tax, total	$246,502	$195,920	$209,762	$222,167	$874,351	$833,842
Domestic	$166,323	$127,935	$143,019	$152,237	$589,514	$574,910
Imported	$80,179	$67,985	$66,743	$69,930	$284,837	$258,932
Beer tax, total	$788,154	$830,369	$1,000,154	$1,126,337	$3,745,014	$3,713,024
Domestic	$655,547	$709,461	$860,663	$972,510	$3,198,181	$3,213,032
Imported	$132,607	$120,908	$139,491	$153,827	$546,833	$499,992
Tobacco tax, total	$1,827,163	$1,632,989	$1,945,241	$2,125,161	$7,530,554	$7,702,164
Domestic						
Regular	$1,724,963	$1,558,644	$1,869,657	$2,040,769	$7,194,033	$7,350,055
Floor stocks	$0	$0	$0	$0	$0	$638
Imported	$102,200	$74,345	$75,584	$84,392	$336,521	$351,471
Unclassified alcohol and tobacco tax (domestic), total	$0.00	$0.05	$0.00	$0.00	$0.05	$0.00
Firearms and ammunition tax, total	$67,796	$67,827	$73,141	$79,072	$287,836	$248,744
Special (occupational) tax, total	$309	$238	$976	$1,286	$2,809	$2,830
Total tax collections	**$4,154,953**	**$3,763,866**	**$4,470,742**	**$4,779,679**	**$17,169,240**	**$17,130,684**

Notes: This is an unofficial report. Official revenue collection figures are stated in the TTB/ATF Chief Financial Officer Annual Report.
All "imported" tax collection figures are obtained from U.S. Customs data.
Addition of current fiscal year prior quarter figures may not agree with cumulative figures for current fiscal year due to the figures being adjusted to reflect classification of unclassified alcohol and tobacco tax collections previously reported, to reflect collection adjustments for prior tax periods and to reflect rounding adjustments.
Source for other tax collection figures on this report is a TTB/ATF database that records tax collection data by tax return period. This data is summarized on this report by the quarter in which an incurred tax liability is satisfied.
Unclassified Alcohol and Tobacco Tax is tax collected, but not yet posted to a taxpayer account due to missing Employer Identification Number (EIN), permit number, and/or other taxpayer identity information.

SOURCE: "Tax Collections TTB S 5630-FY-2007 Cumulative Summary Fiscal Year 2007 Final," in *Alcohol and Tobacco Tax and Trade Bureau Statistical Release*, U.S. Department of the Treasury, Alcohol and Tobacco Tax and Trade Bureau, April 1, 2008, http://www.ttb.gov/statistics/final07.pdf (accessed August 20, 2008)

ments for alcoholic beverage licenses ($442 million in 2007). Taxes on alcohol amounted to about 0.7% of the total state taxes collected in 2007.

Tobacco Taxes

The Census Bureau also reports in "State Government Tax Collections: 2007" that state taxes on tobacco products amounted to $15.3 billion in 2007. States have raised their excise taxes on cigarettes to help defray health care costs associated with tobacco, to discourage young people from starting to smoke, and to motivate smokers to stop. Figure 7.1 shows state cigarette excise tax rates and rankings in 2008. New Jersey had the highest state excise tax on cigarettes at $2.575 per pack. Rhode Island was a close second with $2.46 excise tax per pack. South Carolina (a tobacco-growing state) had the lowest excise tax of $.07 per pack. The average tax in the nation in 2008 was $1.184 per pack.

In addition to state taxes on tobacco, the federal government implements taxes on cigarettes and other tobacco products. On February 4, 2009, President Barack Obama (1961–) signed into law the State Children's Health Insurance Plan (SCHIP) bill, which includes an increase in the federal tobacco tax. According to the National Conference of State Legislatures, in "2009 Proposed State Tobacco Tax Increase Legislation" (April 9, 2009, http://www.ncsl.org/programs/ health/tobacco_tax_bill09.htm), the federal excise tax on cigarettes increased to $1.01 per pack effective April 1, 2009.

GOVERNMENT REGULATION OF ALCOHOL AND TOBACCO

Besides taxation, the alcoholic beverage and tobacco industries are subject to federal and state laws that regulate factors such as sales, advertising, and shipping.

Alcohol Regulation

The best-known pieces of legislation regarding alcohol are the 18th and 21st amendments to the U.S. Constitution. The 18th Amendment prohibited the manufacture, sale, and importation of alcoholic beverages. Ratified in 1919, it took effect in 1920 and ushered in a period in U.S. history known as Prohibition. After 12 years, during which it failed to stop the manufacture and sale of alcohol, Prohibition was repealed in 1933 by the 21st Amendment.

FIGURE 7.1

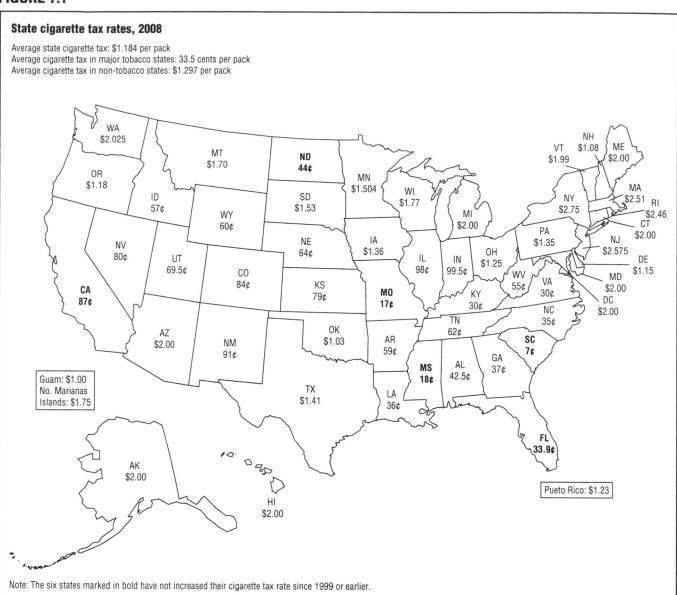

State cigarette tax rates, 2008

Average state cigarette tax: $1.184 per pack
Average cigarette tax in major tobacco states: 33.5 cents per pack
Average cigarette tax in non-tobacco states: $1.297 per pack

WA $2.025
OR $1.18
MT $1.70
ND 44¢
MN $1.504
ID 57¢
WY 60¢
SD $1.53
WI $1.77
NH $1.08
VT $1.99
ME $2.00
NY $2.75
MA $2.51
RI $2.46
CT $2.00
NV 80¢
UT 69.5¢
NE 64¢
IA $1.36
MI $2.00
PA $1.35
NJ $2.575
CA 87¢
CO 84¢
KS 79¢
IL 98¢
IN 99.5¢
OH $1.25
WV 55¢
VA 30¢
DE $1.15
MD $2.00
DC $2.00
AZ $2.00
NM 91¢
OK $1.03
MO 17¢
KY 30¢
NC 35¢
AR 59¢
TN 62¢
SC 7¢
MS 18¢
AL 42.5¢
GA 37¢
TX $1.41
LA 36¢
FL 33.9¢

Guam: $1.00
No. Marianas Islands: $1.75

AK $2.00
HI $2.00

Pueto Rico: $1.23

Note: The six states marked in bold have not increased their cigarette tax rate since 1999 or earlier.

SOURCE: Ann Boonn, "Map of State Cigarette Tax Rates," Campaign for Tobacco-Free Kids, August 1, 2008, http://www.tobaccofreekids.org/research/factsheets/pdf/0222.pdf (accessed August 25, 2008)

Most interpretations of the 21st Amendment hold that the amendment gives individual states the power to regulate and control alcoholic beverages within their own borders. Consequently, every state has its own alcohol administration and enforcement agency. "Control states" directly control the sale and distribution of alcoholic beverages within their borders. According to the TTB, in "Alcohol Beverage Control Boards" (2008, http://www.ttb.gov/wine/control_board.shtml), there are 18 control states: Alabama, Idaho, Iowa, Maine, Michigan, Mississippi, Montana, New Hampshire, North Carolina, Ohio, Oregon, Pennsylvania, Utah, Vermont, Virginia, Washington, West Virginia, and Wyoming. Some critics of this policy question whether such state monopolies violate antitrust laws. The other 32 states are licensure states and allow only licensed businesses to operate as wholesalers and retailers.

DIRECT SHIPMENTS—RECIPROCITY OR FELONY? A legislative controversy has developed over the direct shipment of alcoholic beverages from one state directly to consumers or retailers in another. Under the U.S. Constitution's Interstate Commerce Clause, Congress has the power to regulate trade between states. Nevertheless, the 21st Amendment gives states the authority to regulate the sale and distribution of alcoholic beverages. Furthermore, it allows states to set their own laws governing the sale of alcohol within their borders.

Because the laws of the states are not uniform, several states passed reciprocity legislation, allowing specific states to exchange direct shipments, thus eliminating the state-licensed wholesalers from the exchange. Wholesalers and retailers have charged that reciprocity and direct shipment are violations of the 21st Amendment. They fear being bypassed in the exchange, as do states that prohibit direct shipments of alcohol. Other stakeholders in this issue are consumers and wine producers who want the right to deal directly with each other.

ALCOHOL SALES AND THE INTERNET. In January 2001 the 21st Amendment Enforcement Act became law. This legislation makes it difficult for companies to sell alcohol over the Internet or through mail-order services. It allows state attorneys general in states that ban direct alcohol sales to seek a federal injunction against companies that violate their liquor sales laws.

Within a month of the passage of this act, the high-tech community voiced its concern regarding such legislation, suggesting that if states could ban Internet wine sales they might restrict other electronic commerce as well. Senator Orrin G. Hatch (1934–; R-UT) said he crafted the bill to take other e-commerce concerns into account and insisted that the measure is narrowly tailored to deal with alcohol only.

On May 16, 2005, the U.S. Supreme Court ruled on three cases that had been consolidated under the name *Granholm v. Heald* (544 U.S. 460). At issue were state laws in Michigan and New York that prohibited out-of-state wineries from selling their products over the Internet directly to Michigan and New York residents, but allowed in-state wineries to make such sales. The Michigan and New York state governments argued that these laws were permissible under the 21st Amendment. A group of wineries and business advocates argued that the state laws were unconstitutional restrictions of interstate trade. In a 5–4 decision the Court agreed that the state laws were unconstitutional, stating, "States have broad power to regulate liquor under §2 of the Twenty-first Amendment. This power, however, does not allow States to ban, or severely limit, the direct shipment of out-of-state wine while simultaneously authorizing direct shipment by in-state producers. If a State chooses to allow direct shipment of wine, it must do so on evenhanded terms."

Early Tobacco Regulation and Legislation

Federal tobacco legislation has covered everything from unproved advertising claims and warning label requirements to the development of cigarettes and little cigars that are less likely to start fires. In the past the U.S. Food and Drug Administration (FDA) prohibited the claim that Fairfax cigarettes prevented respiratory and other diseases (1953) and denied the claim that tartaric acid, which was added to Trim Reducing-Aid cigarettes, helped promote weight loss (1959).

The FTC has also been given jurisdiction over tobacco issues in several areas. As early as 1942 the FTC had issued a cease-and-desist order in reference to Kool cigarettes' claim that smoking Kools gave extra protection against or cured colds. In January 1964 the FTC proposed a rule to strictly regulate cigarette advertisements and to prohibit explicit or implicit health claims by cigarette companies.

The tobacco industry has managed to avoid federal regulation by being exempted from many federal health and safety laws. In the Hazardous Substances Act of 1960, the term *hazardous substance* does not include tobacco and tobacco products, nor does the term *consumer product* in the Consumer Product Safety Act of 1972. Tobacco is similarly exempted from regulation under the Fair Packaging and Labeling Act of 1966 and the Toxic Substance Control Act of 1976.

Some of the legislation of the late 1980s included requiring four alternating health warnings to be printed on tobacco packaging, prohibiting smokeless tobacco advertising on television and radio, and banning smoking on domestic airline flights. In 1992 the Synar Amendment was passed. The amendment said that states must have laws that ban the sale of tobacco products to people under 18 years of age.

In 1993 the U.S. Environmental Protection Agency released its final risk assessment on secondhand smoke and classified it as a known human carcinogen (cancer-causing agent). In 1994 the Occupational Safety and Health Administration proposed regulations that would prohibit smoking in workplaces, except in smoking rooms that are separately ventilated. As of spring 2009, the United States did not have federal smoking control legislation, but many states and municipalities did have legislation that banned smoking in a variety of public places and workplaces.

TOBACCO SALES AND THE INTERNET. The Internet plays a role in the distribution of tobacco as well as of alcohol. There are a number of problems with such Web sites. Some online cigarette vendors do not say that sales to minors are prohibited on their site. Many require that the user simply state that he or she is of legal age. According to the Campaign for Tobacco-Free Kids (October 21 2005, http://www.tobaccofreekids.org/reports/internet/) three-quarters of Internet tobacco sellers explicitly say that they will not report cigarette sales to tax collection officials, which is a violation of federal law.

By 2006, according to the Campaign for Tobacco-Free Kids in "Internet Sales of Tobacco Products: Reaching Kids and Evading Taxes" (April 18, 2008, http://www.tobaccofreekids.org/research/factsheets/pdf/0213.pdf), there were at least 770 Web sites selling cigarettes to U.S. tobacco users. "The ongoing increase in illegal Internet sales of tobacco products is stealing away billions of dollars in federal and state tobacco tax revenues and presenting a major challenge to public health efforts to reduce smoking, especially among youth." In the first quarter of 2009 legislation had not been passed to better regulate the sale of tobacco through the Internet.

FDA REGULATION OF TOBACCO PRODUCTS. In 1994 the FDA investigated the tobacco industry to determine whether nicotine is an addictive drug that should be regulated like other addictive drugs. Weeks of testimony before Congress indicated that tobacco companies may have been aware of the addictive effects of nicotine and the likely connection between smoking and cancer as early as the mid-1950s.

In August 1995 the FDA ruled that the nicotine in tobacco products is a drug and, therefore, is liable to FDA regulation. However, the tobacco, advertising, and convenience store industries filed a lawsuit against the FDA, claiming it did not have the authority to regulate tobacco as an addictive drug. After conflicting decisions in the lower courts, the Supreme Court ruled 5–4 in *FDA v. Brown and Williamson Tobacco Corp.* (529 U.S. 120 [2000]) that the government lacks this authority. Even though the ruling did not allow the FDA to regulate tobacco, state laws on selling cigarettes to minors were not affected.

In March 2005 bipartisan bills were introduced in the U.S. House of Representatives and Senate to grant the FDA the authority to regulate tobacco products. The Family Smoking Prevention and Tobacco Control Act would grant the FDA the authority to control tobacco advertising and sales to children, require changes in tobacco products to make them less harmful, prohibit health claims that have no scientific backing, and require the contents and health dangers of tobacco products to be listed on the packaging. The bill never became law during that session of Congress, but legislation to allow the FDA authority over the sale of tobacco products was introduced again in 2009. On April 2 of that year the U.S. House approved the bill—and President Obama subsequently spoke out in favor of it—but the legislation still faced a vote by the U.S. Senate as of May 7, 2009.

ECONOMIC COSTS OF SUBSTANCE USE

Few reports are available on the economic costs of alcohol, tobacco, and other drug use, and many are outdated. As of spring 2009 the latest report calculating the economic costs of alcohol was 2000's *Updating Estimates of the Economic Costs of Alcohol Abuse in the United States: Estimates, Update Methods, and Data* (http://pubs .niaaa.nih.gov/publications/economic-2000/alcoholcost .PDF) by the Lewin Group for the National Institute on Alcohol Abuse and Alcoholism (NIAAA). This report estimated national costs related to alcohol abuse and dependence to be approximately $185 billion in 1998. More research has ensued in the last decade on the costs of drug abuse and tobacco use.

Economic Costs of Drug Abuse

The Office of National Drug Control Policy (ONDCP) asked the Lewin Group to develop data on the costs to society of illicit drug abuse while using data the group had collected from a previous report for the National Institute on Drug Abuse (NIDA) and the NIAAA. The report, *The Economic Costs of Drug Abuse in the United States, 1992–2002* (December 2004, http://www.whitehousedrug policy.gov/publications/economic_costs/economic_costs .pdf), does not include the costs of alcohol abuse or smoking-attributable costs.

Figure 7.2 shows the progression of the economic costs of drug abuse from 1992 to 2002. The overall cost

FIGURE 7.2

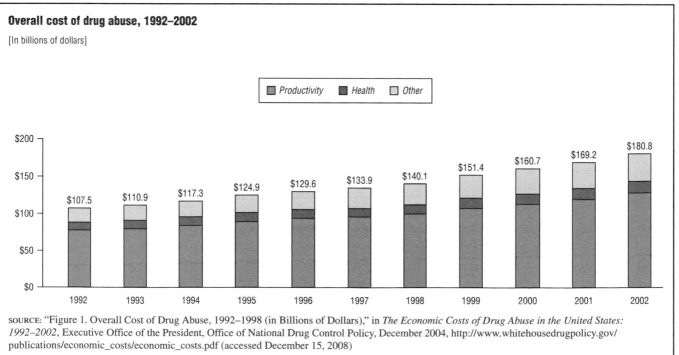

Overall cost of drug abuse, 1992–2002

[In billions of dollars]

SOURCE: "Figure 1. Overall Cost of Drug Abuse, 1992–1998 (in Billions of Dollars)," in *The Economic Costs of Drug Abuse in the United States: 1992–2002*, Executive Office of the President, Office of National Drug Control Policy, December 2004, http://www.whitehousedrugpolicy.gov/ publications/economic_costs/economic_costs.pdf (accessed December 15, 2008)

FIGURE 7.3

Major cost components of drug abuse, 2002

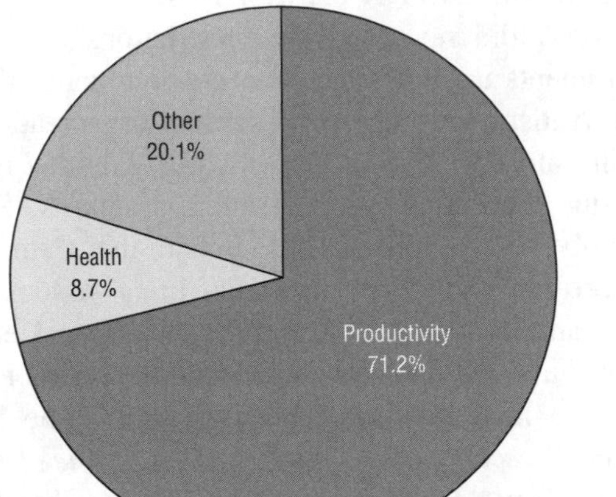

SOURCE: "Figure 2. Distribution of Cost of Drug Abuse, 2002, by Major Cost Components," in *The Economic Costs of Drug Abuse in the United States: 1992–2002*, Executive Office of the President, Office of National Drug Control Policy, December 2004, http://www.whitehousedrugpolicy .gov/publications/economic_costs/economic_costs.pdf (accessed December 15, 2008)

TABLE 7.6

Health care costs resulting from drug abuse, 1992 and 2002

Detailed cost components	1992	2002	Annual change
Community-based specialty treatment	$3,770	$5,997	4.8%
Federally provided specialty treatment			
Department of Defense	$14	$8	−5.8%
Indian Health Services	$26	$54	7.6%
Bureau of Prisons	$17	$39	8.8%
Department of Veterans Affairs	$113	$116	0.2%
Health infrastructure and support			
Federal prevention	$616	$1,203	6.9%
State and local prevention	$89	$148	5.2%
Training	$49	$69	3.5%
Prevention research	$158	$402	9.8%
Treatment research	$195	$564	11.2%
Insurance administration	$268	$476	5.9%
Medical consequences			
Hospital and ambulatory care costs	$518	$1,454	10.9%
Special disease costs			
Drug-exposed infants	$407	$605	4.0%
Tuberculosis	$30	$19	−4.6%
HIV/AIDS	$3,489	$3,755	0.7%
Hepatitis B and C	$462	$312	−3.9%
Crime victim health care costs	$92	$110	1.8%
Health insurance administration	$340	$513	4.2%
Total	**$10,653**	**$15,844**	**4.1%**

SOURCE: "Table III-1. Health Care Costs, 1992 and 2002 (in Millions of Dollars)," in *The Economic Costs of Drug Abuse in the United States 1992–2002*, Executive Office of the President, Office of National Drug Control Policy, December 2004, http://www.whitehousedrugpolicy.gov/ publications/economic_costs/economic_costs.pdf (accessed December 15, 2008). Analysis by The Lewin Group, 2004.

to society of drug abuse in 2002 was estimated to be $180.8 billion, rising approximately 5.3% per year from 1992 to 2002.

The ONDCP report divides the costs of drug abuse into three major cost components: productivity, health, and other. (See Figure 7.2.) The proportion of each cost component remained relatively stable from 1992 to 2002.

Figure 7.3 shows the proportion of each cost component in 2002. Productivity is the largest cost component at 71.2%. In this case, productivity means *loss* from productivity. It is an indirect cost that reflects losses such as work that was never performed because of poor health, premature death, or incarceration. Productivity losses because of drug abuse were estimated to be $128.6 billion in 2002.

The second-largest cost component is "other," which includes drug-related crime costs such as the operation of prisons, state and local police protection, and victim costs. It also includes drug-related costs of the social welfare system. These costs totaled $36.4 billion in 2002.

The third-largest cost component associated with drug abuse is health care. Table 7.6 compares the health care costs between 1992 and 2002 and shows the annual change. The ONDCP report notes that drug abuse-related health care costs are considerable. In 2002 the total health care costs were $15.8 billion, up from $10.7 billion in 1992. The largest share ($3.8 billion) was the cost of treating HIV/AIDS patients who had a history of intra-

venous drug use. Other significant drug-related health care costs in 2002 were hospital and ambulatory care (outpatient) costs at about $1.5 billion and federal effort to prevent drug abuse at $1.2 billion.

Economic Costs of Tobacco Use

In 2008 the Centers for Disease Control and Prevention (CDC) published "Smoking-Attributable Mortality, Years of Potential Life Lost, and Productivity Losses—United States 2000–2004" (*Morbidity and Mortality Weekly Report*, vol. 57, no. 45, November 14, 2008), which included data on the economic costs of tobacco use. The CDC estimates the economic cost of smoking-attributable lost productivity at $96.8 billion annually from 2000 to 2004. The CDC suggests, however, that with smoking-attributable health care expenditures added to this figure, the annual economic cost of cigarette smoking was approximately $193 billion per year.

TOBACCO COMPANIES AND RESPONSIBILITY FOR THE COSTS OF TOBACCO USE

Between 1960 and 1988 approximately 300 lawsuits sought damages from tobacco companies for smoking-related illnesses; courts, though, consistently held that people who choose to smoke are responsible for the health consequences of that decision. This changed in 1988, when a tobacco company was ordered to pay damages for the first time. A federal jury in Newark, New Jersey, ordered Liggett Group Inc. to pay $400,000 to the family of Rose Cipollone, a longtime smoker who died of lung cancer in 1984. The case was overturned on appeal, but the Supreme Court ruled in favor of the Cipollone family in *Cipollone v. Liggett Group, Inc.* (505 U.S. 504 [1992]). In a 7–2 ruling, the Court broadened a smoker's right to sue cigarette makers in cancer cases. The justices decided that the Federal Cigarette Labeling and Advertising Act of 1965, which required warnings on tobacco products, did not preempt damage suits. Despite the warnings on tobacco packaging, people could still sue on the grounds that tobacco companies purposely concealed information about the risks of smoking.

The Master Settlement Agreement

Following the Supreme Court's decision, the tobacco industry was faced with the possibility of never-ending lawsuits and massive damage awards. Many state governments began lawsuits against major cigarette companies, seeking to recover the costs the states had paid in caring for those with smoking-related health problems. The tobacco industry responded by negotiating with the states and offering money and changes in its business practices in exchange for an end to the lawsuits and protection from future lawsuits.

On November 23, 1998, the attorneys general from 46 states (excluding four states that previously settled), five territories, and the District of Columbia signed an agreement with the five largest cigarette companies (Philip Morris, R. J. Reynolds, Brown and Williamson, Lorillard, and Liggett and Myers) to settle all the state lawsuits brought to recover the Medicaid costs of treating smokers. The Master Settlement Agreement (MSA; http://ag.ca.gov/tobacco/msa.php) required the tobacco companies to make annual payments totaling $206 billion over 25 years, beginning in 2000. It also placed restrictions on how the companies could advertise, market, and promote tobacco products. Since the original signing, more than 30 additional tobacco firms have signed the MSA, and Philip Morris has contributed more than half of the payments received by the states under the agreement. Even though the MSA settles all the state and local government lawsuits, the tobacco industry is still subject to class-action and individual lawsuits.

The four states that negotiated their own lawsuit settlements began receiving payments from the tobacco companies in 1998. Payments to other states began in 1999. In the fact sheet "Actual Tobacco Settlement Payments Received by the States (Millions of Dollars)" April 2008, http://www.tobaccofreekids.org/research/factsheets/pdf/0218.pdf), Eric Lindblom of the Campaign

for Tobacco-Free Kids details the amount of money the states have received each year since the start of the agreement. (See Table 7.7.)

HOW ARE STATES USING THE SETTLEMENT FUNDS? The MSA did not place any restrictions on how state governments use the funds they receive under the agreement. Antismoking and public health organizations argue that the most appropriate use for MSA money is to fund smoking prevention and cessation programs. Since the November 1998 tobacco settlement, the Campaign for Tobacco-Free Kids, the American Lung Association, the American Cancer Society, and the American Heart Association have published an annual report to monitor how states are handling the settlement funds. The FY 2009 report *A Decade of Broken Promises: The 1998 State Tobacco Settlement Ten Years Later* (November 18, 2008, http://www.tobaccofreekids.org/reports/settlements/2009/fullreport.pdf) notes that states fell short in their efforts to adequately fund tobacco prevention and cessation programs. It also finds that states that have implemented tobacco prevention and cessation programs in keeping with CDC guidelines have achieved significant reductions in tobacco use among both adults and youth.

According to the report, in FY 2009 no states were funding tobacco prevention and cessation programs at the minimum levels recommended by the CDC. Nine states were funding these programs at about half that level: Alaska, Delaware, Wyoming, Hawaii, Montana, Maine, Vermont, South Dakota, and Colorado. The remaining 41 states and the District of Columbia funded tobacco prevention and cessation programs at less than half the CDC-recommended amount.

What have states done with the tobacco settlement funds not allocated to tobacco prevention and cessation programs? The answer to this question varies among the states; in general, states have used settlement monies to fund other health- and youth-related programs, capital projects (e.g., building hospitals), medical research, medical education, enforcement of tobacco control laws, and expansion of health clinics for low-income citizens. Some states also used part of the money to pay down their debt or to help balance their budgets.

TOBACCO QUOTA SYSTEM ENDED

In 1938 federal tobacco marketing quota and price support loan programs were established during the era of the Great Depression under the Agricultural Adjustment Act of 1933. The act provided funding for farmers who left part of their fields unplanted, thereby reducing crop sizes and crop surpluses and causing prices to rise. This approach helped stabilize crop prices and raise their value so that American farms would remain or become profitable.

TABLE 7.7

Tobacco settlement payments, by state, 1998–2008

[Millions of dollars]

State	1998	1999	2000	2001	2002	2003	2004	2005	2006	2007	2008	State tobacco prevention
Alabama	$0.0	$0.0	$163.0	$104.8	$114.4	$92.7	$100.7	$103.0	$94.3	$98.1	$106.1	$0.77
Alaska	$0.0	$15.8	$19.6	$20.7	$23.7	$19.6	$21.2	$21.8	$19.9	$20.7	$34.7	$7.5
Arizona	$0.0	$0.0	$148.9	$90.2	$105.4	$85.8	$91.6	$94.0	$86.0	$89.5	$115.6	$23.5
Arkansas	$0.0	$0.0	$0.0	$140.1	$57.4	$47.5	$51.5	$52.8	$48.3	$50.3	$57.3	$15.6
California	$0.0	$589.7	$688.6	$773.5	$912.7	$743.4	$793.5	$813.7	$744.5	$774.8	$832.1	$77.4
Colorado	$0.0	$63.3	$78.9	$83.3	$95.0	$78.6	$85.2	$87.4	$80.0	$83.2	$103.6	$26.0
Connecticut	$0.0	$85.8	$100.2	$112.5	$132.7	$108.1	$115.4	$118.4	$108.3	$112.7	$141.3	$0.0
Delaware	$0.0	$18.3	$21.3	$24.0	$28.3	$23.0	$24.6	$25.2	$23.1	$24.0	$30.5	$10.7
DC	$0.0	$28.0	$34.9	$36.9	$42.1	$34.8	$37.7	$38.7	$35.4	$36.9	$43.6	$3.6
Florida	$562.5	$531.0	$640.9	$743.4	$765.7	$546.4	$363.9	$416.7	$389.7	$396.4	$437.8*	$58.0
Georgia	$0.0	$60.6	$141.2	$149.1	$170.0	$140.7	$152.6	$156.5	$143.2	$149.0	$159.5	$2.2
Hawaii	$0.0	$14.9	$32.5	$36.5	$43.0	$35.1	$37.4	$38.4	$35.1	$36.5	$56.1	$10.4
Idaho	$0.0	$9.0	$20.9	$22.1	$25.2	$20.8	$22.6	$23.2	$21.2	$22.1	$28.5	$1.4
Illinois	$0.0	$114.9	$267.8	$282.7	$322.4	$266.9	$289.3	$296.7	$271.5	$282.5	$310.0	$8.5
Indiana	$0.0	$50.4	$117.4	$123.9	$141.3	$117.0	$126.8	$130.0	$119.0	$123.8	$147.4	$16.2
Iowa	$0.0	$21.5	$50.0	$52.8	$60.2	$49.9	$54.1	$55.4	$50.7	$52.8	$75.5	$12.3
Kansas	$0.0	$20.6	$48.0	$50.6	$57.7	$47.8	$51.8	$53.1	$48.6	$50.6	$66.3	$1.4
Kentucky	$0.0	$43.5	$95.0	$106.7	$125.9	$102.6	$109.5	$112.3	$102.7	$106.9	$115.1	$2.4
Louisiana	$0.0	$55.7	$129.8	$137.0	$156.2	$129.3	$140.2	$143.8	$131.5	$136.9	$160.6	$7.7
Maine	$0.0	$19.0	$44.3	$46.7	$53.3	$44.1	$47.8	$49.0	$44.9	$46.7	$58.2	$16.9
Maryland	$0.0	$55.8	$130.0	$137.4	$156.6	$129.6	$140.5	$144.1	$131.8	$137.2	$166.2	$18.4
Massachusetts	$0.0	$99.7	$217.9	$244.8	$288.8	$235.2	$251.1	$257.5	$235.6	$245.2	$288.5	$12.8
Michigan	$0.0	$107.5	$234.8	$263.7	$311.2	$253.5	$270.5	$277.4	$253.8	$264.2	$290.2	$3.6
Minnesota	$0.0	$220.8	$326.7	$351.5	$377.9	$260.2	$168.5	$175.5	$180.8	$183.9	$181.5*	$22.1
Mississippi	$232.1	$109.8	$199.5	$231.1	$229.0	$169.6	$112.5	$116.9	$120.5	$122.6	$123.1*	$8.0
Missouri	$0.0	$0.0	$0.0	$387.8	$159.6	$130.4	$141.4	$145.0	$132.7	$138.1	$153.3	$0.20
Montana	$0.0	$10.5	$24.4	$25.8	$29.4	$24.4	$26.4	$27.1	$24.7	$25.8	$34.6	$8.5
Nebraska	$0.0	$14.7	$34.2	$36.1	$41.2	$34.1	$37.0	$37.9	$34.7	$36.1	$42.9	$2.5
Nevada	$0.0	$15.1	$35.1	$37.0	$42.3	$35.0	$37.9	$38.9	$35.6	$37.0	$46.0	$2.0
New Hampshire	$0.0	$16.4	$38.3	$40.4	$46.1	$38.2	$41.4	$42.5	$38.8	$40.4	$48.4	$1.3
New Jersey	$0.0	$0.0	$402.5	$235.8	$267.9	$221.7	$240.4	$246.5	$225.5	$234.7	$262.2	$11.0
New Mexico	$0.0	$14.7	$34.3	$36.2	$41.3	$34.2	$37.1	$38.0	$34.8	$36.2	$44.9	$9.6
New York	$0.0	$315.1	$688.5	$773.4	$912.5	$743.3	$793.4	$813.6	$744.4	$774.7	$834.5	$85.5
North Carolina	$0.0	$57.6	$125.8	$141.3	$166.8	$135.8	$145.0	$148.7	$136.0	$141.6	$160.0	$17.1
North Dakota	$0.0	$9.0	$21.1	$22.2	$25.4	$21.0	$22.8	$23.3	$21.3	$22.2	$36.5	$3.1
Ohio	$0.0	$124.4	$289.8	$306.0	$348.9	$288.8	$313.1	$321.1	$293.8	$305.8	$334.3	$44.7
Oklahoma	$0.0	$25.6	$59.6	$62.9	$71.8	$59.4	$64.4	$66.1	$60.4	$62.9	$89.0	$14.2
Oregon	$0.0	$28.3	$61.9	$69.5	$82.1	$66.8	$71.3	$73.2	$66.9	$69.7	$90.3	$8.2
Pennsylvania	$0.0	$0.0	$452.3	$348.5	$410.9	$334.7	$357.3	$366.4	$335.2	$348.8	$382.0	$31.7
Rhode Island	$0.0	$17.7	$41.4	$43.7	$49.8	$41.2	$44.7	$45.8	$41.9	$43.6	$53.2	$0.94
South Carolina	$0.0	$29.0	$67.7	$71.5	$81.5	$67.4	$73.1	$76.0	$68.6	$71.4	$83.5	$2.0
South Dakota	$0.0	$8.6	$20.1	$21.2	$24.2	$20.0	$21.7	$22.2	$20.4	$21.2	$27.6	$5.0
Tennessee	$0.0	$0.0	$256.4	$150.4	$169.1	$140.0	$151.7	$155.6	$142.4	$148.2	$157.3	$10.0
Texas	$378.0	$1,018.9	$839.8	$974.2	$1,004.5	$719.0	$479.9	$498.6	$516.1	$524.4	$509.7*	$11.8
Utah	$0.0	$11.0	$25.6	$27.0	$30.8	$25.5	$27.7	$28.4	$25.9	$27.0	$42.1	$7.3
Vermont	$0.0	$10.2	$22.2	$24.9	$29.4	$23.9	$25.6	$26.2	$24.0	$25.0	$39.9	$5.2
Virginia	$0.0	$50.5	$117.6	$124.2	$141.6	$117.2	$127.1	$130.4	$119.3	$124.1	$132.7	$14.5
Washington	$0.0	$50.7	$118.1	$124.7	$142.2	$117.7	$127.6	$130.9	$119.8	$124.6	$173.0	$27.1
West Virginia	$0.0	$21.9	$51.0	$53.8	$61.4	$50.8	$55.1	$56.5	$51.7	$53.8	$73.0	$5.7
Wisconsin	$0.0	$51.2	$111.8	$125.6	$148.2	$120.7	$128.8	$132.1	$120.9	$125.8	$149.2	$15.0
Wyoming	$0.0	$6.1	$13.4	$15.0	$17.8	$14.5	$15.4	$15.8	$14.5	$15.1	$21.4	$5.9
Am. Samoa	$0.0	$0.4	$0.8	$0.9	$1.1	$0.9	$0.9	$1.0	$0.89	$0.9	$2.4	NA
Guam	$0.0	$0.5	$1.2	$1.3	$1.6	$1.3	$1.4	$1.4	$1.28	$1.3	$2.8	NA
No. Mariana	$0.0	$0.2	$0.5	$0.3	$0.4	$0.6	$0.5	$0.5	$0.49	$0.5	$2.0	NA
Puerto Rico	$0.0	$27.7	$60.5	$46.2	$54.6	$83.9	$70.0	$71.5	$65.4	$68.1	$82.6	NA
Virgin Islands	$0.0	$0.4	$0.9	$0.7	$0.8	$1.3	$1.1	$1.1	$1.10	$1.1	$2.5	NA
MSA total	$0.0	$2.4 bill.	$6.0 bill.	$6.4 bill.	$7.0 bill.	$5.8 bill.	$6.2 bill.	$6.4 bill.	$5.8 bill.	$6.1 bill.	$7.0 bill.	$0.6 bill.
Ind. state total	$1.4 bill.	$1.9 bill.	$2.0 bill.	$2.3 bill.	$2.4 bill.	$1.7 bill.	$1.1 bill.	$1.2 bill.	$1.2 bill.	$1.2 bill.	$1.3 bill.*	$0.1 bill.
National total	**$1.4 bill.**	**$4.3 bill.**	**$8.0 bill.**	**$8.7 bill.**	**$9.4 bill.**	**$7.5 bill.**	**$7.3 bill.**	**$7.6 bill.**	**$7.0 bill.**	**$7.3 bill.**	**$8.3 bill.***	**$0.7 bill.**

*Estimated/projected.

SOURCE: Eric Lindblom, "Actual Tobacco Settlement Payments Received by the States (Millions of Dollars)," Campaign for Tobacco-Free Kids, April 2008, http://www.tobaccofreekids.org/research/factsheets/pdf/0218.pdf (accessed August 25, 2008)

Since the 1930s prices for tobacco have been supported through this system of quotas that limited supply and raised market prices to a federally guaranteed price. If the guaranteed price of tobacco was not reached in the marketplace, tobacco farmers were given the guaranteed price, called a nonrecourse loan price. However, in recent years high-priced American tobacco has been losing market share to less-costly foreign-grown tobacco.

In 2004 the Fair and Equitable Tobacco Reform Act ended the quota program and in 2005 established the Tobacco Transition Payment Program (TTPP), which provided 10 years of transitional payments to farmers previously holding quota contracts. Since the termination of the federal tobacco program with the 2005 crop, USDA agencies have also terminated the production of many annual tobacco-related publications.

Bruce Schreiner and Emery P. Dalesio explain in "10 Years after Settlement, Tobacco Rebounds in US" (Asso-

ciated Press, November 25, 2008) that in the first year after the quota and price support system was ended, tobacco production fell 27%. However, by 2008 tobacco production began to rebound and was within 10% of the 2004 level, even though Americans were smoking less. Exports played a large role in the rebound due to cheaper U.S. tobacco and a weak U.S. dollar. Schreiner and Dalesio note that in 2008 the United States was the world's fourth-largest producer of tobacco, behind China, India, and Brazil, and was expected to maintain this rank through 2010.

CHAPTER 8
DRUG TRAFFICKING

Trafficking in drugs refers to commercial activity: the buying and selling of illegal and controlled substances without a permit to do so—a permit that, for example, a physician, pharmacist, or researcher would have. Illegal drugs are those with no currently accepted medical use in the United States, such as heroin, lysergic acid diethylamide (LSD), and marijuana. It is illegal to buy, sell, possess, and use these drugs except for research purposes. (Some states and local jurisdictions have decriminalized certain uses of certain amounts of marijuana, but federal laws supersede these state and local marijuana decriminalization laws. See Chapter 9.)

Legal drugs are those whose sale, possession, and use as intended are not forbidden by law. However, the use of legal psychoactive (mood- or mind-altering) drugs that have the potential for abuse is restricted. These drugs, which include narcotics, depressants, and stimulants, are available only with a prescription and are called controlled substances. Drug trafficking includes all commercial activities that are integral to the buying and selling of illegal and controlled substances, including their manufacture, production, preparation, importation, exportation, supply, offering to supply, distribution, or transportation.

CRIMINAL PENALTIES FOR TRAFFICKING
Federal Penalties

The Controlled Substances Act of 1970 provides penalties for the unlawful trafficking in controlled substances, based on the schedule (rank) of the drug or substance. (See Table 1.2 in Chapter 1 for definitions of the schedules.) Generally, the more dangerous the drug and the larger the quantity involved, the stiffer the penalty. The trafficking of heroin, cocaine, LSD, and phencyclidine (PCP), all Schedule I or II drugs, includes mandatory jail time and fines. A person caught selling at least 500 grams (18 ounces) but less than 5 kilograms (11 pounds) of cocaine powder will receive a minimum

of five years in prison and may be fined up to $2 million for a first offense. (See Table 8.1.) The same penalty is imposed for the sale of 5 to 49 grams (0.2 to 1.7 ounces) of cocaine base (crack). Five grams are equal to the weight of 6 plain M&Ms candies, and 49 grams are a little more than a bag of M&Ms candies (47.9 grams), or about 60 M&Ms. Legislators have imposed the high penalty for selling crack in an effort to curb the use of this drug.

Following the second offense, penalties double to a minimum of 10 years in prison and up to $4 million in fines. When higher quantities are involved (5 or more kilograms [11 or more pounds] of cocaine powder, 50 grams or more [1.8 ounces or more] of crack, etc.), penalties for the first offense are a minimum of 10 years and fines up to $4 million may be levied. For the second offense, a minimum of 20 years and up to $8 million in fines are given, and the third offense results in mandatory life imprisonment. These examples are for an individual. Higher penalties apply if an organized group is involved or if a death or injury is associated with the arrest event.

These penalties also apply to the sale of fentanyl (a powerful painkiller medicine) or similar-acting drugs heroin, LSD, methamphetamine, and PCP. The smallest amount, which can earn someone a minimum sentence of five years in prison and a fine of up to $2 million, involves trafficking in LSD, in which an amount of 1 gram (0.03 of an ounce) carries a five-year-minimum sentence in prison.

Punishments for marijuana, hashish, and hashish oil are shown in Table 8.2. Special penalties exist for marijuana trafficking because it may be traded in large quantities or grown in substantial amounts. The lower the amounts sold or the fewer the plants grown, the lower the sentence. A person cultivating 1 to 49 plants or selling less than 50 kilograms (110 pounds) of marijuana mixture, 10 kilograms (22 pounds) or less of hashish, or 1 kilogram (2.2 pounds) or less of hashish oil may get a maximum sentence of five years in prison and a maxi

TABLE 8.1

Federal drug trafficking penalties, excluding marijuana

Drug/schedule	Quantity	Penalties	Quantity	Penalties
Cocaine (schedule II) Cocaine base (schedule II) Fentanyl (schedule II) Fentanyl analogue (schedule I) Heroin (schedule I) LSD (schedule I) Methamphetamine (schedule II) PCP (schedule II)	500–4999 gms mixture 5–49 gms mixture 40–399 gms mixture 10–99 gms mixture 100–999 gms mixture 1–9 gms mixture 5–49 gms pure or 50–499 gms mixture 10–99 gms pure or 100–999 gms mixture	**First offense**: Not less than 5 yrs, and not more than 40 yrs. If death or serious injury, not less than 20 or more than life. Fine of not more than $2 million if an individual, $5 million if not an individual **Second offense**: Not less than 10 yrs, and not more than life. If death or serious injury, life imprisonment. Fine of not more than $4 million if an individual, $10 million if not an individual	5 kgs or more mixture 50 gms or more mixture 400 gms or more mixture 100 gms or more mixture 1 kg or more mixture 10 gms or more mixture 50 gms or more pure or 500 gms or more mixture 100 gm or more pure or 1 kg or more mixture	**First offense**: Not less than 10 yrs, and not more than life. If death or serious injury, not less than 20 or more than life. Fine of not more than $4 million if an individual, $10 million if not an individual. **Second offense**: Not less than 20 yrs, and not more than life. If death or serious injury, life imprisonment. Fine of not more than $8 million if an individual, $20 million if not an individual. **2 or more prior offenses:** Life imprisonment

Penalties				
Other schedule I & II drugs (and any drug product containing gamma hydroxybutyric acid)	Any amount	**First offense**: Not more that 20 yrs. If death or serious injury, not less than 20 yrs, or more than life. Fine $1 million if an individual, $5 million if not an individual. **Second offense**: Not more than 30 yrs. If death or serious injury, not less than life. Fine $2 million if an individual, $10 million if not an individual		
Flunitrazepam (schedule IV)	1 gm or more			
Other schedule III drugs	Any amount	**First offense**: Not more than 5 years. Fine not more than $250,000 if an individual, $1 million if not an individual.		
Flunitrazepam (schedule IV) All other schedule IV drugs	30 to 999 mgs Any amount	**Second offense**: Not more 10 yrs. Fine not more than $500,000 if an individual, $2 million if not an individual **First offense**: Not more than 3 years. Fine not more than $250,000 if an individual, $1 million if not an individual.		
Flunitrazepam (schedule IV)	Less than 30 mgs	**Second offense**: Not more than 6 yrs. Fine not more than $500,000 if an individual, $2 million if not an individual.		
All schedule V drugs	Any amount	**First offense**: Not more than 1 yr. Fine not more than $100,000 if an individual, $250,000 if not an individual. **Second offense**: Not more than 2 yrs. Fine not more than $200,000 if an individual, $500,000 if not an individual.		

SOURCE: Adapted from "Federal Trafficking Penalties," U.S. Department of Justice, U.S. Drug Enforcement Administration, http://www.usdoj.gov/dea/agency/penalties.pdf (accessed August 25, 2008)

TABLE 8.2

Federal marijuana trafficking penalties

Drug	Quantity	1st offense	2nd offense
Marijuana	1,000 kg or more mixture; or 1,000 or more plants	Not less than 10 years, not more than life. If death or serious injury, not less than 20 years, not more than life. Fine not more than $4 million if an individual, $10 million if other than an individual.	Not less than 20 years, not more than life. If death or serious injury, mandatory life. Fine not more than $8 million if an individual, $20 million if other than an individual
Marijuana	100 kg to 999 kg mixture; or 100 to 999 plants	Not less than 5 years, not more than 40 years. If death or serous injury, not less than 20 years, not more than life. Fine not more than $2 million if an individual, $5 million if other than an individual.	Not less than 10 years, not more than life If death or serious injury, mandatory life Fine not more than $4 million if an individual, $10 million if other than an individual.
Marijuana	More than 10 kgs hashish; 50 to 99 kg mixture More than 1 kg of hashish oil; 50 to 99 plants	Not more than 20 years. If death or serious injury, not less than 20 years, not more than life. Fine $1 million if an individual, $5 million if other than an individual.	Not more than 30 years. If death or seroius injury, mandatory life. Fine $2 million if an individual, $10 million if other than individual.
Marijuana Hashish Hashish oil	1 to 49 plants; less than 50 kg mixture 10 kg or less 1 kg or less	Not more than 5 years. Fine not more than $250,000, $1 million other than individual.	Not more than 10 years. Fine $500,000 if an individual, $2 million if other than individual.

SOURCE: Adapted from "Federal Trafficking Penalties—Marijuana," U.S. Department of Justice, U.S. Drug Enforcement Administration, http://www.usdoj.gov/dea/agency/penalties.pdf (accessed December 15, 2008)

mum fine of $250,000. Sentences for second offenses involving large amounts of marijuana may earn the trafficker up to life imprisonment.

State Laws

States have the discretionary power to make their own drug laws. The possession of marijuana may be a misdemeanor in one state but a felony in another. Prison sentences can also vary for the same charges in different states—the distribution of 500 grams (18 ounces) of cocaine as a Class C felony may specify 10 to 50 years in one state and 24 to 40 years in another. Most states follow the model of the Controlled Substances Act and enforce laws that facilitate the seizure of drug trafficking profits, specify greater penalties for trafficking, and promote user accountability by punishing drug users.

IS THE PROFIT WORTH THE RISK?

Despite the possibility of long prison terms—up to life imprisonment—many drug dealers evidently consider the enormous potential profits of drug trafficking worth the risk. The media often report drug busts and indictments of people involved in multimillion- or billion-dollar operations. Paying fines of hundreds of thousands of dollars, or even millions of dollars, becomes part of doing business when the profits are so high.

THE WORLD'S POPULATION AND ILLICIT DRUGS

The United Nations Office on Drugs and Crime estimates in *2008 World Drug Report* (June 2008, http://www.unodc.org/documents/wdr/WDR_2008/WDR_2008_eng_web.pdf) that 208 million people—slightly less than 5% of the world's population aged 15 to 64—were users of illicit drugs in 2006–07. About half of these 208 million people used drugs at least once per month. About 26 million were addicted to drugs. In 2006, 166 million used cannabis and 25 million used amphetamine-type stimulants, cocaine, and/or opiates.

WORLD PRODUCTION OF PLANT-DERIVED (ORGANIC) DRUGS

In *International Narcotics Control Strategy Report* (March 2008, http://www.state.gov/documents/organization/102583.pdf), the Bureau for International Narcotics and Law Enforcement Affairs (INL), an element of the U.S. Department of State, reports data on the amount of land cultivated to raise opium poppy, the source of heroin and other opioids; coca leaf, from which cocaine is derived; and cannabis, the hemp plant from which marijuana and hashish are derived.

According to the INL, the largest amount of cultivated land was dedicated to the production of opium poppy, followed by coca leaf and cannabis. (See Table 8.3.) In 2006, the most recent year for which data are complete,

TABLE 8.3

Illicit drug production worldwide, by crop and country, 2002–07

[All figures in hectares]

	2007	2006	2005	2004	2003	2002
Poppy						
Afghanistan	202,000	172,600	107,400	206,700	61,000	30,750
Burma	21,700	21,000	40,000	36,000	47,130	77,700
China						
Colombia[a]	in process	2,300	—	2,100	4,400	4,900
Guatemala	—	—	100	330	—	—
India	—	—	—	—	—	—
Iran	—	—	—	—	—	—
Laos	1,100	1,700	5,600	10,000	18,900	23,200
Lebanon						
Mexico	in process	5,000	3,300	3,500	4,800	2,700
Pakistan[b]	—	984	769	—	1,714	213
Thailand	—	—	—	—	—	750
Vietnam	—	—	—	—	—	1,000
Total poppy	**224,800**	**203,584**	**157,169**	**258,630**	**137,944**	**141,213**
Coca						
Bolivia	in process	25,800	26,500	24,600	23,200	21,600
Colombia[c]	in process	157,200	144,000	114,100	113,850	144,450
Peru[d]	in process	37,000	34,000	27,500	29,250	34,700
Total coca	**0**	**220,000**	**204,500**	**166,200**	**166,300**	**200,750**
Cannabis						
Lebanon	—	—	—	—	—	—
Mexico	in process	8,600	5,600	5,800	7,500	4,400
Total cannabis	**0**	**8,600**	**5,600**	**5,800**	**7,500**	**4,400**

[a]In 2007, the survey areas were reduced. The 2005 survey could not be conducted due to cloud-cover. The 2000 survey could not be conducted due to cloud-cover; the reported number is a weighted average of previous years' cultivation.
[b]The 2005 and 2006 surveys included only the Bara River Valley growing area. No estimate was produced in 2002, but cultivation was observed.
[c]Survey areas were expanded greatly between 2004 and 2005, and to a lesser extent between 2005 and 2006.
[d]In the 2006 survey, one growing area could not be completed due to insufficient imagery collection and the value is not comparable to others. In 2007, the Crime and Narcotics Center (CNC) revised the 2005 value due to discovery of an error in the cultivation data. Survey areas were expanded between 2004 and 2005.

SOURCE: "Worldwide Illicit Drug Cultivation: 2002–2007 (All Figures in Hectares)," in *International Narcotics Control Strategy Report: Volume I, Drug and Chemical Control*, U.S. Department of State, Bureau for International Narcotics and Law Enforcement Affairs, March 2008, http://www.state.gov/documents/organization/102583.pdf (accessed August 25, 2008)

220,000 hectares (543,632 acres) of land were used to grow coca. Opium poppy was cultivated on 203,584 hectares (503,067 acres), a sharp increase from the previous year. The largest producer was Afghanistan. Cannabis cultivation, which excludes what is grown domestically in the United States in this tabulation, took place on 8,600 hectares (21,251 acres) in 2006. Over the five-year period from 2002 to 2006, coca leaf cultivation was higher than poppy cultivation in all but one year. Cannabis cultivation is a distant third, reflecting the much lower value of marijuana than of opium, cocaine, and their derivatives.

Data on the production of opium gum, coca leaf, and cannabis are shown for recent years in Table 8.4. The largest tonnage of drug material is coca leaf, followed by cannabis and opium. In 2006, the most recent year for which data are complete, 239,000 metric tons (263,452

TABLE 8.4

Potential illicit drug production worldwide, by crop and country, 2002–07

[In metric tons]

	2007	2006	2005	2004	2003	2002
Opium						
Afghanistan	8,000	5,644	4,475	4,950	2,865	1,278
Burma	270	230	380	330	484	630
China						
Colombia[a]	in process	37		30	63	68
Guatemala			4	12		
India						
Iran						
Laos	5.5	8.5	28	50	200	180
Lebanon						
Mexico	in process	108	71	73	101	58
Pakistan[b]		36	32		44	4.3
Thailand						9
Vietnam						10
Total opium	**8,275.5**	**6,063.5**	**4,990**	**5,445**	**3,757**	**2,237.3**
Coca leaf						
Bolivia	in process	37,000	36,000	37,000	33,000	35,000
Colombia	in process	152,000	136,800	108,000	115,500	147,900
Peru	in process	50,000	52,000	47,900	51,200	58,300
Total coca leaf	**0**	**239,000**	**224,800**	**192,900**	**199,700**	**241,200**
Potential pure cocaine						
Bolivia[c]	in process	115	115	115	100	110
Colombia[d]	in process	610	545	430	460	585
Peru[e]	in process	245	250	230	245	280
Total potential pure cocaine	**0**	**970**	**910**	**775**	**805**	**975**
Cannabis						
Lebanon (hashish)						
Mexico (marijuana)	in process	15,500	10,100	10,400	13,500	7,900
Total cannabis	**0**	**15,500**	**10,100**	**10,400**	**13,500**	**7,900**

[a]In 2007, the survey areas were reduced. The 2005 survey could not be conducted due to cloud-cover. The 2000 survey could not be conducted due to cloud-cover. The reported number is a weighted average of previous years' cultivation.
[b]The 2005 and 2006 surveys included only the Bara River Valley growing area.
[c]In 2006, the Crime and Narcotics Center (CNC) revised the 2001–05 values due to new yield information.
[d]Survey areas were expanded greatly between 2004 and 2005, and to a lesser extent between 2005 and 2006.
[e]In the 2006 survey, one growing area could not be completed due to insufficient imagery collection and the value is not comparable to others. In 2007, CNC revised the 2005 value due to discovery of an error in the cultivation data. Survey areas were expanded between 2004 and 2005. In 2007, CNC revised the 2001–05 values to reflect new yield numbers for immature fields.

SOURCE: "Potential Worldwide Illicit Drug Production: 2002–2007 (All Figures in Metric Tons), in *International Narcotics Control Strategy Report: Volume I Drug and Chemical Control*, U.S. Department of State, Bureau for International Narcotics and Law Enforcement Affairs, March 2008, http://www.state.gov/documents/organization/102583.pdf (accessed August 25, 2008)

tons) of coca leaf, 15,500 metric tons (17,086 tons) of cannabis, and 6,063 metric tons (6,683 tons) of opium gum were produced. Leading producer countries were Colombia for coca leaf, Afghanistan for opium gum, and Mexico for cannabis.

GREATEST DRUG THREAT

The National Drug Intelligence Center (NDIC) surveyed state and local law enforcement agencies nationwide in 2008 to determine what they believed to be the greatest drug threat in the United States and published the results in *National Drug Threat Assessment, 2009* (December 2008, http://www.usdoj.gov/ndic/pubs31/31379/31379p.pdf). Approximately 40.9% of these agencies identified cocaine (powder or crack) as the drug that poses the greatest threat to their area. (See Figure 8.1.) Methamphetamine was identified by 29.4% as the greatest threat,

FIGURE 8.1

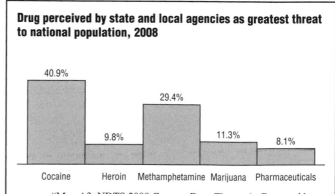

Drug perceived by state and local agencies as greatest threat to national population, 2008

Cocaine 40.9%
Heroin 9.8%
Methamphetamine 29.4%
Marijuana 11.3%
Pharmaceuticals 8.1%

SOURCE: "Map A3. NDTS 2008 Greatest Drug Threat, As Reported by State and Local Agencies," in *National Drug Threat Assessment, 2009*, U.S. Department of Justice, National Drug Intelligence Center, December 2008, http://www.usdoj.gov/ndic/pubs31/31379/31379p.pdf (accessed December 15, 2008)

FIGURE 8.2

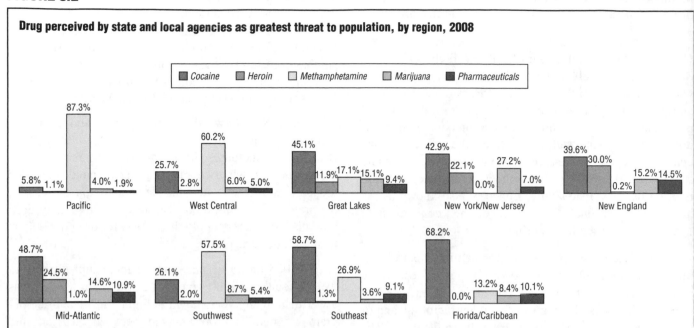

Drug perceived by state and local agencies as greatest threat to population, by region, 2008

SOURCE: "Map A2. NDTS 2008 Greatest Drug Threat by Region, As Reported by State and Local Agencies," in *National Drug Threat Assessment, 2009*, U.S. Department of Justice, National Drug Intelligence Center, December 2008, http://www.usdoj.gov/ndic/pubs31/31379/31379p.pdf (accessed December 15, 2008)

followed far behind by marijuana (11.3%), heroin (9.8%), and illicitly trafficked pharmaceuticals (8.1%).

The NDIC notes that methamphetamine was identified as the greatest threat most often in the western portion of the United States; cocaine was more frequently identified in the eastern portion. Figure 8.2 shows the greatest drug threat by region for 2008.

METHAMPHETAMINE

Methamphetamine (meth) is made in laboratories from precursor drugs rather than directly from plant material. The drug was first synthesized in 1919 and has been a factor on the drug market since the 1960s. The Substance Abuse and Mental Health Services Administration (SAMHSA) reveals in *Results from the 2007 National Survey on Drug Use and Health: National Findings* (September 2008, http://www.oas.samhsa.gov/nsduh/2k7nsduh/2k7Results.pdf) that 529,000 people were current users of methamphetamine in 2007. In addition, 157,000 people aged 12 and older were first-time users of meth.

Methamphetamine Production

Like other synthetics, such as LSD or MDMA (3,4-methylenedioxy-methamphetamine), methamphetamine appeals to small and large criminal enterprises alike because it frees them from dependence on vulnerable crops such as coca or opium poppy. Even a small organization can control the whole process, from manufacture to sale on the street, of methamphetamine. The drug can be made almost anywhere and can generate large profit margins.

Clandestine meth laboratories in the United States are usually operated as temporary facilities. Drug producers make a batch, tear down the lab, and either store the lab and equipment for later use or rebuild it at another site. This constant assembling and disassembling of laboratories is necessary to avoid detection by law enforcement authorities.

The ingredients for making meth are lithium from batteries, acetone from paint thinner, lye, and ephedrine/pseudoephedrine. Anhydrous ammonia, which is used as a fertilizer, can be used to dry the drug and cut the production cycle by 10 hours. According to Celinda Franco of the Congressional Research Service, in *Methamphetamine: Background, Prevalence, and Federal Drug Control Policies* (January 24, 2007, http://assets.opencrs.com/rpts/RL33857_20070124.pdf), this process produces 5 to 7 pounds (2.3 to 3.2 kg) of toxic waste products for every pound of meth. Making meth creates a big stench, forcing producers into remote areas to avoid arousing the suspicion of those living downwind; explosions and fires are also common.

Ephedrine, a stimulant, appetite suppressant, and decongestant, is the key ingredient for making methamphetamine. In 1989 the Chemical Diversion and Trafficking Act gave the U.S. Drug Enforcement Administration (DEA) authority to regulate bulk sales of ephedrine, but over-the-counter (without a prescription) sales were not included. As a result, manufacturers simply bought ephedrine at drugstores and then used it to manufacture meth.

The passage of the Domestic Chemical Diversion Control Act of 1993 made it illegal to sell ephedrine over the counter as well, but pseudoephedrine, a substitute, was not included in the ban. Thus, states have considered and passed legislation placing restrictions on the sale and purchase of over-the-counter medication containing pseudoephedrine; many states also track the names of purchasers. Because of these restrictions on the purchase and sale of ephedrine and pseudoephedrine, the drug ephedra is often used as a substitute. Ephedra, also known as ma huang in traditional Chinese medicine, contains both ephedrine and pseudoephedrine.

The Comprehensive Methamphetamine Control Act of 1996 made it illegal to knowingly possess ephedrine and pseudoephedrine (called precursor chemicals) and doubled the possible penalty for manufacturing and/or distributing methamphetamine from 10 to 20 years. The Methamphetamine Trafficking Penalty Enhancement Act of 1998 further increased penalties for trafficking in meth. Authorities are targeting companies that knowingly supply chemicals that are essential to methamphetamine producers, domestically and internationally. The importance of controlling precursor chemicals has been established in international treaties and laws.

Importation of Methamphetamine and Its Precursors

When the precursors ephedrine and pseudoephedrine became difficult to get in large quantities in the United States, methamphetamine and its precursors flowed into the United States from other countries, primarily Mexico. According to the NDIC, in *National Drug Threat Assessment, 2009*, methamphetamine production in the United States decreased each year from 2002 to 2007, but as this downturn occurred, the synthesis of methamphetamine in Mexico increased, and the drug was smuggled into the United States. However, Mexico trained law enforcement teams to investigate and destroy meth labs in its country and, as a result, methamphetamine production in Mexico declined in 2007 and 2008 as did its flow into the United States. The NDIC notes that production in the United States was expected to increase in 2009, with manufacturers circumventing ephedrine and pseudoephedrine laws by "smurfing," the practice of paying many buyers to purchase small amounts of these precursors for the manufacture of this synthetic drug.

Methamphetamine Prices, Purities, and Supply

The prices and purity of illicit drugs play an important role in understanding and analyzing drug markets. The purity of a drug refers to the extent to which it is diluted, or mixed with, other substances. It is a tremendous challenge to determine prices and purities of illicit drugs accurately, because illicit drugs are not sold in standard quantities and are generally sold at varying purities. In addition, data can only be collected from seizures and purchases by undercover agents. Thus, the data gleaned from the samples collected must be used to estimate these factors for the total drug supply for that year.

Figure 8.3 shows the average price and purity of methamphetamine from April 2005 through June 2008. Drug prices fluctuate with supply and demand. As with other products, when supply outpaces demand, the price drops. Conversely, when the demand outpaces supply, the price rises. In addition, the purity of drugs may drop if demand outpaces supply; it is a way for drug traffickers to stretch the drug resources they have.

In 2005 the price per gram of methamphetamine (a weight equal to slightly more than one plain M&M) was lower than in any year shown in Figure 8.3. The price per gram of meth in 2005 ranged between $101.54 and $111.58. Spikes in the price of the drug occurred in 2006 and 2007, with the highest price in 2007 reaching $284.12 per gram, more than two and a half times as much as the price per gram in 2005. In addition, as the price of meth rose in early 2006 and in 2007, its purity declined. A rise in price of the drug with a concurrent drop in purity is evidence of its decreased availability.

Distribution of Methamphetamine

In *National Drug Threat Assessment, 2009*, the NCIC explains that Mexican drug trafficking organizations (DTOs) control most of the wholesale distribution of both the powder and ice forms of methamphetamine in the United States and are the greatest organized crime threat to this country. Mexican DTOs exist throughout the United States. These groups supply midlevel distributors in at least 230 U.S. cities, which are often Mexican criminal groups as well.

COCAINE

Production and Distribution

The coca plant, from which cocaine is produced, is grown primarily in the Andean region of Colombia, Peru, and Bolivia, with Colombia being the largest producer. The first step in the production of cocaine is to mix the coca leaves with sulfuric acid in a plastic-lined hole in the ground. The leaves are then pounded to create an acidic juice. When this juice is filtered and neutralized, it forms a paste. The paste is purified into cocaine base by the addition of more chemicals and filtering. This cocaine base includes coca paste, freebase cocaine, and crack cocaine. It is transported from the jungles of Bolivia and Peru to southern Colombia, where it is processed into cocaine hydrochloride (white powder) at clandestine

FIGURE 8.3

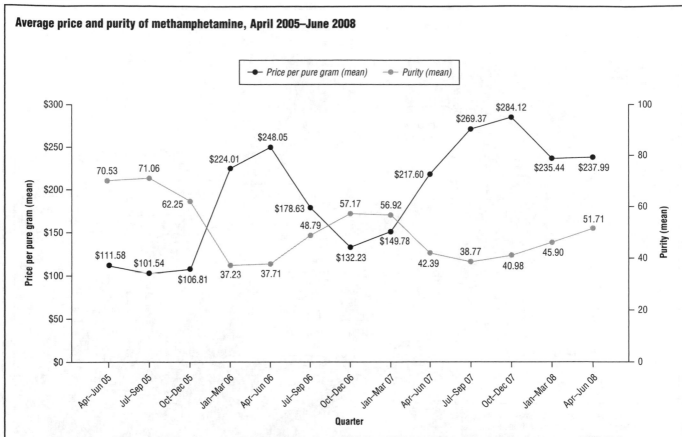

Average price and purity of methamphetamine, April 2005–June 2008

SOURCE: Adapted from "Figure 8. Methamphetamine Price and Purity, April 2005–June 2008," in *National Drug Threat Assessment, 2009*, U.S. Department of Justice, National Drug Intelligence Center, December 2008, http://www.usdoj.gov/ndic/pubs31/31379/31379p.pdf (accessed December 15, 2008)

drug laboratories. Small, independent Bolivian and Peruvian trafficking groups also process some cocaine. It takes 300 to 500 kilograms (661 to 1,102 pounds) of coca leaf to make 1 kilogram (2.2 pounds) of cocaine.

After processing, the powder is shipped to the United States and Europe. Caribbean and Central American countries serve as transit countries for the shipment of drugs into the United States. Drug traffickers shift routes according to law enforcement and interdiction pressures. (Interdiction is the interception of smuggled drugs.) In 2007 approximately 90% of the cocaine transported from South America reached the United States through the Mexico–Central America corridor, which has both an eastern Pacific and a western Caribbean component. (See Figure 8.4.) In the eastern Pacific (a preferred route) the drugs are smuggled primarily on go-fast and fishing boats. Go-fast boats are small boats, usually piloted by and carrying only one person, onto which drugs have been loaded from larger supplies on a ship. Cocaine smugglers are also beginning to use privately built self-propelled semisubmersible low-profile vessels. In the western Caribbean cocaine is smuggled primarily on go-fast boats and private aircraft.

Once cocaine enters the United States, it is transported throughout the country for distribution. Even though cocaine is distributed in nearly every large and midsized city in the United States, principal drug distribution centers are the Colombian DTOs, the locations of which are shown in Figure 8.5. Colombian DTOs are also involved in trafficking multikilogram quantities of the drug. The wholesale-level transportation and distribution of cocaine is primarily controlled by Mexican and Dominican DTOs. The locations of Dominican DTOs are shown in Figure 8.5 as well.

Cocaine Prices, Purities, and Supply

Average prices for cocaine from April 2005 through June 2008 are shown in Figure 8.6. The average price per gram of cocaine increased 40% ($97.01 to $135.57) from the first quarter to the third quarter of 2007. Similarly, the average purity decreased 16% (66.99% to 56.47% pure) from the first quarter to the third quarter of 2007. From the last quarter of 2007 through June 2008 cocaine prices remained higher and purity remained lower than in 2005 or 2006. As mentioned previously, a rise in price of the drug with a concurrent drop in purity is evidence of its decreased availability.

FIGURE 8.4

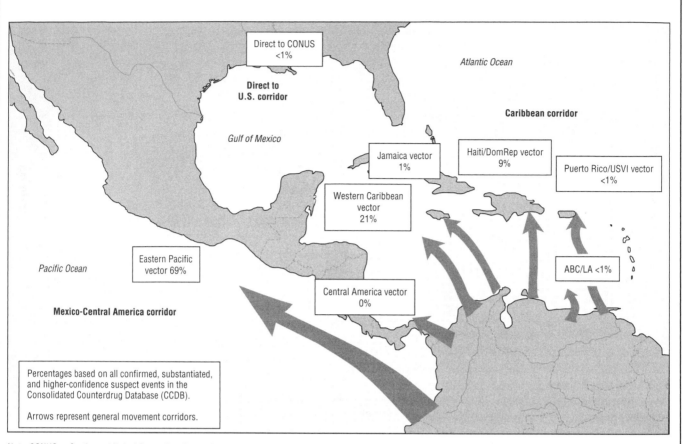

Cocaine flow from South America to the United States, January–December 2007

Direct to CONUS
<1%

**Direct to
U.S. corridor**

Atlantic Ocean

Caribbean corridor

Gulf of Mexico

Jamaica vector
1%

Haiti/DomRep vector
9%

Puerto Rico/USVI vector
<1%

Western Caribbean
vector
21%

Eastern Pacific
vector 69%

Pacific Ocean

ABC/LA <1%

Mexico-Central America corridor

Central America vector
0%

Percentages based on all confirmed, substantiated,
and higher-confidence suspect events in the
Consolidated Counterdrug Database (CCDB).

Arrows represent general movement corridors.

Note: CONUS = Continental United States. DomRep = Dominican Republic. USVI = U.S. Virgin Islands. ABC/LA = Lesser Antilles Vector.

SOURCE: Adapted from "Figure 1. Vectors in the Transit Zone—CCDB-Documented Cocaine Flow Departing South America, January–December 2007," in *National Drug Threat Assessment, 2009*, U.S. Department of Justice, National Drug Intelligence Center, December 2008, http://www.usdoj.gov/ndic/pubs31/31379/31379p.pdf (accessed December 15, 2008)

MARIJUANA

Production, Availability, and Distribution

Marijuana is made from the flowering tops and leaves of the cannabis plant; these are collected, trimmed, dried, and then smoked in a pipe or as a cigarette. Many users smoke "blunts," named after the inexpensive blunt cigars from which they are made. Blunt cigars are approximately 5 inches (12.7 cm) long and can be purchased at any store that sells tobacco products. A marijuana blunt is made from the emptied cigar casing, which is then stuffed with marijuana or a marijuana-tobacco mixture. A blunt may contain as much marijuana as six regular marijuana cigarettes. In some cases blunt users add crack cocaine or PCP to the mixture to make it more potent.

In *Pulse Check: Trends in Drug Abuse* (January 2004, http://www.whitehousedrugpolicy.gov/publications/drug fact/pulsechk/january04/january2004.pdf), the Office of National Drug Control Policy (ONDCP) compiles information from law enforcement and other sources across the country (97 sources in 25 cities). These sources reported that marijuana was readily available in the United States. Domestically grown, Mexican and Canadian grown, hydroponically grown, and the potent seedless marijuana were all available; the domestic variety was the most common. The NDIC confirms in *National Drug Threat Assessment, 2009* that the availability of marijuana was still high throughout the United States in 2007.

Domestic growers cultivate cannabis in remote areas to avoid detection by law enforcement agencies. They surround their plots with camouflaging crops such as corn or soybeans. Based on eradication data collected by the DEA, California, Kentucky, Tennessee, Hawaii, and, to a somewhat lesser extent, Washington and Oregon are the primary source areas for domestic marijuana. Indoor cultivation permits year-round production in a variety of settings. Growers may cultivate a dozen or so plants in a closet or operate elaborate, specially constructed (sometimes underground) greenhouses where thousands of plants grow under intense electric lighting or in sunlight. Indoor cultivators often use hydroponics, in which the

FIGURE 8.5

Cities of influence of drug trafficking organizations, 2006–08

Seattle
Tacoma
Spokane

Schenectady
Albany
Lawrence
Dorchester
Springfield
Hartford
Providence
New Britain
Bridgeport
Scranton
Union City
Patterson
New York
Passaic
Easton
Perth
Jersey City
Allentown
Amboy
Woodbridge
Philadelphia
Newark
Camden
Wilmington
Baltimore
AtlanticCity
Washington

Lowell
Lynn
Boston
New
Bedford

Northeast Coast Inset Map

Salt
Lake City

Denver

Carson City

San Francisco

Springfield

Los Angeles

Albuquerque

San Diego

Phoenix

Dallas

El Paso

Anchorage

McAllen
Brownsville

plants are grown in nutrient solution rather than in soil. The NDIC notes that indoor cannabis cultivation is increasing in the United States, particularly in the western states, Florida, and Georgia.

Nondomestically grown marijuana arrives in the continental United States via the southwestern border with Mexico and the northern border with Canada. Mexican DTOs control most of the wholesale distribution of

FIGURE 8.5

Cities of influence of drug trafficking organizations, 2006–08 [CONTINUED]

Legend
- Colombian
- Cuban
- Dominican
- Italian OC
- La Cosa Nostra

SOURCE: "Map A7. U.S. Cities Reporting the Presence of Colombian, Cuban, and Dominican DTOs; La Cosa Nostra; and Italian Organized Crime, January 1, 2006, through April 8, 2008," in *National Drug Threat Assessment, 2009*, U.S. Department of Justice, National Drug Intelligence Center, December 2008, http://www.usdoj.gov/ndic/pubs31/31379/31379p.pdf (accessed December 15, 2008).

FIGURE 8.6

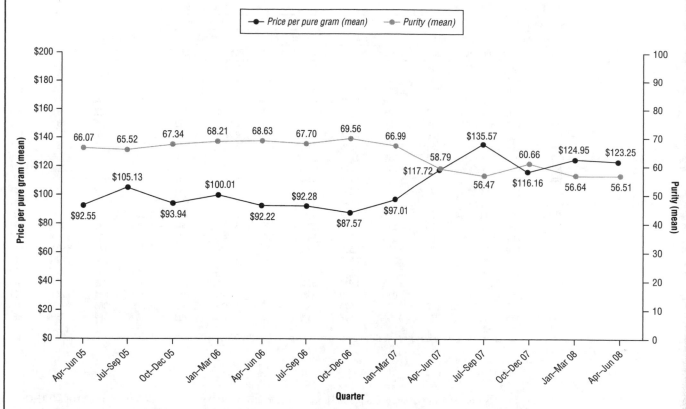

Average price and purity of cocaine, April 2005–June 2008

SOURCE: Adapted from "Figure 3. Cocaine Price and Purity, April 2005–June 2008," in *National Drug Threat Assessment, 2009*, U.S. Department of Justice, National Drug Intelligence Center, December 2008, http://www.usdoj.gov/ndic/pubs31/31379/31379p.pdf (accessed December 15, 2008)

marijuana throughout the United States, and marijuana has become their primary source of income. Mexican DTOs make more money from trafficking in marijuana alone than they do from trafficking in heroin, methamphetamine, and cocaine combined.

Mexican criminal groups control most of the distribution of marijuana in the United States, however, Asian criminal groups—primarily Chinese and Vietnamese—are beginning to control distribution of the Canadian-grown drug and to grow significant quantities of the crop indoors in the United States. Asian DTOs are distributed across the United States, but few are in the western and west-central portions of the country, except for a concentration on the West Coast.

THC Content and Price

The active ingredient in marijuana is THC (delta-9-tetrahydrocannabinol), which is most concentrated in the flowering tops (colas or buds) of the cannabis plants. The flowering tops of female plants that have not yet been pollinated and, therefore, have not yet produced seeds, have the highest THC content. This plant part is called sinsemilla (literally, "without seed"). In contrast, feral

hemp, commonly called ditchweed, contains a low THC content and is generally not a product drug users want.

The ONDCP notes in *National Drug Control Strategy: Data Supplement 2008* (October 2008, http://www.whitehousedrugpolicy.gov/publications/policy/ndcs08_data_supl/ndcs_suppl08.pdf) that from 1985 to 1995 the THC content of marijuana in federal seizure samples averaged less than 4% and in state and local eradication samples less than 3%. (See Table 8.5.) The potency found in federal seizure samples increased dramatically as the years went on; by 2007 the THC content in these samples was 7.2%. Even though the THC content in state and local eradication samples increased through 2000 to 3.9%, it then began to decrease. In 2007 the THC content in these samples was 1.9%.

In 1996 the potency for sinsemilla in federal seizure samples was 11.3%, peaking in 2002 at 14.4%. (See Table 8.5.) In 2007 the potency had dropped to 13.5%, but this level was still considered high. The potency of state and local eradication samples of sinsemilla in 2007 was 7.1%.

The average price of marijuana at the retail level rose from $5.97 per gram in 1981 to $17.57 per gram in

TABLE 8.5

Marijuana potency, 1985–2007

	Federal seizure samples								State and local eradication samples							
	Type of cannabis								Type of cannabis							
	Ditchweed		Marijuana		Sinsemilla		All types[c]		Ditchweed		Marijuana		Sinsemilla		All types[c]	
Year	Potency[a]	Number[b]	Potency[a]	Number[b]	Potency[a]	Number[b]	Potency[a]	Number[b]	Potency[a]	Number[b]	Potency[a]	Number[b]	Potency[a]	Number[b]	Potency[a]	Number[b]
1985	0.30%	9	3.44%	745	7.95%	12	3.48%	767	.50%	102	2.19%	703	7.07%	40	2.22%	845
1986	0.30%	23	2.75%	711	8.78%	14	2.80%	753	.32%	124	1.95%	661	8.16%	18	1.84%	803
1987	0.35%	17	3.16%	1,110	8.29%	17	3.20%	1,147	.34%	86	2.46%	441	7.69%	26	2.38%	553
1988	0.39%	13	3.62%	1,127	8.30%	29	3.70%	1,171	.40%	69	2.20%	513	7.33%	69	2.56%	651
1989	0.30%	7	3.68%	725	7.13%	29	3.78%	761	.29%	104	1.71%	350	6.86%	57	2.00%	511
1990	0.33%	15	3.78%	756	9.59%	16	3.82%	788	.33%	78	2.09%	352	10.29%	45	2.58%	475
1991	0.35%	37	3.18%	1,498	11.20%	29	3.26%	1,564	.31%	246	2.90%	651	10.10%	46	2.57%	943
1992	0.27%	21	3.09%	2,461	9.67%	33	3.16%	2,515	.31%	107	3.05%	875	7.72%	43	2.96%	1,025
1993	0.35%	11	3.67%	1,994	4.64%	5	3.65%	2,010	.37%	189	2.83%	1,039	5.82%	118	2.75%	1,346
1994	0.32%	12	3.76%	2,052	6.92%	10	3.75%	2,074	.39%	136	2.95%	980	7.55%	94	3.02%	1,210
1995	0.44%	14	3.95%	3,729	9.64%	17	3.96%	3,762	.41%	149	2.55%	701	7.26%	147	2.93%	997
1996	0.62%	3	4.40%	1,385	11.30%	22	4.50%	1,405	.37%	115	2.90%	763	8.92%	147	3.48%	1,025
1997	0.57%	3	4.92%	1,313	11.62%	19	5.01%	1,334	.48%	57	3.34%	958	11.61%	102	3.95%	1,117
1998	0.18%	6	4.71%	1,300	11.88%	37	4.91%	1,342	.40%	81	3.38%	775	12.58%	64	3.74%	920
1999	0.56%	13	4.34%	1,759	13.49%	55	4.59%	1,828	.33%	59	3.76%	691	13.31%	81	4.45%	831
2000	0.54%	4	5.10%	1,861	12.87%	62	5.34%	1,930	.34%	69	3.94%	1,066	12.71%	51	4.10%	1,186
2001	0.53%	4	5.77%	1,590	12.05%	95	6.10%	1,690	.42%	59	3.56%	808	7.86%	140	3.98%	1,007
2002	0.30%	8	5.66%	1,381	14.41%	302	7.20%	1,690	.41%	67	3.28%	408	7.29%	226	4.29%	701
2003	0.34%	9	5.63%	1,516	14.00%	347	7.14%	1,871	.35%	57	2.35%	377	7.21%	191	3.70%	625
2004[d]	0.43%	9	6.17%	1,416	13.98%	489	8.13%	1,916	.37%	53	2.55%	395	7.67%	246	4.21%	694
2005	0.79%	4	5.91%	1,606	13.03%	682	8.02%	2,292	.34%	52	2.25%	354	7.81%	251	4.23%	657
2006	0.50%	4	6.51%	1,403	13.58%	660	8.75%	2,070	.29%	49	1.99%	363	6.82%	365	4.16%	419
2007	0.67%	4	7.18%	1,173	13.50%	739	9.60%	1,916	.34%	37	1.92%	363	7.10%	482	4.78%	852

These percentages, indicating potency, are based on simple arithmetic means calculated by dividing the sum of the delta-9THC concentrations of each sample by the number of seizures and are not normalized by weight of seizure.
Number of tested samples that yield the potency in prior column.
All tested samples include a small number of Thai sticks.
Preliminary data through November 8, 2004.

SOURCE: "Table 53. Potency of Tested Cannabis from Federal Seizure and State and Local Eradication Samples, by Type, 1985–2007 (Percent Delta-9 THC Concentrations and Number of Samples Tested)," in *National Drug Control Strategy: Data Supplement 2008*, Executive Office of the President, Office of National Drug Control Policy, October 2008, http://www.whitehousedrugpolicy.gov/publications/policy/ndcs08_data_supl/ndcs_suppl08.pdf (accessed December 15, 2008). Data from *Potency Monitoring Project Quarterly Report 100*. National Center for the Development of Natural Products, Research Institute of Pharmaceutical Sciences Eradication, School of Pharmacy, University of Mississippi (December 16, 2007–March 15, 2008).

1991. (See Table 8.6.) The price then fell to $7.87 per gram in 1998, rose to $11.54 per gram in 2003, and then stabilized at about $10.50 per gram. The average price of marijuana at the retail level in 2007 was $10.41 per gram.

In *National Drug Threat Assessment, 2009*, the NDIC notes that levels of use for marijuana in the United States were higher than for any other drug. (See Figure 4.3 in Chapter 4.) However, the NDIC also indicates that use among adolescents is decreasing. (See Figure 5.7 in Chapter 5.)

HEROIN

Heroin users represent the smallest group using a major drug. According to SAMHSA, in *Results from the 2007 National Survey on Drug Use and Health*, there were 153,000 current heroin users in the United States in 2007, and the rate of use was 0.06%. This was a significant decrease from the number of current users of heroin in 2006 (338,000), which represented 0.14% of the population that year.

Heroin Production and Distribution

PRODUCTION PROCESS. The source of heroin is the opium poppy. After the leaves of the poppy fall off, only the round poppy pods remain. Heroin production begins by scoring the poppy pod with a knife. A gummy substance begins to ooze out. This opium gum is scraped off and collected. The rest of the process is explained by the Central Intelligence Agency (CIA) in "From Flowers to Heroin" (2006, http://www.erowid.org/plants/poppy/poppy _article2.shtml):

Once the opium gum is transported to a refinery, it is converted into morphine, an intermediate product. This conversion is achieved primarily by chemical processes and requires several basic elements and implements. Boiling water is used to dissolve opium gum; 55-gallon drums are used for boiling vessels; and burlap sacks are used to filter and strain liquids. When dried, the morphine resulting from this initial process is pressed into bricks. The conversion of morphine bricks into heroin is also primarily a chemical process. The main chemical used is acetic anhydride, along with sodium carbonate, activated charcoal, chloroform, ethyl alco-

TABLE 8.6

Average price of marijuana, 1981–2007

[In 2007 dollars]

Year	Purchases of 10 grams or less[a] Price per gram ($)	Purchases greater than 10 but less than 100 grams[b] Price per gram ($)
1981	5.97	3.91
1982	6.49	5.58
1983	8.29	9.50
1984	8.39	4.95
1985	7.81	6.94
1986	16.78	10.78
1987	15.44	7.76
1988	14.30	8.90
1989	15.62	9.03
1990	15.87	11.08
1991	17.57	12.35
1992	16.41	8.34
1993	15.04	12.45
1994	12.67	12.03
1995	9.79	8.41
1996	8.83	7.28
1997	8.21	5.40
1998	7.87	6.79
1999	8.87	9.61
2000	8.25	6.02
2001	9.04	6.57
2002	10.83	10.18
2003	11.54	9.34
2004	10.44	7.15
2005	10.38	8.82
2006	10.55	10.26
2007	10.41	10.03

[a]Quantities purchased at the "retail" level.
[b]Quantities purchased at the "dealer" level.

SOURCE: "Table 52. Average Price of Marijuana in the United States, 1981–2007 (2007 Dollars)," in *National Drug Control Strategy: Data Supplement 2008*, Executive Office of the President, Office of National Drug Control Policy, October 2008, http://www.whitehousedrugpolicy.gov/publications/policy/ndcs08_data_supl/ndcs_suppl08.pdf (accessed December 15, 2008)

hol, ether, and acetone. The two most commonly produced heroin varieties are No. 3 heroin, or smoking heroin, and No. 4 heroin, or injectable heroin.

The CIA explains that this generic process produces heroin that may be 90% pure. Variations in the process are introduced as the heroin is diluted to increase its bulk and profits. The pure heroin is mixed with various substances including caffeine, baking soda, powdered milk, and quinine.

OVERVIEW OF THE TRADE. Opium poppies are intensely cultivated in four regions of the world: Southeast Asia, Southwest Asia, Mexico, and South America. In 2006 Southwest Asia, primarily Afghanistan, accounted for approximately 93% of known opium gum production. (See Table 8.4.) In 2001 Afghanistan's production dropped as a consequence of steps taken by the Taliban to suppress the trade. Production went up again to 1,278 metric tons (1,409 tons) in 2002 after the Taliban fell, and more than doubled to 2,865 metric tons (3,158 tons) in 2003. In 2004 production rose to 4,950 metric tons (5,456 tons)—a 73%

increase from 2003. Production was down somewhat in 2005 to 4,475 metric tons (4,933 tons) but nearly doubled to 8,000 metric tons (8,818 tons) by 2007.

Figure 8.7 shows the pattern of opium poppy cultivation in Afghanistan from 2005 through 2007. In 2007 many provinces in the northern, central, and eastern portions of Afghanistan were no longer growing poppies. Additionally most of the Afghan provinces saw a decrease in poppy cultivation from 2005 to 2007. However, the ONDCP states in "Source Countries and Drug Transit Zones: Afghanistan" (2008, http://www.whitehousedrugpolicy.gov/international/afghanistan.html) that "progress in these areas was more than offset by increased opium poppy cultivation in the southwest region, resulting in the production of 8,000 tons of opium in 2007, 42 percent more than in 2006. Approximately 86 percent of Afghanistan's opium poppy cultivation occurred in just 6 provinces with approximately half taking place in a single province, Helmand."

The DEA conducts the Heroin Signature Program. The name of the program comes from the fact that each producing region uses a unique process for deriving heroin from opium, thus the heroin has a unique signature. Under this program heroin seized by federal authorities is analyzed to determine the purity of the heroin and its origin. In *National Drug Threat Assessment, 2009*, the NDIC finds that 76% of all heroin seized in 2006 came from South America, 20% from Mexico, 4% from Southwest Asia, and 0% from Southeast Asia. The NDIC notes that relatively little heroin produced in Afghanistan is distributed in the United States because it is sold, instead, in Asia and Europe. In addition, Colombian and Dominican criminal groups control most of the distribution of heroin in the United States, and they distribute drugs produced in Central and South America.

Mexico produces a variety of heroin called black tar because it looks like roofing tar. It was once considered inferior to Colombian and Asian heroin, but it has reached a level of purity high enough so that it can be snorted or smoked. Mexican heroin is targeted almost exclusively to the U.S. market. The long U.S.-Mexican land border provides many opportunities for drug smugglers to cross. Female couriers are used more frequently than males. Mexican heroin is smuggled in cars, trucks, and buses and may also be hidden on or in the body of the smuggler. Many smugglers send their drugs by overnight package express services.

The bulk of heroin from South America comes from Colombia. Many Colombian coca traffickers have been requiring their dealers to accept a small amount of heroin along with their normal deliveries of coca. This has allowed the Colombian producers to use an existing network to introduce a pure grade of heroin into the U.S. market. Much of the increasing Colombian heroin production is sent through Central America and Mexico by

FIGURE 8.7

Opium poppy cultivation in Afghanistan, 2005–07

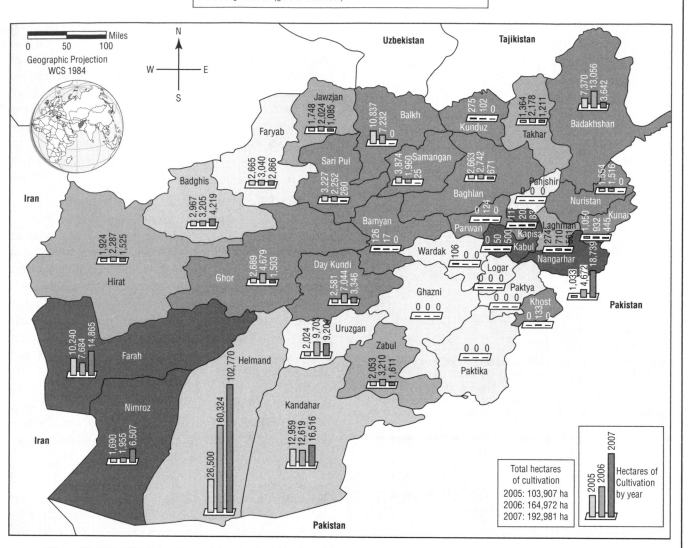

SOURCE: "Figure 25. 2005–2007 Opium Poppy Cultivation in Afghanistan," in *National Drug Control Strategy: 2008 Annual Report*, Executive Office of the President, Office of National Drug Control Policy, February 2008, http://www.whitehousedrugpolicy.gov/publications/policy/ndcs08/2008ndcs.pdf (accessed August 20, 2008). Data from United Nations Office on Drugs and Crime, *Afghanistan Opium Survey 2007*.

mugglers traveling on commercial airline flights into the United States. These smugglers hide the drugs in false-ided luggage, clothing, hollowed-out shoe soles, or nside their bodies. The Colombian-based heroin traf-ickers have established distribution outlets throughout he eastern half of the United States.

Purity and Price

According to the NDIC, in *National Drug Threat Assessment, 2009*, the purity of South American heroin as decreased and the purity of Mexican heroin has increased in recent years. In 2001 South American heroin purity was at 49.7%, whereas Mexican heroin purity was 21%. By 2006 the purity of each was much closer in value to one another: South American heroin purity was 36.1% and Mexican heroin purity was 30%.

Purity is important to heroin addicts because low-purity heroin must be injected to get the most out of the drug. Many people feel uncomfortable using needles and fear contracting the human immunodeficiency virus (HIV), which can be spread by sharing a needle with an infected user. Higher purity heroin can be smoked or snorted, which makes heroin more attractive to potential users who do not want to use needles. Despite these so-called advantages of higher purity heroin, an estimated three out of five heroin users continue to inject the drug no matter what its purity.

The ONDCP explains in *The Price and Purity of Illicit Drugs: 1981 through the Second Quarter of 2003* (November 2004, http://www.whitehousedrugpolicy.gov/publications/price_purity/price_purity.pdf) that heroin purity generally falls into the categories of lower purity (30% to 40%) and higher purity (60% to 75%), depending on the quantity sold. The lower purity is prevalent in purchases of less than 1 to 10 grams (0.03 to 0.4 ounces). The higher purity is prevalent in purchases of 10 to 200 grams (0.4 to 7.1 ounces). The ONDCP suggests that higher purity levels at higher quantity levels likely means that heroin is cut when passed between quantity levels, such as between the distributor and the dealer on the street.

PHARMACEUTICALS

According to the NDIC, in *National Drug Threat Assessment, 2009*, even though the abuse of prescription narcotics, depressants, stimulants, and painkillers exists in the United States, there is little trafficking in these drugs by DTOs. The NDIC notes that those who abuse pharmaceuticals obtain their Schedule II controlled prescription drugs (such as oxycodone, methylphenidate, and dextroamphetamine) primarily through theft, forged prescriptions, doctor shopping (seeking out different doctors to prescribe more medications), and fraudulent practices of some physicians and pharmacists. Abusers generally obtain Schedules III and IV controlled prescription drugs (such as acetaminophen with codeine, hydrocodone with acetaminophen, diazepam, and propoxyphene) through the Internet, although many sites have been shut down. However, the involvement of street gangs and outlaw motorcycle gangs in the distribution of prescription drugs increased from 2004 to 2008.

CHAPTER 9
ANTIDRUG EFFORTS AND THEIR CRITICISMS

The Harrison Narcotic Act of 1914, which outlawed opiates and cocaine, was the first legislation aimed at prohibiting the possession and use of mood-altering drugs. Following that act, laws were passed or amended at intervals, but the war on drugs did not begin in earnest until the early 1970s with the Comprehensive Drug Abuse Prevention and Control Act of 1970. The phrase "war on drugs" was coined in 1971 during the first Nixon administration. A national effort was launched after that to bring illicit drug use under control, and it is still very much under way in the 21st century.

Not everyone agrees with governmental efforts to control or prohibit the use of mood-altering substances. Prohibition came to an end because of massive public disobedience (see Chapter 2). Data from the 2007 National Survey on Drug Use and Health (NSDUH), which are published in *Results from the 2007 National Survey on Drug Use and Health: National Findings* (September 2008, http://www.oas.samhsa.gov/nsduh/2k7nsduh/2k7Results.pdf) by the Substance Abuse and Mental Health Services Administration (SAMHSA), suggest a similar public response to laws that prohibit the use of drugs. In 2007, 46.1% of people aged 12 and older—about 114.2 million individuals—had used illicit drugs at some time in their life. Approximately 35.6 million had done so in the last 12 months, and 19.8 million had used illicit drugs in the past 30 days. According to SAMHSA (February 5, 2009, http://www.oas.samhsa.gov/nhsda/PE1996/artab007 .htm#E8E11), the percentage of lifetime users increased during the preceding three decades; it was 31.3% of the age 12-and-older population in 1979.

One criticism leveled at governmental efforts to control or prohibit the use of mood-altering substances is that they appear to be inconsistent with the public health issues they raise. Tobacco and alcohol, both legal substances, cause many more deaths per year than drugs do. In the fact sheet "Health Effects of Cigarette Smoking" (January 2008, http://www.cdc.gov/tobacco/data_statistics/fact_sheets/health_eff

ects/health_effects.htm), the Centers for Disease Control and Prevention (CDC) estimates that 438,000 premature deaths occur each year as a result of smoking and exposure to secondhand smoke. The CDC reports in "Alcohol-Attributable Deaths and Years of Potential Life Lost—United States, 2001" (*Morbidity and Mortality Weekly Report*, vol. 53, no. 37, September 24, 2004) that in 2001, 75,766 people died prematurely because of excessive alcohol consumption; that same year, 13,674 died in car crashes and other accidents that were alcohol related. In comparison, drug abuse produced 33,541 deaths in 2005, according to the Office of National Drug Control Policy, in *National Drug Control Strategy: Data Supplement 2008* (October 2008, http://www.whitehousedrugpolicy.gov/publications/policy/ndcs08_data_supl/ndcs_suppl08.pdf). SAMHSA states in *Mortality Data from the Drug Abuse Warning Network, 2002* (January 2004, http://oas.samhsa.gov/DAWN2k2/2k2mortality.pdf) that marijuana, which is preponderantly the drug used by most of those classified as illicit drug users, causes few fatalities and virtually none by itself.

NATIONAL DRUG CONTROL STRATEGY

The Anti-drug Abuse Act of 1988 established the creation of a drug-free America as a U.S. policy goal. As part of this initiative, Congress created the Office of National Drug Control Policy (ONDCP; 2008, http://www.whitehousedrugpolicy.gov/about/authorizing_legislation.html) "to set priorities, implement a national strategy, and certify federal drug-control budgets. The law specified that the strategy must be comprehensive and research-based; contain long-range goals and measurable objectives; and seek to reduce drug abuse, trafficking, and their consequences." To stress the importance of the issue, the director of the ONDCP was given a cabinet-level position. John Walters (1952–) was appointed in December 2001 as the ONDCP director and served during most of the administration of President George W. Bush (1946–).

On January 20, 2009, President Barack Obama (1961–) appointed Edward H. Jurith, the former general counsel of the ONDCP, as the office's acting director. As early as spring 2009, only a few months into his presidency, Obama had given indications of the direction his administration would take in the war on drugs, including nominating a "drug czar" who favored treatment over incarceration, as well as developing a major initiative to curtail violent drug trafficking on the Mexican border (see Chapter 1).

The first National Drug Control Strategy was submitted by President George H. W. Bush (1924–) in 1989 and was prepared by William J. Bennett (1943–), the first ONDCP director. Demand reduction was a priority, and has remained such over the years. The strategy also called for directing efforts at countries where cocaine originated, improving the targeting of interdiction (the interception of smuggled drugs), increasing the capacity of treatment providers, accelerating the efforts aimed at drug prevention, and focusing on the education of youth. In its details, the drug strategy laid emphasis on law enforcement activities and the expansion of the criminal justice system.

Since that time the basic building blocks of the national strategy have remained the same, but the specific emphases taken by different administrations, or by the same administration in different years, have changed. Some presidents lean more toward enforcement, others more toward fighting drug traffickers, and yet others more toward treatment and prevention. Whatever the model, all strategies to date have had the same components: prevention and treatment (together constituting demand reduction); and law enforcement, interdiction, and international efforts (together constituting supply disruption). The emphasis given to each of these components has been reflected in federal budgets.

THE FEDERAL DRUG BUDGET

The national drug control budget is shown in Table 9.1. The data span fiscal year (FY) 2002 to the budget request for FY 2009. The federal fiscal year begins October 1 and ends September 30, so that FY 2008 dollars, for example, include funding for the last quarter of calendar year 2007 and the first three quarters of 2008. The budget has grown from $10.8 billion in FY 2002 to $14.1 billion in FY 2009, an increase of 31%.

The budget is divided into two broad components: reducing the demand for drugs and disrupting their supply. Reducing the demand for drugs supports research and programs that help communities work toward a drug-free environment and encourage young people to reject drug use. In Table 9.1, these funding categories are "Drug Abuse Prevention" and "Prevention Research." Reducing the demand for drugs also supports research and treatment for drug abuse and abusers. In Table 9.1, these funding categories are "Drug Abuse Treatment" and "Treatment Research." Funding to disrupt the supply of drugs supports efforts to keep individuals and organizations from profiting from trafficking in illicit drugs, both domestically and internationally. In Table 9.1, these funding categories are "Domestic

TABLE 9.1

Distribution of federal drug control spending, by function, fiscal years 2002–09

[In millions]

Functions	FY 2002 final	FY 2003 final	FY 2004 final	FY 2005 final	FY 2006 final	FY 2007 final	FY 2008 enacted	FY 2009 request
Demand reduction								
Drug abuse treatment	$2,358.3	2,387.7	2,545.5	2,556.9	2,470.4	2,460.1	2,624.7	2,800.9
Treatment research	547.8	611.4	607.2	621.2	600.3	600.8	601.3	601.8
Total treatment	2,906.0	2,999.2	3,152.7	3,178.2	3,070.7	3,060.9	3,226.0	3,402.8
Drug abuse prevention	1,642.5	1,567.2	1,557.3	1,544.0	1,465.4	1,428.4	1,343.4	1,093.2
Prevention research	367.4	382.9	412.4	422.0	411.5	413.4	413.4	413.8
Total prevention	2,010.0	1,950.1	1,969.7	1,966.0	1,876.9	1,841.8	1,756.8	1,507.1
Total demand reduction	**$4,916.0**	**$4,949.2**	**$5,122.5**	**$5,144.2**	**$4,947.6**	**$4,902.7**	**$4,982.8**	**$4,909.8**
Percentage	45.6%	44.1%	42.7%	40.2%	37.6%	35.4%	36.5%	34.8%
Supply reduction								
Domestic law enforcement	2,867.2	3,018.3	3,189.8	3,318.1	3,475.0	3,748.8	3,800.3	3,763.3
Interdiction	1,913.7	2,147.5	2,534.1	2,928.7	3,287.0	3,175.9	3,214.2	3,830.9
International	1,084.5	1,105.1	1,159.3	1,393.3	1,434.5	2,016.6	1,658.1	1,610.4
Total supply reduction	**$5,865.4**	**$6,270.9**	**$6,883.2**	**$7,640.2**	**$8,196.4**	**$8,941.4**	**$8,672.6**	**$9,204.6**
Percentage	54.4%	55.9%	57.3%	59.8%	62.4%	64.6%	63.5%	65.2%
Totals	**$10,781.4**	**$11,220.1**	**$12,005.6**	**$12,784.3**	**$13,144.1**	**$13,844.1**	**$13,655.4**	**$14,114.4**

Note: Detail may not add due to rounding.
In addition to the resources displayed in the table above, the Administration requests $385.1 million in fiscal year (FY) 2008 supplemental funding for counternarcotics support to Mexico and Central America.

SOURCE: "Table 3. Historical Drug Control Funding by Function, FY 2002–FY 2009 (Budget Authority in Millions)," in *National Drug Control Strategy: FY 2009 Budget Summary*, Executive Office of the President, Office of National Drug Control Policy, February 2008, http://www.whitehousedrugpolicy.gov/publications/policy/09budget/tbl_3.pdf (accessed September 2, 2008)

TABLE 9.2

Federal drug control spending, by function, fiscal years 2007–09

[In millions]

	FY 2007 final	FY 2008 enacted	FY 2009 request	08–09 change Dollars	08–09 change Percent
Function					
Treatment (with research)	3,060.9	3,226.0	3.402.8	176.8	5.5%
Percent	22.1%	23.6%	24.1%		
Prevention (with research)	1,841.8	1,756.8	1,507.1	−249.8	−14.2%
Percent	13.3%	12.9%	10.7%		
Domestic law enforcement	3,748.8	3,800.3	3,763.3	−37.0	−1.0%
Percent	27.1%	27.8%	26.7%		
Interdiction	3,175.9	3,214.2	3,830.9	616.7	19.2%
Percent	22.9%	23.5%	27.1%		
International	2,016.6	1,658.1	1,610.4	−47.8	−2.9%
Percent	14.6%	12.2%	11.4%		
Total	**$13,844.0**	**$13,655.4**	**$14,114.4**	**$459.0**	**3.4%**
Supply/demand split					
Supply	8,941.4	8,672.6	9,204.6	531.9	6.1%
Percent	64.6%	63.5%	65.2%		
Demand	4,902.7	4,982.8	4,909.8	−73.0	−1.5%
Percent	35.4%	36.5%	34.8%		
Total	**$13,844.0**	**$13,655.4**	**$14,114.4**	**$459.0**	**3.4%**

Note: Detail may not add due to rounding. In addition to the resources displayed in the table above, the administration requests $385.1 million in fiscal year (FY) 2008 supplementa fundir for counternarcotics support to Mexico and Central America.

SOURCE: "Table 1. Federal Drug Control Spending by Function, FY 2007–FY 2009 (Budget Authority in Millions)," in *National Drug Control Strategy: FY 2009 Budget Summary*, Executive Office of the President, Office of National Drug Control Policy, February 2008, http://www.whitehousedrugpolicy.gov/publications/policy/09budget/tbl_1.pdf (accessed September 2, 2008)

Law Enforcement," "Interdiction," and "International." All the budgets shown were determined during the Bush administration (including the projected budget based on the FY 2009 request).

A high degree of budgetary fluctuation over time has been associated with international programs. (See Table 9.1.) Funds ranged from 10% of the total budget (FY 2002) to 15% (FY 2007). Significant portions of the international budget are spent on supporting international eradication efforts that, in turn, depend on the cooperation of other countries and on the U.S. drug certification program, which may temporarily deny funding to certain regimes.

Table 9.2 shows the overall supply and demand proportions from FY 2007 to FY 2009. Approximately 35% of drug control spending each year is allocated to reducing the demand for drugs. A much larger proportion—approximately 65%—is allocated to disrupting the drug supply. The trend in recent years has been to decrease funding for reducing the demand for drugs (prevention and treatment efforts) and to increase funding for disrupting the drug supply (law enforcement and interdiction).

Table 9.3 summarizes the drug control budget by agency. The agencies that work to reduce the demand for drugs are the ONDCP; the Departments of Health and Human Services, Education, Interior, Veterans Affairs, and Transportation; and the U.S. Small Business Administration. The agen-

cies that work to disrupt the drug supply are the Departments of Defense, Homeland Security, Justice, State, and Treasury

Most domestic law enforcement funds are spent by the U.S. Department of Justice, or on its behalf, and underwrite the operations of the U.S. Drug Enforcement Administration (DEA), the chief domestic drug control agency. Interdiction funds are managed by the U.S. Department of Homeland Security, which now oversees all border-control functions and the U.S. Coast Guard. International funds are divided roughly equally between the U.S. Departments of State and Defense. The Department of State's Bureau of International Narcotics and Law Enforcement Affairs (INL) is the lead agency managing international programs. The Department of Defense is involved in supporting anti-insurgency programs in the Andean region and elsewhere. (Insurgencies are organized, armed rebellions against governments.)

INTERNATIONAL WAR ON DRUGS

The linkages among drugs, organized crime, and insurgencies outside the United States have long been known. A connection to terrorism is a contemporary emphasis that arose in the aftermath of the September 11, 2001 (9/11), terrorist attacks on the United States. In *Fiscal Year 2004 Budget Congressional Justification* (2004, http://www.state.gov documents/organization/22061.pdf), the INL made a case for the convergence between the war on drugs and the war on terror:

TABLE 9.3

Distribution of federal drug control spending, by agency, fiscal years 2007–09

[In millions]

	FY 2007 final	FY 2008 enacted	FY 2009 request
Department of Defense	1,329.8	1,177.4	1,060.5
Department of Education	495.0	431.6	218.1
Department of Health and Human Services (HHS)			
Centers for Medicare & Medicaid Services	—	45.0	265.0
Indian Health Service	148.2	173.2	162.0
National Institute on Drug Abuse	1,000.0	1,000.7	1,001.7
Substance Abuse and Mental Health Services Administration	2,443.2	2,445.8	2,370.6
Total HHS	**3,591.4**	**3,664.8**	**3,799.3**
Department of Homeland Security (DHS)			
Office of Counternarcotics Enforcement	2.5	2.7	4.0
Customs and Border Protection	1,968.5	2,130.9	2,191.9
Immigration and Customs Enforcement	422.8	412.3	428.9
U.S. Coast Guard	1,080.9	1,004.3	1,071.0
Total DHS	**3,474.8**	**3,550.1**	**3,695.8**
Department of the Interior (DOI)			
Bureau of Indian Affairs	2.6	6.3	6.3
Total DOI	**2.6**	**6.3**	**6.3**
Department of Justice (DOJ)			
Bureau of Prisons	65.1	67.2	69.2
Drug Enforcement Administration	1,969.1	2,105.3	2,181.0
Interagency Crime and Drug Enforcement	497.9	497.9	531.6
Office of Justice Programs	245.5	222.8	114.2
Total DOJ	**2,777.7**	**2,893.2**	**2,896.0**
Office of National Drug Control Policy (ONDCP)			
Counterdrug Technology Assessment Center	20.0	1.0	5.0
High Intensity Drug Trafficking Area Program	224.7	230.0	200.0
Other Federal Drug Control Programs	193.0	164.3	189.7
Drug-Free Communities (non-ad)	79.2	90.0	80.0
National Youth Anti-Drug Media Campaign (non-ad)	99.0	60.0	100.0
Salaries and Expenses	26.8	26.4	26.8
Total ONDCP	**464.4**	**421.7**	**421.5**
Small Business Administration	1.0	1.0	1.0
Department of State			
Bureau of International Narcotics and Law Enforcement Affairs	1,055.7	640.8	1,173.2
United States Agency International Development	239.0	361.4	315.8
Total State	**1,294.7**	**1,002.2**	**1,489.0**

TABLE 9.3

Distribution of federal drug control spending, by agency, fiscal years 2007–09 [CONTINUED]

[In millions]

	FY 2007 final	FY 2008 enacted	FY 2009 request
Department of Transportation			
National Highway Traffic Safety Administration	2.9	2.7	2.7
Department of Treasury			
Internal Revenue Service	55.6	57.3	59.2
Department of Veterans Affairs			
Veterans Health Administration	354.1	447.2	465.0
Total	**$13,844.0**	**$13,655.4**	**$14,114.4**

Note: Detail may not add due to rounding.
In addition to the resources displayed in the table above, the administration requests $385.1 million in fiscal year (FY) 2008 supplemental funding for counternarcotics support to Mexico and Central America.

SOURCE: "Table 2. Drug Control Funding by Agency, FY 2007–FY 2009 (Budget Authority in Millions)," in *National Drug Control Strategy: FY 2009 Budget Summary*, Executive Office of the President, Office of National Drug Control Policy, February 2008, http://www.whitehousedrugpolicy.gov/publications/policy/09budget/tbl_2.pdf (accessed September 2, 2008)

The September 11 attacks and their aftermath highlight the close connections and overlap among terrorists, drug traffickers, and organized crime groups. The nexus is far-reaching. In many instances, such as Colombia, the groups are the same. Drug traffickers benefit from terrorists' military skills, weapons supply, and access to clandestine organizations. Terrorists gain a source of revenue and expertise in the illicit transfer and laundering of money for their operations. All three groups seek out weak states with feeble justice and regulatory sectors where they can corrupt and even dominate the government. September 11 demonstrated graphically the direct threat to the United States by a narcoterrorist state such as Afghanistan where such groups once operated with impunity. Although the political and security situation in Colombia is different from the Taliban period in Afghanistan—the central government is not allied with such groups but rather is engaged in a major effort to destroy them—the narcoterrorist linkage there poses perhaps the single greatest threat to the stability of Latin America and the Western Hemisphere and potentially threatens the security of the United States in the event of a victory by the insurgent groups. The bottom line is that such groups invariably jeopardize international peace and freedom, undermine the rule of law, menace local and regional stability, and threaten both the United States and our friends and allies.

The key to the international war on drugs is disruption of the drug supply. The ONDCP states in *National Drug Control Strategy, 2006* (February 2006, http://www.usdoj.gov/olp/pdf/ndcs06.pdf) that market disruption "contributes to the Global War on Terrorism, severing the links between drug traffickers and terrorist organizations in countries such as Afghanistan and Colombia, among others. It renders support to allies such as the courageous administration of President Alvaro Uribe [1952–] in Colombia. Market disruption initiatives remove some of the most violent criminals from society, from kingpins such as the remnants of the Cali Cartel to common thugs such as the vicious MS-13 street gang."

DISRUPTING THE DRUG SUPPLY

Internationally, the federal effort is concentrated on what the INL calls the Andean ridge, the northwestern part of South America where Colombia, Ecuador, and Peru, running north to south, touch the Pacific and where landlocked Bolivia lies east of Peru. In *International Narcotics*

Control Strategy Report: Volume I Drug and Chemical Control (March 2008, http://www.state.gov/documents/organiz ation/102583.pdf), the INL estimates that 90% of all cocaine entering the United States comes from Colombia. The remaining cocaine comes from Bolivia and Peru. Besides focusing on Colombia, the INL also concentrates on Mexico, not only because the country is a major transmission route of drugs to the United States but also because Mexico is a significant source of heroin, marijuana, and methamphetamine.

The centerpiece of the effort is eradication of coca and poppy by providing airplanes and funds for spraying herbicides that kill the plants. Efforts also include assisting foreign law enforcement agencies and foreign governments with counternarcotics and anticorruption activities, and providing financial support through the U.S. Agency for International Development (USAID) for the planting of legal crops and improving infrastructure (roads and bridges) so that farm goods can be delivered to market. The latter measures are necessary because many of the people involved in cultivating drug-producing plants live in remote and undeveloped regions and this is the only source of income. The USAID programs are intended to give them alternatives.

Elsewhere, the INL is concentrating on Afghanistan and Pakistan. In all, INL programs extend to about 150 countries and involve assistance in law enforcement and in the fight against money laundering (making illegally acquired cash seem as though it was legally acquired). What follows is a brief encapsulation of the INL strategy in selected high-focus areas.

Colombia

The primary effort to disrupt the drug supply in Colombia is coca eradication. The coca tree (*Erythroxylon coca*) is a densely leafed plant native to the eastern slopes of the Andes mountains and is heavily cultivated in Colombia.

Table 9.4 shows how many hectares of Colombian coca bushes were sprayed with herbicide and manually eradicated from 1987 to 2004. The area eradicated nearly tripled from 42,283 hectares (104,484 acres) in 2000 to 120,714 hectares (298,290 acres) in 2004. The INL states in *International Narcotics Control Strategy Report* that 219,529 hectares (542,468 acres) had been eradicated in 2007. The hectares of coca bushes cultivated fell to 1987 levels by 2006.

When the source of a drug such as cocaine is diminished, two things happen: the purity of the finished product (the drug) declines and the price of it rises. There is a lag time, however, between the eradication of source plants and the detection of the decline in purity and rise in price of the drug in the United States. Figure 8.6 in Chapter 8 shows the decline in purity and the rise in price of cocaine beginning in the first quarter of 2007, reflecting the result of coca eradication from years prior.

TABLE 9.4

Amount of coca leaf cultivated and eradicated, 1987–2006

[In hectares]

Year	Cultivated			Eradicated		
	Bolivia[a]	Colombia	Peru	Bolivia	Colombia	Per
1987	41,300	25,600	108,800	1,040	460	3
1988	48,900	34,000	110,400	1,475	230	5,1
1989	52,900	42,400	120,400	2,500	640	1,2
1990	50,300	40,100	121,300	8,100	900	
1991	47,900	37,500	120,800	5,486	972	
1992	45,500	37,100	129,100	3,152	959	
1993	47,200	39,700	108,800	2,397	793	
1994	48,100	45,000	108,600	1,058	541[b]	
1995	48,600	50,900	115,300	5,493	3,243[b]	
1996	48,100	67,200	94,400	7,512	15,407[b]	1,2
1997	45,800	79,500	68,800	7,026	31,663[b]	3,4
1998	38,000	101,800	51,000	11,621	49,641[b]	7,8
1999	21,800	122,500	38,700	16,999	39,113[b]	13,8
2000	14,600	136,200	34,200	7,653	42,283[b]	6,2
2001	19,900	169,800	34,000	—	77,165[b]	3,9
2002	21,600	144,450	34,700	11,839	102,225[b]	7,0
2003	23,200	113,850	29,250	10,000	116,342[b]	11,3
2004	24,600	27,500	27,500	8,437	120,714[b]	10,3
2005	26,500	26,500	34,000	6,073	—	
2006	25,800	25,800	37,000	5,070	—	

—Data not available.
[a]Beginning in 2001, U. S. government surveys of Bolivian coca take place over the period June to June.
[b]Colombian figures pertain to aerial eradication from 1994 to 2004.

SOURCE: "Table 99. Amount of Coca Leaf Cultivated and Eradicated, Calendar Years 1987–2006 (Hectares)," in *National Drug Control Strategy: Data Supplement 2008*, Executive Office of the President, Office of National Drug Control Policy, October 2008, http://www.whitehousedrugpolicy.gov/ publications/policy/ndcs08_data_supl/ndcs_suppl08.pdf (accessed December 15, 2008)

TABLE 9.5

Amount of opium poppy cultivated and eradicated, 1990–2007

[In hectares]

Year	Afghanistan	Pakistan	Burma	Laos	Thailand	Colombia	Guatemala	Mexico[a]
Cultivated								
1990	12,370	8,220	150,100	30,580	3,435	—	845	5,450
1991	17,190	8,205	160,000	29,625	3,000	1,160	1,145	3,765
1992	19,470	8,170	153,700	25,610	2,050	—	—	730
1993	21,080	6,280	146,600	18,520	2,110	—	440	438
1994	29,180	7,270	154,070	19,650	2,110	—	—	50
1995	38,740	6,950	154,070	19,650	1,750	6,540	150	5,050
1996	37,950	3,400	163,100	25,250	2,170	6,300	90	5,100
1997	39,150	4,100	155,150	28,150	1,650	6,600	—	4,000
1998	41,720	3,030	130,300	26,100	1,350	6,100	—	5,500
1999	51,500	1,570	89,500	21,800	835	7,500	—	3,600
2000	64,510	515	108,700	23,150	890	7,500	—	1,900
2001	1,685	213	105,000	22,000	820	6,500	—	4,400
2002	30,750	213	77,700	23,200	750	4,900	—	2,700
2003	61,000	1,714	47,130	18,900	—	4,400	—	4,800
2004	206,700		36,000	10,000	—	2,100	330	3,500
2005	107,400	769	40,000	5,600	—	—	100	3,300
2006	172,600	984	21,000	1,700	—	2,300	—	5,000
2007	202,000		21,700	1,100	—	—	—	
Eradicated								
1990	—	185		0	720	—	1,085	4,650
1991	—	440	1,012	0	1,200	1,156	576	6,545
1992	—	977	1,215	0	1,580	12,858	470	11,583
1993	—	856	604	0	0	9,821	426	13,015
1994	—	463	3,345	0	0	3,906	150	11,036
1995	—	0	0	0	580	3,760	86	15,389
1996	—	867	0	0	880	6,028	12	14,671
1997	—	654	10,501	0	1,050	6,972	3	17,732
1998	—	2,194	16,194	—	715		5	17,449
1999	—	1,197	9,800	—	808	5,947[b]	1	15,469
2000	—	1,704	0	—	757	7,540[b]	1	15,300
2001	—	1,484	9,317	—	832	1,819[b]	1	19,115
2002	—	—	25,862	—	507	3,043[b]	1	19,157
2003	—	3,000	683	18,900	767	2,821[b]	1	20,034
2004	—	—	—	—	—	2,899[b]	—	15,925
2005	—	—	—	—	—	—	—	21,609
2006	—	—	—	—	—	—	—	16,889
2007	—	—	—	—	—	—	—	11,046

—Data not available.

The eradication figures shown for 1992–2001 are derived from data supplied by Mexican authorities to the International Narcotics Control Strategy Report (INCSR). The effective eradication figure is an estimate of the actual amount of crop destroyed—factoring in replanting, repeated spraying of one area, and other factors. Eradication figures shown for Colombia represent aerial eradication from 1999 to 2004.

SOURCE: "Table 95. Amount of Opium Poppy Cultivated and Eradicated, Calendar Years 1990–2007 (Hectares)," in *National Drug Control Strategy: Data Supplement 2008*, Executive Office of the President, Office of National Drug Control Policy, October 2008, http://www.whitehousedrugpolicy.gov/publications/policy/ndcs08_data_supl/ndcs_suppl08.pdf (accessed December 15, 2008). Data for Colombian eradication for 1999–2004 from the Policia Nacional de Colombia (CNP)/US Department of State INL Air Wing.

Poppy eradication takes place in Colombia as well, because this country supplies a great deal of the heroin entering the United States. Table 9.5 shows there was a 9% increase in Colombian opium poppy eradication from 2001 to 2004. In 2001 eradication efforts removed 1,819 hectares (4,495 acres) of the plants and in 2004 they removed 2,899 hectares (7,164 acres). Colombian cultivation of opium poppy declined by 68% between 2001 and 2004, from 6,500 hectares (16,062 acres) to 2,100 hectares (5,189 acres). Cultivation slightly rose in 2006 to 2,300 hectares (5,683 acres).

Along with eradication in Colombia, USAID has been conducting the Alternative Livelihoods Program, which is aimed at providing drug farmers with alternative crops. USAID began operations in Colombia late in 2000, although this idea started in some areas more than 30 years ago.

Besides Colombia's aggressive seizure of drugs within its borders, the country is working with the United States in the resumption of the Air Bridge Denial (ABD) program. The ABD program works by forcing or shooting down aircraft that appear to be taking part in drug trafficking activities. The program was halted in 2001, when a civilian aircraft was downed in Peru and two U.S. citizens were killed. It was resumed in 2003. According to the INL, in *International Narcotics Control Strategy Report*, the ABD program was instrumental in decreasing suspected and known illegal flights over Colombia by 73% between 2003 and 2007, from 637 flights to 171.

Colombia, however, illustrates some of the fundamental dilemmas of interdiction. The drug trade there has been one symptom of a festering civil war. Through the 1990s and into the first decade of the 21st century antigovernment insurgent groups and illegal paramilitary groups were heavily funded by the drug trade. However, the Central Intelligence Agency notes in *World Factbook: Colombia* (February 24, 2009, https://www.cia.gov/library/publications/the-world-factbook/geos/co.html) that "more than 31,000 former paramilitaries had demobilized by the end of 2006 and the United Self Defense Forces of Colombia (AUC) as a formal organization had ceased to function. In the wake of the paramilitary demobilization, emerging criminal groups arose, whose members include some former paramilitaries. The Colombian Government has stepped up efforts to reassert government control throughout the country, and now has a presence in every one of its administrative departments." The Associated Press reported on March 6, 2009 ("Colombia Drug Kingpin Extradited to U.S.," http://www.cbsnews.com/stories/2009/03/06/world/main4847765.shtml), that "Colombia extradited reputed cocaine kingpin Miguel Angel Mejia…, making him the 16th paramilitary warlord dispatched to the United States on drug trafficking charges in less than a year." Noting the progress the Colombian government has made in drug arrests, the report went on to state that Uribe, since taking office in 2002, has extradited more than 800 criminal suspects to stand trial in the United States.

With an internal conflict that has lasted more than 40 years, however, quite some time may pass before civil order is totally restored in Colombia and economic development has advanced enough to make drug-plant cultivation unattractive.

Bolivia and Peru

According to the INL, in *International Narcotics Control Strategy Report*, similar problems have hampered efforts to bring coca production under control in Bolivia, the third-largest producer of cocaine. The country is poor and has had an unsettled history (nearly 200 coups since its independence in 1825). The country has been under democratic rule since the 1980s, but successive governments have been reluctant to support eradication programs energetically. Coca is a traditional crop, and the coca leaf is chewed by the inhabitants; eradication has resulted in a popular antiestablishment movement. Table 9.4 shows the number of hectares of coca leaf that have been eradicated, from 11,839 hectares (29,255 acres) in 2002 to 5,070 hectares (12,528 acres) in 2006. However, these eradication efforts are paralleled by replanting, and eradication is sometimes violently opposed by the population. As a result, the number of hectares of coca leaf cultivated in Bolivia increased during this period, from 21,600 hectares (53,375 acres) in 2002 to 25,800 hectares (63,753 acres) in 2006.

The INL explains that Peru is a major producer of cocaine and a major importer of cocaine precursor chemicals. The country has organized bodies of *cocaleros* (coca growers) who enjoy sufficient popular support to hamper government action. In Peru as in Bolivia, replanting frequently follows eradication efforts. Nonetheless, Table 9.4 shows that the cultivation of coca leaf in Peru decreased dramatically from a peak of 129,100 hectares (319,01? acres) in 1992 to 37,000 hectares (91,429 acres) in 2006 Meanwhile, eradication has increased. Data are unavailable for many years, but eradication increased eightfold between 1996 and 2004, from 1,259 hectares (3,110 acres) to 10,339 hectares (25,537 acres).

Mexico

Mexico is one of the principal producers of marijuana and heroin that enter the United States. From 2000 to 2006 the Mexican president Vicente Fox (1942–) and the Mexican government were energetic both in the eradication of the marijuana and poppy crops and in the arrest and prosecution of the members of drug cartels, even though efforts were hampered by severe budget constraints, corruption, and inefficiencies within law enforcement and criminal justice institutions. In December 2006 Felipe Calderón (1962–) succeeded Fox. According to the INL, in *International Narcotics Control Strategy Report*, during the first year of the Calderón administration significant progress was made in attacking drug trafficking and consumption. In October 2007 Presidents Bush and Calderón announced the Merida Initiative, a plan to achieve stronger law enforcement cooperation between the United States and Mexico. President Obama in March 2009 expanded this initiative.

Table 9.6 shows the eradication of 29,606 hectares (73,158 acres) of the Mexican marijuana crop in 2004 and the cultivation of only 5,800 hectares (14,332 acres). The hectares of cultivated marijuana rose to 8,600 (21,25? acres) in 2006. Table 9.5 shows the eradication of 15,92? hectares (39,352 acres) of the Mexican opium poppy crop in 2004 and 11,046 hectares (27,295 acres) in 2007. In spite of eradication efforts, poppy cultivation was higher in 2007 than in the previous seven years; the climate and terrain of this country are such that up to three opium poppy growing seasons are possible. The 5,000 hectares (12,355 acres) grown in 2006 almost matched the 5,500 hectares (13,591 acres) cultivated in 1998.

Mexico is also a major shipping thoroughfare for illicit drugs that are destined for the United States and Canada. Along with marijuana and heroin, one of the drugs that comes to the United States over the U.S.-Mexican border is methamphetamine, a synthetic drug that is made in illegal laboratories. This drug has become an increasing problem in the United States (see Chapter 4). U.S. law enforcement agencies have done much to combat the spread of this drug domestically, but they are also active in stopping the flow of methamphetamine and its precursors (other substances used to make methamphetamine) into the country. In general

TABLE 9.6

Amount of cannabis cultivated and eradicated by foreign countries, 1990–2007

[In hectares]

	Cultivated				Eradicated		
Year	Mexico	Jamaica	Colombia		Mexico*	Jamaica	Colombia
1990	35,050	1,220	1,500		6,750	1,030	500
1991	17,915	950	2,000		10,795	833	0
1992	16,420	398	2,000		16,872	811	49
1993	21,190	1,200	5,050		16,645	456	50
1994	19,045	1,000	5,000		14,227	692	14
1995	18,650	1,000	5,000		21,573	695	20
1996	18,700	1,000	5,000		22,961	473	—
1997	15,300	1,060	5,000		23,576	743	—
1998	4,600	—	5,000		23,928	705	—
1999	3,700	—	5,000		33,583	894	—
2000	3,900	—	5,000		33,000	517	—
2001	4,100	—	5,000		28,699	332	—
2002	4,400	—	5,000		30,775	80	—
2003	7,500	—	5,000		—	445	—
2004	5,800	—	5,000		29,606	—	—
2005	5,600	—	—		—	—	—
2006	8,600	—	—		—	—	—
2007	—	—	—		—	—	—

—Data not available.

*The eradication figures shown for 1992–2001 are derived from data supplied by Mexican authorities to the International Narcotics Control Strategy Report (INCSR). The effective eradication figure is an estimate of the actual amount of crop destroyed—factoring in replanting, repeated spraying of one area, and other factors.

SOURCE: "Table 103. Amount of Cannabis Cultivated and Eradicated by Foreign Countries, Calendar Years 1990–2007 (Hectares)," in *National Drug Control Strategy: Data Supplement 2008*, Executive Office of the President, Office of National Drug Control Policy, October 2008, http://www.whitehousedrugpolicy.gov/publications/policy/ndcs08_data_supl/ndcs_suppl08.pdf (accessed December 15, 2008)

increased production of methamphetamine within Mexico is indicated by increased seizures at the U.S. southwest border. Figure 9.1 shows that methamphetamine seizures were up in 2005 and 2006, dropped significantly in 2007, and rose again in 2008.

By 2009 Mexico drew world scrutiny as drug violence flared. CNN reported ("Obama to Beef Up Mexico Border Policy, March 25, 2009, http://www.cnn.com/2009/POLITICS/03/24/obama.mexico.policy) that, in 2008, 6,500 Mexicans were killed by drug cartels. The Obama administration pledged to address the crisis: "The new federal plan, developed by the departments of Justice and Homeland Security, calls for doubling the number of border security task force teams and moving a significant number of other federal agents, equipment and resources to the border. It also involves greater intelligence sharing aimed at cracking down on the flow of money and weapons into Mexico that helps fuel the drug trade."

Afghanistan

In *International Narcotics Control Strategy Report*, the INL indicates that trafficking in opium provided over one-third of Afghanistan's gross domestic product in 2007. This country is the world's largest supplier of opium. When Afghanistan was under the control of the fanatically religious and conservative Taliban regime, cultivated poppy acreage dropped precipitously, from 64,510 hectares (159,408 acres) in 2000 to 1,685 hectares (4,163 acres) in 2001. (See

FIGURE 9.1

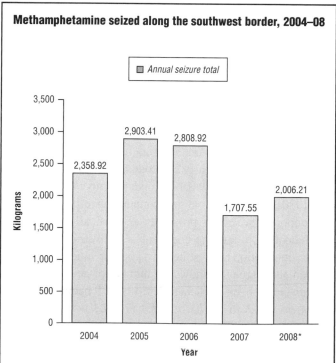

Methamphetamine seized along the southwest border, 2004–08

Note: Data run November 13, 2008.

SOURCE: "Figure 7. Methamphetamine Seized along the Southwest Border, in Kilograms, 2004–2008," in *National Drug Threat Assessment, 2009*, U.S. Department of Justice, National Drug Intelligence Center, December 2008, http://www.usdoj.gov/ndic/pubs31/31379/31379p.pdf (accessed December 15, 2008)

Table 9.5.) The United States invaded Afghanistan in 2001, in a response to the 9/11 terrorist attacks, and the Taliban was driven from power. An unintended consequence of this was that poppy cultivation resumed, rising to 30,750 hectares (75,985 acres) in 2002. By 2004 poppy cultivation reached a staggering 206,700 hectares (510,767 acres) but then dropped by nearly half to 107,400 hectares (265,391 acres) in 2005. The recultivation of poppy was in part a response to the continuing drought in the region: opium poppy is hardy and can grow under adverse conditions, supplying income to farmers. By 2007 poppy cultivation in Afghanistan had nearly reached 2004 levels at 202,000 hectares (499,153 acres).

Afghanistan's post-9/11 government officially banned opium poppy cultivation and has pressured its regional governors to suppress the drug trade. Despite these efforts, the situation in Afghanistan was, in the immediate post-Taliban era, similar to the situation in Colombia, with a weak central government unable to assert itself in areas where autonomous warlords hold de facto (virtual) power. Other countries and organizations have tried to help. For example, USAID has been active in establishing alternative development programs. The United Kingdom has conducted some eradication efforts and established a counternarcotics mobile force; Germany has provided training and equipment to establish an Afghan security force; and Italy has been involved in strengthening the country's judicial system.

The DEA developed the Foreign-Deployed Advisory Support Teams program in Afghanistan to identify, target, investigate, and disrupt or dismantle transnational drug trafficking operations in the region. A major goal of this program is to help develop Afghanistan's antidrug abilities. Training began in 2004 and operations began in 2005. Even though results were initially positive, the INL indicates in *International Narcotics Control Strategy Report* that in 2007 "narcotics law enforcement was hampered by corruption and incompetence within the justice system as well as the absence of governance in large sections of the country. Although narcotics make up one-third of Afghanistan's GDP, no major drug traffickers have been arrested and convicted in Afghanistan since 2006. In addition, too few high-level drug traffickers served terms in Afghanistan's prisons during 2007." Furthermore, since 2004, Taliban support in Afghanistan was growing, aided in part by neighboring Pakistan.

In March 2009 efforts were stepped up to combat the drug trade in Afghanistan. "American authorities are planning a broad new campaign to choke off the prime source of financing for terrorists in Afghanistan, sending in dozens of federal drug enforcement agents to disrupt the country's massive opium trade and the money that streams to the Taliban and al-Qaida," reported Lolita C. Baldor for the Associated Press ("US Launches New Fight against Afghan Drug Trade," March 30, 2009, http://www.google.com/hostednews/ap/article/ALeqM5hCUxKbunroDLpz-QKfiKnqI0i

AWQD978J8OG0). "The surge of narcotics agents, which would boost the number of anti-drug officials inside Afghanistan from a dozen to nearly 80, would bolster a strategy laid out . . . by the Obama administration to use U.S. and NATO troops to target 'higher level drug lords.'"

FOSTERING INTERNATIONAL COOPERATION: THE DRUG CERTIFICATION PROCESS

The United States uses a drug certification process to promote international cooperation in controlling drug production and trafficking. Section 490 of the Foreign Assistance Act of 1961 requires the president to annually submit to Congress a list of major drug-producing and drug-transiting countries. The president must also assess each country's performance in battling narcotics trade and trafficking based on the goals and objectives of the 1988 United Nations Convention against Illicit Traffic in Narcotic Drugs and Psychotropic Substances. Countries that have fully cooperated with the United States or that have taken adequate steps to reach the goals and objectives of the United Nations convention are "certified" by the president. U.S. aid is withheld to countries that are not certified. Many countries resent the process, but most work toward certification.

TRANSIT-ZONE AGREEMENTS

Other countries not on the list are frequently reluctant to cooperate with the United States to stop drug traffickers. The Caribbean basin, for example, is a major transit zone for drug trafficking. The Caribbean basin countries are those that border, or lie in, the Gulf of Mexico and the Caribbean Sea, such as the island nations of the West Indies, Mexico, Central American nations, and northern South American nations. Bermuda is also included, even though it is in the Atlantic Ocean. Most of the islands have bilateral agreements with the United States, but these agreements are limited to maritime matters that permit U.S. ships to seize traffickers in the territorial waters of particular Caribbean islands. Few transit-zone countries permit U.S. planes to fly in their airspace to force suspected traffickers to land. Some transit-zone countries have no maritime agreements with the United States, including Ecuador and Mexico.

Bilateral agreements are not the same in each country, and some provide limited rights to U.S. law enforcement authorities. For example, a U.S.-Belize agreement allows the U.S. Coast Guard to board suspected Belizean vessels on the high seas without prior notification. The agreement with Panama requires U.S. Coast Guard vessels in Panamanian waters to be escorted by a Panamanian government ship.

DOMESTIC DRUG SEIZURES

The DEA is also at work within the United States to disrupt the drug supply. Table 9.7 shows drug seizures across the United States from 1989 to 2007. Seizures of cocaine, heroin, methamphetamine, and cannabis have varied during

TABLE 9.7

Cocaine, heroin, methamphetamine, and cannabis seizures, 1989–2007

[in kilograms]

				Cannabis	
Year	Cocaine	Heroin	Methamphetamine	Marijuana	Hashish
1989	114,903	1,311	—	393,276	23,043
1990	96,085	687	—	233,478	7,683
1991	128,247	1,448	—	224,603	79,110
1992	120,175	1,251	—	344,899	111
1993	121,215	1,502	7	409,922	11,396
1994	129,378	1,285	178	474,856	561
1995	111,031	1,543	369	627,776	14,470
1996	128,555	1,362	136	638,863	37,851
1997	101,495	1,624	1,099	698,799	756
1998	118,436	1,458	2,559	827,149	241
1999	132,063	1,151	2,779	1,075,154	797
2000	106,619	1,674	3,470	1,235,938	10,867
2001	105,748	2,496	4,051	1,214,188	161
2002	102,515	2,773	2,477	1,101,459	621
2003	117,024	2,381	3,853	1,229,615	155
2004	172,804	2,116	3,899	1,180,688	166
2005	174,679	1,692	4,772	1,117,189	388
2006	154,047	1,790	4,739	1,143,924	178
2007	145,103	2,517	2,871	1,461,474	338

—Data not available.

SOURCE: "Table 54. Federal-Wide Cocaine, Heroin, Methamphetamine, and Cannabis Seizures, 1989–2007 (Kilograms)," in *National Drug Control Strategy: Data Supplement 2008*, Executive Office of the President, Office of National Drug Control Policy, October 2008, http://www.whitehousedrugpolicy.gov/publications/policy/ndcs08_data_supl/ndcs_suppl08.pdf (accessed December 15, 2008)

the time span shown but, in general, have risen. For example, seizures of cocaine have ranged from a low of 96,085 kilograms (211,831 pounds) in 1990 to a high of 174,679 kilograms (385,101 pounds) in 2005. Table 9.8 shows domestic seizures of MDMA from 2000 to 2007. These seizures varied widely as well. The year in which domestic seizures were the greatest was 2001 with 10.7 million dosage units; the year in which domestic seizures were the lowest was 2003 with 1.9 million dosage units.

In 2006 the Combat Methamphetamine Epidemic Act was signed into law, establishing stricter national controls for the over-the-counter sale of products containing the methamphetamine precursor drugs ephedrine and pseudoephedrine. Before this act, many states had imposed restrictions on the retail sale of pseudoephedrine. These state and national restrictions have resulted in a significant decline in methamphetamine lab seizures, because without these precursor drugs the labs cannot manufacture methamphetamine. The INL also reports in *International Narcotics Control Strategy Report* that the number of superlab seizures—those labs capable of producing more than 10 pounds (4.5 kg) of methamphetamine per production run—has decreased as well. Table 9.9 shows that 245 superlabs were seized in 2001, compared with 14 in 2006.

WHY IS THE WAR ON DRUGS SO HARD TO WIN?

The goal of the international war on drugs is a difficult one. The United States and other countries are attempting to

TABLE 9.8

MDMA (ecstasy) seizures, 2000–07

Year	Reported in dosage units	Reported in kilograms	Total in dosage units*
2000	8,289,023	0	8,289,023
2001	10,710,509	80	10,982,509
2002	4,715,098	1,056	8,305,498
2003	1,888,475	484	3,534,075
2004	2,326,434	107	2,690,234
2005	4,357,631	242	5,180,431
2006	5,168,566	477	6,790,366
2007	4,121,389	463	5,695,589

*Conversion of seizures reported in kilograms to dosage units assumes 1 kilogram equals 3,400 impure dosage units, based on the Drug Enforcement Agency's MDMA Drug Intelligence Brief (June 1999).

SOURCE: "Table 57. Domestic Seizures of MDMA, 2000–2007," in *National Drug Control Strategy: Data Supplement 2008*, Executive Office of the President, Office of National Drug Control Policy, October 2008, http://www.whitehousedrugpolicy.gov/publications/policy/ndcs08_data_supl/ndcs_suppl08.pdf (accessed December 15, 2008)

stop the flow of a product that is in high demand, generally cheap to produce, and offers enormous profits. In reference to the United States, it is undeniably the case that a significant number of Americans want drugs, are affluent, and thus create a vast market for drug traffickers.

Production costs for drugs are so low and the profit so great that even if a trafficker loses most of his or her product, he or she can earn a huge amount of money on the remainder. When one drug policy is put in place, drug traffickers change their operations to circumvent it. When

TABLE 9.9

Methamphetamine superlab seizures by state, 2000–06

[Ten pounds of methamphetamine or more]

State	2000	2001	2002	2003	2004	2005	2006
Alabama	0	0	1	0	0	0	0
Arizona	0	0	1	0	0	0	0
Arkansas	0	0	2	0	0	0	0
California	122	223	124	125	43	29	12
Colorado	0	0	2	0	0	0	0
Georgia	0	0	0	0	0	1	0
Illinois	0	0	0	2	0	0	0
Indiana	0	0	1	0	0	0	0
Louisiana	0	0	1	0	0	0	0
Missouri	0	0	0	1	1	1	0
Nevada	0	3	1	0	0	0	0
New Hampshire	0	0	0	0	0	0	0
North Dakota	0	0	1	0	0	0	0
Ohio	0	0	0	0	1	0	0
Oklahoma	1	0	2	0	1	2	0
Oregon	3	5	2	1	4	1	0
South Carolina	0	0	0	0	1	0	0
South Dakota	0	0	0	0	0	0	0
Tennessee	0	0	0	1	0	0	2
Texas	3	9	1	0	2	1	0
Vermont	0	0	0	0	1	1	0
Washington	1	5	2	0	1	0	0
West Virginia	0	0	1	0	0	0	0
Wisconsin	0	0	0	0	1	0	0
Total	**130**	**245**	**142**	**130**	**56**	**36**	**14**

*2006 numbers for the first half of the year (January to June) only.

SOURCE: "Table 74. States with Methamphetamine Seizures of Super Labs (10 Pounds or More) by State, 2000–2006," in *National Drug Control Strategy: Data Supplement 2008*, Executive Office of the President, Office of National Drug Control Policy, October 2008, http://www.whitehousedrugpolicy.gov/publications/policy/ndcs08_data_supl/ndcs_suppl08.pdf (accessed December 15, 2008)

one route is blocked or one method of production shut down, traffickers change to another. When one drug trafficker or grower is captured, or even if a major trafficking group is shut down, others quickly arise.

Critics of the U.S. drug policy feel that so long as demand persists, suppliers will find a way to deliver the product. Even though they may, or may not, support eradication and interdiction efforts, these critics believe that ultimately the most successful policies are those that reduce the demand for drugs.

MARIJUANA LEGALIZATION MOVEMENT

In the United States the legalization of drugs almost invariably refers to the legalization of marijuana rather than, for instance, heroin and cocaine. The use of "hard drugs" such as these is relatively limited, and most Americans consider them to be highly addictive and damaging to one's physical and mental health. Marijuana's situation is different. According to SAMHSA, in *Results from the 2007 National Survey on Drug Use and Health*, 72.8% of all current drug users in 2007 were using marijuana, and 53.3% of all current drug users used only marijuana and no other drugs. Some studies suggest significant harm from marijuana use, including effects on the heart, lungs, brain, and social and learning capabilities. Other studies find little or no harm from moderate marijuana use. Regardless of what the research says, marijuana is generally thought of as a relatively mild drug, an opinion supported in Canada by those who introduced repeated initiatives to decriminalize marijuana possession, or in the Netherlands, where marijuana sales are tolerated in coffee shops.

Public Opinion

The polling data that the Gallup Organization gathered for selected years from 1969 to 2005 show public opinion increasingly favoring the legalization of marijuana. (See Figure 9.2.) In 1969, 84% of the public opposed legalization and 12% favored it. By 2005 those opposed had declined to 60% of the public, whereas 36% were in favor. As of the first part of 2009, Gallup had not conducted a more recent survey of public attitudes on this question.

It is with the support of this population that a number of initiatives and referenda attempting to legalize marijuana for medical purposes or to decriminalize possession of modest quantities have appeared on state ballots. Many states and local jurisdictions *have* decriminalized certain uses of certain amounts of marijuana. Decriminalization means that the state or local jurisdiction no longer considers uses of marijuana in the amounts and manners it specifies as illegal, but the jurisdiction may still consider these uses as civil infractions and may impose civil fines, drug education, or drug treatment. Nevertheless, the possession and

FIGURE 9.2

Public opinion on legalizing marijuana use, selected years 1969–2005

DO YOU THINK THE USE OF MARIJUANA SHOULD BE MADE LEGAL, OR NOT?

Numbers shown in percentages

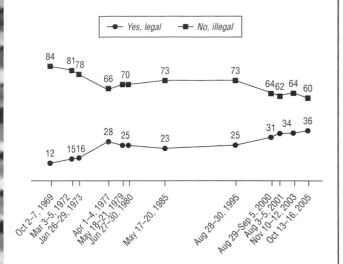

SOURCE: Joseph Carroll, "Do You Think the Use of Marijuana Should Be Made Legal, or Not?" in *Who Supports Marijuana Legalization? Support Rising; Varies Most by Age and Gender*, The Gallup Organization, November 1, 2005, http://www.galluppoll.com (accessed January 7, 2009). Copyright © 2005 by The Gallup Organization. Reproduced by permission of The Gallup Organization.

TABLE 9.10

Top ten facts on legalization of drugs cited by the Drug Enforcement Administration (DEA), 2003

Fact 1:	We have made significant progress in fighting drug use and drug trafficking in America. Now is not the time to abandon our efforts.
Fact 2:	A balanced approach of prevention, enforcement, and treatment is the key in the fight against drugs.
Fact 3:	Illegal drugs are illegal because they are harmful.
Fact 4:	Smoked marijuana is not scientifically approved medicine. Marinol, the legal version of medical marijuana, is approved by science.
Fact 5:	Drug control spending is a minor portion of the U.S. budget. Compared to the social costs of drug abuse and addiction, government spending on drug control is minimal.
Fact 6:	Legalization of drugs will lead to increased use and increased levels of addiction. Legalization has been tried before, and failed miserably.
Fact 7:	Crime, violence, and drug use go hand-in-hand.
Fact 8:	Alcohol has caused significant health, social, and crime problems in this country, and legalized drugs would only make the situation worse.
Fact 9:	Europe's more liberal drug policies are not the right model for America.
Fact 10:	Most nonviolent drug users get treatment, not jail time.

SOURCE: "Summary of the Top Ten Facts on Legalization," in *Speaking out against Drug Legalization*, U.S. Department of Justice, Drug Enforcement Administration, May 2003, http://www.dea.gov/demand/speakout/index.html (accessed January 7, 2009)

use of marijuana is still illegal under federal law, and this law supersedes state and local marijuana decriminalization laws. Therefore, a person residing in a state that has decriminalized the possession and use of marijuana can still be arrested and prosecuted by federal officials under federal law.

Arguments for and against Legalization

FOR LEGALIZATION. Most of those who favor legalization in some form (for medical use, decriminalization, or regulation) use two arguments in combination. The first is that an approach to drugs based on prohibition and criminalization does not work, produces excessive rates of incarceration, and costs a lot of money that could be more productively spent on treatment and prevention. The second is that drug use is an activity arbitrarily called a crime. It is imposed by law on some drugs and not on others, and can be seen as criminal at one time but perhaps not at another. Murder, rape, and robbery have always been considered inherently criminal acts, but drug use is just a consumption of substances; its control is arbitrary and follows fashions. Alcohol consumption was once prohibited but is now legal. Likewise, in the early 1900s opiates were sold in pharmacies and Coca-Cola contained small quantities of cocaine.

Some who advocate the legalization of drugs believe the government has no right telling people what they may and may not ingest. However, most legalization proponents recognize that many drugs can be harmful (though many dispute the degree), but they do not see this as a reason to make their use illegal. They point out that tobacco use and alcohol abuse are harmful—possibly more harmful or addictive than some drugs that are illicit—but their use is legal. The policy these legalization advocates recommend is based on educational and public health approaches such as those used for tobacco and alcohol. They feel that a greater harm is imposed on society by prohibiting such substances, as evidenced by the consequence of the Prohibition period of the early 20th century, during which alcohol was banned and crime, racketeering, and homicide rates soared.

Many proponents argue that legalization will result in decreased harm and crime from trafficking, gang wars, and crimes committed to obtain drugs; lower incarceration rates and associated cost savings; and more funds available for treatment from savings and from taxes on legally distributed drugs. Legalization of drugs is also seen as making available marijuana in medical applications, such as relieving the suffering of cancer and acquired immune deficiency syndrome (AIDS) patients.

AGAINST LEGALIZATION. The federal government's case against legalization is summarized in the DEA brochure *Speaking Out against Drug Legalization* (May 2003, http://www.usdoj.gov/dea/demand/speakout/speaking_out-may03.pdf). The 10 arguments presented by the DEA are shown in Table 9.10.

Like legalization proponents, the DEA's position is organized around the concept of harm. Certain drugs are illegal or controlled because they cause harm. In the DEA's view, the legalization of drugs—even if only marijuana—

will increase the harm already suffered by the drug-using public by spreading use to ever larger numbers of people. The DEA points to National Institute on Drug Abuse studies that show that smoking a marijuana joint introduces four times as much tar into the lungs as a filtered cigarette. The agency makes the point that drugs are much more addictive than alcohol and invites the public to contemplate a situation in which commercial interests might be enabled to promote the sale of presently illicit substances.

Would legalization reduce crime? The DEA does not believe it would. Under a regulated drug-use system, age restrictions would apply. A criminal enterprise would continue to supply those under age. If marijuana were legalized, trade in heroin and cocaine would continue. If all three of the major drugs were permitted to be sold legally, other substances, such as phencyclidine and methamphetamine, would still support a criminal trade. The DEA does not envision that a black market in drugs could be eliminated entirely, because health authorities would never permit potent drugs to be sold freely on the open market.

For all these reasons, the DEA advocates the continuation of a balanced approach to the control of drugs including prevention, enforcement, and treatment.

Contradictions and Inconsistencies

Proponents of legalization sometimes find the question of where to draw the legal line problematic. How harmful must a drug be before it should be made illegal? In an environment where public pressures are mounting against the use of tobacco, the legalization of marijuana has a contradictory aspect. Funds expended now on incarcerating drug offenders may have to be expended in some future time on public health programs to treat ills caused by newly legalized drugs, though whether or how much the use of drugs such as marijuana would increase if they were legal remains entirely unknown.

Opponents of legalization have similar difficulties in addressing the issues of alcohol and tobacco. How can their legality be justified when the use of comparably harmful substances is not legal and can yield long prison sentences?

Arguments claiming that the war on drugs is succeeding because drug use is down as measured against some point in the past ignore the fact that drug use is a cyclical phenomenon that ebbs and flows. For example, in *Speaking Out* the DEA notes that the overall number of drug users declined from 25.4 million 1979 to 15.9 million in 2001. However, during this period current drug use first declined to 12 million people in 1992, according to SAMSHA (June 1, 2008, http://www.oas.samhsa.gov/nhsda/ar18tbl.htm), and then rose again to 15.9 million by 2001, according to the DEA, while the same policies were being pursued. If the DEA had used 1992 as its base year, it would have had to concede that its programs are not working.

MEDICAL MARIJUANA

The medicinal value of THC (delta-9-tetrahydrocannabinol), the active ingredient in marijuana, has long been known to the medical community. The drug has been shown to alleviate the nausea and vomiting caused by chemotherapy, which is used to treat many forms of cancer. Marijuana has also been found useful in alleviating pressure on the eye in glaucoma patients. Furthermore, the drug has been found effective in helping to fight the physical wasting that usually accompanies AIDS. AIDS patients lose their appetite and can slowly waste away because they do not eat. Complicating matters, many of the newer AIDS remedies must be taken on a full stomach. Marijuana has been found effective in restoring the appetite of some AIDS patients. This is not to say that all scientists agree that marijuana is healthy or useful. For example, some studies find that marijuana suppresses the immune system and contains a number of lung-damaging chemicals. Still, the potentially beneficial uses of marijuana as a medicine have led to a movement for it to be made legally available by prescription.

Opponents of the medical legalization of marijuana often point to dronabinol (a laboratory-made form of THC found in marijuana) as a superior alternative. Dronabinol provides a standardized THC content and does not contain impurities, such as leaves, mold spores, and bacteria, which are generally found in marijuana. However, many patients do not respond to dronabinol, and the determination of the right dose is variable from patient to patient. Nonresponding patients claim that smoking marijuana allows them to control the dosage they get.

Marijuana has been used illegally by an unknown number of cancer and AIDS patients on the recommendation of their doctors. Nonetheless, the medical use of marijuana is not without risk. The primary negative effect is diminished control over movement. In some cases users may experience unpleasant emotional states or feelings. In addition, the usefulness of medicinal marijuana is limited by the harmful effects of smoking, which can increase a person's risk of cancer, lung damage, and problems with pregnancies (such as low birth weight). However, these risks are usually not important for terminally ill patients or those with debilitating symptoms.

Some states and local jurisdictions have decriminalized the cultivation of marijuana for personal medical use. As mentioned previously, however, the cultivation of marijuana is still illegal under federal law, which supersedes state and local marijuana decriminalization laws. In addition, such state and local rulings do not necessarily establish that the use of marijuana is medically appropriate. That issue is hotly debated in the media and among Americans but no nationally recognized medical organization—including the American Medical Association, the American Cancer Society, or the American Academy of Pediatrics—has endorsed the medical use of smoked marijuana.

IMPORTANT NAMES
AND ADDRESSES

AAA Foundation for Traffic Safety
607 Fourteenth St. NW, Ste. 201
Washington, DC 20005
(202) 638-5944
FAX: (202) 638-5943
E-mail: info@aaafoundation.org
URL: http://www.aaafoundation.org/

Action on Smoking and Health
2013 H St. NW
Washington, DC 20006
(202) 659-4310
URL: http://www.ash.org/

Adult Children of Alcoholics
PO Box 3216
Torrance, CA 90510
(310) 534-1815
E-mail: info@AdultChildren.org
URL: http://www.adultchildren.org/

Al-Anon Family Group Headquarters
1600 Corporate Landing Pkwy.
Virginia Beach, VA 23454-5617
(757) 563-1600
FAX: (757) 563-1655
E-mail: wso@al-anon.org
URL: http://www.al-anon.alateen.org/

Alcoholics Anonymous World Services
475 Riverside Dr. at W. 120th St., 11th Floor
New York, NY 10115
(212) 870-3400
URL: http://www.aa.org/

Beer Institute
122 C St. NW, Ste. 350
Washington, DC 20001
(202) 737-2337
1-800-379-2739
E-mail: info@beerinstitute.org
URL: http://www.beerinstitute.org/

**Bureau for International Narcotics and
Law Enforcement Affairs
U.S. Department of State**
2201 C St. NW
Washington, DC 20520

(202) 647-4000
URL: http://www.state.gov/p/inl

Campaign for Tobacco-Free Kids
1400 Eye St., Ste. 1200
Washington, DC 20005
(202) 296-5469
URL: http://www.tobaccofreekids.org/
index.php

**Centers for Disease Control
and Prevention
National Center for Chronic Disease
Prevention and Health Promotion
Office on Smoking and Health**
1600 Clifton Rd.
Atlanta, GA 30333
1-800-232-4636
E-mail: tobaccoinfo@cdc.gov
URL: http://www.cdc.gov/tobacco/

Cocaine Anonymous World Services
3740 Overland Ave., Ste. C
Los Angeles, CA 90034
(310) 559-5833
FAX: (310) 559-2554
E-mail: cawso@ca.org
URL: http://www.ca.org/

Distilled Spirits Council
1250 Eye St. NW, Ste. 400
Washington, DC 20005
(202) 628-3544
URL: http://www.discus.org/

Drug Enforcement Administration
Mailstop: AES
8701 Morrissette Dr.
Springfield, VA 22152
(202) 307-1000
URL: http://www.usdoj.gov/dea/

Drug Policy Alliance Network
70 W. Thirty-sixth St., Sixteenth Floor
New York, NY 10018
(212) 613-8020
FAX: (212) 613-8021

E-mail: nyc@drugpolicy.org
URL: http://www.dpf.org/

Nar-Anon Family Groups
22527 Crenshaw Blvd., Ste. 200B
Torrance, CA 90505
(310) 534-8188
1-800-477-6291
FAX: (310) 534-8688
E-mail: naranonWSO@gmail.com
URL: http://nar-anon.org/index.html

Narcotics Anonymous World Services
PO Box 9999
Van Nuys, CA 91409
(818) 773-9999
FAX: (818) 700-0700
E-mail: fsmail@na.org
URL: http://www.na.org/

**National Clearinghouse for Alcohol and
Drug Information**
PO Box 2345
Rockville, MD 20847-2345
1-800-729-6686
URL: http://ncadi.samhsa.gov/

**National Council on Alcoholism
and Drug Dependence**
244 E. Fifty-eighth St., Fourth Floor
New York, NY 10022
(212) 269-7797
FAX: (212) 269-7510
E-mail: national@ncadd.org
URL: http://www.ncadd.org/

**National Drug and Alcohol Treatment
Referral Routing Service**
1-800-662-HELP

**National Institute on Alcohol Abuse
and Alcoholism**
5635 Fishers Ln., MSC 9304
Bethesda, MD 20892-9304
(301) 443-3860
URL: http://www.niaaa.nih.gov/

National Institute on Drug Abuse
5001 Executive Blvd., Rm. 5213
Bethesda, MD 20892-9561
(301) 443-1124
E-mail: information@nida.nih.gov
URL: http://www.nida.nih.gov/

National Organization for the Reform of Marijuana Laws
1600 K St. NW, Ste. 501
Washington, DC 20006-2832
(202) 483-5500
FAX: (202) 483-0057
E-mail: norml@norml.org
URL: http://www.norml.org/

Office of National Drug Control Policy
Drug Policy Information Clearinghouse
PO Box 6000
Rockville, MD 20849-6000
1-800-666-3332
FAX: (301) 519-5212
URL: http://www.whitehousedrugpolicy.gov/

Office of Safe and Drug-Free Schools
U.S. Department of Education
400 Maryland Ave. SW
Washington, DC 20202
1-800-872-5327
URL: http://www.ed.gov/about/offices/list/osdfs

Substance Abuse and Mental Health Services Administration
One Choke Cherry Rd.
Rockville, MD 20857
(240) 276-2000
FAX: (240) 276-2010
URL: http://www.samhsa.gov/

Wine Institute
425 Market St., Ste. 1000
San Francisco, CA 94105
(415) 512-0151
FAX: (415) 957-9479
URL: http://www.wineinstitute.org/

RESOURCES

The various agencies of the U.S. Department of Health and Human Services (HHS) produce important publications on the consumption of alcohol, tobacco, and drugs in the United States and their health effects. Reports of the U.S. surgeon general and special reports to Congress are published through this office.

The Substance Abuse and Mental Health Services Administration (SAMHSA) produces the annual National Survey on Drug Use and Health. SAMHSA also tracks treatment services. The most recent report is *National Survey of Substance Abuse Treatment Services (N-SSATS): 2006—Data on Substance Abuse Treatment Facilities* (October 2007). SAMHSA also tracks reported episodes of drug abuse; the most recent published results are in *Treatment Episode Data Set (TEDS) 1996–2006: National Admissions to Substance Abuse Treatment Services* (July 2008). The agency also operates the Drug Abuse Warning Network, which collects data from emergency rooms.

The HHS also publishes the bimonthly *Public Health Reports*, the official journal of the U.S. Public Health Service. The journal is a helpful resource on health problems, including those caused by alcohol and tobacco. The Association of Schools of Public Health has been a partner in the publication of *Public Health Reports* since 1999.

The National Institute on Alcohol Abuse and Alcoholism (NIAAA) publishes the journal *Alcohol Research and Health*. The journal contains current scholarly research on alcohol addiction issues. The NIAAA also publishes the quarterly bulletin *Alcohol Alert*, which disseminates research findings on alcohol abuse and alcoholism.

The National Center for Health Statistics, in its annual *Health, United States*, reports on all aspects of the nation's health, including tobacco- and alcohol-related illnesses and deaths. *Morbidity and Mortality Weekly Report* is published by the Centers for Disease Control and Prevention (CDC), which also publishes many studies on the trends and health risks of smoking and drinking. Additionally, the American Cancer Society and the American Lung Association provide many facts on cancer and heart disease.

The U.S. Department of Agriculture (USDA) was responsible for several helpful reports concerning tobacco up until 2005. Its publications *Tobacco Outlook* and *Tobacco Briefing Room* monitored tobacco production, consumption, sales, exports, and imports. These publications were discontinued in 2005 after the government ended the decades-old tobacco quota system (see Chapter 7). The USDA still publishes the annual *Agricultural Statistics*, which provides valuable information about farming, and *Food Consumption, Prices, and Expenditures*, which compiles data on how the nation spends its consumer dollars. Other useful information is provided by the Economic Research Service of the USDA and the U.S. Department of Labor's Bureau of Labor Statistics, which examines how people spend their income, including spending on cigarettes and alcohol.

The National Highway Traffic Safety Administration of the U.S. Department of Transportation produces the annual *Traffic Safety Facts*, which includes data on alcohol-related accidents.

The Bureau of Justice Statistics monitors crime in the United States and focuses on criminal prosecutions, prisons, sentencing, and related subjects. Particularly helpful are *Drug Use and Dependence, State and Federal Prisoners, 2004* (October 2006, Christopher J. Mumola and Jennifer C. Karberg) and the annual publications *Compendium of Federal Justice Statistics* and *Sourcebook of Criminal Justice Statistics*. The Federal Bureau of Investigation's annual *Crime in the United States* provides arrest statistics for the United States. The U.S. Department of the Treasury's Alcohol and Tobacco Tax and Trade Bureau provides alcohol and tobacco tax information.

Other important annual surveys of alcohol, tobacco, and drug use in the United States are conducted by both public and private organizations. The CDC's Youth Risk Behavior Surveillance monitors not only alcohol, tobacco, and drug use but also other risk behaviors, such as teenage sexual activity and weapons possession. The Monitoring the Future survey of substance abuse among students from middle school through college is by the National Institute on Drug Abuse and the University of Michigan Institute for Social Research. The *PRIDE Questionnaire Report*, based on a survey of youth and parents, is produced by PRIDE Surveys.

The Wine Institute, the Distilled Spirits Council of the United States, and the Beer Institute are private trade organizations that track alcoholic beverage sales and consumption, as well as political and regulatory issues. Action on Smoking and Health publishes reviews concerned with the problems of smoking and the rights of nonsmokers. The Campaign for Tobacco-Free Kids provides information on tobacco-related federal, state, and global initiatives; cigarette taxes; tobacco advertisements; tobacco and smoking statistics; and tobacco-related special reports.

The Gallup Organization and the Robert Wood Johnson Foundation provide important information about the attitudes and behaviors of the American public.

The national policy on combating drug abuse is centered in the Office of National Drug Control Policy (ONDCP). The ONDCP, which prepares a drug control policy each year for the president and coordinates efforts across the federal bureaucracy, is an excellent source for statistics that are collected from many other agencies. Publications consulted for this volume include *National Drug Control Strategy: Data Supplement 2008* (October 2008), *National Drug Control Strategy: FY 2009 Budget Summary* (February 2008), and *National Drug Control Strategy* documents published in earlier years.

Domestic law enforcement and interdiction activities fall under the U.S. Department of Justice. The U.S. Drug Enforcement Administration (DEA) oversees all domestic drug control activities. The DEA publishes *Drugs of Abuse* (2005), a resource tool that educates the public about drug facts and the inherent dangers of illegal drugs.

The effort to control drugs beyond the nation's borders is largely under the supervision of the U.S. Department of State. The agency within the Department of State in charge of the drug control effort is the Bureau for International Narcotics and Law Enforcement Affairs. An excellent source of information is the bureau's annual *International Narcotics Control Strategy Report*.

Gale, a part of Cengage Learning, sincerely thanks all the organizations listed here for the valuable information they provide.

INDEX

Page references in italics refer to photographs. References with the letter t following them indicate the presence of a table. The letter f indicates a figure. If more than one table or figure appears on a particular page, the exact item number for the table or figure being referenced is provided.

A

AA (Alcoholics Anonymous), 94, 139

AAA Foundation for Traffic Safety, 139

ABD (Air Bridge Denial) program, 130

Abuse
  commonly abused drugs, 3t–4t
  definition of, 2, 5–6
  factors of, 3–5
  See also Alcohol abuse; Drug abuse

Accidents. *See* Motor vehicle accidents

Acquired immune deficiency syndrome (AIDS)
  crack cocaine use and, 13
  medical marijuana for, 137

Action on Smoking and Health, 139

"Actual Tobacco Settlement Payments Received by the States (Millions of Dollars)" (Lindblom), 106

Addiction (dependence)
  addictive nature of nicotine, 37–38
  to alcohol, 18–19
  to cocaine, 55
  definition of, 2
  disease model of, 81–82
  drug abuse/addiction, 81–82
  drug use, abuse, dependence, 8f
  genetic component of, 2–3
  progression from use to, 7
  risk factors for drug addiction, 65
  to synthetic stimulants, 53
  to tranquilizers, 53
  See also Alcohol dependence

Addresses/names, of organizations, 139–140

"Administration Officials Announce U.S.-Mexico Border Security Policy: A Comprehensive Response and Commitment" (White House press release), 14–15

Admissions, for treatment
  admitted patients, statistics on, 88, 91
  drug treatment admissions by sex, race/ethnicity, age, 83
  See also Drug treatment

Adult Children of Alcoholics
  contact information, 139
  for drug treatment help, 94

Adult Drug Courts: Evidence Indicates Recidivism Reductions and Mixed Results for Other Outcomes (U.S. GAO), 94

Advertising
  for alcohol, tobacco, 98–100
  of cigarettes, 9, *10f*
  youth tobacco use and, 73

Afghanistan
  drug supply, disruption of, 129
  opium poppy cultivation in, 121, 122f
  war on drugs and, 14

African-Americans
  alcohol consumption by, 18
  drug abuse arrestees, 61
  drug treatment admissions, 83, 88
  drug use by prisoners, 64
  drug violation convictions, 61
  early use of alcohol, tobacco, marijuana, 65, 66
  illicit drug users, 47
  smoking by, 35
  war on drugs and, 62
  youth alcohol use, 70
  youth tobacco use, 74

Age
  adult smokers, by age group/gender, 36(f3.4)

alcohol, cigarettes, high school students who drank/smoked before age 13, 66(t5.1)

alcohol consumption and, 17

of cocaine users, 55

current, binge, and heavy alcohol use among persons aged twelve and older 20f

current alcohol use by high school students, 67

drinking age, 8–9, 28

drug treatment admissions and, 83, 88

drug use by prisoners and, 64

early use of alcohol, tobacco, marijuana 65–66

of first illicit drug use, 75

of first use of alcohol, 66–67

of first use of tobacco, 72

health consequences of early tobacco use, 71–72

of illicit drug users, 47, 79–80

of illicit pain reliever users, 52

of inhalant users, 57

marijuana, high school students who tried, before age 13, 66(t5.2)

marijuana, new users of, over age 12, mean age at first use, 51f

marijuana use among persons aged 18–45, by time of use, age group, 50f

marijuana use and, 50–51

methamphetamine, new users of, over age 12, mean age at first use, 54(f4.6)

methamphetamine use among persons aged 18–30, by time of use and age group, 54(f4.7)

of methamphetamine users, 53

past-month illicit drug use among persons aged 12 and older, 48f

problem drinking and, 18, 20

smoking by, 35

tobacco use among college students, 73

top problems of youth and, 65

substance abuse, economic costs of, 104–105

See also Spending

Court cases

Cipollone v. Liggett Group, Inc., 106

FDA v. Brown and Williamson Tobacco Corp., 104

Granholm v. Heald, 103

Crack cocaine

age of first use of, 75

description of, 55

drug treatment effectiveness, 91

introduction of, 13

penalties for trafficking, 109

Craving, 38

Crime

drug use as, 136

illicit drugs and, 62–64

international war on drugs, 127–128

marijuana legalization and, 137

prisoners, state/federal, drug use among, 64(*t*4.6)

sentences for violation of drug laws, by type/length of sentence, U.S. District Courts, 63*t*–64*t*

state prison populations, impact of drugs on, 61*f*

state prisons, number of sentenced offenders in, by race, gender, offense, 62*t*

substance abuse treatment and, 93

Crime Control Act of 1984, 13

Criminal penalties. *See* Penalties

Crispo, Anna, 45

CSA. *See* Controlled Substances Act

CSPI (Center for Science in the Public Interest), 98

"The Cumulative Risk of Lung Cancer among Current, Ex- and Never-Smokers in European Men" (Crispo et al.), 45

D

Dalesio, Emery P., 108

D'Amico, Elizabeth J., 66

Dangers, of alcohol, 8–9

DARP (Drug Abuse Reporting Program), 91

Date rape drug (flunitrazepam), 53

DEA. *See* U.S. Drug Enforcement Administration

Deaths

from alcohol, 24, 25, 27–28

from alcohol, tobacco, drugs, 125

death rates for five leading causes of death, 42*f*

drug-related deaths, 49

drug-related homicides, 62

motor vehicle crashes, pedestrians killed in, by age group/percent BAC, 30(*t*2.13)

from motor vehicle/pedestrian accidents, 28, 71

from sedatives, 54

smoking cessation and, 45

from tobacco use, 41, 43

"Deaths: Final Data for 1998" (Murphy), 49

"Deaths: Final Data for 2005" (Kung et al.), 27–28, 49

"Deaths: Preliminary Data for 2006" (Heron), 45

A Decade of Broken Promises: The 1998 State Tobacco Settlement Ten Years Later (Campaign for Tobacco-Free Kids), 106

"The Definition of Alcoholism" (Morse & Flavin), 18

Dehydration, 23

Delta-9-tetrahydrocannabinol. *See* THC

Demand reduction, 126–127

Dementia, 25

Denial, 18, 19

Dependence, 6–7

See also Addiction (dependence); Alcohol dependence

Depressants

alcohol as depressant, 17

commonly abused drugs, 3*t*–4*t*

as controlled substances, 1

definition of, 2

nicotine as, 33

regulation of, 12

See also Alcohol

Depression

drinking for, 22

sexual function and, 25

DeRoo, Lisa A., 25–26

Designer drugs

description of, use of, 56–57

high school students' use of MDMA, 79

Detoxification

distribution of drug treatment patients, 87–88

from drugs, 87

See also Drug treatment; Withdrawal

Diagnostic and Statistical Manual of Mental Disorders (DSM) (APA)

definition of alcoholism/alcohol abuse, 19

definitions of abuse/dependence, 5–7

Diagnostic and Statistical Manual of Mental Disorders–IV Text Revision (DSM-IV-TR) (APA)

definition of abuse/dependence, 5–7

definition of alcohol dependence/abuse, 19

on substance abuse, substance dependence, 81

Diazepam, 53

Dick, Danielle, 37–38

Direct shipments, of alcohol, 102–103

Disease model of addiction

description of, 81–82

drug treatment, 83, 87

Diseases

adverse health effects caused by cigarette smoking, 39*t*–40*t*

from alcohol consumption, 24

alcoholism, definition of, 18–19

early tobacco use and, 72

linked to tobacco use, 38, 40, 41

Dispelling the Myths about Addiction: Strategies to Increase Understanding and Strengthen Research (Institute of Medicine), 18

Distillation, 7

Distilled spirits (liquor)

consumption of, 17, 18*t*

sales/consumption of, 95–96

Distilled Spirits Council 2007 Industry Review (Distilled Spirits Council of the United States), 95–96

Distilled Spirits Council of the United States, 100, 139

"Distilled Spirits Taxes" (Distilled Spirits Council of the United States), 100

Distribution

of cocaine, 115

of marijuana, 117, 119

of methamphetamine, 114

See also Drug trafficking

Ditchweed, 49

Doescher, Mark P., 74

Domestic Chemical Diversion Control Act of 1993, 114

Dopamine

MAO inhibitors and, 38

nicotine triggers release of, 33

release of, 4

Dorsey, Tina L., 60–61

Downers. *See* Depressants

Drinking

in colonial America, 8

influences on decision to drink, 67

intoxication from, 23–24

motives for, 21–22

See also Alcohol

Drinking age, 8–9, 28

Drinks

intake recommendations, 25

standard drink equivalents, 17

Driver's license, revocation of, 28

Driving. *See* Motor vehicle accidents

Driving under the influence (DUI)

arrests for, 28–29, 31*t*

drinking and young drivers, 71

motor vehicle crashes, drivers with BAC of 0.08 or higher involved in, 30(*t*2.12)

motor vehicle/pedestrian accidents and, 28

Dronabinol, 137

Drug abuse

deaths from, 125

definition of, 81